THE EARLY LIVES OF MILTON

Nectens aut Paphia Myrti, aut Parnaſside Lauri
Fronde comas, at ego secura pace quiescam.
J. R. sen f.   MILTON's Mansus.
From an Excelᵗ Orig: (Crayons) in his Collection.

PORTRAIT OF JOHN MILTON, FRONTISPIECE TO J. RICHARDSON'S
EXPLANATORY NOTES AND REMARKS ON
MILTON'S "PARADISE LOST"

THE EARLY LIVES
OF MILTON

Edited with Introduction
and Notes by

HELEN DARBISHIRE

LONDON

CONSTABLE & CO LTD

1932

Republished 1972
Scholarly Press, Inc., 22929 Industrial Drive East
St. Clair Shores, Michigan 48080

PUBLISHED BY
Constable and Company Ltd
LONDON

·

Oxford University Press
BOMBAY CALCUTTA MADRAS

·

*The Macmillan Company
of Canada, Limited*
TORONTO

rary of Congress Cataloging in Publication Data

rbishire, Helen, 1881-1961, ed.
 The early lives of Milton.

 The anonymous life, printed from Bodleian MS. Wood
4, is ascribed by the editor to John Phillips.
 CONTENTS: Aubrey, J. Mr. John Milton: minutes,
31.--Phillips, J. The life of Mr. John Milton.--
d, A. à. John Milton, master of arts: from Fasti
nienses, 1691. [etc.]
 1. Milton, John, 1608-1674--Biography. I. Title.
3579.D3 1972   821'.4 [B]   77-144966
BN 0-403-00935-6

PREFACE

A MODERN edition of the early Lives of Milton is long overdue. I have attempted first, to give an acceptable text of the six Lives chosen, as true to the original writings as the modern printers' art permits ; secondly to throw into a clearer light certain matters of authorship and the relation between authors, which have hitherto remained obscure—(I hope that I have established John Phillips as the author of the anonymous Life)—and thirdly to put together a few grains of information collected in various places whilst I searched the field for the earliest authentic records of Milton. I have, with Dr. Johnson, regarded Notes as a necessary evil, and have aimed to reduce them to a minimum, inserting information only when it was new or not easily accessible. For my text of the first two Lives, by Aubrey and by John Phillips, I have returned to the original manuscripts; for the other Lives I have followed the first printed editions. I should like to express to the Printers my high appreciation of the skill and patience with which they have constructed a printed text of Aubrey's Life which preserves far more faithfully than I should have supposed possible the appearance of the original manuscript.

I am able to illustrate, from photographs of manuscripts in the Bodleian, Aubrey's handiwork and handwriting, along with that of Edward and of John Phillips; and by the courtesy of the Master and Fellows of Trinity College, Cambridge, I am permitted to reproduce from the facsimile of the Trinity College Manuscript of Milton's poems a page on which, as I believe, John Phillips transcribed a sonnet for his uncle.

I am grateful to Sir Charles Firth who has read my Introduction and helped to confirm my conjectures on one or two historical points; and to Professor de Sélincourt who has given me the benefit of his tonic criticism. If the book brings its readers a little nearer to Milton himself, I shall be content.

HELEN DARBISHIRE.

June 1932.

CONTENTS

ILLUSTRATIONS

INTRODUCTION

MILTON is the first of our great poets to have his life written by contemporaries, a distinction which he does not owe to his genius alone. It was by a hard-hitting political pamphlet and not by *Paradise Lost* that he became a European celebrity; and it was his chance to be born into an age when the art of biography began to flourish in England. The early Lives of Milton ought to be better known. To publish them is to restore the character and person of Milton in his habit as he lived. Later biographers have quarried the historical records of his time to build a formidable monument, from which in the end the living man has escaped.

" Nobody can write the life of a man," said Johnson, " but those who have eat and drunk and lived in social intercourse with him." Three of Milton's first biographers had this inalienable claim, and from two of these the fourth had the wit to draw his main matter. These four first biographers, John Aubrey, the anonymous writer of the manuscript life in Wood's collection, Edward Phillips, and Anthony à Wood himself, stood close to Milton. They left a record of his life and character which has not been, and cannot be superseded. The personal record does not end with them: its last notes were not written till the middle of the eighteenth century, and I have thought well to publish Toland's Life and Richardson's along with the first four, since both Toland and Richardson could add fresh touches from surviving witnesses, and had themselves the living sense of Milton's personality. But the first four biographers stand together and form the first authority.   Scanning the originals closely, two of them in manuscript, I have found intimate and vital connections between the writers, and a chance crossing of two different lines of inquiry revealed to me in one moment the identity of the nameless biographer.   The relation of the four is intricate, but every knot and join is significant; and the tangled tale must be carefully unwound.

Milton died in 1674.   In 1691 Anthony à Wood, Oxford's famous antiquary, published a trenchant account of his life and works in the *Fasti Oxonienses*. In 1694 appeared an anonymous volume of Milton's *State Letters*, translated into English and prefaced by a Life: the editor and biographer was known to his contemporaries as Milton's nephew, Edward Phillips. Wood had no acquaintance with Milton himself, but he took pains to get his facts from those who had.   His life of Milton in the *Fasti* comes under the year 1635, in which year Milton was incorporated as M.A. Oxon. This fact Wood says he got " not from the Register, (from which the Registrar a careless man tho a good Scholar had omitted throughout all his time the incorporations of the Cantabrigians) but from Milton's own mouth, to my friend who was well acquainted with and *had from him, and from his relations after his death, most of this account of his life and writings following.*"

The " friend " is John Aubrey, and Wood's account is in fact partly based on a few pages of untidy notes [1] sent him by Aubrey in the year 1681, but more largely upon a Life of Milton in Manuscript which has been preserved among Wood's papers in the Bodleian.[2]

[1] Bodl. MS. Aubrey 8.   [2] Bodl. MS. Wood D. 4.

This is an unsigned, undated composition evidently by one who had personal knowledge of his subject. Warton described Wood's Life as " the first and the groundwork of all the lives of Milton." But the groundwork of Wood's Life in its turn was this anonymous Life in manuscript, whose merit and authenticity I hope to make good. It has been estimated that nearly one half of Wood's Life has been taken almost verbatim from the manuscript, whilst a valuable tenth part was furnished out of Aubrey's notes. Mr. Parsons, who edited the manuscript for the *English Historical Review* in 1902, was unable to find out who wrote it, but conjectured that it was one of Milton's friends, an elderly man, not a clergyman, not an Oxford man, probably a doctor and possibly Dr. Paget.

Each of these first four biographies has its own stamp and value. Of the four compilers, Aubrey and the anonymous biographer—the two who provided Wood with his material—are independent of one another; and Edward Phillips, writing last, is independent both of Wood and of them. Wood has a few points of his own. As an Oxford man he can set right the account he got from Aubrey and the anonymous biographer of the local connection of Milton's family with Halton and Shotover and Milton. He has a fuller list of Milton's works than the others and he makes it from the works themselves. But his independence of his two informants breaks out blatantly in his indictment of Milton for siding with the faction. Aubrey had written that " whatever Milton wrote against monarchy was out of no animosity to the King's person or out of any faction or interest, but out of a pure zeal to the liberty of mankind." Wood hits out as a party man against a man of the opposite party, and is the first of a long line of biographers who let political prejudice discolour their estimate of Milton's character. Milton had already been alluded to in William Winstanley's *Lives of the most famous English Poets*, a biographical dictionary issued in 1687. Under the name of John Milton he writes this and no more: " John Milton was one, whose natural parts might deservedly give him a place amongst the principal of our English Poets, having written two Heroick Poems and a Tragedy; namely Paradise Lost, Paradise Regain'd and Sampson Agonistes; But his Fame is gone out like a Candle in a snuff, and his Memory will always Stink, which might have lived in honourable repute, had he not been a notorious Trayter, and most impiously and villanously bely'd that blessed Martyr, King Charles the First." Winstanley wrote no life, gave no facts and attempted no character. Wood, who wrote the first printed biography of Milton, began the evil work of twisting facts and misinterpreting motives. He says—and no falser word has been said of Milton—that he " did great matters to obtain a name and wealth." The anonymous biographer had insisted that Milton's " labours for the glory of God and some public good " were wholly disinterested. Wood tells us that in *Regii Sanguinis Clamor* " Salmasius was highly extolled and Milton *had his just character given*,"—maliciously re-writing the anonymous biographer's sentence: " Salmasius was here hugely extolled, and Mr. Milton *as falsely defamed.*" And, as we shall see, Wood's omissions are as telling as his revisions.

Aubrey interested himself in Wood's great enterprise of the biographical dictionary and undertook to collect information on the many persons about whom Wood was groping for facts. He was a delightful, sociable gossip, who made a business as well as a pleasure of knowing everything about everybody. There is no mystery about Aubrey's notes on Milton, except the fitful shadow of mystery cast by a somewhat irregular handwriting. They are dated incidentally 1681 and were sent to Wood in that year. Aubrey was an impatient man and particularly disliked the habit—only too frequent in his learned acquaintances —of procrastination in the answering of letters. He gives an amusing, exasperated account in one letter of his efforts to get an answer out of Dr. Birkett. He wrote, called, wrote again: still no answer. Finally he comments: " 'Tis strange that a man of letters should be *so horribly dull and slow*." He never seems to have reconciled himself to this weakness of literary men. On 2nd April, 1681, he writes to Wood: " My good friend Mr. Wood, what a God's name are you asleep or dead, or what is become of you? I wrote a letter, or two, to you not long since desiring you to let me know by what friend or by what carrier I might conveigh my MS. of Lives."

In September Wood had the manuscript in his hands. The notes on Milton are set down in Aubrey's seemingly higgledy-piggledy but really methodical fashion on three sheets of paper. His personal acquaintance with Milton is clinched by the following: " He was scarce as high as I am (*Quaere*, Quot feet am I high? *Resp*. Of middle Stature)." He draws at various times upon the poet's brother, Christopher

Milton, his widow, and his nephew, Edward Phillips, for dates, facts, and personal details, and is usually careful to note his authority. He learnt from Christopher Milton that in John Milton's early school-days when he studied hard, and sat up late, often till twelve or one o'clock at night, " his father ordered the maid to sitt up for him " : from Edward Phillips that " he made his nephews songsters, and sing from the time they were with him," and that it was these same nephews, John and Edward Phillips, his first scholars, that Milton's young bride heard beaten and cry in the large silent house " where no company came to her." He gives a time-table of Milton's day, evidently in his later years, and some notes for a character —thus: " Extreme pleasant in his conversation, and at dinner, supper, etc. but satyricall . . . Of a very cheerful humour. . . . He would be cheerful even in his gowt-fits and sing."

When Aubrey began his notes he did not know Edward Phillips, was ignorant even of his Christian name; but he made his acquaintance, evidently at a suggestion from Mrs. Milton, on purpose to sound him, and was amply rewarded. I read this story in the notes themselves. On the second leaf of the first sheet Aubrey writes, " *vidua affirmat* she gave all his papers to his Nephew, that he brought up, a sister's son . . . Phillips, who lives near the Maypole in the Strand." Lower down on the same page he writes " *Quaere* Mr. . . . Phillips for a perfect Catalogue of his writings," and at another time in different ink he has written *Edw.* in the blank space. On the second sheet of notes Edward Phillips has with his own hand written the list of Milton's writings which Aubrey wanted, and over-leaf a paragraph about his travel abroad and his tuition of his two nephews, himself and his brother, John. He told Aubrey some interesting facts about his uncle's writing of *Paradise Lost*—that it was begun as a Tragedy about fifteen or sixteen years before the Epic was thought of: that during the composition of it he, Edward Phillips, was his chief amanuensis—this is a note in his own hand—and that " all the time of writing it the poet's vein began at the autumnal equinoctial and ceased at the vernal."

This last curious piece of information is one of the few things generally remembered in Edward Phillips's own Life of Milton, written later as Preface to the *Letters of State*. But we owe more to it than this. It is twice the length of the anonymous Life, which is itself longer than Wood's, and it is fuller and more detailed than either. Though he is not to be trusted with dates— he gets wrong both the year of Milton's birth, writing 1606 instead of 1608, and the year of his death, writing 1673 for 1674—he has a good memory for places. Dr. Johnson remarked upon " the respect paid to Milton by his biographers: every house in which he resided is mentioned." It was Edward Phillips who made it possible for later biographers to do this, for he notices in its place in the story every one of the eleven houses, including temporary lodgings, in which Milton lived in London.[1] He introduces some of Milton's friends whom we should not other-wise have met, notably Dr. Davis's daughters, one of whom he says Milton designed to marry when his wife had deserted him, and he had written his mind on

[1] He omits the temporary lodging with Millington for which we have only Richardson's authority, *vide* p. 203 *infra*.

THE EARLY LIVES OF MILTON

divorce, " a very handsome and witty gentlewoman,
but averse, as it is said, to this motion: " and Mr.
Alphry and Mr. Miller, " young sparks . . ." with
whom in the early days of his schoolmastering " he
would now and then keep a Gaudy day." It is he
who tells us that after he was blind Milton used his
two youngest daughters as readers, until they protested
and were put to learn embroidery. He attempts no
" character " of his uncle, though he tells us incidentally of his " insuperable industry," his generous
disposition, and his frugal and temperate life.

The anonymous writer's biography has an importance of its own. His first paragraph combines a plea
for the biography of good men with an ardent eulogy
of Milton's character, and his aim throughout is a
sympathetic portrait of Milton both as a public and
a private person. Like Aubrey he asserts the high-
minded and philosophical character of Milton's political principles. Milton acted on a disinterested belief
in liberty, and " was not concerned in the corrupt
designs of his masters." Of Cromwell's government
he says categorically that Milton was " a stranger to
their inner counsels." He alone gives chapter and
verse for Milton's impartial generosity to men of both
parties. " And as he was not linked to one party by
self-interest, so neither was he divided from the other
by animosity; but he was forward to do any of them
good offices, when their particular cases afforded him
ground to appear on their behalf. . . . He procured
relief for a grandchild of Spenser's, a papist, and for
Sir Wm. Davenant when taken prisoner." He notes
that though frugal in his life, he loved to buy books,
and was generous in relieving the wants of his friends.

Wood suppresses all this.   The anonymous biographer
ends with a character sketch, the chief part of which
Wood took over word for word:

" He was of a moderate stature, and well-propor-
tioned, of a ruddy complexion, light brown hair and
handsome features; save that his eyes were none of
the quickest.   But his blindness, which proceeded
from a *gutta serena*, added no further blemish to them.
His deportment was sweet and affable;—(Wood leaves
out ' sweet ')—and his gate erect and manly, bespeaking
courage and undauntedness (or a Nil conscire) on which
account he wore a sword while he had his sight, and
was skilled in using it.   He had an excellent ear, and
could bear a part both in vocal and instrumental
music."   He tells us how Milton divided his day,
consecrating the early hours to the composition of
poetry.   Aubrey spoke of Milton's wit and pleasantry:
the anonymous biographer gives us an example.
Waking early in the morning, he says, " he commonly
had a good stock of verses ready against his amanuensis
came, which if it happened to be later than ordinary
he would complain, saying *he wanted to be milked.*"
And finally from the anonymous biographer we learn
that Milton's death " happened with so little pain or
emotion that the time of his expiring was not to be
perceived by those in the room,"—a fact which was
seized by Wood, and repeated by later biographers.
Dr. Johnson's stately and beautiful phrase, " He died
by a quiet and silent expiration," is his own characteristic rendering of the simple fact first recorded by
the anonymous biographer.   The man who recorded
it must have been of Milton's inner circle, or he was
intimate with those who were, and his affectionate

b

tribute carries weight in either case. It carries still
more weight when we know who he was. By chance,
on a different quest, I discovered that he was John
Phillips, Milton's younger and scapegrace nephew.

I had set out to track down Milton's amanuenses,
who, as we know from Edward Phillips and the anonymous biographer, were often his pupils. I was also
interested to know whether any of his pupils adopted
his peculiar spellings. Milton's unusual spelling of
thir for the possessive pronoun *their* was one good test.
The famous erratum in the first edition of *Paradise
Lost*, Book II, line 14, " for *we* read *wee*," records his
attempt to distinguish, by spelling, the emphatic from
the unemphatic forms of the personal pronouns. *Their*
he spelt *thir* normally, only writing *their* when he required a special emphasis. So far as I knew, no one
before Milton had spelt the possessive pronoun *thir*.
My pursuit of handwritings and spellings led me at
once to the two Phillips nephews.

There is plenty of Edward Phillips's handwriting in
the Bodleian, for he transcribed and translated for
Ashmole. He writes a clear Italian hand, uses the
Greek form of *e*, and spells *their* in the normal way.
His hand is not found in the Trinity manuscript of
Milton's poems, but it appears in Milton's Commonplace book in the British Museum. In both these
manuscript notebooks, Milton employed various hands
to write for him after he was blind.

Of John Phillips only one manuscript is catalogued
in the Bodleian, his *Satyr against Hypocrites*.[1] Three
hands are at a glance distinguishable in this manuscript: first, the Dedication, filling two pages, signed

[1] Bodl. MS. Rawl. Poet. 30.

by John Phillips, is written in a formal Italian hand, whose calligraphic character becomes considerably modified towards the close; secondly, the text of the poem is in a careful formal hand, mixed Italian-English; and finally, the marginal headings or gloss to the text, along with certain corrections and inserted passages, are in a third more cursive and " characteristic " hand, again mixed Italian-English. Was any of these hands the author's ? The scribe of the text of the poem seemed to be a formal copyist: no corrections of any interest are in his hand. But I soon became convinced that the writer of the marginal gloss, the corrections and additions to the text, was John Phillips himself. In one place [1] the scribe has left a blank in the text, and into it this third hand has inserted the bars of music and accompanying words which satirize the Presbyterian manner of Church-singing. Now Phillips alone would know exactly how he wished this to stand: naturally he would tell the scribe to leave a space, and would write in the staves and words himself. The writer of the marginal glosses strikes out a word and substitutes another in a manner which betrays the composer rather than the copier. But the clinching proof to my mind was that this writer spelt *thir* in Milton's unusual manner. The scribe of the text spells *their* throughout. On turning to the Dedication signed by John Phillips I found once more the peculiar spelling of *thir* used consistently, and after a close study of the handwriting in comparison with that of the corrector and annotator to the text, I satisfied myself that John Phillips also wrote the two pages of Dedication. He chose here to use an Italian script

[1] f. 5 verso.

as formal and decorative as he could manage, whereas he wrote the marginal glosses and textual corrections in his more ordinary cursive hand. Though the general effect of the two hands is different, each has a tendency to approach the other: the formal Italian script of the Dedication to which the Italian *e* is proper becomes more cursive at the end of the second page, and the inverted English *e* slips in: on the other hand, the writer of the marginal glosses, who commonly uses the inverted English *e* or Greek *e*, will occasionally write an important word in Italian script, employing there the correct Italian *e*. The word *sermon* in the margin of the third folio will at once be found to be in a similar hand to that of the Dedication. It seems then that John Phillips wrote his Dedication in calligraphic hand, that he got a careful scribe to copy out the text of the poem for him, and that he afterwards inserted in his own more cursive " mixed " hand various corrections and annotations. A reference in the poem dates it 1654. John Phillips was then twenty-three.

Happening for another purpose to turn at this time to the anonymous Life of Milton in Wood's collection in the Bodleian,[1] I was struck at once by the similarity of the handwriting to that of John Phillips's Dedication to the *Satyr*, and further by the appearance here again of Milton's peculiar spelling of *thir*. I became convinced also that the writer of the anonymous Life not only wrote but composed it: more than once he alters his mind in the middle of a sentence. I was now reminded of one of the amanuenses' hands in the Trinity manuscript, and looking up the facsimile found the two sonnets to Cyriack Skinner, written

[1] *Vide* facsimile facing p. 19 *infra*.

they hold forth thir false lights, thro' signes ratus=
os, men, are lead, or rather gulld by them into thir
destruction. Yet to vaile thir Ignoran:e, urge, all they
can, an outward formality. and strictnes', by which they
domineer over the Consitences of deluded People, wth a
tyramous and glossd religion, as wth Barnacles, holding
thir auditors by the noses, and powring th'invenomd Potion
of Cæbe's vain Woman. down the throats of thir cre=
dulous slaves. What a Contempt this hath brought
upon, religion is too well experienced. And that these
men are the authors of it is too manifest, For there is
no rational man that despises religion, for it self, onely
is angrie that that religion which, he sees so full, of
mockery toward God, should be esteemd a right worship. And
This may suffice to shew the limits of my intentions, who
since I meddle not wth ye Indifferent men, can no way, be
thought to reflect at all upon ye best. Wth this fortifi=
cation I though it necessary to pallisado these few sheets
against the batteries of slander, expecting for my attempt
to be saluted wth yᵉ names of Atheist & Prophane. Sr I
shall cease to trouble you any furder, onely crave the boldnes
to subscribe my self

                    Sr
                        Your most obedient
                            Servant
                                J. Phillips

JOHN PHILLIPS'S DEDICATION TO HIS *SATYR AGAINST
HYPOCRITES.* Bodl. MS. Rawl. Poet. 30

(to face p. xviii)

indubitably by the same hand that wrote the anonymous Life.[1] The word *their* occurring twice in the
second sonnet is spelt the first time *their*, corrected to
thir, and the second time *thir* without hesitation. This
is the only place in the whole manuscript where *thir* is
spelt thus in any hand but Milton's. In judging the
handwritings we must remember that John Phillips
was a young man of twenty-three when in 1654 he
wrote the *Satyr against Hypocrites*, and that the anonymous Life was written, according to Malone, in 1686
or 1687, more than thirty years later. A man's hand
may change much in thirty years. The handwriting
of the sonnets is much more evidently like that of the
anonymous Life than either is like the handwriting of
the Dedication to the *Satyr against Hypocrites*. I am
fully aware of this, and I am not so rash as to swear by
first impressions, powerful and compelling as they
sometimes are. But a prolonged study of these manuscripts over a period of years has left me still more
surely convinced that the same hand wrote all three.
My conclusion is that John Phillips learnt to spell *thir*
in his uncle's peculiar fashion, that he acted as his
amanuensis at least once in later years, and that he
wrote the anonymous Life.

If John Phillips is the author, then Wood's statement may be strictly true that Aubrey got from
Milton *and from his relations after his death* most of the
account of his life and writings which he, Wood, was
able to print. Though Aubrey, as we saw, went out
of his way to make Edward Phillips's acquaintance, the
notes he sent Wood in 1681 make no mention at all of
the other Phillips nephew. John Phillips's biography
is of the short formal kind suitable for a Preface to a

[1] *Vide* facsimile facing p. xxvi *infra*.

volume of Milton's works. Perhaps it was composed for
some such purpose and the enterprize came to nought.
Then, we may imagine, Aubrey chanced to meet John
Phillips, found he had written a Life of his uncle, obtained it from him, and sent it in triumph to Wood.

Mr. Parson's conjectures about the anonymous
author are right in so far as they are negative.   John
Phillips was not an Oxford man.   His brother Edward
studied at Magdalen College, though he left without
taking his degree; Milton formed a poor opinion of
the University of Oxford, and it was the fate of John
to receive all his academic education from his uncle,
who took the boy after his father's death " under his
special charge and care."   Neither was he a clergyman.
He became a witty satirist, and his shafts were aimed
first at the Presbyterian clergy in his *Satyr against
Hypocrites*, and later at the High Churchmen in his
Speculum Crape Gownorum.   I had always thought ill-
founded Mr. Parson's conjecture that the anonymous
biographer was a doctor.   The details he gives of
Milton's optical trouble, on which Mr. Parsons
hazards his guess, are such as might be familiar to
the sufferer's lay friends.   Compared with ourselves,
intelligent people in those days seem to have known
more—and possibly did not talk less—about their
physical ailments.   In my ramblings among manuscripts of the period I came upon a sheet headed " On
the present ill State of my health," dated 1677, which
turned out to be written by Pepys—a full account, in
a vocabulary inexhaustibly rich and expressive, of every
physical symptom and sensation which he experienced
in each part of his anatomy.   Milton's anonymous
biographer need not have been a doctor.   Neither did

I detect the marks which stamped him as an elderly man, of an age to be Milton's contemporary. But if John Phillips is the author, the Life has a fresh value. Of all the early Lives it is the most outspoken in admiration of Milton as a man. Now John Phillips lived with him through the impressionable years of his childhood and youth, the years of his uncle's unhappy first marriage and of the turmoil of civil war; he knew the good and the bad of his uncle's character.

John and Edward Phillips have received unequal treatment at the hands of their biographers. While Edward has been white-washed, John has been much reviled. Godwin, in his Lives of the brothers, writes thus of Milton's funeral: " It is obvious to conjecture that Edward Phillips, his nearest male relative and afterward the historian of his life, probably filled the place of chief mourner, in this last farewell to the ashes of his adored preceptor and uncle. John Phillips, on the contrary, did not, I trust, pollute the sad solemnity with his unhallowed presence." What are we to think ? Edward, in his biography, says Milton died in 1673 towards the latter end of the summer: whereas in fact he died on 8th November, 1674. And he tells us that he had a very decent interment according to his quality. John gives us the date right, and tells of the rare quietness—a matter of wonder to those who were present—with which Milton breathed his last breath. John must have been present, Edward unexpectedly absent.

John Phillips's Life is yet to be written. His relations with his uncle must be put straight. Born in 1631, he was adopted by Milton at the age of nine, educated by him and brought up under his roof. When he was

twenty, he wrote under his uncle's direction a Latin
reply to an attack on Milton in the great Salmasius
controversy.   This maiden effort is described by Wood
thus: " John Phillips, having early imbibed in a most
plentiful manner the rankest anti-monarchical Principles, from that villanous leading incendiary, Joh.
Milton his uncle, but not in any university, proved in a
short time so notable a Proficient in his bloody School
of King-killing, that he judged himself sufficiently
qualified publicly to engage in his master's quarrel;
and this he did in his *Miltoni Defensio*."   In 1653
Milton made both his musically-trained nephews
compose complimentary poems to his friend Henry
Lawes, the musician.   The poems are printed in
Henry Lawes's volume of *Ayres* of that year.   Two
years later appeared the *Satyr against Hypocrites*,
anonymously published but certainly the work of John
Phillips.   This poem ran through a number of editions
after the Restoration, and its popularity is easy to
understand.   Masson calls it an anti-Puritan and anti-
Miltonic production, and thinks that by the time it
was published Phillips must have got quite beyond his
uncle's control.   Among new acquaintance, he states
dogmatically, he had forsworn his uncle's politics, and
from this time onwards was alienated from him.   Let
us look a little closer at the facts.   The *Satyr against
Hypocrites* is not " anti-Miltonic," nor " anti-Puritan "
as Masson suggests.   It is a satire against the Presbyterians.   The third edition of it, 1661, has actually
the title *The Religion of the Hypocritical Presbyterians*.
By 1655 Milton himself had long been thoroughly
disgusted with the Presbyterians; their bigotry and
hypocrisy had gone home to him when he found him-

self preached against for his own assumption of liberty
of conscience and opinion in his pamphlets on divorce;
and so long ago as 1644 he had charged them in his
Areopagitica with assuming a tyranny exactly as bad
as that of the Bishops.   Later, in his *Tenure of Kings
and Magistrates* of 1649, he attacked the Presbyterian
divines in strong and scathing words for their neglect
of their true duties, urging them to " study harder,
and attend the office of good Pastors, knowing that
he whose flock is least among them hath a dreadful
charge, not performd by mounting twise into the chair
with a formal preachment huddl'd up at the odd hours
of a whole lazy week."   When they meet, " let them
assemble with thir Elders and Deacons to the preserving
of Church discipline," and not " a pack of Clergiemen
by themselves to belly-cheare . . ." or to " abuse and
gull the simple Laity."

John Phillips's dedication to the *Satyr against
Hypocrites* sounds like an echo:

" While [the hypocritical divines] hold forth thir
false lights, men are lead or rather gulld by them into
thir destruction.   Yet to vaile thir Ignorance they
urge, all they can, an outward formality and strictnes,
by which they domineer over the . . . People with a
tyrannous and gloss'd religion." [1]   The satire itself
gives only too vivid a picture of the addiction of these
pastors to " belly-cheer."

Phillips's *Satyr* is not written as Milton would have
written it: that goes without saying.   Phillips, with
his incurably coarse mind, revels in the sheer human
fun, the gross comedy and crude ironic contrasts dis-
played in the life of the Presbyterians as he watched it in

[1] Bodl. MS. Rawl. Poet. 30.

its natural centre, the Parish Church.   The Presbyterian manner of church-singing, out of tune and out
of time, may well have been a family jest in Milton's
musical household.   John Phillips lets fly in the following lines—part of the tale of the Sunday service:

> Straight then the Clerk began with potsheard voice
> To grope a tune, singing with woful noise,
> Like a crackt Sans-bell jarring in the Steeple,
> Tom Sternhold's wretched Pricksong to the people:
> Then out the people yaul an hundred parts,
> Some rore, some whine, some creake like wheeles of Carts;
> Such notes the Gamut never yet did know,
> Nor num'rous keyes of Harps'call in a rowe
> Their heights and depths could ever comprehend,
> Now below double *A re* some descend
> 'Bove *E la* squealing now ten noates some fly,
> Straight then as if they knew they were too high
> With headlong haste downstairs again they tumble,
> Discords and concords O how thick they jumble,
> Like untam'd horses tearing with their throats
> One wretched stave into a hundred notes.
> Some lazie throated fellowes thus did bawle:

Here in the manuscript Phillips wrote in the staves
and the ill-joined words in his own hand, and drew
attention in the margin to " Thir excellent manner of
singing."   The sanctimonious " Sunday Levite " with
his double cap, his white cuffs, and whiter gloves, is
before us in a few excellent satiric touches: and when
he mounts the pulpit,

> Out comes his kerchief then, which he unfolds
> As gravely as his text, and fast he holds
> In's wrath-denouncing hand ; then marke when he prayed
> How he rear'd his reverend whites, and softly sayd
> A long " most merciful " or " O allmighty."

In the manuscript Phillips has altered " merciful " to
" *mur*ciful," and again, in the Ash Wednesday Sermon
that follows, the affected parsonical utterance comes
through in the delightful spellings, " The *Laud* " and
" most gl*au*rious Truth." Much of the satire is
unquotably gross. But grossness belonged to the age,
and Milton's own polemical writings are disfigured by
it. John Phillips went too far, but we can see now
that Masson was wrong when he assumed that the
Satyr against Hypocrites must have been the death-blow
to Milton's friendly relations with his clever young
nephew. Milton may have disliked the coarse in-
decencies of the *Satyr*, but who can think that he failed
to be diverted by its wit ?

Of John Phillips's long life it is not easy to piece
together many facts. He was evidently employed by
his uncle in some sort as assistant during the fifties
when Milton was Latin Secretary to the Council.
Much later he was mixed up with Titus Oates and the
Popish Plot. He was a voluminous writer, and we can
follow, spasmodically, his literary career. Aubrey says
he was happy at jiggish poetry. Wood dislikes him
and dismisses him with bad words, " a man of very
loose principles, atheistical, deserts his wife and
children." John Dunton, the eccentric bookseller,
notices Phillips among his " hackney authors "—" a
Gentleman of good learning and well born. He'll
write you a design off in a very little time, if the gout
(or Claret) don't stop him." This was written in
1705, thirty years after Milton's death, when Phillips
was an old man of seventy-four. Along with the gout,
he inherited good learning and good breeding from his
uncle. He must have had a warm impulsive tempera-

ment, good wits and a capacity for hard, quick work. Certainly he was no ascetic; and there is a strain of gross indecency in his books which is repellent to modern taste. But we may guess that he was an amusing and affectionate nephew, and that his uncle would not easily break with him. If I am right about John Phillips's handwriting, we have a glimpse of him on a certain page in the manuscript of Milton's poems preserved in the Library of Trinity College, Cambridge. On this page John Phillips has copied out two sonnets for his uncle, clearly, it seems, for the edition of poems to be published in 1673. The second sonnet is that on his blindness addressed to Cyriack Skinner, and Phillips has not only made the fair copy, but has returned to it and written in at his uncle's request what must be the poet's second thoughts. He first wrote:

> " Yet I argue not
> Against Gods hand or will, nor bate a jot
> Of heart or hope ; but still attend to steer
> Uphillward."

But Milton made three improvements which Phillips put in for him, and the corrected version runs:

> " Yet I argue not
> Against heavns hand or will, nor bate a jot
> Of heart or hope ; but still bear up and steer
> Right onward."

John Phillips came to see his uncle, then, about the year 1673, and made himself useful, as a friendly nephew should. And this was surely one of many times.

Both the Phillips brothers became hack writers—or in the more graceful phrase of the period, hackney

⑦

To day deep thoughts resolve with me to drench
In mirth, that after no repenting draws,
Let Euclid rest and Archimedes pause,
And what the Swede intends and what the French.
To measure life learn thou betimes, and know
Toward solid good what leads the nearest way;
For other things mild Heavn a time ordains,
And disapproves that care, though wise in show,
That with superfluous burden loads the day,
And when God sends a cheerfull houre, refrains.

22

Cyriack, this three years day these eys though clear
To outward view, of blemish or of spot;
Bereft of light their seeing have forgot,
Nor to their idle orbs doth sight appear
Of Sun or Moon or Starre throughout the year,
Or man, or woman. Yet I argue not
Against heavns hand or will, nor bate a jot
Of heart or hope; but still bear up and steer
Right onward. What supports me, dost thou ask?
The conscience, Friend, to have lost them overplyd
In libertyes defence, my noble taske,
Of which all Europe talks from side to side.
This thought might lead me through the worlds vain mask
Content though blind, had I no better guide.

SONNETS TRANSCRIBED BY JOHN PHILLIPS.   Trin. MS. f. 49

(to face p. xxvi)

authors—and picked up a living as they could, sometimes in ways not reputable. Fate played them a
malicious trick in making them the nephews of so
great a man and forbidding them to join their names
with his for their own profit and honour. Daniel
Skinner, to whom Milton entrusted his manuscript of
De Doctrina Christiana, cannot have been the only
young man whose career was blocked by the ill-repute
of his friendship with Milton the regicide. Edward
Phillips did not risk putting his name to the volume
which commemorated his uncle, and John Phillips
had to see his biography used by a man who took over
the bulk of his composition word for word without
acknowledgment, yet omitted every fact and reversed
every sentiment which did special honour to his uncle's
noble character.

On a certain page of one of Anthony à Wood's books
in the Bodleian three of Milton's first biographers
come together in a humorous conjunction. On
1st August, 1681, Wood bought for 1s. 6d. a copy of
Edward Phillips's *Theatrum Poetarum* from a stationer
" newlie sett up in Holywell." He annotated it with
his crabbed pen and reddish ink in his usual fashion.
Phillips had done his brother John a good turn by
introducing him among the modern poets with somewhat inflated praise. In the first sentence of this
brotherly " puff " of John Phillips, Wood has under-
lined a phrase—" *maternal nephew and disciple of an
Author of most deserv'd Fame late deceas't,*" and has
written in the margin, " John Milton, a rogue." We
witness the first clash of sympathies and antipathies
which were to conflict for more than a century in the
biography and criticism of Milton.

The poet's next biographer, John Toland, never knew Milton, but he followed close on the heels of those who did; he knew Aubrey, he looked through Edward Phillips's papers, talked with John Phillips, and learnt some particulars from one of Milton's amanuenses and from his widow. Toland, author of *Christianity not Mysterious*, deist, free-thinker, " prompt at priests to jeer," was an ardent admirer of Milton's political writings. In the quaint epitaph which he composed for his own tombstone a few days before his death he calls himself " Veritatis propugnator, Libertatis asser-tor, Nullius autem sectator aut cliens," and it is in this character that he found Milton a kindred spirit. His Life of Milton appeared in 1698 as preface to the first collected edition of the poet's prose works. In the main narrative he follows Edward Phillips with an occasional glance at Wood, but he gives much more space to political events, viewing them from his own side; he lets in a larger and freer air by quoting fully from Milton's prose and verse—he sets out indeed, for the first time, the great passages of self-revelation; and he supplies here and there some new matter. His ears and mind were open to all that concerned the Milton he chiefly loved, the Milton of *Areopagitica*, champion of freedom and free thought. He judges, from his own bias, that " to display the different effects of liberty and tyranny was the chief design of his *Paradise Lost*." He records, what the first bio-graphers omitted to tell, that the *Paradise Lost* was in danger of having its licence refused, because the licenser, ignorant or malicious, saw treason in the lines about the eclipse, which " with fear of change perplexes monarchs." He notes that in his later years Milton was not a professed member of any Christian sect, that he frequented none of their assemblies, nor made use of their rites in his family—an illuminating fact which neither of the nephews had thought fit to expose. He tells us of the generous direction and help which Milton gave to other writers; he lights up the shrewd, practical side of Milton's character in a flash when he says that he sold his library before his death, partly because the heirs he left could not make use of it, partly because he thought he might sell it more to their advantage than they would be able to do themselves. His sketch of Milton's character and personal life is fuller and truer than any that went before, except that of John Phillips in the manuscript which Wood so freely plundered. Toland not only collected matter from those who knew Milton at first-hand and from Milton's own writings: he had the sympathy to see its significance, and the wit to select what revealed the man himself. His portrait has a glow about it, and the faithful details fall into their place.

In the first half of the eighteenth century Milton's fame grew and prospered, his works were frequently edited and his life was as often written. Fenton in 1725 wrote a short account of Milton's life as preface to an edition of his poems. This, " Mr. Fenton's elegant abridgement," as Johnson rightly called it, —it was one of those " honeysuckle lives " of Milton whose smooth and gracious tone exasperated him,— supplies no new matter; but three other biographers, Jonathan Richardson the painter, Thomas Birch, and Bishop Newton, took the trouble to make minute inquiries of Milton's descendants and acquaintance and were able to record fresh details that have the stamp of personal knowledge. Richardson's Life, prefixed to his *Explanatory Notes and Remarks on Milton's* PARADISE LOST, rambles in the manner of a discursive essay, reflecting the eccentric, charming character of its author, but it gives here and there an unforgettable glimpse of Milton himself. " Other stories I have heard concerning the posture he was usually in when he dictated,—that he sat leaning backward obliquely in an easy chair, with his leg flung over the elbow of it." Richardson had the good fortune to meet several people who had known or seen Milton. His warm admiration and his personal affection for Milton,—for such indeed it is, though he never met him in the life,—moved him to record many a scene, or incident, to note down many a trivial detail, such as bring the living man before us. Through Richardson's eyes, the eyes of a painter, we see Milton led along the streets in his blindness by Millington, the seller of old books in Little Britain, who at that time gave Milton a lodging in his house. We see him in a grey Camblet coat in cold weather; and in warm sunny weather sitting in a grey coarse cloth coat outside his house near Bunhill Fields to enjoy the fresh air. With the old Dorsetshire clergyman we stumble up the staircase of a certain small London house and enter a room hung with rusty green to find Milton sitting in an elbow chair in neat black clothes, pale but not cadaverous, his hands and fingers gouty. Richardson was interested in the technicalities of other arts than his own: he is the first to draw intelligent attention to Milton's care for spelling and other typographical points, and so he lays bare more than the fastidious pains, the noble patience with which Milton laboured to perfect his text after he was blind. " This is all I intend," he writes, " not a Panegyrick, not to give my own sense of what a man should be, but what This Man Really was."

Birch and Newton compiled in more pedestrian fashion all the matter available, and yet collected a few new facts. Both talked with a granddaughter of Milton, Deborah's daughter Elizabeth. Here the personal tradition ends. What is the value of the evidence, and how does Milton himself emerge from it ?

We know now that the three first independent accounts of Milton's life and character were written by men who knew him intimately,—the two nephews, Edward and John Phillips, and Aubrey, a personal acquaintance, who took pains to get his facts from the family. These Lives are original; the Lives of Wood and Toland drew their chief facts from them, and through Wood and Toland the original matter passed into the main stream. Our new knowledge that the anonymous Life was written by Milton's own nephew, John Phillips, gives a fresh strength and vitality to the essential core of the biography. This was the scapegrace nephew who got into trouble with the Council over a licentious book of songs, wrote a coarse *Satyr* upon the Presbyterians that was to enjoy a prolonged popularity with the Royalists, and as far as we can see had nothing at all of the Puritan in his composition. Yet his Life of Milton is, in the words of its first editor, who was ignorant of the author, " the one seventeenth century biography of the poet in which he is treated with entire sympathy." That Milton kept on friendly terms with him till the last year of his life is, I think, clear; liking must have been mutual, and it speaks as

c

well for the uncle's genial tolerance, as for the light-
hearted nephew's discernment.   We must remember
that both the nephews suffered the extreme rigours of
Milton's educational system: he beat them, he taught
them to sing, he taught John to spell in his peculiar
fashion, he put them through a drastic curriculum.
Both speak of the strictness of his discipline, which
though they bore it themselves was such, as John
Phillips suggests, that " the temper of our gentry could
not bear."   Yet, as Edward conveyed to Aubrey,
Milton was a delightful companion out of school hours:
" as he was severe on the one hand, so he was most
familiar and free in his conversation, to those to whom
most severe in his way of education." [1]   Something
of the affection they felt for their uncle comes through
in each of their biographies, but it is warmer and less
reserved in John's.   We must make up our minds
about the integrity of these first witnesses.   How far
are they to be trusted in their facts and judgments ?

We know very little of the reputation of the two
nephews, rather too much perhaps of Aubrey's.   John
Phillips seems to have been clever and reckless, Edward
more serious and steady-going.   John Evelyn thought
Edward a quiet, decent person, fit to take into his house
as tutor to his son;   John Dunton thought John
Phillips a man of learning and well-born, whose clever
pen could always be relied upon, unless the gout (or
claret) stopped him.   From their published works we
get an impression of Edward as a respectable scholar
for his day, of John as a nimble-witted and industrious

---

[1] This sentence has been misread : the printed texts give wrongly :
" to whom most *sowre* in his way of education."   No one who knew
Milton ever called him sour.

hack-writer.   Each, as we have seen, wrote his uncle's Life independently.   While Wood adopts sentence after sentence nearly verbatim from John Phillips, and Toland does the same with Edward Phillips and Wood, there is no verbal correspondence between the biographies of the two nephews.   It is plain, I think, that neither saw what the other wrote.   But their evidence on vital points is found to tally.   This says much for their integrity as witnesses: in the issue each silently vindicates the other.   And further, where their information is independent, it is often supported by other evidence.   John Phillips, alone of the first biographers, mentions these four facts: first, that Milton's grandfather had an estate of £500 at Stanton St. John; second, that Milton saved Davenant's life when he was in danger; third, that Milton was arrested by the Sergeant-at-Arms shortly after the Restoration; fourth, that he was invited to be Latin Secretary under Charles II.   Now Masson, independently—for he had not read the anonymous Life—identified Milton's grandfather as a yeoman of Stanton St. John.   The second fact, about the saving of Davenant's life, is corroborated by Richardson, and quite independently and on good evidence by Jacob Tonson, who had heard it from Davenant's own son.[1]   The third, about the arrest, is attested by the Journals of the House of Commons for that year.   The fourth is again corroborated by Richardson.   All that John Phillips tells us of Milton's habits of composition is supported by the best of witnesses, Milton himself.   " The Evenings," writes

[1] See letter from Jacob Tonson : *The Manuscript of Milton's Paradise Lost, Book I*, edited by Helen Darbishire, p. xiv, and cf. J. Phillips, p. 30 and note p. 338 *infra*.

Phillips, " he spent in reading some choice Poets, by way of refreshment after the days toyl, and to store his Fancy against Morning." . . . " And David's Psalms were in esteem with him above all Poetry." . . . " And he waking early had a good stock of verses ready against his Amanuensis came."   Now Milton tells us in his lofty poetical way that he makes a habit of reading Hebrew and Greek poetry at night, and that this provides him with thoughts that move him easily to compose:

> Thee *Sion* and the flowrie Brooks beneath
> That wash thy hallowd feet, and warbling flow,
> Nightly I visit : nor sometimes forget
> Those other two equal'd with me in Fate,
> So were I equal'd with them in renown,
> Blind *Thamyris* and blind *Mæonides*,
> And *Tiresias* and *Phineus* Prophets old.
> Then feed on thoughts, that voluntarie move
> Harmonious numbers.

Edward Phillips alone of the first biographers speaks of the tasks to which he set his daughters of reading aloud to him in languages which they did not understand, and he tells us that when they found this too irksome they were sent out to learn embroidery. These facts are fully supported by the evidence taken in the dispute on Milton's nuncupative will, first published by Thomas Warton.

Aubrey's accuracy and fidelity have been often discredited.   Wood, after a quarrel, wrote of him as " a shiftless person, roving and magotie headed, and sometimes little better than crazed. And being exceedingly credulous, would stuff his many letters sent to A. W. with folliries and misinformations. . . ."

But the truth is that Anthony à Wood, deeply in trouble for his own indiscreet use of Aubrey's confidential notes, and worn out with illness and overwork, was, by the time he wrote this, little better than crazed himself. Aubrey, no less than Wood, was tormented by the antiquary's restless desire for knowledge and more knowledge: both were enamoured of the mere fact. Aubrey was different from Wood in his warm love for human oddities, and in a liveliness of vision, which prompts him now and then to a phrase like a poet's. There was a custom—he noted—in his schooldays of binding the books as they fell to pieces in the parchment of old manuscripts: " in my grandfather's days," he adds, " the Manuscripts flew about like butterflies." But poets are not necessarily liars. Toland pays tribute in his *History of the Druids* to Aubrey's faithful and manifold knowledge of the Druid temples: he says that he appeared to be extremely superstitious, yet insists " he was a very honest man and most accurate in his accounts of matters of fact." Malone paid Aubrey his weighty tribute on the same score. Anyone who will take the trouble to read through Aubrey's notes on Milton's life as he wrote them will be struck by the pains he took to get his facts from the best sources, and the systematic way he went about it. The crowded sheets, with queries stuffed into the margins, new facts or afterthoughts written between the lines, correcter information superseding less correct, are at first puzzling to read; but anyone who has slowly mastered them—and a necessary part of the process is to return again and again to every page and paragraph— will be rewarded by daylight at last. I think I see now how Aubrey went to work, and though it would be

absurd to be dogmatic about every detail, the main
order in which he wrote things down is clear. Wood
tells us that Aubrey was well acquainted with Milton.
In making his notes for his Life, he first blocked out the
frame-work on his first sheet, writing in the few facts
and impressions he had got from Milton himself, and
leaving spaces, as his habit was, for the details that he
hoped to fill in later. Thus, " Mr. John Milton was
of an Oxfordshire familie, his Grandfather . . . of . . .
in Oxfordshire near Whately. His father was brought
up. . . . He was born A° Dom . . . the . . . day of
. . . about . . . aclock in the . . ." In the margin
above this paragraph he writes, " Quaere Christopher
Milton his brother, the Inner Temple." And he must
have gone to Christopher for the details he afterwards
inserted in the gaps. He also made a first sketch for
a family tree from what he had heard from Milton
himself and afterwards filled in missing names with the
help of Christopher. At the same time or soon after
he must have visited Milton's widow, and seen the
portraits and found out many things that he wanted to
know. Perhaps he got from her the time-table of
Milton's day. Naturally he asked her whether she
had any manuscripts of Milton's, and she told him that
she gave all his papers to his nephew that he brought
up, Mr. Phillips, who lived near the Maypole in the
Strand. Aubrey then looked up Mr. Phillips, and
found he had struck a rich vein indeed. We can see
from the notes he made before, and at, and after the
meetings he had with Edward Phillips, that he knew
exactly what questions he should ask, and what information he hoped to get. He wanted a completer
catalogue of Milton's writings than he could make

unaided.   Mr. Phillips, who had been entrusted with
Milton's literary papers after his death, was evidently
the right person to apply to.   " Quaere his nephew,
Mr. Edw. Philips," he writes, " for a perfect Catalogue
of his writings."   Mrs. Milton had told him that
Milton educated the Phillips nephews.   Aubrey made
a mental note to ask Phillips about his experience as a
schoolboy: how did the boys like Milton as a schoolmaster, what did they learn, and in what order?
Aubrey was interested in education and had his own
theories.   The manuscript of his *Idea of the Education
of Young Gentlemen* is still in the Bodleian.   He found
that Phillips had acted as Milton's amanuensis during
the writing of *Paradise Lost*, a fact that Phillips was
proud to record in his own hand on Aubrey's manuscript.   He questioned him then about the composition of the poem, how long did it take, when begun,
when finished?   The answers to all these questions
are to be found either in Aubrey's or Edward Phillips's
hand on the second and third sheets of Aubrey's notes.

Aubrey was, as we all know, fond of company and
of the cheerful glass, and after he lost his fortune he
was much tied to the society of those wealthier friends
and kinsmen who would take him under their roof.
Critics are too fond of assuming that he scribbled his
notes for the Lives in the forenoons after late hours and
drunken carouses, and that he wrote them helter-skelter,
leaving gaps like " drunken hiccups." [1]   The truth
is, his notes for many of the Lives are essentially
methodical, though they look untidy and erratic.
When he leaves gaps, as I have shown, he does so

[1] *Vide The Scandals & Credulities of John Aubrey*, edited by John
Collier, 1931.

systematically. The trouble he took not only to obtain the best information but to record it correctly is to be read in every page of the sheets reserved for Milton's Life. To get the exact particulars of Milton's birth, he makes a note: " Quaere Mr. Christopher Milton," and the details appear later in Mrs. Milton's hand, copied word for word from the front page of the family Bible. To make sure of the circumstances and day of his death he called on Milton's apothecary. He had first written: " He died of a feaver at his house in Juinn Street about the 64th yeare of his age ; " struck this out when he had better information, and wrote in its place: " gowt struck in, he died the 9th or 10th of November 1674, as appeares by his Apothe- caryes Booke." His careful deletions and corrections inspire confidence. He had an uneasy conscience about over-statement. He wrote of Milton, " He had an extraordinary memory," and afterwards struck out " extraordinary " and substituted " very good." Of his proficiency in music he first wrote " He had great skill," but returned to strike out " great " and insert " good." There can be no question, I think, that Aubrey tried in his lively, human way to get a true portrait of Milton.

But there is a stumbling-block for the modern reader on the threshold of both the nephews' biographies. " To write the Lives of Single Persons," writes John, " is then a commendable Undertaking, when by it some Moral benefit is design'd to Mankind." And Edward: " Of all the several parts of History, that which sets forth the Lives, and Commemorates the most remarkable Actions, Sayings, or Writings of Famous and Illustrious Persons, . . . as it is not the

least useful in itself, so it is in highest Vogue and
Esteem among the Studious and Reading part of
Mankind." Are we to look for a true portrait and a
trustworthy version of the facts in biography thus
conceived ?

Biography for edification still flourished in the
seventeenth century, with the mediaeval examples of
innumerable Saints' Lives behind it, and the classical
model of Plutarch towering above, to remind it of
nobler proportions and humaner scope. When Johnson came to write Lives of the English Poets, he made
short work of the old school of biography. The first
sentence of his first Life dismisses Sprat's Life of
Cowley as a funeral oration rather than a history. But
the new conception was already alive and growing,
already transforming the old, a century before Johnson.
Walton's Lives of Hooker and Donne are Saints'
Lives indeed, yet they are also histories of living men.
Clarendon and Dryden studied and wrote the characters of contemporary persons with a freer psycho-
logical interest. And while the historians and poets
invaded biography from one border, the antiquaries
invaded it from another. Wood and Aubrey carried
their passion for the mere fact into their biographical
records. Bishop Sprat wrote that Cowley's parents
were " citizens of virtuous life and sufficient estate ":
Johnson writes : " His father was a grocer." Now
Johnson got this from Wood, who himself used a
note of Aubrey's: " He was born in Fleet Street, near
Chancery Lane ; his father a grocer." Aubrey, let
us be thankful, had no purpose of edification: all he
wanted was the living fact. Sir Walter Raleigh's
beard, he tells us, turned up naturally. It is enough.

Make what you will of it, the inviolable fact remains.
Jotting down his untidy notes from here, there and
everywhere, Aubrey is superbly disengaged from the
decent conventions of biography under which Milton's
nephews wrote.   But happily for us they, too, were not
untouched by the spirit of the new biography.   Though
their bias was for the noble portrait and the moral life,
they knew the value of trivial human facts.   If they tell
us little or nothing discreditable to Milton, that is not
simply because they were writing for edification.   Perhaps there was little discreditable to tell.   Aubrey was
frankly unbiassed and incurably indiscreet, yet he has
nothing worse to report than that Milton was whipped
by his tutor at Cambridge and that he in his turn
whipped his nephews.   And Wood, who was harshly
disposed to Milton, gives evil interpretations but no
evil facts.

There are indeed two passages in Edward Phillips's
Life of Milton which, interpreted and re-interpreted by
later biographers, have cast a shadow upon Milton's
character.   It is generally assumed that two months
after his first marriage and before his wife left him,
Milton wrote a pamphlet pleading for greater freedom
of divorce ; and that he tyrannized cruelly over his
daughters.   The evidence ought to be freshly scanned.
All we know of the circumstances of Milton's marriage
is derived from the accounts given by the two nephews.
Edward's account is the fuller.   The tale he tells is
briefly this: that at Whitsuntide, sometime after 1641
(he does not say in what year) Milton went to Forrest
Hill near Oxford and returned in a month's time a
married man; that his wife, Mary Powell, daughter of
Richard Powell, stayed with him a little more than a

month, and then went home on a visit, promising to come back at Michaelmas ; that when Michaelmas came, she refused to return and Milton's messenger was dismissed with contempt ; that finding her family were determined to keep her from him—they were Royalists, and the Royalist fortunes seemed in the ascendant—he resolved on his part never to take her back, and to support this resolution he wrote the treatises on divorce. At the same time he entered on a project of marrying another wife. Later biographers have dated the marriage Whitsuntide, 1643. Now *The Doctrine and Discipline of Divorce*, the first of the pamphlets, was in print on 1st August, 1643. Whitsuntide fell on May 26th that year, so that if this interpretation is right, Milton's bride must have left him just after or just before the pamphlet was published, and Milton must have been writing it in the first weeks of his marriage. But Edward Phillips says distinctly that the pamphlets on divorce were the outcome of his resentment at his wife's refusal to return to him : " however, it so incensed our Author, that he thought it would be dishonourable ever to receive her again, after such a repulse ; so that he forthwith prepared to Fortify himself with Arguments for such a Resolution, and accordingly wrote two Treatises by which he undertook to maintain, That it was against Reason . . . for any Married Couple disagreeable in Humour and Temper . . . to be forc'd to live yok'd together all their Days."

John Phillips agrees with him about the sequence of events, though he interprets differently Milton's immediate motive for writing the pamphlets : " Hee in this interval, who had entred into that state for the end

design'd by God and Nature, and was then in the full
vigor of his Manhood, could ill bear the disappointment hee mett with by her obstinate absenting . And
therefore thought upon a Divorce, that he might be
free to marry another : concerning which hee also was
in treaty. The lawfulness and expedience of this, only
regulat in order to all those purposes for which Marriage was at first instituted, had upon full consideration
and reading good Authors bin formerly his Opinion :
And the necessity of justifying himselfe now concurring with the opportunity, acceptable to him of
instructing others in a point of so great concern to the
peace and preservation of Families; and so likely to
prevent temptations as well as mischiefs, hee first writt
The Doctrine and Discipline of Divorce. . . ."

Later biographers have found these facts hard to
digest. I think the remedy is to re-read what Edward
Phillips wrote. He never says the marriage took
place in 1643, as the biographers one after the other
have assumed. What he says is that after settling in
London Milton moved into a house in Aldersgate
Street, in one or two of the first years of his residence
writing *Of Reformation in England*, *Against Prelatical
Episcopacy*, *The Reason of Church Government*, *The
Defence of Smectymnuus* : (the first three of these books
were published in 1641, the fourth in 1642): that
" during the time of his continuance in this House there
fell out several Occasions of the Increasing of his
Family; " and these he proceeds to enumerate. His
father came to live with him, on the dissettlement of
his other son Christopher after the taking of Reading.
Then he had an addition of some scholars. No date
is given for this. " To which may be added his

entring into matrimony " . . . " About *Whitsuntide*
it was or a little after " . . . he proceeds with the story.
Now Edward Phillips is unreliable about dates as we
have seen, and he is writing of events that happened
more than fifty years back, when he was a boy of
twelve or thirteen. All that he says is that these
different accessions to his uncle's household happened
while they were living in Aldersgate Street, after 1641.
We can date only one of the events he names. Reading
fell before Essex on 26th April, 1643. From this
date the biographers have proceeded to assume that
Edward Phillips means to date the marriage at Whitsuntide the same year. Now this does not fit the
other facts. If old Mr. Milton were to be dislodged
at all, he surely would move at once. Yet Edward
Phillips says that Milton was able to receive the Bride's
friends on their return to his house after the wedding,
since " his father nor anybody else were yet come."

In the light of public events Whitsuntide 1643 is a
difficult if not impossible date for Milton's marriage.
The Civil War began in August, 1642, and Oxford
at once became a military centre. Journeys to and fro
between Oxford and London would be dangerous and
difficult for civilians at any time during 1643, except
during the twenty days' truce which ended on 15th
April, when Essex laid siege to Reading. At Whitsuntide Milton could not have gone to Forest Hill and
brought his wife and her relations back to London to
prolong the marriage festivities.[1]

[1] Since writing the above I have read Mr. R. A. Wright's two
articles on " Milton's First Marriage " in the *Modern Language Review*,
Oct. 1931 and Jan. 1932, where my point is made fully and con-
clusively. It seemed better, notwithstanding, to let my own argument
stand.

I believe that Milton was married in the spring or summer of 1642. I do not take my stand on Whitsuntide, for if Edward Phillips can describe the time of Milton's death—which really happened on 8th November—as " towards the latter end of the summer " we cannot trust him very closely on the seasons. John Phillips's account of the marriage also fits the date 1642. After describing Milton's first group of pamphlets, on the ecclesiastical controversy, all written in 1641 and 1642, he proceeds, " *In this while* his manner of Settlement fitting him for the reception of a Wife, hee in a moneths time . . . courted, marryed, and brought home . . . a Daughter of Mr. Powell." And he says she returned to him about four years afterwards, connecting that event with the surrender of the Royalist garrison at Oxford in 1646. If Milton was married in 1642, the other events fall into place and the whole story becomes credible. His wife left him in the summer of 1642 and refused to return to him at Michaelmas. He recoiled in anger and disgust, threw himself into his studies, and found himself irresistibly drawn back to a subject which had interested him long before, as John Phillips reports and his own Commonplace Book attests,—marriage and liberty of divorce. His personal wrongs and sufferings drove him to a deeper probing of the essential matter; he saw in it something that vitally concerned the commonweal; he brooded over it all the following spring, and he poured out his thoughts in the first Divorce pamphlet published in August, 1643. Mr. Chilton Powell has recently shown, quoting an array of evidence, that according to Puritan theory and practice, Milton had sufficient grounds for divorce in his wife's desertion

alone.[1]   He thinks that Milton's first book on Divorce
was planned before he was married, and had no connection with his own situation.   I find this impossible
to believe.   The overwhelming testimony of the first
biographers is against it, and we have among them not
only a friend and gossip like Aubrey, but two members
of his own household closely in touch with him all his
life.   And further, Milton's pleading in the pamphlet
has the authentic ring of personal feeling.   Milton
suffered in body as well as in spirit;   his pamphlets
reveal in their burning phrases the whole man suffering;
but there is no final truth in the vulgar interpretations
of his plight, or of the actions that sprang out of it.
Critics of our own day think that the worst shock for
him was his wife's refusal of the physical consummation
of marriage: one of the nephews thought that he wrote
the Divorce pamphlets to justify his step in proceeding
to another union: many writers assume that he wrote
them with the practical end of freeing himself from his
own chains.   There is room, I think, for an interpretation more in keeping with Milton.   Let the first
accounts be read side by side in the light of Milton's
own pamphlets.   A critical re-reading of the two
nephews' biographies should first put us right about
the dates, and when the dates are clear, we see Milton
slowly preparing to speak his mind on the question of
marriage and divorce after he has accepted his personal
defeat.   We have independent evidence from Milton's
own Commonplace Book to support John Phillips's
statement that Milton had long before, and apart from
personal experience, made up his mind about the

[1] *English Domestic Relations*, 1487-1653.   Chilton Latham Powell,
1917.

right to divorce; we ought to believe him also when he says that Milton wrote partly to enlighten and assist his fellow-men. This is consistent with Milton's own explicit account in *Defensio Secunda*; but what is more, it is of one piece with the character that he reveals in his writings from first to last. It is hard to read a great man aright, but we begin to learn his alphabet when we put mind and spirit first, and recognize that he sets a higher value on the life of these than the rest of us can apprehend. "For what is life," Milton cries, "without the vigour and spiritual exercise of life?" As the *Areopagitica* is a plea for free thought rather than a protest against Press Censorship, so *The Doctrine and Discipline of Divorce* is not a tirade against the marriage laws but an eloquent plea for true marriage : communion of mind and spirit based on joyful companionship,—that, Milton would have us know, is the only marriage worth having.

Both nephews praise Milton's forgiveness of his first wife, seeing in it a signal example of his humanity and generosity. With the failure of the Royalist cause, the Powell family fortunes were ruined, and Milton took under his roof not only his wife, but her father and mother and several brothers and sisters. At the time when Milton married his daughter, Richard Powell owed Milton's father a debt of £300: he arranged to give her a dowry of £1000. None of this money ever came to Milton. Richard Powell was guilty of many deceitful dealings, not only with his son-in-law. As soon as he died in Milton's house in December, 1646, his creditors began to take action for recoveries from his estate, and his son-in-law must have become acquainted with the long and tangled tale of his unscrupulous chicanery.[1] Milton suffered much from his wife's family, now the noisy, uncongenial inmates of his quiet house. They were with him from the summer of 1646 for nearly a year. On 21st April, 1647, in a letter to his friend Carlo Dati in Florence he pours forth something of the poignant sense he has of the irony of his lot. " It is often a matter of sorrowful reflection with me," he writes, " that those with whom I have been linked by chance or the law, by propinquity or some connection of no real meaning, are continually at hand to invest my home, to stun me with their noise and wear out my temper, whilst those who are endeared to me by the closest sympathy of tastes and pursuits are almost all withheld from my embrace either by death or an insuperable distance of place." He is thinking not only of his Italian friends in Florence, of whom Dati was perhaps the dearest, but of Charles Diodati, the intimate friend of his youth, who died in England when he himself was in Italy. And more deeply still he is lamenting the loss of his father, who died only a month before. It was a bad beginning to his second attempt at married life with Mary Powell. We cannot tell whether he found happiness with her in the six years that she was with him. The human probabilities point the other way. She died in 1652, and their son John, on whom his father must surely have set his heart and hopes, died at the age of two years and three months, about six weeks after his mother. Milton was left, just at the time when total blindness closed in on him, with three daughters, of whom the eldest was lame and infirm. They were never sent to school

[1] *Vide Milton Papers* by David Harrison Stevens.

d

but had a mistress to teach them at home, so Deborah the youngest declared.   But this was not all: for, says Edward Phillips, he made his children " serviceable to him in that very particular in which he most wanted their Service, and supplied his want of Eye-sight by their Eyes and Tongue; for though he had daily about him one or other to Read to him, some persons of Man's Estate, who of their own accord greedily catch'd at the opportunity of being his Readers . . . yet excusing only the Eldest Daughter by reason of her bodily Infirmity, and difficult utterance of Speech, (which to say truth I doubt was the Principal cause of excusing her) the other two were Condemn'd to the performance of Reading, and exactly pronouncing of all the Languages of whatever Book he should at one time or other think fit to peruse, *viz.* the *Hebrew*, (and I think the *Syriac*), the *Greek*, the *Latin*, the *Italian*, *Spanish* and *French*.   All which sorts of Books to be confined to Read, without understanding one word, must needs be a Tryal of Patience, almost beyond endurance; yet it was endured by both for a long time, yet the irksomeness of this imployment could not be always concealed, but broke out more and more into expressions of uneasiness; so that at length they were all (even the Eldest also) sent out to learn some Curious and Ingenious sorts of Manufacture, that are proper for Women to learn, particularly Imbroideries in Gold or Silver."   This paragraph of Edward Phillips has done more perhaps than any other single statement in any of the biographies to damage Milton's character, and to cut him off from the affection of posterity. Ninety-nine people know him as the harsh parent who condemned his daughters to read aloud to him in

languages they did not understand, for one who
knows him as the wronged but generous husband that
took under his roof in a time of political danger not
only his rebellious wife, but her parents and eight tire-
some brothers and sisters. The story of Milton's
relations with his daughters is unhappy to the end, and
we may be very sure that there were faults on both
sides. Too much has been made of the harshness of
his conduct in this business of training them to read
in foreign languages. Manners and customs were
different in Milton's time; and even to-day daughters
must make themselves useful where means are
straitened. After he was blind Milton required a
reader for many hours of the day; the alternative for
the girls was either to do this service for their father,
who could then dispense with a hired man, or to go
out and learn a wage-earning trade. Perhaps in the
beginning they chose the first, or perhaps their father
chose it for them. Can we blame him much if he did?
At any rate when they found it irksome, he released
them and sent them out to learn what they were more
capable of learning, "some Curious and Ingenious
sorts of Manufacture," that, as Edward Phillips says,
"are proper for Women to learn." Did Milton
attempt to teach them any of the languages that he
wished them to read, and were they too lazy or too
stupid to learn? This we shall never know. Deborah's daughter, Elizabeth Foster, gave Birch a
garbled version of things recounted of Milton by her
Mother, and amongst others reported that he "kept
his daughters at a great distance, and would not allow
them to learn to write, which he thought unnecessary
for a woman." Now we happen to know that two of

the daughters, Deborah and Mary, could write, for
they signed their names, ill-spelt it is true, to a docu-
ment which has survived.[1]   Anne, who suffered from
some infirmity, has only made her mark.   Deborah
told Dr. Ward, from whom Dr. Birch quotes in his life
of Milton, that her father used often to say in their
hearing, " *one Tongue was enough for a Woman.*"   This
saying, again, is often solemnly quoted against Milton
as a proof of his harshness to his daughters, and yet
more of his contempt for women.   How strange is
the fate of the living word!   Do we ever reflect that
these stray phrases, handed down to posterity from the
lips of living men, have been torn from their context
of human talk and lively feeling, dropped into a fixed
mould and hardened to take one tone and serve one
purpose ?   I can imagine that Deborah and Mary
chattered, that their father vainly tried to teach them
enough concentration to learn a language, that he gave
it up,—perhaps with humorous relief,—and would
quote against them till it became a family jest, " *one
tongue is enough for a woman!*"   When Milton
married his third young wife in 1663, Anne was
sixteen and Deborah eleven years old.   The daughters
and the stepmother did not live happily together.
We hear from Elizabeth Foster that Deborah left
home because she received very ill treatment from
Milton's last wife.   After their father's death the
daughters disputed his will, given by word of mouth,
which his widow was trying to prove.   This will,
written down by his lawyer brother Christopher, was
as follows: " The portion due to me from Mr. Powell,
my former wife's father, I leave to the unkind children

[1] *Vide Chetham Soc. Misc.*, vol. i. p. 1.

I had by her, having received no parte of it: but my meaning is, they shall have no other benefit of my estate than the said portion, and what I have besides done for them ; they having been very undutifull to me. All the residue of my estate I leave to the disposall of Elizabeth, my loving wife." When the case came on and Christopher was cross-questioned, he declared that his brother had " complained, but without passion, that his children had been unkind to him, but that his wife had been very kind and careful of him; " that the daughters had lived apart from their father for the last four or five years, and that " in former times he had heard him complain that they were careless of him being blind, and made nothing of deserting him."

The wheel has come full circle. From the beginning to the end Mary Powell and her children brought him unhappiness. His first marriage was made in haste on a visit to Richard Powell, of which the purpose was, perhaps, to recover a large outstanding family debt. Mr. Powell offered his beautiful daughter, promised a dowry of £1000, and Milton took everything in good faith. He was quickly undeceived; his wife deserted him; no penny of the dowry ever came to him ; the debt was never paid.

Milton was bred by a generous and honourable father. It is easy to imagine the annoyance and distress that he felt at the miserable deceits and shabby dealings of Richard Powell. Such things ought not to have a deep or lasting effect upon a noble mind. But human nature is what it is, and experience tells that where transactions like this have been connected with a man's intimate feelings, they take on an importance which they should not have. Milton appears

vindictive. He who was naturally generous with
money ought not, when he made his Will, to have
harked back to the ill-dealings of his father-in-law over
his first marriage. He would have done better to
forget the long miserable tale. But it was interwoven
with his intimate sufferings, with wounds to his
affections which can never have healed. He married
knowing little of women, sensitive, idealistic, looking
for an exquisite peace and solace in marriage. His
wife deserted him at the very beginning; and in the
end his daughters deserted him, when he merited pity
as well as love. If the witness, Elizabeth Fisher, a
maidservant in Milton's house, is to be trusted—and
probably she is not wholly to be trusted—we must
believe that Milton's daughters took after their grandfather, the unscrupulous Richard Powell, for she says
they " did combine together and counsel the maid to
cheat Milton in his markettings, and made away with
some of his books, and would have sold the rest to the
dung-hill women." But, as Richardson remarks,
" there is no end of going into Family affairs, in which
'tis impossible to come at materials to be sufficiently
instructed." We shall never know the truth. Milton's
last testament shows hard dealing with his daughters,
but we can at least remember that he had been hardly
dealt with. He found it difficult, we can easily
believe, to live in close sympathy with the daughters
of Mary Powell, whose memory was bound up for
him with so bitter ánd prolonged an experience of
disillusion.

Years after his death Deborah spoke of her father
with great tenderness. She admired him; she said
he was delightful company, " the life of the conversa-

tion, and that on account of a flow of subject and an unaffected cheerfulness and civility." This is the man that Aubrey knew, " extreme pleasant in his conversation, and at dinner, supper etc."; the man who " would be cheerful even in his gowt fitts and sing," whose deportment, according to his scapegrace nephew, was " sweet and affable." He is much unlike the " acrimonious and surly republican " whom Dr. Johnson pictured, harsh in his domestic relations, gloomy in his religion. To his remark that Milton was extreme pleasant in his conversation Aubrey added " but satyricall," noting that he pronounced the letter *r* very hard, " a certain sign of a Satyricall Wit." Richardson gives us a glimpse of him in the satirical mood. Milton, he says, had a servant who was a very honest silly fellow, and a zealous follower of the Presbyterians. " When he came back from the meeting his master would frequently ask him what he had heard, and divert himself with ridiculing their fooleries, or it may be the poor fellow's understanding, both one and t'other probably." This Milton, who could mercilessly mock and tease, might be a formidable father to dull-witted daughters. Deborah at any rate seems to have harboured no resentment. Aubrey tells us that she acted as his amanuensis. From all we hear, she must have been the most intelligent of the three. In appearance she was much like her father.

Across the pages of the first biographies pass a number of people, young and old, men and women, Puritans, Royalists, men of fashion, men of science, statesmen, artists, poets, who were Milton's friends. He had the genius for friendship. And he had another gift and passion, reflected vividly in these first records, the gift and passion for teaching. It was not merely that he had theories about education and liked to try experiments. He loved teaching for itself, and enjoyed the relationship of teacher and pupil. His pupils were his friends—Aubrey puts Daniel Skinner, " his disciple," along with Andrew Marvell among his familiar acquaintance. The two nephews, who underwent Milton's hard discipline as schoolboys, freely admired and loved him. Thomas Elwood the Quaker tells in his delightful rambling autobiography how he went to school with Milton at mature years to make up the Humane Learning he was ashamed to have lost, and of the friendship which grew out of the schooling. Since Elwood's lively reminiscences are a part of the contemporary record of Milton, I shall quote from them at length. They give a picture, which as it happens, none of the early biographers attempted, of Milton at work with one of his grown-up pupils. It was after an illness in 1661 that Thomas Elwood, now converted to the Quaker doctrine, found himself ashamed of his lack of learning and consulted his friend Isaac Pennington about getting some assistance to his solitary labours; Pennington had intimate acquaintance with Dr. Paget, and he with John Milton, " a Gentleman," writes Elwood, " of great note for Learning throughout the Learned World."

" This person, having filled a Publick Station in the former Times, lived now a private and retired life in *London* : and having wholly lost his Sight, kept always a Man to read to him; which usually was the Son of some Gentleman of his Acquaintance, whom in his Kindness, he took to improve in his Learning. Thus by the Mediation of my Friend *Isaac Pennington* with

Dr. *Paget*, and of Dr. *Paget* with *John Milton*, was I admitted to come to him; not as a Servant to him (which at that time he needed not) nor to be in the House with him: but only to have the Liberty of coming to his House, at certain Hours, when I would, and to read to him what Books he should appoint me ; which was all the Favour I desired. . . . He received me courteously ; as well for the sake of Dr. *Paget* as of *Isaac Pennington* to both of whom he bore a good Respect . . . I went therefore and took myself a Lodging as near to his House (which was then in Jewen Street) as conveniently as I could, and from thenceforward went every Day in the Afternoon (except on the *First Days* of the Week), and sitting by him in his Dining Room, read to him in such Books in the *Latin Tongue* as he pleased to hear me read. At my first sitting to read to him, observing that I used the *English Pronunciation,* he told me ' If I would have the benefit of the *Latin* Tongue (not only to read and understand *Latin* authors but) to Converse with Foreigners either abroad or at home, I must learn the Foreign Pronunciation.' "

Milton expounded this, and Elwood tried to learn it. He proceeds:

" He, perceiving with what earnest Desire I pursued Learning, gave me not only all the Encouragement, but all the Help he could. For, having a curious Ear, he understood by my Tone when I understood what I read, and when I did not: and accordingly would stop me, Examine me, and open the most difficult Passages to me. Thus I went on, for about six weeks time reading to him in the Afternoons."

An illness of Elwood's interrupted the lessons, and he was obliged to go away. On his return, he writes:

" I was kindly received by my Master, who had conceived so good an Opinion of me, that my Conversation, I found, was acceptable to him; and he seem'd heartily glad of my Recovery and Return ; and into our old method of Study we fell again."

Later the friendship bore memorable fruit.

"Some little time before I went to *Alesbury* Prison, I was
desired by my quondam Master *Milton* to take an House for
him, in the Neighbourhood where I dwelt, that he might get
out of the City, for the Safety of himself and his Family, the
Pestilence then growing hot in *London*.   I took a pretty Box for
him in *Giles-Chalfont*, a Mile from me ; of which I gave him
notice : and intended to have waited on him, and seen him well
settled in it ; but was prevented by that Imprisonment.

But now being released, and returned Home, I soon made a
Visit to him, to welcome him into the Country.

After some common Discourses had passed between us, he
called for a Manuscript of his ; which being brought he delivered
it to me, bidding me take it home with me, and read it at my
Leisure : and when I had so done, return it to him, with my
Judgment thereupon.

When I came home, and had set myself to read it, I found it
was that Excellent Poem, which he entituled PARADISE LOST.
After I had, with the best Attention, read it through, I made
him another Visit, and returned him his Book, with due
Acknowledgement of the Favour he had done me, in Com-
municating it to me.   He asked me how I liked it, and what I
thought of it ; which I modestly, but freely told him : and after
some further Discourse about it, I pleasantly said to him, Thou
hast said much here of *Paradise lost* ; but what hast thou to say
on *Paradise found*?   He made me no Answer, but sate some
time in a Muse : then brake of that Discourse, and fell upon
another Subject.

After the Sickness was over, and the City well cleansed and
become safely habitable again, he returned thither.   And when
afterwards I went to wait on him there (which I seldom failed
of doing, whenever my Occasions drew me to *London*) he
shewed me his Second Poem, called PARADISE REGAINED ; and
in a pleasant Tone said to me, *This is owing to you: for you put
it into my Head, by the Question you put to me at Chalfont; which
before I had not thought of.*"

Milton's advice to Elwood about the foreign pronunciation of Latin is repeated in his Letter *Of Education*: the speech of the boys in his Academy " is to be
fashion'd to a distinct and cleer pronunciation, as neer
as may be to the *Italian*, especially in the vowels. For
we Englishmen being farre Northerly, do not open our
mouthes in the cold air, wide enough to grace a South-
ern tongue; but are observ'd by all other nations to
speak exceeding close and inward: So that to smatter
Latin with an English mouth, is as ill hearing as law
French." He is drawing upon his own experience in
Italy.

Every reader of the early biographies of Milton
must be struck by the fulness with which his visit to
Italy is described: the biographers are in fact following
Milton's own careful account in the *Defensio Secunda*:
the visit to Italy bulks large because Milton himself
set so high a value on it. He felt himself at home
in Italy, at home physically in the sunny air and
climate, at home intellectually in the society of kindred
spirits and " choicest wits." He found at once that
with them he could interchange ideas and literary
projects more freely and more fruitfully than in any
society he knew in England. His mind and genius
were recognized with quick responsive sympathy.
In later life he kept up a correspondence with some of
the members of the Academy in Florence with whom he
had become intimate. The surviving letters tell their
own tale. Milton brought back from Italy a nostalgia
for the warm South and for the easy lively society of
Italian wits and scholars. All his life after, he felt a
sense of exile in the cold Northern climate of our
island, where neither mouths nor minds open wide

enough for gracious interchange. In his Poem to
Mansus, he speaks of his Muse barely nourished in
the icy North ; " For the sun, which we want," he
complains in his *History of Britain*, " ripens wits as well
as fruits." He seems to have felt a misgiving lest
genius might be quenched by the chill and damp air
of our shores. Thus in the *Reason of Church Government*, he vows to accomplish his great poem, " *if there
be nothing adverse in our climate*, or the fate of the
age," a thought that was with him still, twenty-five
years later, when in the exordium to the eighth book
of *Paradise Lost*, he approached the scene of the
Temptation, a fitting theme, he believed, to give
Heroic name to Person or to Poem . . .

> . . . higher Argument
> Remaines, sufficient of it self to raise
> That name unless an age too late, or cold
> Climat, or Years damp my intended wing
> Deprest. . . .

Milton's sympathy with the Italian temperament and
Italian climate is a part of his lifelong sympathy with
easy pleasure-loving natures. He had a natural
liking for his nephew John. He could enjoy a gaudy-
day with the two young sparks of the town, Mr. Alphry
and Mr. Miller. His feeling for the fresh, balmy air of
spring was akin to his feeling for the youthful ardour
and vivacity of sensuous natures. It is not by accident
that he described such natures, " those of soft and
delicious temper,"—" others of a more delicious and
airy spirit," with the same epithets that bring to life
the " soft, delicious air " breathing its balm in *Paradise
Lost*. Let it not be forgotten by those who condemn
Milton for overloading, as a scholar will, the time-table

of his ideal school, that he recommended a shutting up
of books in springtime and a rushing forth into the
country-side, when the warm air calls irresistibly:
" There is another opportunity of gaining experience
to be won from pleasure itselfe abroad; in those vernal
seasons of the yeer when the air is calm and pleasant,
it were an injury and sullennesse against nature not
to go out, and see her riches, and partake in her rejoycing with heaven and earth.   I should not therefore
be a persuader to them of studying much then. . . ."
Another genial provision of Milton's for his young
pupils is to delight their travailed spirits, in the interim
before meals, with music heard or learned.   Music
was a necessary part of Milton's daily life, and his
trained skill and permanent pleasure in it he owed,
with other cherished gifts, to his father.   Mr. John
Milton, senior, was a musician and composer of repute.
The sympathy between father and son must have been
strong and enduring.   The elder Milton stands out
clearly in the first Lives.   All four have the story of his
being disinherited by the Roman Catholic grandfather
for reading the Bible; Milton must have been proud of
this tale, and fond of relating it.   All four make much
of the father's enthusiastic care for his clever son's
education.   John Phillips notes the generous un-
worldly character of the man in retiring early from his
prosperous trade, once he had provided a competency
for his children, to live peacefully in the country and
devote himself to his music.   The Civil War broke
into his tranquil life, and he was driven to London
where his son John found a quiet corner for him under
his roof, for, as Edward Phillips tells us from his own
memory, in that house well-filled and busy with pupils,

" the old gentleman lived retired to his rest and devotion without the least trouble imaginable." Milton inherited from his father his passion for liberty, his love of learning and the arts, and most surely also his love of quiet. In the letter I have quoted to his Italian friend, written soon after his father's death, he contrasts the quiet companionship he has lost and would fain recall with the noisy society of his wife's family. " They stun me with their noise." The incompatible differences of taste and temper between Milton and his first wife would perhaps be summed up if we set against these words of his, complaining of his wife's noisy family, those other words in which Aubrey tells, not without friendly sympathy, of the young bride's first horror of Milton's silent house: " His first wife was brought up and lived where there was a great deal of company and merriment, dancing etc. And when she came to live with her husband in St. Bride's church-yard, she found it very solitary; no company came to her, . . . This life was irksome to her." Aubrey is in error about the house. It was not the lodgings in St. Bride's Church-yard to which Milton brought his wife. It was the " good handsome house " in Aldersgate Street, " at the end of an entry, and therefore the fitter for his turn," says Edward Phillips, " by reason of the Privacy, and besides that there are few streets in London more free from Noise than that." Milton, like his musical father, loved quiet and hated noise: his wife liked noise and cheerful clatter, and silence preyed upon her nerves.

When Milton left the still air of delightful studies to plunge into public warfare, he was fully aware of what he sacrificed. He abandoned, he says, " a calme and pleasing solitarynes fed with cheerful and confident thoughts, to imbark in a troubl'd sea of noises and hoars disputes." He found the world of politics harsh, ugly, full of conflict and confusion, a thing to be summed up in words and images of noise. In another apology, he addresses his readers thus: " I may hope one day to have ye again in a still time when there shall be no more chiding. *Not in these Noises.*" John Phillips chose his words advisedly and perhaps with some underlying sense of poetic justice fulfilled, when he described Milton's last years, the years that brought to light his greatest works in prose and verse, as a period of serenity, ending in a quiet close. " In these Works, and the instruction of some Youth or other at the intreaty of his friends, hee in great Serenity spent his time, and expired no less calmly in the yeare 1674."

I have made no attempt to draw a full portrait of Milton. I have simply desired to throw into relief some features of his character which the early biographers saw clearly at close range, and which have grown dim or obscure to posterity. Milton's ardent spirit was austere, his character as a political fighter not only indomitably courageous but also hard and unbending. In public controversy he could be harsh, coarse and brutal. But in his private life his friends and relatives knew a different man—a man of culture and breeding, generous, companionable, witty, peaceable, loving music and good talk, loving quiet and all the delights of intercourse with affectionate, intelligent companions. This is the Milton with whom the first biographers were familiar, and who comes alive in their pages.

MINUTES OF THE LIFE OF MR JOHN MILTON

BY JOHN AUBREY

His mother was a Bradshaw.
Crest an Arme dexter
holding an Eagles
head & Neck erased G.

Q. Xpr. Milton
[his brother the
Inner Temple]
Bencher.
~~Barrister.~~

Mʳ John Milton

was of an Oxfordshire familie his Grandfather . . . . . .
neer Shotover
[a Rom: Cath:] of Holton in Oxfordshire ~~neer Whately.~~
at Christchurch
His father was brought-up in yᵉ Univ^{ty} of Oxon: ^and
his gr.father disinherited him because he kept not the
Q. he found a Bible in English in his chamber
Catholique Religion so ~~that~~ therupon he came to
London, and became a Scrivener [brought up by a
friend of his, was not an Apprentice] and gott a plentiful
estate by it & left it off many yeares before he dyed.
he was an ingeniose man, delighted in Musiq. composed many Songs now in print especially that of
Oriana. his son Jo: was borne in Bread street in
Spread Eagle
London at ye ~~Rose,~~ wch was his house, he had also
in yᵗ street   the Rose and other houses in other places
~~there~~ another house.

A   I

He was borne A° D^m . . . . . . the . . . day of . . .
about . . . . a clock in the . . . . . .

He went to schoole to ~~Dr~~ old Mr Gill at Paules schoole; went
at his own chardge only   at
ʌ to Christs College in Cambr: ~~very young~~ [~~Sc. about~~
fifteen   at least
~~thirteen was the most~~] where he stayed eight yeares:

then he travelled into Franc & Italie. At Geneva he

contracted a great friendship with ~~Carolo Diodati,~~ . . .

Had Sr H. Wotton's comēendatory lrs
~~son of~~ the learned Dr Diodati of Geneva   [vide his
                                          who delighted
Poems.] He was acquainted beyond sea with Sr Henry
in his company
Wotton Ambassador at Venice. He   was   severall
Q. how many.   Resp. two yeares.   just upon
yeares beyond sea, & returned to England ~~a~~ . . . ~~little~~
the breaking out of the   stet.
~~before the~~ Civill warres ~~brake out.~~ He was ~~Latin~~
                    the parliament
Secretary to ~~Oliver Cromwell.~~

          D^m   his schoolmaster was a puritan in
     A° ~~aetatis~~ 1619, he was ten yeares old, as by his
Essex, who cutt his haire short
picture: & was then a Poet.
🔖 she went from him to her Mother at . . . ye Kings quarters neer Oxford
~~He parted from her~~ A° D^m . . . and wrote the triple chord, about Divorce
He married his first wife . . . . . . Powell of . . Fosthill
without her husband's consent
She went ʌ to her mother in the Kings quarters. Shee dyed A° D^m . . .
in Oxonshire A° D^m . . . . . . by whom he had 4 children:

hath two daughters living: Deborah was his Amanu-

ensis, he taught her Latin, & to read Greeke ~~and~~

Q.

~~Hebrew~~ to him, when he had lost his eiesight, wch was
A° D^m . . . .

Resp. of middle stature
Q.quot feet I am high.   abroun
He was scarce so tall as I am. he had light browne
              exceeding   his eye a dark gray
hayre, his complex^n very faire*. ovall face. His
                    very well & like
widowe has his picture drawne ʌ when a Cambridge
scholler [* he was so faire y^t they called him the Lady
of X^ts coll:] She has his picture when a Cambridge
scholler, wch ought to be engraven: for the Pictures
before his bookes are not *at all* like him.

                    Mris Eliz: Minshull
He mar^d his 2^d wife A° . . . . . . ye yeare before the
a gent. person a peacefull & agreable humour.
Sicknesse.

After he was blind he wrote these following Bookes
viz.

                Paradise lost
                Paradise regained
                Gram͞ar
                Dictionarie—impfect Q+

he was a Spare man

~~He married Eliz. 2^d wife A° D^m 16 . . .~~   *Sheet A. f.2*
different Rell:
    Two opinions doe not well on the same Boulster.
                                        the K's
She was a . . . . . . Royalist, & went to hr mother near
Quarters
Oxford. I have so much charity for her y^t she might

not wrong his bed but what man (especially contem-
plative) w^d like to have a young wife environ'd ~ stormd~ by the
sons of Mars[1] and those of the enemi partie.

He lived in several places. e.g. Holborn neer K's
gate.

He died in Bunhill opposite to the Artillery garden-
wall.

His harmonicall, and ingeniose soule ~did lodge~ dwelt in a
beautifull & well proportioned body—In toto nusquam
corpore menda fuit.   Ovid.

He had an ~extraordinary~ *a very good* memory: but I believe y^t
his excellent method of thinking & disposing did much
to helpe his memorie.

I heard that after he was blind, that he was writing
in the hands of Moyses Pitt
a Latin Dictionary. vidua Affirmat she gave all his
among wch this Dict. imperfect
papers ~ to his Nephew, that he brought up, a sister's
son: ...... Philips, who lives neer the Maypole in
Q
the Strand. She has a great many letters by her from
learned men his acquaintance, both of England &
beyond sea.

His eiesight was decaying *about* 20 yeares before his death.
starke
Q. when quite Blind. his father read wth out spectacles

1 Aubrey used a sign for Mars.

at 84. his mother had very weake eies, & used spectacles psently after she was thirty yeares old.

Of a very cheerfull humour.

seldome tooke any Physique, only sometimes he tooke Manna
He was very healthy, & free from all diseases, and only
towards his later end he was visited wth the Gowte
spring & Fall : he would be chearfull even in his Gowte-
fitts ; & sing.

ye gow^t struck in
He died of a ~~feaver at his house in Juinn street~~
the 9th or 10th of Novemb. 1674 as appeares by his Apothecaryes Booke.
~~about the 64th yeare of his age~~

upper end of
He lies buried in St Giles Cripplegate ∧ chancell at
gravestone
the right hand ~~v. his stone~~. md̄m his stone is now
removed ; ~~for~~ about 2 yeares since [now 1681] the
steppes to the com̄union table were raysed. I ghesse
Jo : Speed & He lie together.

Q. his nephew Mr Edw. Philips for a perfect
Catalogue of his writings. md̄m. he wrote a little
Tract. of *Education*.

md̄m Mr Theodore Haak R.S.S. hath translated
halfe his Paradise lost into High Dutch in such blank
verse, wch is very well liked of by Germanus Fabricius
Professor at Heidelberg, who sent to Mr Haak a letter
upon this Translation—Incredible est quantum nos
omnes effecerit gravitas styli, & copia lectissimorum
verborum et . . . . . . v. the letter.

Sc: at 4 a clock manè
He was an early riser. yea, after he lost his sight.
He had a man read to him: the first thing he read was
the Hebrew bible, & y^t was at 4^h manè $- \frac{4^h}{2} +$. then
contemplated
he ~~thought~~. At 7 his man came to him again & then
and wrote
read to him ∧ till dinner: the writing was as much
2 Maried in Dublin to one
as the reading. His da: Deborah could read to
sells silke etc
Mr Clarke [a mercer] very like her father.
him Latin: Ital. & French & Greeke. The other
I
sister is Mary, more like hr mother. After dinner he
at a time
used to walke 3 or 4 houres ∧ he alwayes had a Garden
where he lived: went to bed about 9. Temperate ~~man~~,
rarely dranke between meales. Extreme pleasant in his
conversation, & at dinner, supper &c: but Satyricall.
He pronounced ye letter R very hard † [1]

Littera canina

† a certaine signe of a Satyricall Witt fr. Jo: Dreyden [2]

good
He had a delicate tuneable Voice & had ~~great~~ skill:
his father instructed him: he had an Organ in his
house: he played on that most. His exercise was
chiefly walking.

by learned
He was visited much: more then he did desire.

[1] but Satyricall . . . hard. This note has been added, first in pencil,
at a different time.
[2] This is written on the opposite page A. f. 2, with tallying mark.

He had a very good extraordinary memory: but I beleeve of his excellent method of thinking, &

disposing did much helpe his memorie.

I heard that after he was blind, that he was writing
a Latin Dictionary. [among all his bookes, of the losse whereof]
in the hands of Maister Pitt. Nephew, that he brought up, a sisters son? — — Phillips, who
lives neer the Maypole in the Strand. She shewd letters to her
of from learned men his acquaintance, both of England &
forraign lea.

His eie-sight was decaying about 20 yeares before his death. Q when quite blind.
his father read without spectacles at 84. his mother had very weake eies, & used spectacles presently after she was
of a very cheerfull humour.
He was very healthy & free from all disease, only sometymes he tooke Manna.
He died of the Gout-struck & Fall. he would be chearfull even in his Gout fitts: & sing.
He died about the 10th of Novemb. 1674, as appears by his Apothecaryes Booke
He lies buried in S.t Giles Cripplegate. the next at the right hand
& his stone with his stone is now removed, for about 2 yeares since now 1681 the
stepps to the communion table were raysed. J.Speed & he lie together.

Q. his nephew m' Philips for a perfect Catalogue of
his Writings. m'n he wrote a little tract of Education

m'n m' Theodore Haake S.S. hath translated halfe his Paradise lost into

He was mightily importuned to goe into Fr. &
Italie [foraigners came much to see him] and much
admired him, & offered to him great pfermts. to come
over to them, & the only inducement of severall
foreigners that came over into England, was chiefly to
see O. Protector & Mr. J. Milton, & would see the
house & chamber wher he was borne: he was much
more admired abrode then at home.

His familiar learned Acquaintance were

> Mr. Andrew Marvell, Mr. Skinner, Dr. Pagett M.D.
>
> Mr. . . . . . Skinner, who was his disciple.
>
> Jo: Dreyden Esq. Poet Laureate, who very much
> admires him, & went to him to have leave to
> putt his Paradise-lost into a Drama in
> Rhyme: Mr. Milton received him civilly,
> & told him he would give him leave to
> tagge his Verses.

His widowe assures me that Mr. Hobbs was not one
of his acquaintance: y^t her husband did not like him at
all: but he would acknowledge him to be a man of
great parts, a learned man. Their Interests & tenets
did run counter to each other
were diametrically $\int$ ^{1}. v. Mr. Hobbes Behemoth.

---

^{1} $\int$ is Aubrey's sign for opposite.

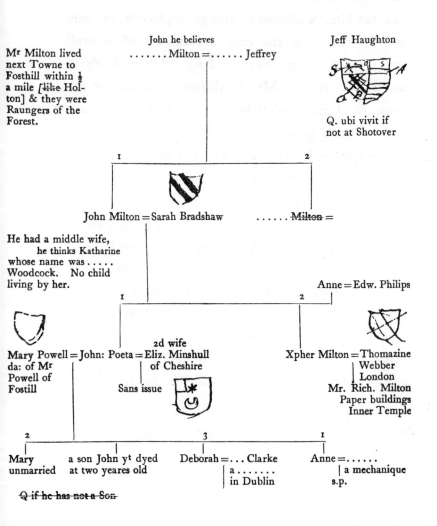

Mr Milton lived
next Towne to
Fosthill within ½
a mile [like Hol-
ton] & they were
Raungers of the
Forest.

John he believes
...... Milton = ... Jeffrey

Jeff Haughton

Q. ubi vivit if
not at Shotover

1   2

John Milton = Sarah Bradshaw   ...... ~~Milton~~ =

He had a middle wife,
     he thinks Katharine
whose name was .....
Woodcock. No child
living by her.

Anne = Edw. Philips

1   2

          2d wife

Mary Powell = John: Poeta = Eliz. Minshull
da: of Mr   of Cheshire
Powell of
Fostill   Sans issue

Xpher Milton = Thomazine
             Webber
             London
   Mr. Rich. Milton
   Paper buildings
   Inner Temple

2   3   1

Mary   a son John yt dyed   Deborah = ... Clarke   Anne = ...
unmarried at two yeares old   a .... | a mechanique
                            in Dublin   s.p.

~~Q if he has not a Son~~

Catalog^s Librorum.

Set them downe according to order of time

twice printed. Some writt but at 18.

1. Poems 8° printed at . . . . . .

Of Reformacōn.

2. Εἰχονοκλασης printed at . . . . . .

3. Pro. Pop. Ang. Defensio contra Salmasium.

4. Tetrachordon: 4to of Divorce.

5.
6. Paradise {lost 4to.
{regaind 4to. Edw. Philips his $_\wedge$ Aman-

cheif

uensis[1]

7. Latin Epistles. 8vo. {Familiar
{Politique

8. Latin Gram̄ar in English. 8°.

9. The History of Britain from y^e first tradiconall
beginning, continued to the Norman Conquest.
4to Lōdon. MDCLXX. for James Alestry.
Rose & Crowne P's ch-yard. Scripsit prout p̢
effigiem [sed falsam] 1670. aetate 62.

10. A Letter,[2] of Education to Mr S. Hartlib. [wth
his Poëms]

11. A Brief History of Muscovia: and other less
Advertisement
known Countries lyeing Eastward. writt by
the Author's owne hand before he lost his Sight:
and intended to have printed it before his death.

12. His Logick. 13. Idea Theologiae in M̄S. in y^e

14. He wrote a Dictionary called *Idioma Linguae Latinae*, from Mr Packer who was his Scholar.

---

[1] Edw. . . . . Amanuensis is written in Edward Phillips's own hand.

[2] Aubrey first wrote: 10. . . . . . . of Education: afterwards filled in:
" A Letter " (rather crowded into the narrow space left) and then
wrote " to Mr S. Hartlib . . . . . . Poëms."

hands of Mr Skinner ∧ in Marke Lane. Mďm,
_{a merchant's sonne}

a merchant's sonne

hands of Mr Skinner ∧ in Marke Lane. Mďm,
there was one Mr Skinner of ye Jerkers office
up 2 paire of stayres at the Custome-house. Q.

heet B. f.1.   from his Bro: Chr. Milton.

When he went to Schoole, when he was very
young he studied very hard and sate-up very late,
com̄only till 12 or one aclock at night, & his father
ordered ye mayde to sitt-up for him, and in those
[10]
yeares composed many Copies of verses, wch might well
become a riper age.   And was a very hard student in the
University, & pformed all his exercises there wth very
good Applause.   His 1st Tutor there was Mr Chapell,
whip't him
from whom receiving some unkindnesse, he was afterwards (though it seemed ∫ ye Rules of ye Coll:) trans-
ferred to the Tuition of one Mr Tovell, who dyed
Parson of Lutterworth.

I have been told, that the Father composed a Song
of fourscore parts, for the Lantgrave of Hess, for w^cb
or a noble present   about 1647
Highnesse sent a medall of Gold.   He dyed ~~in that
yeare that the Army marched thorough the City~~ buried
in Cripple-gate-ch: from his house in the Barbican.

Q. Mr. Chr. Milton to see the date of his Bro: Birth.

qr whither   1. Of Reformation.[1]
2 books.
                 Against prelatical Episcopacy.

              2. The reason of church government.

              3. A defence of Smectymnuus.

              4. The Doctrin & disciplin of divorce.

All these in prose-   5. Colasterion.
cution of yᵉ same
subject[2]   6. The Judgement of Martin Bucer.

              7. Tetrachordon [of Divorce [2]].

              8. Areopagitica, viz. for yᵉ libertie of ye Presse.

                 Of Education

                 Iconoclastes

                 Tenure of Kings & Magistrates.

                 Defensio populi anglicani

                                His Logick [2]
                 Defensio 2ᵈ contra Morum

                 Defensio 3ᵗⁱᵃ

                 Of yᵉ powr of yᵉ civil Magistrate in Ecclesiastical affairs

                 Against Hirelings   [against Tithes]

                 Of a Comonwealth

                 Against Dʳ Griffith

                 Of Toleration Heresie & Schisme.

[1] This list is in Edward Phillips's hand.
[2] These words are written in afterwards in Aubrey's hand.

He went to travell about ye year 1638 & was abroad

about a years space cheifly in Italy   imediately after

his return he took a lodging at Mr Russell's a Taylour

in St Brides churchyard & took into his tuition his

sisters two sons Edw: & John Philips ye first 10 the

other 9 years of age & in a years time made them capable

of interpreting a Latin authour at sight & within 3

years they went through ye best of Latin & Greec

*and some
Rudiments
of Arithm:
& Geom:

& wth him the use of the Globes *

Poetts Lucretius & Manilius of ye Latins; Hesiod,

Apollonii Argonautica

Aratus, Dionysus Afer, Oppian . . . . &

Quintus Calaber.   Cato, Varro, & Columella de Re

rusticâ were the very first Authors they learn't. [1]

As he was severe on one hand, so he was most

familiar and free in his conversation to those to whome

most severe in his way of education—NB. He made

his Nephews Songsters, and sing from the time they

were with him.

John Milton was born the 9th of december 1608 die

veneris half an howr after 6 in the morning.[2]

[1] This paragraph from " He went " to " Calaber " is written by
Edward Phillips, with the exception of the additions, in small print
above, which are by Aubrey. Aubrey then takes up the pen and writes
from " Cato " to the end of the paragraph " were with him."

[2] This sentence is written in a hand which I identify as Mrs.
Milton's, the widow.

H/e w'ent to travell about ye year 1638
ou abroad about a years space chiefly
imediately after his return he took a
Mr Russell's a Taylour in St Brides ch
& took into his tuition his Sisters two
& John philips ye first 10 the other 9
& in a years time made them then capab
prcking a Latin authour at sight &c &
years they went through ye best of
poëts Lucretius &c with him the use of the Globes
Aratus Dionysius After. Oppian Apollony
Quintus Calaber. Cato Varro & Column
ruftica were the very first authors they learn'd.
As he was severe on one hand, so he was most favour
in his conversation to those to whome most severe in
Education. — NB. He made his Nephews &c
sing from ye time they were with him.

and some Rudim̃ts
of Arithm: & Geom:

Why do ye not set downe where Joh. Milton
was borne ?[1]

from Mr E. Philips.

　　† His Invention was much more free and easie
in the Æquinoxes than at the Solstices; as he more
particularly found in writing his Paradise lost.　M^r
Edw. Philip his, [his Nephew and Amanuensis] hath †
All the time of writing his *Paradise lost*, his veine began
at the Autumnall Æquinoctiall and ceased at the Vernall or thereabouts (I believe about May) and this was
4 or 5 yeares of his doeing it.　He began about 2 yeares
before the K. came-in, and finished about 3 yeares after
the K's Restauracōn.

　　Q. Mr J. Playford p̄ Wilby's sett of *Oriana's*.

In the 2^d or 3^d 4th Booke of Paradise lost, there are
about 6 verses of Satan's exclamation to the Sun, w^{ch}
Mr E. Ph. remembers, about 15 or 16 yeares before
ever his Poëm was thought of, wch verses were intended
for the Beginning of a Tragoedie wch he had designed,
but was diverted from it by other businesse.

Whatever he wrote against Monarchie was out of no *Sheet C. f.*
　　or out of any faction, or Interest　　　　verso
animosity to the King's person, but out of a pure zeall

---

[1]This sentence is written by Anthony à Wood.
† This is roughly crossed out from " His Invention " to " hath."

to the Liberty of[1] Mankind, wch he thought would be greater under a free state than under a Monarchall goverment. His being so conversant in Livy and the Rom: authors and the greatnes he saw donne by the Rom: com̄onwealth & the virtue of their great

Captaines
Com̄anders induc't him to.

a Royalist
*Sheet C. f.*2.   His first wife (Mrs Powell) was brought up & lived

dancing &c
where there was a great deale of company & merriment, and when she came to live wth her husband at Mr Russells in St Brides ch: yd, she found it very solitary: no company came to her, often-times heard his Nephews

2   1
cry, and beaten. This life was irkesome to her; & so she went to her Parents at Fosthill: he sent for her (after some time) and I think his servant was evilly entreated, but as for ~~matter of~~ wronging his bed, I never heard the least suspicion: nor had he of that, any Jealousie.

*Sheet C. f.*2.   from Mr Abr. Hill.
verso.

mēm his sharp writing against Alexander More of Holland upon a mistake notwithstanding he had given him by the *Ambassador* all satisfaction to the contrary,

[1] Aubrey omitted 'of'.

☙ ~~viz that~~

☞ Q. the Ambassadors name of Mr Hill
Resp. Newport ye Dutch Ambassador

Q. Mr Allam of Edm: hall Oxon. of Mr J. Milton's life writt by himselfe v. pagg.

☙ viz. that the booke [called Clamor ~~Coeli~~] was
writt by Peter du Moulin. well that was all one, ~~when~~
~~he had~~ he having writt it, it should goe into the world.
one of them was as bad as the other.

his sight began to faile him at first, upon his writing
against Salmasius, and before 'twas fully compleated
one eie absolutely failed; upon the writing of other
books after that his other eie decayed.

write his name in red letters on his Pictures, wth his
widowe, to pserve.

THE LIFE OF MR. JOHN MILTON

BY JOHN PHILLIPS

To write the Lives of Single Persons is then a commendable Undertaking, when by it some Moral benefit is design'd to Mankind. Hee who has that in aim, will not imploy his time or Pen, to record the history of bad men, how sucessful or great soever they may have bin; unless by relating thir Tragical ends (which, through the just Judgment of the Almighty, most commonly overtakes them) or by discriminating, with a due note of Infamy, whatever is criminal in thir actions, hee warn the Reader to flee thir example.

But to celebrate, whether the Guifts or Graces, the natural Endowments, or acquir'd laudable Habitts of Persons eminent in thir Generations, while it gives glory to God, the bestower of all good things, and (by furnishing a Modell) tends to the edification of our Brethren, is little less then the duty of every Christian: Which seems acknowleg'd by the late Supervisors of our Common Prayer; when they added to the Collect for the Church militant, a clause commemorating the *Saints and Servants of God departed this life in his Fear.*

That Hee who is the subject of this discourse, made it his endeavor to bee thought worthy of that high Character, will, I make no doubt, appeer to the impartial Reader from the particulars, wch I shall with all sincerity relate of his life and Works.

The learned Mr. John Milton, born about the yeer sixteen hundred and eight, is said to bee descended from an antient Knightly Family in Buckinghamshire, that gave name to the chief place of thir abode. However that bee, his Father was entitled to a true Nobility in the Apostle Pauls Heraldry; having bin disinherited about ye beginning of Queen Elizabeths reign by his Father a Romanist, who had an estate of five hundred pound a yeer at Stainton St. John in Oxfordshire, for reading the Bible. Upon this occasion hee came yong to London, and beeing taken care of by a relation of his a Scrivenor, hee became free of that profession; and was so prosperous in it, and the Consortship of a prudent virtuous Wife, as to bee able to breed up in a liberal manner, and provide a competency for two Sons, and a Daughter: After which, out of a moderation, not usual with such as have tasted the sweets of gain, and perhaps naturally inclin'd rather to a retir'd life by his addiction to Music (for his skill in which hee stands registred among the Composers of his time) hee gave over his trade, and went to live in the Country.

This his eldest Son had his institution to learning both under public, and private Masters; under whom, through the pregnancy of his Parts, & his indefatigable industry (sitting up constantly at his Study till midnight) hee profited exceedingly; and early in that time wrote several grave and religious Poems, and paraphras'd some of Davids Psalms.

At about eighteen Yeers of age hee went to Christs College in Cambridge; where for his diligent study, his performance of public exercises, and for choice Verses, written on the occasions usually solemniz'd by the

hee was not farr distant, her learning, Musick and the Mathematics.

Being now become Master of what usefull knowlege was to bee had in Books: and competently skilld amongst others, in the Italian language, hee made choice of that Country to travail into, in order to polish his Conversation, & learn to know Men. And having receivd instructions how to demean himselfe with that wise observing Nation, as well as how to shape his Journy, from Sr Henry Wotton, whose esteem of him appeers in an elegant letter to him upon that Subject, hee took his way thorough France: In wch Kingdom (haveing the mann: & the Genius of which hee had no admiration) hee made small stay, nor contracted any Acquaintance; save that with the recommendation of the Lord Scudamore, then our Kings Ambassador at Paris, hee waited on Hugo Grotius, who was there under that Character from the Crown of Sweden.

Hasting to study by the way & Nice & passing through Genoa Ligorn & Pisa hee arrivd at Florence: Here hee stayd two monetts in familiar and elegant conversation with the choice Witts of that city, and was admitted by them to thir Academies; an Oeconomy much practisd among the virtuosi of those parts, for the communication of Polite literature as well as for the cementing of friendships. The reputation hee had with them they exprest in several Commendatory Verses, wch are extant in his book of Poems.

From Florence hee went to Rome, where, as in all places, hee spent his time in the choicest company, and amongst others there, in that of Lucas Holstein, Library keeper at the Vatican.

JOHN PHILLIPS'S *LIFE OF MILTON.*   Bodl. MS. Wood D. 4., f. 140. verso.

(to face page 19)

Universities, as well as for his virtuous and sober life, hee was in high esteem wth the best of his time.

After taking his degree of Master of Arts hee left the University, and, having no design to take upon him any of the particular learned Professions, apply'd him-selfe for five yeers, at his Fathers house in the Country, to the diligent reading of the best Classic Authors, both Divine and Humane; sometimes repairing to London, from wch hee was not farr distant, for learning Music and the Mathematics.

Beeing now become Master of what useful knowlege was to bee had in Books, and competently skill'd, amongst others, in the Italian language, hee made choice of that Country to travel into; in order to polish his Conversation, & learn to know Men. And having receiv'd instructions how to demean himselfe with that wise observing Nation, as well as how to shape his Journy, from Sr Henry Wotton, whose esteem of him appeers in an elegant letter to him upon that Subject, hee took his way [1] thorough France. In this [2] King-dom,[3] the manners & Genius of which hee had in no admiration, hee made small stay, nor contracted any Acquaintance; save that, with the recommendation of the Lord Scudamore,[4] our Kings Ambassador at Paris, hee waited on Hugo Grotius, who was there under that Character from the Crown of Sweden.

Hasting to Italy by the way of Nice, & passing through Genua Ligorn & Pisa hee arriv'd at Florence. Here hee liv'd [5] two moneths in familiar & elegant con-

---

[1] Substituted for " journy."   [2] Substituted for " w^{ch} ."

[3] " hee made no stay, having " crossed out.

[4] " hee waited " crossed out.   [5] Substituted for " pass'd."

versation with the choice Witts of that Citty, and
was admitted by them to thir private Academies; an
Oeconomy much practis'd among the Virtuosi of those
parts, for the communication of Polite literature, as
well as for the cementing of friendships. The reputation hee had with them they express'd in several
Commendatory Verses, wch are extant in his book of
Poems.

From Florence hee went to Rome, where, as in all
places, hee spent his time in the choicest company; and
amongst others there, in that of Lucas Holstein.[1]

At Naples, which was his next remove, hee became
acquainted wth Marquis Manso, a learned Person, and
so aged as to have bin Contemporary and intimate w^th
Torquato Tasso, the famous Italian Heroic.   This
Noble-man oblig'd him by very particular civilities,
accompanying him to see the rarities of the place, and
paying him Visitts at his lodging;   Also sent him the
testimony of a great esteem in this Distich

> *Ut Mens, Forma, Decor, Facies, Mos, si Pietas sic,*
> *Non Anglus, verum herclè Angelus ipse fores.*

Yet excus'd himselfe at parting for not having bin able
to do him more honour, by reason of his resolute owning his Religion: This hee did whensoever by any ones
enquiry occasion was offred; not otherwise forward to
enter upon discourses of that Nature.   Nor did hee
decline its defense in the like circumstances even in
Rome it self, on his return thether; though hee had
bin advis'd by letters from som friends to Naples, that

---

[1] After Holstein he has written and then crossed out " Library keeper
at the Vatican."   Over Library a mark refers to the margin, where he
has written and crossed out " for I am not certain that he was Library
keeper."

the English Jesuits design'd to do him mischief on that
account. Before his leaving Naples hee return'd the
Marquis an[1] acknowlegement of his great favors in an
elegant Copy of Verses entitl'd Mansus wch is extant
amongst his other latin Poems.[2]

From Rome hee revisited Florence for the sake of
his charming friends there; and then proceeded to
Venice, where hee shippd what books he had bought,
& through the delicious[3] country of Lombardy, and
over the Alps to Geneva, where hee liv'd in familiar
conversation with the famous Diodati. Thence through
France hee returnd home, having, with no ill management of his time, spent about fifteen moneths abroad.

Hee had by this time laid in a large stock of knowlege, which as design'd not for the purchase of Wealth,
so neither intended hee[4] it, as a Misers hoard, to ly
useless: Having therefore[5] taken a house, to bee[6] at
full ease and quiet, & gotten his books about him, hee
sett himselfe upon Compositions, tending either to the
public benefit of Mankind, and especially his Countrymen, or to the advancement of the Commonwealth of
Learning. And his first labours were very happily
dedicated to, what had the chiefest place in his affections, and had bin no small part of his Study, the service
of Religion.

It was now the Year 1640: And the Nation was
much divided upon the Controversies about Church

[1] Substituted for " a large."

[2] He first wrote "an elegant Poem wch is amongst his other latin
Verses."

[3] Substituted for " pleasant."   [4] " that " crossed out after " hee."

[5] " gotten his Books about him " crossed out.

[6] " full " crossed out.

Government, between the Prelatical party, and the Dissenters, or, as they were commonly then calld, Puritans.
Hee had study'd Religion in the Bible and the best
Authors, had strictly livd up to it's Rules, and had no
temporal concern depending upon any Hierarchy, to
render him suspected, either to himselfe, or others, as
one that writt for Interest; and therefore [1] with great
boldness, and Zeal offer'd his Judgment, first in two
Books of Reformation [2] by way of address to a friend,
And then in answer to a Bishop hee writt of *Prelatical
Episcopacy* and *The Reason of Church Government.* After
that [3] *Animadversions upon the Remonstrants defence* (the
work of Bishop Hall) *against Smectymnyus* and *Apology
for those Animadversions.*

In this while, his manner of Settlement fitting him
for the reception of a Wife, hee in a moneths time
(according to his practice of not wasting that precious
Talent) courted, married, and brought home from
Forrest-hall near Oxford a Daughter of Mr Powell.
But shee, that was very Yong, & had bin bred in a
family of plenty and freedom, beeing not well pleas'd
with his reserv'd manner of life, within a few days left
him, and went back [4] into the Country with her Mother:
Nor though hee sent severall pressing invitations could
hee prevayl wth her to return, till about foure yeers
after, when Oxford was surrendr'd (the nighness of her
Fathers house to that Garrison having for the most part
of the mean time hindred any communication between
them) shee of her own accord came, & submitted to
him; pleading that her Mother had bin the inciter of

---

[1] Substituted for " thence."   [2] " And then " crossed out.
[3] Substituted for " After that for a first and second."
[4] Substituted for " return'd."

her to that frowardness. Hee in this Interval,[1] who had entred into that State for the end design'd by God & Nature, and was then in the full vigor of his Manhood, could ill bear the disappointment hee mett with by her obstinate absenting: And therefore thought upon a Divorce, that hee might bee free to marry another; concerning which hee also was in treaty. The lawfulness and expedience of this, duly regulat in order to all those purposes, for which Marriage was at first instituted; had upon full consideration & reading good Authors bin formerly his Opinion: And the necessity of justifying himselfe now concurring with the opportunity, acceptable to him, of instructing others in a point of so great concern [2] to the peace and preservation of Families; and so likely to prevent temptations as well as mischiefs,[3] hee first writt *The Doctrine and Discipline of Divorce*, then *Colasterion*, and after *Tetrachordon*: In these [4] hee taught the right use and design of Marriage; then the Original and practise of Divorces amongst the Jews, and [5] show'd that our Savior, in those foure places of the Evangelists, meant not the abrogating, but rectifying the abuses of it; [6] rendring to that purpose another Sense of the word Fornication (and wch is also the Opinion amongst others of Mr. Selden in his *Uxor Hebræa*) then what is commonly received. Martin

[1] " in this Interval " read originally " in this mean time." " Interval " was substituted for " mean time," and " the " changed to " this."

[2] " of so great concern " substituted for " so necessary."

[3] " as well as mischiefs " substituted for " to Sin."

[4] Substituted for " which."

[5] " by expounding after other ... divines the foure passages in the Evangelists " crossed out.

[6] " among the Jews " crossed out.

Bucers Judgment in this matter hee likewise translated into English. The Assembly of Divines then sitting at Westminster, though formerly obliged by his learned Pen in the defense of Smectymnyus, and other thir controversies with the Bishops, now impatient of having the Clergies [1] Jurisdiction, as they reckon'd [2] it, invaded, instead of answering, or disproving what those books [3] had asserted, caus'd him to be summon'd [4] for them before the Lords: But that house, whether approving [5] the Doctrin, or not favoring his Accusers, soon dismiss'd him.

This was the mending of a decay in the Superstructure, and had for object onely the well beeing of private Persons, or at most of Families; His small treatise *of Education*, address'd to Mr Hartlib, was the laying a Foundation also of Public Weale: In it hee prescrib'd an easy and delightful method for training up Gentry in such a manner to all sorts of Literature, as that they might at the same time by like degrees advance in Virtue, and Abilities to serve their Country; subjoyning directions for their attayning other necessary, or Ornamental accomplishments: And it seem'd hee design'd in some measure to put this in practise. Hee had from his first settling taken care of instructing his two Nephews by his Sister Phillips, and, as it happen'd, the Sonn of some friend: Now hee took a large house, where the Earle of Barrimore, sent by his Aunt

---

[1] Originally " thir Jurisdiction ": " thir " was changed to " the Clergies."

[2] Substituted for " term'd."

[3] " those books " substituted for " he."

[4] " caus'd ... summon'd " substituted for " summon'd him."

[5] Substituted for " not misliking."

the Lady Ranalagh, Sr Thomas Gardiner of Essex, and others were under his Tuition: But whether it were that the tempers of our Gentry would not beare the strictness of his Discipline, or for what other reason, hee continud that course but a while.

His next public work, and which seem'd to bee his particular Province, who was so jealous in promoting Knowlege, was *Areopagitica*, written in manner of an Oration, to vindicate the Freedom of the Press from the Tyranny of Licensers; Who either inslav'd to the Dictates of those that put them into Office, or prejudic'd by thir own Ignorance, are wont to hinder ye comming out of any thing [1] which is not consonant to the common receiv'd Opinions, and by that means deprive the public of the benefit of many usefull labours.

Hitherto all his Writings had for subject the propagation of Religion or [2] Learning, or the bettering some more private concerns of Mankind: In Political matters hee had publish'd nothing. And it was now the time for the King's comming upon his Tryal, when some of the Presbiterian Ministers, out of malignity to the Independent Party, who had supplanted them, more than from any principles of Loyalty, asserted clamorously in thir Sermons and Writings the Privilege of Kings from all accountableness, Or (to speak in the Language of this time) Non resistance & Passive Obedience to bee the Doctrine of all the Reformed Churches. This general Thesis, which incourag'd all manner of Tyranny, hee opposed by good Arguments, and the Authorities of several eminently learned Protestants in a Book titled *The Tenure of Kings*, but without any par-

---

[1] " New or " crossed out.
[2] Substituted for " &."

ticular application to the dispute then on foot in this Nation.

Upon the change of Government which succeeded the King's death hee was, without any seeking of his, by the means of a private Acquaintance, who was then a member of the new Council of State, chosen Latin Secretary. In this public Station his abilities & the acuteness of his parts, which had lyen hid in his privacy, were soon taken notice of, and hee was pitch'd upon to elude the Artifice of Ἐικὼν βασιλικὴ. This hee had no sooner perform'd, answerably to the expectation from his Witt & Pen, in Ἐικονοκλάςης, but another Adventure expected him.

Salmasius a Professor in Holland, who had in a large Treatise, not long before, maintain'd the parity of Church Governors against Episcopacy, put out *Defensio Caroli Regis*, and in it, amongst other absurdities, justify'd (as indeed it was unavoidable in the defense of that cause, which was styl'd Bellum Episcopale) to the contradiction of his former Book, the pretensions of the Bishops. Him Mr. Milton by the order of his Masters answerd in [1] *Defensio pro populo Anglicano*; both in more correct Latin, to the shame of the others Grammership, and by much better reasoning. For Salmasius beeing a Forrainer, & grossly ignorant of our Laws & Constitution (which in all Nations are the respective distinguishing Principles of Government) either brought no arguments from thence, or such onely (and by him not seldom mistaken or misapply'd) as were partially suggested to him by those whose cause hee had undertaken; and which, having during the many yeers of our divisions been often ventilated, receiv'd an

[1] Substituted for " by."

easy solution. Nor had hee given proof of deeper learning in that which is properly call'd Politics, while hee made use of trite Instances, as that of the Government of Bees, & such like to prove the preeminency of Monarchy: and all along so confounded it with Tyranny (as also hee did the Episcopal with the Papal Government) that hee might better have pass'd for a Defender of the grand Signor, and the Council of Trent, then of a lawful King and a Reformed Church. For this and reneging his former Principles hee was by Mr. Milton facetiously expos'd: Nor did hee ever reply, though hee liv'd three yeers after.

But what hee wisely declin'd, the further provoking such an Adversary, or persisting to defend a Cause hee so ill understood, was attempted in *Clamor Regij Sanguinis &c*: in which Salmasius was hugely extoll'd, and Mr Milton as falsly defam'd. The Anonymous Author, Mr. Milton, who had by his last book gain'd great esteem and many friends among the Learned abroad, by whom, and by public Ministers comming hether hee was often visited, soon discover'd to bee Morus, formerly a Professor & Minister at Geneva, then living in Holland. Him, in *Secunda Defensio pro populo Anglicano* he rendr'd ridiculous for his trivial and weak Treatise under so Tragical a title, conteyning little of Argument, which had not before suffr'd with Salmasius. And because it consisted most of Railing & false Reproches, hee, in no unpleasant manner, from very good testimonies retorted upon him the true history of his notorious Impurities, both at Geneva, and Leyden. Himselfe hee also, by giving a particular ingenuous account of his whole life Vindicated from those scurrilous aspersions, with which that Book had indevor'd to blemish him: Adding perhaps thereby also reputation to the cause hee defended, at least, with impartial Readers, when they should reflect upon the different qualifications of the respective Champions. And when Morus afterwards strove to cleer himselfe of beeing the Author, & to represent Mr. Milton as an injurious Defamer in that particular, hee in *Defensio pro se* by very good testimonies, and other circumstantial proofs justify'd his having fixd it there, and made good sport of the others shallow Evasions.

While hee was thus employ'd his Eysight totally faild him; not through any immediat or sudden Judgment, as his Adversaries insultingly affirm'd; but from a weakness which his hard nightly study in his youth had first occasion'd, and which by degrees had for some time before depriv'd him of the use of one Ey: And the Issues and Seatons, made use of to save or retrieve that, were thought by drawing away the Spirits, which should have supply'd the Optic Vessells, to have hasten'd the loss of the other. Hee was indeed advis'd by his Physitians of the danger, in his condition, attending so great intentness as that work requir'd. But hee, who was resolute in going through with what upon good consideration hee at any time design'd, and to whom the love of Truth and his Country was[1] dearer then all things, would not for any danger decline thir defense.

Nor did his Darkness discourage or disable him from prosecuting, with the help of Amanuenses,[2] the former design of his calmer Studies. And hee had now more leisure, beeing dispens'd with, by having a Substitute allowd him, and sometimes Instructions sent

---

[1] Substituted for " were."   [2] " his " crossed out.

home to him, from attending in his office [1] of Secretary.

It was now that hee began that laborious work of amassing out of all the Classic Authors, both in Prose and Verse, a [2] *Latin Thesaurus* to the emendation of that done by Stephanus; Also the composing *Paradise Lost* And the framing a *Body of Divinity* out of the Bible: All which, notwithstanding the several Calamities befalling him in his fortunes, hee finish'd after the Restoration: As also the *Brittish history* down to the Conquest, *Paradise regaind, Samson Agonistes,* a Tragedy, *Logica* & *Accedence commenc'd Grammar* & had begun a *Greek Thesaurus*; having scarce left any part of learning unimprov'd by him: As in *Paradise lost & Regain'd* hee more especially taught all Virtue.

In these Works, and the instruction of some Youth or other at the intreaty of his friends, hee in great Serenity spent his time & expir'd no less calmly in the Yeare 1674.

He had naturally a Sharp Witt, and steddy Judgment; which helps toward attaining Learning hee improv'd by an indefatigable attention to his Study; and was supported in that by a Temperance, allways observ'd by him, but in his Youth even with great Nicety. Yet did hee not reckon this Talent but as intrusted with him; and therefore dedicated all his labours to the glory of God, & some public Good; Neither binding himselfe to any of the gainfull Professions, nor having any worldly Interest for aim in what he taught. Hee made no address or Court for the emploiment of Latin Secretary, though his eminent fittness for it appeer by his printed Letters of that time.

---

[1] Substituted for " place."   [2] " that " crossed out.

And hee was so farr from beeing concern'd in the
corrupt designs of his Masters, that whilst in his first
and second *Defensio pro populo Anglicano* he was an
Advocate for Liberty against Tyranny & Oppression
(which to him seem'd the case, as well by the public
Declarations on the one side [and hee was a Stranger
to thir private Counsels] as by the Arguments on the
other side, which run mainly upon the justifying of
exorbitant & lawless power) hee took care all along
strictly to define, and persuade to true Liberty, and
especially in very solemn Perorations at the close of
those Books; where hee also, little less than Prophetically, denounc'd the Punishments due to the abusers of
that Specious name.   And as hee was not link'd to one
Party by self Interest,[1] so neither was hee divided from
the other by Animosity; but was forward to do any of
them good Offices, when their particular Cases afforded
him ground to appeer on thir behalf.   And especially,
if on the score of Witt or Learning, they could lay
claim to his peculiar Patronage.   Of which were instances, among others, the Grand child of the famous
Spencer, a Papist suffering in his concerns in Ireland,
and S[r] William Davenant when taken Prisoner, for
both of whom hee procur'd relief.

[1] On the back of the last page are five lines of writing carefully
crossed out, which were evidently the first draft of the passage, " Perorations ... self Interest."   They are as follows :

" Perorations at the close of those Books at the close of those Books where
       so firmly   &   denounc'd
hee ∧ denounc'd ∧ little less then Prophetically ∧ the Punishments
w[ch]   due to
∧ often befell ∧ the abusers of that Specious name whether by
enlarging   serve
stretching it to licentiousness or by inverting it to ye corrupt ends of
Amb[ition]   And as hee was not link'd to one Party by selfe."

This his Sincerity, and disentanglement of any private ends with his Sentiments relating to the Public, proceeded no doubt from a higher Principle, but was in great part supported,[1] and temptations to the contrary avoided by his constant Frugality; which enabl'd him at first to live within compass of the moderate Patrimony his Father left him, and afterwards to bear with patience, and no discomposure [2] of his way of living, the great losses which befell him in his Fortunes. Yett he was not sparing to buy good Books; of which hee left a fair Collection; and was generous in relieving the wants of his Friends. Of his [3] Gentleness and Humanity hee likewise gave signal proof in receiving home, and living in good accord till her death with his first wife, after shee had so obstinately absented from him: During which time, as neither in any other Scene of his life, was hee blemish'd with the least Unchastity.

From so Christian a Life, so great Learning, and so unbyass'd a search after Truth it is not probable any errors in Doctrine should spring. And therefore his Judgment in his Body of Divinity concerning some speculative points, differing perhaps from that commonly receivd, (and which is thought to bee the reason that never was printed) neither ought rashly to bee condemnd, and however himselfe not to bee uncharitably **censur'd**; who by beeing a constant Champion [4] **for** the liberty of Opining, expressd much Candor **towards** others. But that this Age is

---

[1] " by his frugality " crossed out.

[2] " no discomposure " substituted for " small alteration."

[3] " genero " crossed out.

[4] Originally " so constant a."

insensible of the great obligations it has to him, is too
apparent in that hee has no better a Pen to celebrate
his Memory.

Hee was of a moderate Stature, and well proportion'd, of a ruddy Complexion, light brown Hair, &
handsom Features; save that his Eyes were none of the
quickest. But his blindness, which proceeded from a
Gutta Serena, added no further blemish to them. His
deportment was sweet and affable; and his Gate erect
& Manly, bespeaking Courage and undauntedness
(or a Nil conscire) On which account hee wore a
Sword while hee had his Sight, and was skill'd in using
it. Hee had an excellent Ear, and could bear a part
both in Vocal & Instrumental Music. His moderate
Estate left him by his Father was through his good
Oeconomy sufficient to maintain him. Out of his
Secretary's Salary hee had sav'd two thousand pounds,
which being logd'd in the Excise, and that Bank failing upon the Restoration, hee utterly lost; Beside
which, and the ceasing of his Imploiment hee had no
damage by that [1] change of Affairs.[2] For hee early
sued out his Pardon; and by means of that, when the
Serjeant of the house of Commons had officiously seisd
him, was quickly set at liberty. Hee had too at the first
return of the Court in good manners [3] left his house in
Petty France, which had a door into the Park; and in
all other things demeaning himselfe peaceably, was so
farr from being reckon'd disaffected, that hee was
visited at his house on Bun-hill by a Chief Officer of
State, and desir'd to imploy his Pen on thir behalfe.

[1] Substituted for " the."
[2] Substituted for " Government."
[3] " good manners " substituted for " prudently."

And when the Subject of Divorce was under consideration with the Lords, upon the account of the Lord Ross,
hee was consulted by an eminent [1] Member of that
house. By the great fire in 1666 hee had a house in
Bread street burnt: wch was all the Real Estate hee
had. Hee rendred his Studies and various Works
more easy & pleasant by allotting them thir several
portions of the day. Of these the time friendly to the
Muses fell to his Poetry; And hee waking early (as is
the use of temperate men) had commonly a good Stock
of Verses ready against his Amanuensis came; which
if it happend to bee later than ordinary, hee would complain, Saying *hee wanted to bee milkd*. The Evenings
hee likewise spent in reading some choice Poets, by
way of refreshment after the days toyl, and to store his
Fancy against Morning. Besides his ordinary lectures
out of the Bible and the [2] best Commentators on the
week day, That was his sole subject on Sundays. And
Davids Psalms were in esteem with him above all
Poetry. The Youths that hee instructed from time to
time servd him often as Amanuenses, & some elderly
persons were glad for the benefit of his learned Conversation, to perform that Office. His first Wife dy'd a
while after his blindness seizd him, leaving him three
Daughters, that liv'd to bee Women. Hee marry'd
two more, whereof one surviv'd him. Hee dy'd in a
fitt of the Gout, but with so little pain or Emotion, that
the time of his expiring was not perceiv'd by those in
the room. And though hee had bin long troubl'd with
that disease, insomuch that his Knuckles were all call-
ous, yet was hee not ever observ'd to be very impatient.

[1] " an eminent " substituted for " no mean."
[2] Substituted for " its."

c

Hee had this Elogy in common with the Patriarchs and Kings of Israel that he was gather'd to his people; [1] for hee happen'd to bee bury'd in Cripplegate where about thirty yeer before hee had by chance also interrd his Father.

[1] " was gather'd to his people " substituted for " slept with his Fathers."

FROM *FASTI OXONIENSES* OR *ANNALS* OF THE UNIVERSITY OF OXFORD.

By ANTHONY à WOOD, 1691.

1635. THIS year was incorporated Master of Arts *John Milton*, not that it appears so in the Register, for the reason I have told you in the Incorporations 1629, but from his own mouth to my friend, who was well acquainted with, and had from him, and from his Relations after his death, most of this account of his life and writings following. (1) That he was born in *Breadstreet* within the City of *London*, between 6 and 7 a clock in the morning of the ninth of *Decemb.* an. 1608. (2) That his father *Joh. Milton* who was a Scrivner living at the *Spread Eagle*[1] in the said street, was a Native of *Halton* in *Oxfordshire*, and his mother named *Sarah* was of the antient family of the *Bradshaws*. (3) That his Grandfather *Milton* whose Christian name was *John*, as he thinks, was an Under-Ranger or Keeper of the Forest of *Shotover* near to the said town of *Halton*, but descended from those of his name who had lived beyond all record at *Milton* near *Halton* and *Thame* in *Oxfordshire*. Which Grandfather being a zealous Papist, did put away, or, as some say, disinherit, his Son, because he was a Protestant, which made him retire to *London*, to seek, in a manner, his fortune. (4) That he the said *John Milton* the Author, was educated mostly in *Pauls* school under

[1] The arms that *Joh. Milton* did use and seal his letters with, were, *Argent a spread eagle with two heads gules, legg'd and beak'd sable.*

35

Alex. Gill senior, and thence at 15 years of age was sent to *Christs* Coll. in *Cambridge*, where he was put under the tuition of *Will. Chappell*, afterwards Bishop of *Ross* in *Ireland*, and there, as at School for 3 years before, 'twas usual with him to sit up till midnight at his book, which was the first thing that brought his eyes into the danger of blindness. By this his indefatigable study he profited exceedingly, wrot then several Poems, paraphras'd some of *David's Psalms*, performed the collegiate and academical exercise to the admiration of all, and was esteemed to be a vertuous and sober person, yet not to be ignorant of his own parts. (5) That after he had taken the degrees in Arts, he left the University of his own accord, and was not expelled for mis-demeanors, as his Adversaries have said. Whereupon retiring to his Fathers house in the Country, he spent some time in turning over Latin and Greek Authors, and now and then made [1] excursions into the great City to buy books, to the end that he might be instructed in Mathematicks and Musick, in which last he became excellent, and by the help of his Mathematicks could compose a Song or Lesson. (6) That after five years being thus spent, and his Mother (who was very charit-able to the poor) dead, he did design to travel, so that obtaining the rudiments of the Ital. Tongue, and Instructions how to demean himself from Sir *Hen. Wotton*, who delighted in his company, and gave him Letters of commendation to certain persons living at *Venice*, he travelled into *Italy*, an. 1638. (7) That in his way thither, he touched at *Paris*, where *Joh. Scuda-moure*, Vicount *Slego*, Embassador from K. *Ch.* I. to

---

[1] See in Joh. Milton's book intit. *Defensio secunda*: edit. *Hag. Com.* 1654, p. 61, &c.

the French king, received him kindly, and by his means became known to *Hugo Grotius*, then and there Embassador from the Qu. of *Sweden*; but the manners and genius of that place being not agreeable to his mind, he soon left it. (8) That thence by *Geneva* and other places of note, he went into *Italy*, and thro *Legorne*, *Pisa*, &c. he went to *Florence*, where continuing two months, he became acquainted with several learned men, and familiar with the choicest Wits of that great City, who introduced and admitted him into their private Academies, whereby he saw and learn'd their fashions of literature. (9) That from thence he went to *Sena* and *Rome*, in both which places he spent his time among the most learned there, *Lucas Holsteinius* being one; and from thence he journied to *Naples*, where he was introduced into the acquaintance of *Joh. Bapt. Mansus* an Italian Marquess (to whom *Torquatus Tassus* an Italian poet wrot his book *De Amicitia*) who shewed great civilities to him, accompanied him to see the rarities of that place, visited him at his Lodgings, and sent to, the testimony of his great esteem for, him, in this Distich,

> *Ut mens, forma, decor, mos, si pietas sic,*
> *Non Anglus, verum herculè Angelus ipse fores.*

And excus'd himself at parting for not having been able to do him more honour, by reason of his resolute owning his (Protestant) religion: which resoluteness he using at *Rome*, many there were that dared not to express their civilities towards him, which otherwise they would have done: And I have heard it confidently related, that for his said Resolutions, which out of policy, and for his own safety, might have been then spared, the English Priests at *Rome* were highly disgusted, and it was question'd whether the Jesuits his Countrymen there, did not design to do him mischief. Before he left *Naples* he return'd the Marquess an acknowledgment of his great favours in an elegant copy of verses entit. *Mansus*, which is among the Latin poems. (10) That from thence (*Naples*) he thought to have gone into *Sicily* and *Greece*, but upon second thoughts he continued in *Italy*, and went to *Luca*, *Bononia*, *Ferrara*, and at length to *Venice*; where continuing a month, he went and visited *Verona* and *Millan*. (11) That after he had ship'd the books and other goods which he had bought in his travels, he returned thro *Lombardy*, and over the *Alpes* to *Geneva*, where spending some time, he became familiar with the famous *Joh. Deodate* D.D. Thence, going thro *France*, he returned home, well fraught with Knowledge and Manners, after he had been absent one year and three months. (12) That soon after he setled in an house in *S. Bride's* Churchyard, near *Fleetstreet*, in *London*, where he instructed in the Lat. Tongue two Youths named *John* and *Edw. Philips*, the Sons of his Sister *Anne* by her Husband *Edward Philips*: both which were afterwards Writers, and the eldest princip'd as his Uncle. But the times soon after changing, and the Rebellion thereupon breaking forth, *Milton* sided with the Faction, and being a man of parts, was therefore more capable than another of doing mischief, especially by his pen, as by those books which I shall anon mention, will appear. (13) That at first we find him a Presbyterian and a most sharp and violent opposer of Prelacy, the established ecclesiastical Discipline and the orthodox Clergy. (14) That shortly after he did set on foot and maintained very odd and novel Positions concerning Divorce, and then taking part with the Independents, he became a great Antimonarchist, a bitter Enemy to K. *Ch.* I. and at length arrived to that monstrous and unparallel'd height of profligate impudence, as in print to justify the most execrable Murder of him the best of Kings, as I shall anon tell you. Afterwards being made Latin Secretary to the Parliament, we find him a Commonwealths man, a hater of all things that looked towards a single person, a great reproacher of the Universities, scholastical degrees, decency and uniformity in the Church. (15) That when *Oliver* ascended the Throne, he became the Latin Secretary, and proved to him very serviceable when employed in business of weight and moment, and did great matters to obtain a name and wealth. To conclude, he was a person of wonderful parts, of a very sharp, biting and satyrical wit. He was a good Philosopher and Historian, an excellent Poet, Latinist, Grecian and Hebritian, a good Mathematician and Musitian, and so rarely endowed by nature, that had he been but honestly principled, he might have been highly useful to that party, against which he all along appeared with much malice and bitterness. As for the things which he hath published, are these, (1) *Of Reformation, touching Church Discipline in England, and the causes that hitherto have hindred it*, &c. Lond. 1641. qu. At which time, as before, the Nation was much divided upon the Controversies about Church Government between the prelatical party, and Puritans, and therefore *Milton* did with great boldness and zeal offer his judgment as to those matters in his said book of Reformation. (2) *Animadversions upon the Remonstrants*

defence against Smectymnus. Lond. 1641. qu. Which
Rem. defence was written (as 'tis said) by Dr. *Jos. Hall*,
Bishop of *Exeter*. (3) *Apology against the humble Remonstrant.* This was written in vindication of his *Animadversions*. (4) *Against prelatical Episcopacy.* This I
have not yet seen. (5) *The reason of Church Government;*
nor this. (6) *The doctrine and discipline of divorce*, &c.
in two books. Lond. 1644-45. qu. To which is added
in some copies a translation of *The judgment of Mart.
Bucer concerning Divorce*, &c. It must be now known,
that after his settlement, upon his return from his
Travels, he in a months time courted, married, and
brought home to his house in *London*, a Wife from
Forsthill lying between *Halton* and *Oxford*, named
Mary the daughter of Mr. — *Powell* of that place,
Gent. But she, who was very young, and had been
bred in a family of plenty and freedom, being not well
pleas'd with her Husband's retired manner of life, did
shortly after leave him and went back in the Country
with her Mother. Whereupon, tho he sent divers
pressing invitations, yet he could not prevail with her
to come back, till about 4 years after when the Garrison
of *Oxon* was surrendred (the nighness of her Father's
house to which having for the most part of the mean
time hindred any communication between them) she of
her own accord returned and submitted to him, pleading
that her Mother had been the chief promoter of her
frowardness. But he being not able to bear this abuse,
did therefore upon consideration, after he had consulted
many eminent Authors, write the said book of Divorce,
with intentions to be separated from her, but by the
compromising of her Relations the matter did not take
effect: so that she continuing with him ever after till

her death, he had several Children by her, of whom *Deborah* was the third daughter, trained up by the Father in Lat. and Greek, and made by him his *Amanuensis.* (7) *Tetrachordon: Expositions upon the four chief places in Scripture, which treat on marriage,* on Gen. 1, 27, 28, &c. Lond. 1646. qu. (8) *Colasterion: A reply to a nameless answer against the doctrine and discipline of divorce* &c. printed 1645. qu. Upon his publication of the said three books of Marriage and Divorce, the *Assembly of Divines* then sitting at *Westminster* took special notice of them, and thereupon, tho the Author had obliged them by his pen in his defence of *Smectymnus* and other their Controversies had with the Bishops, they impatient of having the Clergies jurisdiction (as they reckon'd it) invaded, did, instead of answering, or disproving what those books had asserted, cause him to be summoned before the House of Lords: but that House, whether approving the Doctrine, or not favouring his Accusers, did soon dismiss him. To these things I must add, that after his Majesty's Restauration, when the subject of Divorce was under consideration with the Lords upon the account of *John* lord *Ros* or *Roos* his separation from his Wife *Anne Pierpont* eldest daughter to *Henry* Marquess of *Dorchester*, he was consulted by an eminent Member of that House, as he was about that time by a chief Officer of State, as being the prime person that was knowing in that affair. (9) *Of Education*, written or addressed to Mr. *Sam. Hartlib.* In this Treatise he prescrib'd an easy and delightful method for the training up of Gentry to all sorts of Literature, that they might at the same time by like degrees advance in virtue and abilities to serve their Country, subjoyning directions for their obtaining

other necessary or ornamental Accomplishments. And
to this end that he might put it in practice, he took a
larger house, where the Earl of *Barrimore* sent by his
Aunt the lady *Rannelagh*, Sir *Thomas Gardiner* of
Essex, to be there with others (besides his two Nephews)
under his Tuition. But whether it were that the tempers of our Gentry would not bear the strictness of his
discipline, or for what other reasons I cannot tell, he
continued that course but a while. (10) *Areopagetica:
A speech for the Liberty of unlicensed printing, to the
Parliament of England.* Lond. 1644. qu. written to
vindicate the freedom of the Press from the Tyranny of
Licensers, who for several Reasons deprive the public
of the benefit of many useful Authors. (11) *Poemata:
quorum pleraque intra annum aetatis vigesimum conscripsit
author*, &c. Lond. 1645, oct. (12) *A mask.*—printed
1645. oct. (13) *Poems*, &c.—printed the same year.
Hitherto we find him only to have published political
things, but when he saw, upon the coming of K.
Charles I. to his Tryal, the Presbyterian Ministers
clamorously to assert in their Sermons and Writings
the privileges of Kings from all accountableness, or (to
speak in the language of that time) Non-resistance and
Passive obedience to be the Doctrine of all the reformed
Churches (which he took to be only their malignity
against the Independents who had supplanted them,
more than for any principles of Loyalty) he therefore
to oppose that *Thesis* (which as he conceiv'd did en-
courage all manner of Tyranny) did write and publish
from divers Arguments and Authorities, (13) *The
tenure of Kings and Magistrates: proving that it is lawful,
&c. to call to account a Tyrant or King, and after due
conviction to depose and put him to death*, &c. Lond.

1649-50. qu. Soon after the King being beheaded to
the great astonishment of all the World, and the Government thereupon changed, he was, without any seeking
of his, by the endeavours of a private acquaintance, who
was a member of the new *Council of State*, chosen Latin
Secretary, as I have before told you. In this publick
station his abilities and acuteness of parts, which had
been in a manner kept private, were soon taken notice
of, and he was pitch'd upon to elude *the artifice* (so it
was then by the Faction called) of *Eikon Basilice*.
Whereupon he soon after published (14) *Iconoclastes in
answer to a book entit*. Eikon Basilice, the portrature
of his sacred Majesty in his Sollitudes and Sufferings.
Lond. 1649-50. qu. *ib*. 1690. oct. which being published to the horror of all sober men, nay even to the
Presbyterians themselves, yet by the then dominant
party it was esteemed an excellent piece, and perform'd
answerably to the expectation of his Wit and Pen.
After the Return of King *Charles* 2, this book was
called in by Proclamation, dated 13 *Aug*. 1660, at
which time the Author (who a little before had left his
house in *Petty France* which had a door going into
S. *James's* park) absconded, for fear of being brought
to a legal Tryal, and so consequently of receiving con-
dign Punishment. At the same time also, was called
in a book of *John Goodwin*, then lately a Minister in
Colemanstreet in *Lond*. entit. *The Obstructors of Justice;*
written in defence of the Sentence against his Majesty
Charles I.[1] At which time also the said *Goodwin*

---

[1] From a MS. note of Wood, the editors of the second edition of the
Fasti, 1721, insert here: " Mr. John Milton is also thought to be
" the author of *The grand Case of Conscience concerning the Engagement
" stated and resolv'd*, &c. *Lond*. 1650. qu. 3.sh."

absconded to prevent Justice.   Soon after the publication of *Iconoclastes*, *Salmasius*, a professor in *Holland*,
who had in a large treatise not long before, maintain'd, as 'tis said, the parity of Church Governours
against Episcopacy, did publish *Defensio regia, pro
Carolo I. Rege Angliæ*, wherein he justified several
matters, as *Milton* conceived, to the contradiction of
his former book.   Whereupon he wrot and published,
(15) *Pro populo Anglicano defensio contra Claudii Anonymi
alias Salmasii defensionem regiam.* Lond. 1651. fol. said
to be written in more correct Latin than that of *Salmasius*.   While *Milton* was writing the said book, his
sight began to fail him, and before it was fully compleated, one of his eyes did absolutely perish.   In the
month of *June* the same year (1651) the said book was
burnt at *Tholouse* by an arrest from the Parliament,
under the Government of the Duke of *Orleans:* And
in *Sept.* following it was the usual practice of *Marchm.
Nedham* a great crony of *Milton*, to abuse *Salmasius* in
his publick Mercury called *Politicus*, (as *Milton* had done
before in his *Defensio*) by saying among other things
that *Christina* Qu. of *Sweden* had cashiered him her
favour, by understanding that he was " *a pernicious
parasite, and a promoter of Tyranny.*"   After his Majesty's
Restauration, this book also was called in by the same
proclamation before mention'd.   But so it was, that in
1652, a certain book entit. *Regii sanguinis clamor*, &c.
being published, *Salmasius* was highly extol'd in it, and
Milton had his just character given therein.   The
nameless Author of which being for a considerable time
sought out, but in vain, by *Milton*, he at length learn'd
by certain Ministers of State sent to the Republick of
England, (who would sometimes visit him as a learned

man) that it was written by one *Alex. More*, formerly
a Professor and Minister at *Geneva*, then living in
Holland. Whereupon he published (16) *Pro populo
Anglicano defensio secunda, contra infamem libellum Anonymum, cui titulus*, Regii sanguinis clamor ad cœlum
adversus patricidas Anglicanos. *Lond.* 1654, and at
Hag. Com. the same year, in oct. Upon the writing
of this book, the Author *Milton* lost the other eye; and
tho to his charge he used many means, yet he could
never recover either of his eyes. This book, entit.
Reg. sang. clam. &c. tho written by Dr. *Peter du
Moulin*, Prebendary of *Canterbury*, as it afterwards
well appeared, yet Milton upon the reports before
mention'd could not be convinced to the contrary, but
that it was written by the said *More*, and therefore not
only abused him in his Answers, but by his friend
Nedham in his *Politicus* whereby the reputation of that
learned person was severely touched. (17) *Pro se
Defensio contra Alex. Morum Ecclesiasten, libelli famosi,
cui tit.* Regii sanguinis clamor, &c. *Lond.* 1655 oct.
In this book he is exceeding bitter against *Morus*, and
pretends to give a true history of his notorius Impurities
both at *Geneva* and *Leyden*, and an account of his own
particular life to vindicate himself from what, as he
thought, was scurrilously said of him by *Morus*. At
the end of the said book, the Author *Milton* added
Ad Alex. Mori supplementum responsio. About the time
that he had finished these things, he had more leisure,
and time at command, and being dispenced with by
having a substitute allowed him, and sometimes Instructions sent home to him from attending his office of
Secretary, he began that laborious work of amassing
out of all the classick Authors both in prose and verse a

Latin *Thesaurus*, to the emendation of that done by *Stephanus*; also the composing of *Paradise lost*, and of the framing a *Body of Divinity* out of the Bible. All which, notwithstanding the several troubles that befell him in his fortunes, he finished after his Majesty's Restauration. But to go on with the Cat. of his Books according to time, take these as they follow; (18) *Treatise of civil power in ecclesiastical causes*, &c. Lond. 1659. in tw. (19) *Considerations touching the likeliest means to remove Hirelings out of the Church*. Lond. 1659. in tw. (20) *Ready and easie way to establish a free Commonwealth, and the excellencies thereof compared with*, &c. Lond.1659. in two sheets and an half in qu. This being published in *Feb*. the same year, was answer'd by *G. S.* in his *Dignity of Kingship*. (21) *Brief notes upon a late Sermon titled*, The Fear of God and the King, &c. *Lond.* 1660. qu. See more in *Matthew Griffith* among the Writers, *an*. 1665. (22) *Accedence commenced Grammar*, &c. pr. 1661 in oct. (23) *Paradise lost:* a Poem in 10 books, Lond. 1669. qu. pr. in fol. with cuts, *an*. 1688. (24) *Paradise regain'd:* a Poem in four books. Lond. 1670. qu. pr. in fol. with cuts, *an*. 1688. (25) *History of Britany from the first traditional beginning, continued to the Norman Conquest*. Lond. 1670. qu. This History, when it first came abroad, had only the reputation of the putting of our old Authors neatly together in a connex'd story, not abstaining from some lashes at the ignorance, or I know not what, of those times. (26) *Artis Logicæ plenior institutio ad Petri Rami Methodum concinnata*. Lond. 1672, in tw. (27) *Of true Religion, Heresy, Schism, Toleration, and what best means may be used against the Growth and increase of Popery*, Lond. 1673. qu. (28) *Poems, &c. on several occasions,*

both English and Latin, &c. *composed at several times.*
Lond. 1673-4. oct. Among these are mixed some of
his Poems before mention'd, made in his youthful years.
(29) *Epistolarum familiarium lib.* 1. Lond. 1674. oct.
(30) *Prolusiones quædam Oratoriæ in Coll. Christi habitæ,*
printed with the *familiar Epistles.* (31) *Literæ Pseudo
senatus Anglicani, Cromwellii, reliquorum perduellium
nomine ac jussu conscriptæ.* printed in 1676. in tw.
(32) *Character of the Long Parliament, and of the Assembly of Divines.* Lond. 1681. in 2 sheets in qu. In
which book is a notable account of their Ignorance,
Treachery, and Hypocrisie. (33) *Brief History of Muscovia and of other less known Countries, lying eastward of
Russia as far as Cathay,* &c. Lond. 1682. oct. (34) *The
right of the People over Tyrants,* printed lately in qu.
These, I think, are all the things that he hath yet extant:
those that are not, are *The body of Divinity,* which my
friend calls Idea *Theologiæ,* now, or at least lately, in the
hands of the Author's Acquaintance called *Cyr. Skinner,* living in *Mark lane, London,* and the *Latin
Thesaurus* in those of Edw. Philipps his Nephew. At
length this great Scholar and frequent Writer dying in
his house at *Bunhill* near *London,* in a fit of the Gout,
but with so little pain, that the time of his expiring was
not perceived by those in the room, on the ninth or
tenth day of *Novemb.* 1674, was buried in the grave
of his Father, (who died very aged about 1647) in the
Chancel of the Church of St. *Giles* near *Cripplegate,
London.* See more of him in Sir *Walter Raleigh* among
the Writers, Numb. 458. He was of a moderate
Stature, and well proportion'd, of a ruddy Complexion,
light brown hair, and had handsome features, yet his
eyes were none of the quickest. When he was a

Student in *Cambridge* he was so fair and clear, that many called him the *Lady of Christ's Coll.* His deportment was affable, and his gate erect and manly, bespeaking courage and undauntedness. On which account he wore a sword while he had his sight, and was skill'd in using it. He had a delicate tuneable voice, an excellent ear, could play on the Organ, and bear a part in vocal and instrumental Musick. The Estate which his Father left him was but indifferent, yet by his frugality he made it serve him and his. Out of his Secretary's Salary he saved 2000 *l.* which being lodg'd in the Excise, and that bank failing upon his Majesty's Restauration, he utterly lost that sum. By the great Fire which hapned in *London* in the beginning of *Sept.* 1666, he had a house in *Breadstreet* burnt, which was all the real Estate that he had then left. To conclude, he was more admired abroad, and by Foreigners, than at home; and was much visited by them when he liv'd in *Petty France*, some of whom have out of pure devotion gone to *Breadstreet* to see the house and chamber where he was born, *&c.*

THE LIFE OF MR. JOHN MILTON

BY EDWARD PHILLIPS

1694

Of all the several parts of History, that which sets forth the Lives, and Commemorates the most remarkable Actions, Sayings, or Writings of Famous and Illustrious Persons, whether in War or Peace; whether many together, or any one in particular, as it is not the least useful in it self, so it is in highest Vogue and Esteem among the Studious and Reading part of Mankind.

The most Eminent in this way of History were among the Ancients, *Plutarch* and *Diogenes Laertius* of the *Greeks;* the first wrote the Lives, for the most part, of the most Renowned Heroes and Warriours of the *Greeks* and *Romans;* the other the Lives of the Ancient *Greek* Philosophers. And *Cornelius Nepos* (or as some will have it *Æmilius Probus*) of the *Latins*, who wrote the Lives of the most Illustrious *Greek* and *Roman* Generals. Among the Moderns, *Machiavel* a Noble *Florentine*, who Elegantly wrote the Life of *Castrucio Castracano*, Lord of *Luca*. And of our Nation, Sir *Fulk Grevil*, who wrote the Life of his most intimate Friend, Sir *Philip Sidney:* Mr. *Thomas Stanly* of *Cumberlo-Green*, who made a most Elaborate improvement to the foresaid *Laertius*, by adding to what he found in him, what by diligent search and enquiry he Collected from other Authors of best Authority; *Isaac Walton*, who wrote the Lives of Sir *Henry Wotton*, Dr. *Donne;* and for his Divine Poems, the admired Mr. *George Herbert*. Lastly,

D

not to mention several other Biographers of considerable Note, the Great *Gassendus* of *France*, the worthy Celebrator of two no less worthy Subjects of his impartial Pen; *viz.* the Noble Philosopher *Epicurus*, and the most politely Learned Virtuoso of his Age, his Countryman, Monsieur *Periesk*. And pitty it is the Person whose memory we have here undertaken to perpetuate by recounting the most memorable Transactions of his Life, (though his Works sufficiently recommend him to the World), finds not a well-informed Pen able to set him forth, equal with the best of those here mentioned; for doubtless had his Fame been as much spread through *Europe* in *Thuanus*'s time as now it is, and hath been for several Years, he had justly merited from that Great Historian, an Eulogy not inferiour to the highest, by him given to all the Learned and Ingenious that liv'd within the compass of his History. For we may safely and justly affirm, that take him in all respects, for Acumen of Wit, Quickness of Apprehension, Sagacity of Judgement, Depth of Argument, and Elegancy of Style, as well in *Latin* as *English*, as well in Verse as Prose, he is scarce to be parallel'd by any the best of Writers our Nation hath in any Age brought forth.

He was Born in *London*, in a House in *Breadstreet*, the Lease whereof, as I take it, but for certain it was a house in *Breadstreet*, became in time part of his Estate, in the year of our Lord 1606. His Father *John Milton*, an Honest, Worthy, and Substantial Citizen of *London*, by Profession a Scrivener; to which Profession he voluntarily betook himself, by the advice and assistance of an intimate Friend of his, Eminent in that Calling, upon his being cast out by his Father, a bigotted *Roman Catholick*, for embracing, when Young, the Protestant Faith, and abjuring the Popish Tenets; for he is said to have been Descended of an Ancient Family of the *Miltons*, of *Milton* near *Abington* in *Oxfordshire*; where they had been a long time seated, as appears by the Monuments still to be seen in *Milton* Church, till one of the Family having taken the wrong side, in the Contests between the Houses of *York* and *Lancaster*, was sequestred of all his Estate, but what he held by his Wife. However, certain it is, that this Vocation he followed for many Years, at his said House in *Breadstreet*, with success suitable to his Industry and prudent conduct of his Affairs; yet he did not so far quit his own Generous and Ingenious Inclinations, as to make himself wholly a Slave to the World; for he sometimes found vacant hours to the Study (which he made his recreation) of the Noble Science of Musick, in which he advanc'd to that perfection, that as I have been told, and as I take it, by our Author himself, he Composed an *In Nomine* of Forty Parts: for which he was rewarded with a Gold Medal and Chain by a *Polish* Prince, to whom he presented it. However, this is a truth not to be denied, that for several Songs of his Composition, after the way of these times, three or four of which are still to be seen in Old *Wilby's* set of Ayres, besides some Compositions of his in *Ravenscrofts* Psalms, he gained the Reputation of a considerable Master in this most charming of all the Liberal Sciences: Yet all this while, he managed his Grand Affair of this World with such Prudence and Diligence, that by the assistance of Divine Providence favouring his honest endeavours, he gained a Competent Estate, whereby he was enabled to make a handsom Provision both for the

Education and Maintenance of his Children; for three he had, and no more, all by one Wife, *Sarah*, of the Family of the *Castons*, derived originally from *Wales*, a Woman of Incomparable Vertue and Goodness; *John* the Eldest, the Subject of our present Work, *Christopher*, and an onely Daughter *Ann*.

Christopher being principally designed for the Study of the Common-Law of *England*, was Entered Young a Student of the *Inner-Temple*, of which House he lived to be an Ancient Bencher, and keeping close to that Study and Profession all his Life-time, except in the time of the Civil Wars of *England*; when being a great favourer and assertor of the King's Cause, and Obnoxious to the Parliament's side, by acting to his utmost power against them, so long as he kept his Station at *Reading*; and after that Town was taken by the Parliament Forces, being forced to quit his House there, he steer'd his course according to the Motion of the King's Army. But when the War was ended with Victory and Success to the Parliament Party, by the Valour of General *Fairfax*, and the Craft and Conduct of *Cromwell*; and his composition made by the help of his Brother's Interest, with the then prevailing Power, he betook himself again to his former Study and Profession, following Chamber-Practice every Term, yet came to no Advancement in the World in a long time, except some small Employ in the town of *Ipswich*, where (and near it) he lived all the latter time of his Life. For he was a person of a modest quiet temper, preferring Justice and Vertue before all Worldly Pleasure or Grandeur: but in the beginning of the reign of K. *James* the II., for his known Integrity and Ability in the Law, he was by some Persons of Quality recommended to the King, and at a Call of Serjeants received the Coif, and the same day was Sworn one of the Barons of the Exchequer, and soon after made one of the Judges of the Common Pleas; but his Years and Indisposition not well brooking the Fatigue of publick Imployment, he continued not long in either of these Stations, but having his *Quietus est*, retired to a Country Life, his Study and Devotion.

Ann, the onely Daughter of the said *John Milton* the Elder, had a considerable Dowry given her by her Father, in Marriage with *Edward Philips*, (the Son of *Edward Philips* of *Shrewsbury*,) who coming up Young to Town, was bred up in the Crown-Office in Chancery, and at length came to be Secondary of the Office under Old Mr. *Bembo*; by him she had, besides other Children that dyed Infants, two Sons yet surviving, of whom more hereafter; and by a second Husband, Mr. *Thomas Agar* (who, upon the Death of his Intimate Friend Mr. *Philips*, worthily succeeded in the place, which, except some time of Exclusion before and during the *Interregnum*, he held for many Years, and left it to Mr. *Thomas Milton*, the Son of the aforementioned Sir *Christopher*, who at this day executes it with great Reputation and Ability), two Daughters, *Mary* who died very Young, and *Ann* yet surviving.

But to hasten back to our matter in hand; *John* our Author, who was destin'd to be the Ornament and Glory of his Countrey, was sent, together with his Brother, to *Paul's* School, whereof Dr. *Gill* the Elder was then Chief Master; where he was enter'd into the first Rudiments of Learning, and advanced therein with that admirable Success, not more by the Discipline of the School and good Instructions of his Masters (for that he had another Master possibly at his Father's house, appears by the Fourth Elegy of his Latin Poems written in his 18th year, to *Thomas Young*, Pastor of the *English* Company of Merchants at *Hamborough*, wherein he owns and stiles him his Master), than by his own happy Genius, prompt Wit and Apprehension, and insuperable Industry ; for he generally sate up half the Night, as well in voluntary Improvements of his own choice, as the exact perfecting of his School-Exercises: So that at the Age of 15 he was full ripe for Academick Learning, and accordingly was sent to the University of *Cambridge;* where in *Christ's College*, under the Tuition of a very Eminent Learned man, whose Name I cannot call to mind, he Studied Seven years, and took his Degree of Master of Arts; and for the extraordinary Wit and Reading he had shown in his Performances to attain his Degree, (some whereof, spoken at a Vacation-Exercise in his 19th year of Age, are to be yet seen in his Miscellaneous Poems), he was lov'd and admir'd by the whole University, particularly by the Fellows and most Ingenious Persons of his House. Among the rest there was a Young Gentleman, one Mr. *King*, with whom, for his great Learning and Parts, he had contracted a particular Friendship and Intimacy; whose death (for he was drown'd on the *Irish* Seas in his passage from *Chester* to *Ireland*) he bewails in that most excellent Monody in his forementioned Poems, Intituled *Lycidas*. Never was the loss of Friend so Elegantly lamented; and among the rest of his Juvenile Poems, some he wrote at the Age of 15, which contain a Poetical Genius scarce to be parallel'd by any *English* Writer.

Soon after he had taken his Master's Degree, he

thought fit to leave the University: Not upon any disgust or discontent for want of Preferment, as some
Ill-willers have reported; nor upon any cause whatsoever forc'd to flie, as his Detractors maliciously feign;
but from which aspersion he sufficiently clears himself
in his Second Answer to *Alexander Morus*, the Author of
a Book call'd, *Clamor Regii Sanguinis ad Cœlum*, the
chief of his Calumniators; in which he plainly makes it
out, that after his leaving the University, to the no
small trouble of his Fellow-Collegiates, who in general
regretted his Absence, he for the space of Five years
lived for the most part with his Father and Mother at
their house at *Horton* near *Colebrook* in *Barkshire;*
whither his Father, having got an Estate to his content,
and left off all business, was retir'd from the Cares and
Fatigues of the world. After the said term of Five years,
his Mother then dying, he was willing to add to his
acquired Learning the observation of Foreign Customs,
Manners, and Institutions; and thereupon took a resolution to Travel, more especially designing for *Italy*; and
accordingly, with his Father's Consent and Assistance, he
put himself into an Equipage suitable to such a Design;
and so, intending to go by the way of *France*, he set out
for *Paris*, accompanied onely with one Man, who attended him through all his Travels; for his Prudence was
his Guide, and his Learning his Introduction and Pres-
entation to Persons of most Eminent Quality. However,
he had also a most Civil and Obliging Letter of Direction and Advice from Sir *Henry Wootton*, then Provost
of *Eaton*, and formerly Resident Embassador from king
James the First to the State of *Venice;* which Letter is
to be seen in the First Edition of his Miscellaneous
Poems.

At *Paris*, being Recommended by the said Sir *Henry* and other Persons of Quality, he went first to wait upon my Lord *Scudamore*, then Embassador in *France* from King *Charles* the First. My Lord receiv'd him with wonderful Civility; and understanding he had a desire to make a Visit to the great *Hugo Grotius*, he sent several of his Attendants to wait upon him, and to present him in his Name to that Renowned Doctor and Statesman, who was at that time Embassador from *Christina*, Queen of *Sweden*, to the *French* King. *Grotius* took the Visit kindly, and gave him Entertainment suitable to his Worth, and the high Commendations he had heard of him. After a few days, not intending to make the usual Tour of *France*, he took his leave of my Lord, who at his departure from *Paris*, gave him letters to the *English* Merchants residing in any part through which he was to Travel, in which they were requested to shew him all the Kindness, and do him all the Good Offices that lay in their Power.

From *Paris* he hastened on his Journey to *Nicæa*, where he took Shipping, and in a short space arrived at *Genoa*; from whence he went to *Leghorn*, thence to *Pisa*, and so to *Florence:* In this City he met with many charming Objects, which Invited him to stay a longer time than he intended; the pleasant Scituation of the Place, the Nobleness of the Structures, the exact Humanity and Civility of the Inhabitants, the more Polite and Refined sort of Language there, than else-where. During the time of his stay here, which was about Two Months, he Visited all the private Academies of the City, which are Places establish'd for the improvement of Wit and Learning, and maintained a Correspondence and perpetual Friendship among

Gentlemen fitly qualified for such an Institution: and such sort of Academies there are in all or most of the most noted Cities in *Italy*. Visiting these Places, he was soon taken notice of by the most Learned and Ingenious of the Nobility, and the Grand Wits of *Florence*, who caress'd him with all the Honours and Civilities imaginable; particularly *Jacobo Gaddi*, *Carolo Dati*, *Antonio Francini*, *Frescobaldo*, *Cultellino*, *Bonmatthei* and *Clementillo:* Whereof *Gaddi* hath a large Elegant *Italian Canzonet* in his Praise: *Dati*, a Latin Epistle; both Printed before his Latin Poems, together with a Latin Distich of the Marquess of *Villa*, and another of *Selvaggi*, and a Latin *Tetrastick* of *Giovanni Salsilli*, a *Roman*.

From *Florence* he took his Journey to *Siena*, from thence to *Rome;* where he was detain'd much about the same time he had been at *Florence;* as well by his desire of seeing all the Rarities and Antiquities of that most Glorious and Renowned City, as by the Conversation of *Lucas Holstenius*, and other Learned and Ingenious men; who highly valued his Acquaintance, and treated him with all possible Respect.

From *Rome* he Travelled to *Naples*, where he was introduced by a certain Hermite, who accompanied him in his Journey from *Rome* thither, into the knowledge of *Giovanni Baptista Manso*, Marquess of *Villa*, a *Neapolitan* by Birth, a Person of high Nobility, Vertue, and Honour, to whom the famous *Italian* Poet, *Torquato Tasso*, Wrote his Treatise *de Amicitia;* and moreover mentions him with great Honour in that Illustrious Poem of his, Intituled, *Gierusalemme Liberata*. This Noble Marquess received him with extraordinary Respect and Civility, and went with him himself to give him a sight of all that was of Note and Remark in the City, particularly the Viceroys Palace, and was often in person to Visit him at his Lodging. Moreover, this Noble Marquess honoured him so far, as to make a Latin Distich in his Praise, as hath been already mentioned; which being no less pithy then short, though already in Print, it will not be unworth the while here to repeat.

Ut Mens, Forma, Decor, Facies, mos, si Pietas [1] *sic,*
Non Anglus, Verum Hercle Angelus ipse foret.

In return of this Honour, and in gratitude for the many Favours and Civilities received of him, he presented him at his departure with a large Latin Eclogue, Intituled, *Mansus*, afterwards Published among his Latin Poems. The Marquess at his taking leave of him, gave him this Complement, That he would have done him many more Offices of Kindness and Civility, but was therefore rendered incapable, in regard he had been over-liberal in his speech against the Religion of the Country.

He had entertain'd some thoughts of passing over into *Sicily* and *Greece*, but was diverted by the News he receiv'd from *England*, that Affairs there were tending towards a Civil War; thinking it a thing unworthy in him to be taking his Pleasure in Foreign Parts, while his Countreymen at home were Fighting for their Liberty: But first resolv'd to see *Rome* once more; and though the Merchants gave him a caution that the Jesuits were hatching designs against him, in case he should return thither, by reason of the freedom he took in all his discourses of Religion; nevertheless he ven-

[1] This word relates to his being a Protestant not a *Roman*-Catholick.

tured to prosecute his Resolution, and to *Rome* the second time he went, determining with himself not industriously to begin to fall into any Discourse about Religion; but, being ask'd, not to deny or endeavour to conceal his own Sentiments. Two Months he staid at *Rome;* and in all that time never flinch'd, but was ready to defend the Orthodox Faith against all Opposers; and so well he succeeded therein, that, Good Providence guarding him, he went safe from *Rome* back to *Florence,* where his return to his Friends of that City was welcomed with as much Joy and Affection, as had it been to his Friends and Relations in his own Countrey, he could not have come a more joyful and welcome Guest. Here, having staid as long as at his first coming, excepting an excursion of a few days to *Luca,* crossing the *Apennine,* and passing through *Bononia* and *Ferrara,* he arriv'd at *Venice;* where when he had spent a Month's time in viewing of that Stately City, and Shipp'd up a Parcel of curious and rare Books which he had pick'd up in his Travels; particularly a Chest or two of choice Musick-books of the best Masters flourishing about that time in *Italy,* namely, *Luca Marenzo, Monte Verde, Horatio Vecchi, Cifa,* the Prince of *Venosa,* and several others, he took his course through *Verona, Milan,* and the *Pœnine Alps,* and so by the lake *Leman* to *Geneva,* where he staid for some time, and had daily converse with the most Learned *Giovanni Deodati,* Theology-Professor in that City; and so returning through *France,* by the same way he had passed it going to *Italy,* he, after a Peregrination of one compleat Year and about Three Months, arrived safe in *England,* about the time of the Kings making his second Expedition against the *Scots.*

Soon after his return, and visits paid to his Father and other Friends, he took him a Lodging in St. *Brides* Church-yard, at the House of one *Russel*, a Taylor, where he first undertook the Education and Instruction of his Sister's two Sons, the Younger whereof had been wholly committed to his Charge and Care. And here by the way, I judge it not impertinent to mention the many Authors both of the Latin and Greek, which through his excellent judgment and way of Teaching, far above the Pedantry of common publick Schools (where such Authors are scarce ever heard of) were run over within no greater compass of time, then from Ten to Fifteen or Sixteen Years of Age. Of the Latin, the four Grand Authors, *De Re Rustica, Cato, Varro, Columella* and *Palladius; Cornelius Celsus,* an Ancient Physician of the *Romans;* a great part of *Pliny's* Natural History; *Vitruvius* his Architecture; *Frontinus* his Stratagems; with the two Egregious Poets, *Lucretius* and *Manilius.* Of the Greek; *Hesiod,* a Poet equal with *Homer; Aratus* his *Phænomena,* and *Diosemeia; Dionysius Afer de situ Orbis; Oppian's Cynegeticks* & *Halieuticks; Quintus Calaber* his Poem of the *Trojan* War continued from *Homer; Apollonius Rhodius* his *Argonauticks*: and in Prose, *Plutarch's Placita Philosophorum,* and Περι Παιδων 'Αγογιας; *Geminus's* Astronomy; *Xenophon's Cyri Institutio,* and *Anabasis; Ælian's Tacticks;* and *Polyænus* his Warlike Stratagems. Thus by teaching he in some measure increased his own knowledge, having the reading of all these Authors as it were by Proxy; and all this might possibly have conduced to the preserving of his Eye-sight, had he not, moreover, been perpetually busied in his own Laborious Undertakings of the Book or Pen. Nor did the time thus Studiously imployed in conquering the *Greek* and *Latin* Tongues, hinder the attaining to the chief Oriental Languages, *viz.* The *Hebrew*, *Caldee* and *Syriac*, so far as to go through the *Pentateuch*, or Five Books of *Moses* in *Hebrew*, to make a good entrance into the *Targum*, or *Chaldee* Paraphrase, and to understand several Chapters of St. *Matthew* in the *Syriac* Testament: besides an Introduction into several Arts and Sciences, by reading *Urstisius* his Arithmetick, *Riffs* Geometry, *Petiscus* his Trigonometry, *Joannes de Sacro Bosco de Sphæra;* and into the *Italian* and *French* Tongues, by reading in *Italian*, *Giovan Villani's* History of the Transactions between several petty States of *Italy;* and in French a great part of *Pierre Davity*, the famous Geographer of *France* in his time. The *Sunday's* work was for the most part the Reading each day a Chapter of the *Greek* Testament, and hearing his Learned Exposition upon the same, (and how this savoured of Atheism in him, I leave to the courteous Backbiter to judge). The next work after this, was the writing from his own dictation, some part, from time to time, of a Tractate which he thought fit to collect from the ablest of Divines, who had written of that Subject; *Amesius*, *Wollebius*, &c. *viz.* A perfect System of Divinity, of which more hereafter. Now persons so far Manuducted into the highest paths of Literature both Divine and Human, had they received his documents with the same Acuteness of Wit and Apprehension, the same Industry, Alacrity, and Thirst after Knowledge, as the Instructer was indued with, what Prodigies of Wit and Learning might they have proved! The Scholars might in some degree have come near to the equalling of the Master, or at least

have in some sort made good what he seems to predict
in the close of an Elegy he made in the Seventeenth
Year of his Age, upon the Death of one of his Sister's
Children (a Daughter), who died in her Infancy:

> Then thou, the Mother of so sweet a Child,
> Her false Imagin'd Loss cease to Lament,
> And Wisely learn to curb thy Sorrows Wild;
> This if thou do, he will an Offspring give,
> That to the Worlds last end shall make thy Name to live.

But to return to the Thread of our Discourse; he
made no long stay in his Lodgings in St. *Brides* Church-
yard; necessity of having a place to dispose his Books
in, and other Goods fit for the furnishing of a good
handsome House, hastning him to take one; and
accordingly a pretty Garden-House he took in *Aldersgate*-Street, at the end of an Entry, and therefore the
fitter for his turn, by the reason of the Privacy, besides
that there are few Streets in *London* more free from
Noise then that. Here first it was that his Academick
Erudition was put in practice, and Vigorously proceeded, he himself giving an Example to those under
him, (for it was not long after his taking this House,
e're his Elder Nephew was put to Board with him also)
of hard Study, and spare Diet; only this advantage he
had, that once in three Weeks or a Month, he would
drop into the Society of some Young Sparks of his
Acquaintance, the chief whereof were Mr. *Alphry*, and
Mr. *Miller*, two Gentlemen of *Gray's*-Inn, the *Beau's* of
those Times, but nothing near so bad as those now-a-
days; with these Gentlemen he would so far make bold
with his Body, as now and then to keep a Gawdy-day.

In this House he continued several Years, in the one
or two first whereof, he set out several Treatises, *viz.*

That of *Reformation;* that against *Prelatical Episcopacy;*
The *Reason of Church-Government;* The *Defence of
Smectimnuus,* at least the greatest part of them, but as I
take it, all; and some time after, one Sheet of Education, which he Dedicated to Mr. *Samuel Hartlib,* he that
wrote so much of Husbandry; this sheet is printed at
the end of the Second Edition of his Poems; and
lastly, *Areopagitica.* During the time also of his continuance in this House, there fell out several Occasions
of the Increasing of his Family. His Father, who till
the taking of *Reading* by the Earl of *Essex* his Forces,
had lived with his other Son at his House there, was
upon that Son's dissettlement necessitated to betake
himself to this his Eldest Son, with whom he lived
for some Years, even to his Dying Day. In the next
place he had an Addition of some Scholars; to which
may be added, his entring into Matrimony; but he
had his Wife's company so small a time, that he may
well be said to have become a single man again soon
after.

About *Whitsuntide* it was, or a little after, that he
took a Journey into the Country; no body about him
certainly knowing the Reason, or that it was any more
than a Journey of Recreation: after a Month's stay,
home he returns a Married-man, that went out a Bat-
chelor; his Wife being *Mary,* the Eldest Daughter of
Mr. *Richard Powell,* then a Justice of Peace, of *Forrest-
hil,* near *Shotover* in *Oxfordshire;* some few of her
nearest Relations accompanying the Bride to her new
Habitation; which by reason the Father nor any body
else were yet come, was able to receive them; where
the Feasting held for some days in Celebration of the
Nuptials, and for entertainment of the Bride's Friends.

At length they took their leave, and returning to *Forresthill*, left the Sister behind; probably not much to her satisfaction, as appeared by the Sequel; by that time she had for a Month or thereabout led a Philosophical Life (after having been used to a great House, and much Company and Joviality). Her Friends, possibly incited by her own desire, made earnest suit by Letter, to have her Company the remaining part of the Summer, which was granted, on condition of her return at the time appointed, *Michalemas*, or thereabout: In the mean time came his Father, and some of the foremention'd Disciples. And now the Studies went on with so much the more Vigour, as there were more Hands and Heads employ'd; the Old Gentleman living wholly retired to his Rest and Devotion, without the least trouble imaginable. Our Author, now as it were a single man again, made it his chief diversion now and then in an Evening to visit the Lady *Margaret Lee*, daughter to the ―― *Lee*, Earl of *Marlborough*, Lord High Treasurer of *England*, and President of the Privy Councel to King *James* the First. This Lady being a Woman of great Wit and Ingenuity, had a particular Honour for him, and took much delight in his Company, as likewise her Husband Captain *Hobson*, a very Accomplish'd Gentleman; and what Esteem he at the same time had for Her, appears by a Sonnet he made in praise of her, to be seen among his other Sonnets in his Extant Poems.

Michalemas being come, and no news of his Wife's return, he sent for her by Letter; and receiving no answer, sent several other Letters, which were also unanswered; so that at last he dispatch'd down a Foot-Messenger with a Letter, desiring her return; but the

Messenger came back not only without an answer, at least a satisfactory one, but to the best of my remembrance, reported that he was dismissed with some sort of Contempt. This proceeding, in all probability, was grounded upon no other Cause but this, namely, that the Family being generally addicted to the Cavalier Party, as they called it, and some of them possibly ingaged in the King's Service, who by this time had his Head Quarters at *Oxford*, and was in some Prospect of Success, they began to repent them of having Matched the Eldest Daughter of the Family to a Person so contrary to them in Opinion; and thought it would be a blot in their Escutcheon, when ever that Court should come to Flourish again; however, it so incensed our Author, that he thought it would be dishonourable ever to receive her again, after such a repulse; so that he forthwith prepared to Fortify himself with Arguments for such a Resolution, and accordingly wrote two Treatises, by which he undertook to maintain, That it was against Reason, (and the enjoyment of it not proveable by Scripture), for any Married Couple disagreeable in Humour and Temper, or having an aversion to each other, to be forc'd to live yok'd together all their Days. The first was, his *Doctrine and Discipline of Divorce;* of which there was Printed a Second Edition, with some Additions. The other in prosecution of the first, was styled *Tetrachordon.* Then the better to confirm his own Opinion by the attestation of others, he set out a Piece called *the Judgement of Martin Bucer*, a Protestant Minister, being a Translation, out of that Reverend Divine, of some part of his Works, exactly agreeing with him in Sentiment. Lastly, he wrote in answer to a Pragmatical Clerk, who would needs give himself the

E

Honour of Writing against so great a Man, his *Colasterion*, or Rod of Correction for a Sawcy Impertinent.

Not very long after the setting forth of these Treatises, having application made to him by several Gentlemen of his acquaintance for the Education of their Sons, as understanding haply the Progress he had infixed by his first undertakings of that nature, he laid out for a larger House, and soon found it out; but in the interim before he removed, there fell out a passage, which though it altered not the whole Course he was going to Steer, yet it put a stop or rather an end to a grand Affair, which was more than probably thought to be then in agitation: It was indeed a design of Marrying one of Dr. *Davis's* Daughters, a very Handsome and Witty Gentlewoman, but averse, as it is said, to this Motion; however, the Intelligence hereof, and the then declining State of the King's Cause, and consequently of the Circumstances of Justice *Powell's* family, caused them to set all Engines on Work, to restore the late Married Woman to the Station wherein they a little before had planted her; at last this device was pitch'd upon. There dwelt in the Lane of St. *Martins Le Grand*, which was hard by, a Relation of our Author's, one *Blackborough*, whom it was known he often visited, and upon this occasion the visits were the more narrowly observ'd, and possibly there might be a Combination between both Parties; the Friends on both sides concentring in the same action though on different behalfs. One time above the rest, he making his usual visit, the Wife was ready in another Room, and on a sudden he was surprised to see one whom he thought to have never seen more, making Submission and begging Pardon on her Knees before him; he might probably at first make some shew of aversion and rejection; but partly his own generous nature, more inclinable to Reconciliation than to perseverance in Anger and Revenge; and partly the strong intercession of Friends on both sides, soon brought him to an Act of Oblivion, and a firm League of Peace for the future; and it was at length concluded, That she should remain at a Friends house, till such time as he was settled in his New house at *Barbican*, and all things for her reception in order; the place agreed on for her present abode, was the Widow *Webber's* house in St. *Clement's* Churchyard, whose Second Daughter had been Married to the other Brother many years before. The first fruits of her return to her Husband was a brave Girl, born within a year after; though, whether by ill Constitution, or want of Care, she grew more and more decrepit. But it was not only by Children that she increas'd the number of the Family, for in no very long time after her coming, she had a great resort of her Kindred with her in the House, *viz.* her Father and Mother, and several of her Brothers and Sisters, which were in all pretty Numerous; who upon his Father's Sickning and Dying soon after went away.

And now the House look'd again like a House of the Muses only, tho the accession of Scholars was not great. Possibly his proceeding thus far in the Education of Youth may have been the occasion of some of his Adversaries calling him Pædagogue and Schoolmaster: Whereas it is well known he never set up for a Publick School to teach all the young Fry of a Parish, but only was willing to impart his Learning and Knowledge to Relations, and the Sons of some Gentlemen that were his intimate Friends; besides, that neither his Converse, nor his Writings, nor his manner of Teaching ever savour'd in the least any thing of Pedantry; and probably he might have some prospect of putting in Practice his Academical Institution, according to the Model laid down in his Sheet of Education. The Progress of which design was afterwards diverted by a Series of Alteration in the Affairs of State; for I am much mistaken, if there were not about this time a design in Agitation of making him Adjutant-General in Sir *William Waller's* army; but the new modelling of the Army soon following, prov'd an obstruction to that design; and Sir *William*, his Commission being laid down, began, as the common saying is, to turn *Cat in Pan*.

It was not long after the March of *Fairfax* and *Cromwel* through the City of *London* with the whole Army, to quell the Insurrections *Brown* and *Massy*, now Malecontents also, were endeavouring to raise in the City against the Armies proceedings, ere he left his great House in *Barbican*, and betook himself to a smaller in *High Holbourn*, among those that open backward into *Lincolns-Inn* Fields. Here he liv'd a private and quiet Life, still prosecuting his Studies and curious Search into Knowledge, the grand Affair perpetually of his Life; till such time as, the War being now at an end, with compleat Victory to the Parliament's side, as the Parliament then stood purg'd of all it's Dissenting Members, and the King after some Treaties with the Army, *re Infecta*, brought to his Tryal; the form of Government being now chang'd into a Free State, he was hereupon oblig'd to Write a Treatise, call'd the *Tenure of Kings and Magistrates*.

After which his thoughts were bent upon retiring

again to his own private Studies, and falling upon such Subjects as his proper Genius prompted him to Write of, among which was the History of our own Nation from the Beginning till the *Norman* Conquest, wherein he had made some progress. When for this his last Treatise, reviving the fame of other things he had formerly Published, being more and more taken notice of for his excellency of Stile, and depth of Judgement, he was courted into the Service of this new Commonwealth, and at last prevail'd with (for he never hunted after Preferment, nor affected the Tintamar and Hurry of Publick business) to take upon him the Office of *Latin* Secretary to the Counsel of State for all their Letters to Foreign Princes and States; for they stuck to this Noble and Generous Resolution, not to write to any, or receive Answers from them, but in a Language most proper to maintain a Correspondence among the Learned of all Nations in this part of the World; scorning to carry on their Affairs in the Wheedling, Lisping Jargon of the Cringing *French*, especially having a Minister of State able to cope with the ablest any Prince or State could imploy for the Latin tongue; and so well he acquitted himself in this station, that he gain'd from abroad both Reputation to himself, and Credit to the State that Employed him; and it was well the business of his Office came not very fast upon him, for he was scarce well warm in his Secretaryship, before other Work flow'd in upon him, which took him up for some considerable time. In the first place there came out a Book said to have been written by the King, and finished a little before his Death, Entituled Ἐικων Βασιλικη, that is, *The Royal Image;* a Book highly cryed up for it's smooth Style, and pathetical Composure;

wherefore to obviate the impression it was like to make among the *Many*, he was obliged to Write an Answer, which he Entituled Εικονωκλασης, or *Image-Breaker*; and upon the heels of that, out comes in Publick the great Kill-cow of *Christendom*, with his *Defensio Regis contra Populum Anglicanum:* a Man so Famous and cryed up for his *Plinian Exercitations*, and other Pieces of reputed Learning, that there could no where have been found a Champion that durst lift up the Pen against so formidable an Adversary, had not our little *English David* had the Courage to undertake this great *French Goliah*, to whom he gave such a hit in the Forehead, that he presently staggered, and soon after fell; for immediately upon the coming out of the Answer, Entituled, *Defensio Populi Anglicani, contra Claudium Anonymum*, &c. he that till then had been Chief Minister and Superintendant in the Court of the Learned *Christina* Queen of *Sweden*, dwindled in esteem to that degree, that he at last vouchsafed to speak to the meanest Servant.   In short, he was dismiss'd with so cold and slighting an Adieu, that after a faint dying Reply, he was glad to have recourse to Death, the remedy of Evils, and ender of Controversies.

And now I presume our Author had some breathing space; but it was not long; for though *Salmasius* was departed, he left some stings behind; new Enemies started up, Barkers, though no great Biters; who the first Assertor of *Salmasius* his Cause was, is not certainly known, but variously conjectur'd at, some supposing it to be one *Janus* a Lawyer of *Grays-Inn*, some Dr. *Bramhal*, made by King *Charles* the Second after his Restauration Archbishop of *Armagh* in *Ireland*; but whoever the Author was, the Book was thought fit to be taken into correction, and our Author not thinking it worth his own undertaking, to the disturbing the progress of whatever more chosen work he had then in hands, committed this task to the youngest of his Nephews, but with such exact Emendations before it went to the Press, that it might have very well passed for his, but that he was willing the person that took the pains to prepare it for his Examination and Polishment, should have the Name and Credit of being the Author; so that it came forth under this Title, *Joannis Philippi Angli Defensio pro Populo Anglicano contra*, &c. During the Writing and Publishing of this Book he lodg'd at one *Thomson's* next door to the *Bull-head* tavern at *Charing-Cross*, opening into the *Spring-Garden*, which seems to have been only a Lodging taken, till his designed Apartment in *Scotland-Yard* was prepared for him; for hither he soon removed from the foresaid place; and here his third Child, a Son, was born, which through the ill usage, or bad Constitution of an ill chosen Nurse, died an Infant.

From this Apartment, whether he thought it not healthy, or otherwise convenient for his use, or whatever else was the reason, he soon after took a pretty Garden-house in *Petty-France* in *Westminster*, next door to the Lord *Scudamore's* and opening into St. *James's* Park; here he remain'd no less than Eight years, namely, from the year 1652, till within a few weeks of King *Charles* the 2d's Restoration. In this House his first Wife dying in Childbed, he Married a Second, who after a Year's time died in Childbed also; this his Second Marriage was about Two or Three years after his being wholly depriv'd of Sight, which was just going, about the time of his Answering *Salmasius*;

whereupon his Adversaries gladly take occasion of imputing his blindness as a Judgment upon him for his Answering the King's Book, &c. whereas it is most certainly known, that his Sight, what with his continual Study, his being subject to the Head-ake, and his perpetual tampering with Physick to preserve it, had been decaying for above a dozen years before, and the sight of one for a long time clearly lost. Here he wrote, by his *Amanuensis*, his Two Answers to *Alexander More;* who upon the last Answer quitted the field. So that being now quiet from State-Adversaries and publick Contests, he had leisure again for his own Studies and private Designs; which were his foresaid *History of England*, and a New *Thesaurus Linguæ Latinæ*, according to the manner of *Stephanus;* a work he had been long since Collecting from his own Reading, and still went on with it at times, even very near to his dying day; but the Papers after his death were so discomposed and deficient, that it could not be made fit for the Press; However, what there was of it, was made use of for another Dictionary. But the Heighth of his Noble Fancy and Invention began now to be seriously and mainly imployed in a Subject worthy of such a Muse, *viz.* A Heroick Poem, Entituled, *Paradise Lost;* the Noblest in the general Esteem of Learned and Judicious Persons, of any yet written by any either Ancient or Modern: This Subject was first designed a Tragedy, and in the Fourth Book of the Poem there are Ten Verses, which several Years before the Poem was begun, were shewn to me, and some others, as designed for the very beginning of the said Tragedy. The Verses are these;

O Thou that with surpassing Glory Crown'd!
Look'st from thy sole Dominion, like the God
Of this New World; at whose sight all the Stars
Hide their diminish'd Heads; to thee I call,
But with no friendly Voice; and add thy Name,
O Sun! to tell thee how I hate thy Beams
That bring to my remembrance, from what State
I fell; how Glorious once above thy Sphere;
Till Pride and worse Ambition threw me down,
Warring in Heaven, against Heaven's Glorious King.

There is another very remarkable Passage in the Composure of this Poem, which I have a particular occasion to remember; for whereas I had the perusal of it from the very beginning; for some years, as I went from time to time, to Visit him, in a Parcel of Ten, Twenty, or Thirty Verses at a Time, which being Written by whatever hand came next, might possibly want Correction as to the Orthography and Pointing; having as the Summer came on, not been shewed any for a considerable while, and desiring the reason thereof, was answered, That his Vein never happily flow'd, but from the *Autumnal Equinoctial* to the *Vernal*, and that whatever he attempted was never to his satisfaction, though he courted his fancy never so much; so that in all the years he was about this Poem, he may be said to have spent but half his time therein.

It was but a little before the King's Restoration that he Wrote and Published his book in *Defence of a Commonwealth;* so undaunted he was in declaring his true Sentiments to the world; and not long before, his Power of the *Civil Magistrate in Ecclesiastical Affairs;* and his *Treatise against Hirelings*, just upon the King's coming over; having a little before been sequestred from his Office of *Latin* Secretary, and the Salary thereunto belonging, he was forc'd to leave his House also, in *Petty-France*, where all the time of his abode there, which was eight years, as above-mentioned, he was frequently visited by persons of Quality, particularly my lady *Ranala*, whose Son for some time he instructed; all Learned Foreigners of Note, who could not part out of this City, without giving a visit to a person so Eminent; and lastly, by particular Friends that had a high esteem for him, *viz.* Mr. *Andrew Marvel*, young *Laurence* (the Son of him that was President of *Oliver's* Council) to whom there is a Sonnet among the rest, in his Printed Poems; Mr. *Marchamont Needham*, the Writer of *Politicus ;* but above all, Mr. *Cyriak Skinner* whom he honoured with two Sonnets, one long since publick among his Poems; the other but newly Printed.

His next removal was, by the advice of those that wisht him well, and had a concern for his preservation, into a place of retirement and abscondence, till such time as the current of affairs for the future should instruct him what farther course to take; it was a Friend's House in *Bartholomew-Close*, where he liv'd till the Act of Oblivion came forth; which it pleased God, prov'd as favourable to him as could be hop'd or expected, through the intercession of some that stood his Friends both in Council and Parliament; particularly in the House of Commons, Mr. *Andrew Marvel*, a member for *Hull*, acted vigorously in his behalf, and made a considerable party for him; so that, together with *John Goodwin* of *Coleman-Street*, he was only so far excepted as not to bear any Office in the Commonwealth. Soon after appearing again in publick, he took a House in *Holborn* near *Red Lyon Fields;* where he stay'd not long before his Pardon having pass'd the Seal, he remov'd to *Jewin Street;* there he liv'd when he married his 3d Wife, recommended to him by his old Friend Dr. *Paget* in *Coleman-street;* but he stay'd not long after his new Marriage, ere he remov'd to a House in the *Artillery*-walk leading to *Bunhill Fields*. And this was his last Stage in this World, but it was of many years continuance, more perhaps than he had had in any other place besides. Here he finisht his noble Poem, and publisht it in the year 1666. The first Edition was Printed in Quarto by one *Simons*, a Printer in *Aldersgate-Street;* the other in a large Octavo, by *Starky* near *Temple-Bar*, amended, enlarg'd, and differently dispos'd as to the Number of Books, by his own Hand, that is by his own appointment; the last set forth, many years since his death, in a large Folio with Cuts added by *Jacob Tonson*. Here it was also that he finisht and publisht his History of our Nation till the Conquest, all compleat so far as he went, some Passages only excepted, which, being thought too sharp against the Clergy, could not pass the Hand of the Licencer, were in the Hands of the late Earl of *Anglesey* while he liv'd; where at present is uncertain.

It cannot certainly be concluded when he wrote his excellent Tragedy entitled *Samson Agonistes*, but sure enough it is that it came forth after his publication of *Paradice lost*, together with his other Poem call'd *Paradice regain'd*, which doubtless was begun and finisht and Printed after the other was publisht, and that in a wonderful short space considering the sublimeness of it; however it is generally censur'd to be much inferiour to the other, though he could not hear with patience any such thing when related to him; possibly the Subject may not afford such variety of Invention, but it is thought by the most judicious to be little or nothing inferiour to the other for stile and decorum. The said Earl of *Anglesy* whom he presented with a Copy of the unlicens'd Papers of his History, came often here to visit him, as very much coveting his society and converse; as likewise others of the Nobility, and many persons of eminent quality; nor were the visits of Foreigners ever more frequent than in this place, almost to his dying day. His Treatise of true Religion, Heresy, Schism and Toleration, &c. was doubtless the last thing of his writing that was publisht before his Death. He had, as I remember, prepared for the press an answer to some little scribing Quack in *London*, who had written a Scurrilous Libel against him; but whether by the disswasion of Friends, as thinking him a Fellow not worth his notice, or for what other cause I know not, this Answer was never publisht.

He died in the year 1673, towards the latter end of the Summer, and had a very decent interment according to his Quality, in the Church of St. *Giles Cripplegate*, being attended from His house to the Church by several Gentlemen then in Town, his principal well-wishers and admirers.

He had three Daughters who surviv'd him many years (and a Son) all by his first Wife (of whom sufficient mention hath been made): *Anne* his Eldest as abovesaid, and *Mary* his Second, who were both born at his House in *Barbican ;* and *Debora* the youngest, who is yet living, born at his House in *Petty-France*, between whom and his Second Daughter, the Son, named *John*, was born as above-mention'd, at his Apartment in *Scotland Yard*. By his Second Wife, *Catharine* the Daughter of Captain *Woodcock* of *Hackney*, he had only one Daughter, of which the Mother the first year after her Marriage died in Child bed, and the Child also within a Month after. By his Third Wife *Elizabeth* the daughter of one Mr. *Minshal* of *Cheshire* (and Kinswoman to Dr. *Paget*), who surviv'd him, and is said to be yet living, he never had any Child; and those he had by the First he made serviceable to him in that very particular in which he most wanted their Service, and supplied his want of Eye-sight by their Eyes and Tongue; for though he had daily about him one or other to Read to him, some persons of Man's Estate, who of their own accord greedily catch'd at the opportunity of being his Readers, that they might as well reap the benefit of what they Read to him, as oblige him by the benefit of their reading; others of younger years sent by their Parents to the same end; yet excusing only the Eldest Daughter by reason of her bodily Infirmity, and difficult utterance of Speech, (which to say truth I doubt was the Principal cause of excusing her), the other two were Condemn'd to the performance of Reading, and exactly pronouncing of all the Languages of whatever Book he should at one time or other think fit to peruse; *Viz.* The *Hebrew* (and I think the *Syriac*), the *Greek*, the *Latin*, the *Italian*, *Spanish* and *French*. All which sorts of Books to be confined to Read, without understanding one word, must needs be a Tryal of Patience, almost beyond endurance; yet it was endured by both for a long time; yet the irksomeness of this imployment could not always be concealed, but broke out more and more into expressions of uneasiness; so that at length they were all (even the Eldest also) sent out to learn some Curious and Ingenious sorts of Manufacture, that are proper for Women to learn, particularly Imbroideries in Gold or Silver. It had been happy indeed if the Daughters of such a Person had been made in some measure Inheritrixes of their Father's Learning; but since Fate otherwise decreed, the greatest Honour that can be ascribed to this now living (and so would have been to the others, had they lived) is to be Daughter to a man of his extraordinary Character.

He is said to have dyed worth 1500 l. in Money (a considerable Estate, all things considered) besides Houshold Goods; for he sustained such losses as might well have broke any person less frugal and temperate then himself; no less then 2000 l. which he had put for Security and improvement into the Excise Office, but neglecting to recal it in time, could never after get it out, with all the Power and Interest he had in the Great ones of those Times; besides another great Sum, by mismanagement and for want of good advice.

Thus I have reduced into form and order what ever I have been able to rally up, either from the recollection of my own memory, of things transacted while I was with him, or the Information of others equally conversant afterwards, or from his own mouth by frequent visits to the last.

I shall conclude with two material passages, which though they relate not immediately to our Author, or his own particular concerns; yet in regard they hapned during his publick employ, and consequently fell most especially under his cognisance; it will not be amiss here to subjoin them. The first was this,

Before the War broke forth between the States of *England* and the *Dutch*, the *Hollanders* sent over Three Embassadours in order to an accommodation; but they returning *re infecta*, the *Dutch* sent away a *Plenipotentiary*, to offer Peace upon much milder terms, or at least to gain more time. But this *Plenipotentiary* could not make such haste, but that the Parliament had procured a Copy of their Instructions in *Holland*, which were delivered by our Author to his Kinsman that was then with him, to Translate for the Council to view, before the said *Plenipotentiary* had taken Shipping for *England ;* an Answer to all he had in Charge lay ready for him, before he made his publick entry into *London*.

In the next place there came a person with a very sumptuous train, pretending himself an Agent from the Prince of *Conde*, then in Arms against Cardinal *Mazarine :* The Parliament mistrusting him, set their Instrument so busily at work, that in Four or Five Days they had procured Intelligence from *Paris*, that he was a Spy from K. *Charles :* whereupon the very next Morning our Author's Kinsman was sent to him, with an Order of Councel commanding him to depart the Kingdom within Three Days, or expect the Punishment of a Spy.

By these two remarkable passages, we may clearly discover the Industry and good Intelligence of those Times.

To *OLIVER CROMWELL*

CROMWELL our Chief of Men, that through a Croud,
Not of War only, but distractions rude;
Guided by Faith, and Matchless Fortitude:
To Peace and Truth, thy Glorious way hast Plough'd,
And Fought God's Battels, and his Work pursu'd,
While *Darwent* Streams with Blood of *Scots* imbru'd;
And *Dunbarfield* resound thy Praises loud,
And *Worcester's* Laureat Wreath; yet much remains
To Conquer still; Peace hath her Victories
No less than those of War; new Foes arise
Threatning to bind our Souls in secular Chains,
Help us to save Free Conscience from the paw
Of Hireling Wolves, whose Gospel is their Maw.

To my Lord *FAIRFAX*

FAIRFAX, whose Name in Arms through *Europe* rings,
And fills all Mouths with Envy or with Praise,
And all her Jealous Monarchs with Amaze.
And Rumours loud which daunt remotest Kings,
Thy firm unshaken Valour ever brings
Victory home, while new Rebellions raise
Their Hydra-heads, and the false *North* displays
Her broken League to Imp her Serpent Wings:
O yet! a Nobler task awaits thy Hand,
For what can War, but Acts of War still breed,

Till injur'd Truth from Violence be freed;
And publick Faith be rescu'd from the Brand
Of publick Fraud; in vain doth Valour bleed,
While Avarice and Rapine shares the Land.

To Sir *HENRY VANE*.

VANE, Young in years, but in Sage Councels old,
Then whom a better Senator ne're held
The Helm of *Rome*, when Gowns, not Arms, repell'd
The fierce *Epirote*, and the *African* bold,
Whether to settle Peace, or to unfold
The Drift of hollow States, hard to be Spell'd;
Then to advise how War may best be upheld,
Mann'd by her Two main Nerves, Iron and Gold,
In all her Equipage: Besides, to know
Both Spiritual and Civil, what each means,
What serves each, thou hast learn'd, which few have
     done.
The bounds of either Sword to thee we owe;
Therefore on thy Right hand Religion leans,
And reckons thee in chief her Eldest Son.

To Mr. *CYRIAC SKINNER*

Upon his Blindness.

CYRIAC this Three years day, these Eyes though clear
To outward view of blemish or of Spot,
Bereft of Sight, their Seeing have forgot:
Nor to their idle Orbs doth day appear,
Or Sun, or Moon, or Star, throughout the Year;
Or Man, or Woman; yet I argue not

F

Against Heaven's Hand, or Will, nor bate one jot
Of Heart or Hope; but still bear up, and steer
Right onward.   What supports me, dost thou ask ?
The Conscience, Friend, to have lost them over ply'd
In Liberties Defence, my noble task;
Of which all *Europe* rings from side to side.
This thought might lead me through this World's
      vain mask
Content, though blind, had I no other Guide.

THE LIFE OF JOHN MILTON

By JOHN TOLAND 1698

TO THOMAS RAULINS OF KILREAG IN HEREFORDSHIRE, ESQ;

I send You at length, my best Friend, what you have so
often and earnestly sollicited me to write, the Life of
JOHN MILTON, a Man eminent at home and famous
abroad for his universal Learning, Sagacity and solid
Judgment: but particularly noted as well for those
excellent Volumes he wrote on the behalf of Civil,
Religious, and Domestic Liberty; as for his divine and
incomparable Poems, which, equalling the most beautiful Order and Expression of any antient or modern
Compositions, are infinitly above them all for Sublimity and Invention. Observing in this performance
the Rules of a faithful Historian, being neither provok'd
by Malice, nor brib'd by Favor, and as well daring to
say all that is true, as scorning to write any Falshood, I
shall not conceal what may be thought against my
Author's Honor, nor add the least word for his Reputation: but three things I would have you specially
observe. First, I shall not be too minute in relating the
ordinary Circumstances of his Life, and which are common to him with all other Men. Writings of this
nature should in my opinion be design'd to recommend
Virtue, and to expose Vice; or to illustrate History, and
to preserve the memory of extraordinary things. That
a Man, for example, was sick at such a time, or well at

another, should never be mention'd; except in the Causes or Effects, Cure or Continuance, there happens somthing remarkable, and for the benefit of Mankind to know. I had not therfore related *Milton's* Headachs in his Youth, were it not for the influence which this Indisposition had afterwards on his Eys, and that his Blindness was rashly imputed by his Enemies to the avenging Judgment of God. Secondly, In the Characters of Sects and Parties, Books or Opinions, I shall produce his own words, as I find 'em in his Works; that those who approve his Reasons, may ow all the Obligation to himself, and that I may escape the blame of such as may dislike what he says. For it is commonly seen, that Historians are suspected rather to make their Hero what they would have him to be, than such as he really was; and that, as they are promted by different Passions, they put those words in his mouth which they might not speak themselves without incurring som danger, and being accus'd perhaps of Flattery or Injustice: but I am neither writing a Satyr, nor a Panegyric upon *Milton*, but publishing the true History of his Actions, Works, and Opinions. In the third place, I would not have it expected that when I quote a few Verses or Passages in a different Language, I should always pretend to translate 'em, when the whole turn or fancy absolutely depends upon the force of the Original words; for the Ignorant could be nothing the wiser, and the best Translation would spoil their Beauty to the Learned. But this happens so rarely, and almost only during his Travels abroad, that it scarce deserv'd an Advertisement. The amplest part of my Materials I had from his own Books, where, constrain'd by the Diffamations of his Enemys, he often gives an account of himself. I learnt som Particulars from a Person that had bin once his Amanuensis, which were confirm'd to me by his Daughter now dwelling in *London*, and by a Letter written to one at my desire from his last Wife, who is still alive. I perus'd the Papers of one of his Nephews, learnt what I could in Discourse with the other; and lastly consulted such of his acquaintance, as, after the best inquiry, I was able to discover. Thus completely furnish'd, I undertook, most ingenious Sir, the following Work, as well to oblige you, as to inform Posterity; and perform'd what I knew would be acceptable to my Friend with as much pleasure as ever you perus'd our Author's excellent Sheets.

JOHN MILTON, the Son likewise of *John Milton*, and *Sarah Caston*, a Woman exemplary for her Liberality to the Poor, was born in *London* in the Year of Christ 1606. a Gentleman by his Education and Family, being descended from the *Miltons* of *Milton* in *Oxford-shire*; tho if you consider him in his admirable Works or Genius, he was truly and eminently noble. But he had too much good Sense to value himself upon any other Qualities except those of his Mind, and which only he could properly call his own: for all external and adventitious Titles, as they may at the pleasure of a Tyrant, or by an unfortunat Attemt against his Government, be quite abolish'd; so we often find in hereditary Honors, that those Distinctions which the Brave and the Wise had justly obtain'd from their Country, descend indifferently to Cowards, Traytors, or Fools, and spoil the Industry of better Souls from indeavoring to equal or excede the Merits of their Ancestors. His Father was a polite Man, a great Master of Music, and by Profession a Scrivener, in which Calling, thro his

Diligence and Honesty, he got a competent Estate in a small time: for he was disinherited by his bigotted Parents for imbracing the Protestant Religion, and abjuring the Popish Idolatry. He had two other Children, *Anna* marry'd to *Edward Philips;* and *Christopher* bred to the Common Law, who, more resembling his Grandfather than his Father or Brother, was of a very superstitious nature, and a man of no Parts or Ability. After the late Civil Wars, tho he was intirely addicted to the Royal Cause, no notice was taken of him, till the late King *James*, wanting a set of Judges that would declare his Will to be superior to our Legal Constitution, created him the same day a Serjeant and one of the Barons of the Exchequer, knighting him of course, and making him next one of the Judges of the Common Pleas: But he quickly had his *quietus est*, as his Master not long after was depos'd for his Maladministration by the People of *England*, represented in a Convention at *Westminster*. To return now to the Person who makes the Subject of this Discourse, *John Milton* was destin'd to be a Scholar; and partly under domestic Teachers (whereof one was *Thomas Young*, to whom the first of his familiar Letters is inscrib'd) and partly under Dr. *Gill*, the chief Master of *Paul's* School (to whom likewise the fifth of the same Letters is written) he made an incredible Progress in the knowlege of Words and Things, his Diligence and Inclination outstripping the care of his Instructors. After the twelfth Year of his Age, such was his insatiable thirst for Learning, he seldom went to bed before midnight. This was the first undoing of his Eys, to whose natural debility were added frequent Headachs, which could not retard or extinguish his laudable Passion for Letters. Being thus

initiated in several Tongues, and having not slightly
tasted the inexpressible Sweets of Philosophy, he was
sent at 15 to *Christ's College* in *Cambridg* to pursue more
arduous and solid Studies.   This same Year he gave
several Proofs of his early Genius for Poetry, wherin he
afterwards succeded so happily, that to all Ages he'l
continue no less the Ornament and Glory of *England*,
than *Homer* is own'd to be that of *Greece*, and *Virgil* of
Italy.   He first translated som Psalms into English
Verse, wherof the 114*th* begins in this manner.

> When the blest Seed of *Terah*'s faithful Son,
> After long toil their Liberty had won,
> And past from *Pharian* Fields to *Canaan* Land,
> Led by the strength of the Almighty's Hand;
> Jehovah's Wonders were in *Israel* shown,
> His Praise and Glory was in *Israel* known.

In his seventeenth Year he wrote a handsom Copy of
English Verses on the Death of a Sister's Child that
dy'd of a Cough; and the same Year a Latin Elegy on
the Death of the Bishop of *Winchester*, with another on
that of *Ely*.   'Twas then also that he compos'd his fine
Poem on the Gunpouder-Treason; concerning all
which and the rest of his Juvenil pieces, the judicious
Morhof, in his *Polyhistor Literarius*, says, that *Milton's*
Writings shew him to have bin a Man in his very
Childhood; and that these Poems are excedingly
above the ordinary Capacity of that Age.   He continu'd in *Cambridg* seven years, where he liv'd with
great Reputation, and generally belov'd, till taking the
degree of Master of Arts, and performing his Exercises
with much applause, he left the University; for he
aim'd at none of those Professions that require a longer
stay in that place.   Som of his Academic Performances

are still extant among his occasional Poems, and at the
end of his familiar Letters. The five succeding years
he liv'd with his Father in his Country Retirement at
Horton near *Colebrook* in *Barkshire*, where at full leisure
he perus'd all the *Greec* and *Latin* Writers; but was not
so much in love with his Solitude, as not to make an
excursion now and then to *London*, somtimes to buy
Books, or to meet Friends from *Cambridg* ; and at other
times to learn som new thing in the Mathematics or in
Music, with which he was extraordinarily delighted.
It was about this time he wrote from *London* a Latin
Elegy to his intimat Friend *Charles Diodati*, wherein
som Verses reflecting on the University, and preferring
the Pleasures of the Town, gave a handle afterwards to
certain Persons no less ignorant than malitious to report
that either he was expel'd for som Misdemeanor from
Cambridg, or left it in discontent that he obtain'd no
Preferment: and that at *London* he spent his time with
leud Women, or at Playhouses. But the falsity of this
story we shall in due place demonstrat, and in the
mean time insert those lines for the satisfaction of the
curious.

> *Me tenet urbs reflua quam Thamesis alluit unda,*
>   *Meque nec invitum patria dulcis habet.*
> *Jam nec arundiferum mihi cura revisere Camum,*
>   *Nec dudum vetiti me laris angit amor.*
> *Nuda nec arva placent, umbrasque negantia molles,*
>   *Quem malè Phoebicolis convenit ille locus!*
> *Nec duri libet usque minas perferre Magistri,*
>   *Caeteraque ingenio non subeunda meo.*
> *Si sit hoc exilium patrios adisse penates,*
>   *Et vacuum curis otia grata sequi,*
> *Non ego vel profugi nomen, sortemve recuso,*
>   *Laetus & exilii conditione fruor.*

O utinam vates nunquam graviora tulisset
   Ille Tomitano flebilis exul agro ;
Non tunc Ionio quicquam cessisset Homero,
   Neque foret victo laus tibi prima, Maro.
Tempora nam licet hic placidis dare libera Musis,
   Et totum rapiunt me mea vita libri.
Excipit hinc fessum sinuosi pompa Theatri,
   Et vocat ad plausus garrula scena suos.

Et paulo post:

Sed neque sub tecto semper, nec in urbe, latemus,
   Irrita nec nobis tempora veris eunt.
Nos quoque lucus habet vicino consitus ulmo,
   Atque suburbani nobilis umbra loci.
Saepius hic blandas spirantia Sydera flammas
   Virgineos videas praeteriisse Choros.

He wrote another Latin Elegy to *Charles Diodati;* and in his twentieth year he made one on the approach of the Spring: but the following year he describes his falling in love with a Lady (whom he accidentally met, and never afterwards saw) in such tender Expressions, with those lively Passions, and Images so natural, that you would think Love himself had directed his Pen, or inspir'd your own Breast when you peruse them. We shall see him now appear in a more serious Scene, tho yet a Child in comparison of the Figure he afterwards made in the World. The Death of his Mother happening likewise about this time facilitated his design, which was with his Father's leave to travel into foren Regions, being persuaded that he could not better discern the Preeminence or Defects of his own Country, than by observing the Customs and Institutions of others; and that the study of never so many Books, without the advantages of Conversation, serves only to render a

Man either a stupid Fool, or an insufferable Pedant.
First therfore he procedes to *France* with one Servant,
and no Tutor: for such as still need a Pedagog are not
fit to go abroad; and those who are able to make a right
use of their Travels, ought to be the free Masters of
their own Actions, their good Qualifications being
sufficient to introduce 'em into all places, and to present
'em to the most deserving Persons. He had an elegant
Letter of Direction and Advice from the famous Sir
Henry Wotton, who was a long time Ambassador from
King *James* the First to the Republic of *Venice*. Being
arriv'd at *Paris*, he was most kindly receiv'd by the
English Ambassador, who recommended him to the
famous *Grotius*, then Ambassador also from Queen
Christina of *Sweden*, at the French Court: for we may
easily imagin that *Milton* was not a little desirous to be
known to the first Person then in the World for reading
and latitude of Judgment, to speak nothing of his other
meritorious Characters. From hence he parted for
Italy, where after passing thro several noted Places, he
came at length to *Florence* ; a City for the Politeness of
the Language, and the Civility of the Inhabitants, he
always infinitly admir'd. In this place he staid about
two months, and was daily assisting at those learned
Conferences which they hold in their privat Academys,
according to the laudable Custom of *Italy*, both for the
improvement of Letters, and the begetting or maintaining of Friendship. During this time he contracted
an intimat Acquaintance with several ingenious Men,
most of which have since made a noise in the World,
and deserve a mention in this place: I mean *Gaddi*,
*Dati, Frescobaldo, Francini, Bonmattei, Coltellino, Chi-
mentelli*, and several others. With these he kept a

constant Correspondence, particularly with *Carolo Dati*, a Nobleman of *Florence*, to whom he wrote the tenth of his Familiar Epistles, and who gave him the following Testimonial of his Esteem.

Joanni Miltoni Londinensi,
Juveni patria et virtutibus eximio.

VIRO qui multa peregrinatione, studio cuncta orbis terrarum perspexit, ut novus Ulysses omnia ubique ab omnibus apprehenderet. Polyglotto, in cuius ore linguæ jam deperditæ sic reviviscunt, ut idiomata omnia sint in ejus laudibus infacunda ; & jure ea percallet, ut admirationes & plausus populorum ab propria sapientia excitatos, intelligat. Illi, cujus animi dotes corporisque sensus ad admirationem commovent, & per ipsam motum cuique auferunt ; cujus opera ad plausus hortantur, sed venustate vocem auditoribus adimunt. Cui in memoria totus orbis : in intellectu sapientia : in voluntate ardor gloriæ : in ore eloquentia. Harmonicos cœlestium Sphærarum sonitus, Astronomia duce, audienti ; characteres mirabilium naturæ, per quos Dei magnitudo describitur, magistra Philosophia legenti ; antiquitatum latebras, vetustatis excidia, eruditionis Ambages, comite assidua autorum lectione, exquirenti, restauranti, percurrenti. At cur nitor in arduum ? Illi in cujus virtutibus evulgandis ora famæ non sufficiant, nec hominum stupor in laudandis fatis est, reverentiæ et amoris ergo hoc ejus meritis debitum admirationis tributum offert

Carolus Datus Patricius Florentinus,
Tanto homini Servus, tantæ virtutis Amator.

I don't think the Italian Flourishes were ever carry'd further than in this Elogy, which notwithstanding is sincere, and pen'd by an honest Man. *Francini* is not less liberal of his Praises in the long Italian Ode he compos'd in his Honor, which because it dos Justice to the English Nation, and foretold the future Greatness of *Milton*, I have annex'd to this Discourse. That he corresponded afterwards with Bonmattei, appears from

the eighth of his familiar Letters, which he wrote to
him on his design of publishing an *Italian* Grammar,
and is not more elegant than pertinent. But he attain'd
that perfection himself in the *Italian* Language, as to
make som Songs on a real or feign'd Mistress, in one
of which he gives a handsom account of his writing in
this Tongue.

> *Qual in colle aspro, al imbrunir di sera,*
> *L'avezza giovinetta pastorella*
> *Va bagnando L'herbetta strana e bella,*
> *Che mal si spande a disusata spera*
> *Fuor di sua natia alma prima vera :*
> *Cosi amor meco insu la lingua snella*
> *Desta il fior nuovo di strania favella ;*
> *Mentre io di te, vezzozamente altera,*
> *Canto dal mio buon popol non inteso,*
> *E'l bel Tamigi cangio col bel arno :*
> *Amor lo volse, ed io a l'altrui peso ;*
> *Seppi ch'amor cosa mai volse indarno.*
> *Deh ! foss'il mio cuor lento, e'l duro seno*
> *A chi pianta dal ciel si buon terreno.*

From his beloved *Florence* he took his Journy next to
Rome, where he stay'd two other Months to see the
miserable Remains of that famous City, once the glorious
Mistress of the World, and deservedly so, as being then
not only the fairest thing under Heaven; but that, till
the Ambition of a few Persons corrupted her equal
Government, she extended Liberty and Learning as far
as the Glory of her Name, or the Terror of her Arms.
Here, no doubt, all the Examples he had hitherto read
of the Virtue, Eloquence, Wisdom, or Valor of her
antient Citizens, occur'd to his mind, and could not but
oppress with grief his generous Soul, when with his
own eys he saw *Rome* now the chief Seat of the most

exquisit Tyranny exercis'd by effeminat Priests, not
reigning in the World thro any conceiv'd opinion of
their Justice, or dread of their Courage; for to these
Qualities they are known and sworn Enemys: but
deluding men with unaccountable Fables, and disarm-
ing 'em by imaginary Fears, they fill their heads first
with Superstition, and then their own Pockets with their
Mony. Here he became acquainted with the celebrated
Lucas Holstenius the *Vatican* Librarian, who us'd him
with great Humanity, and readily shew'd him al the
Greec Authors, whether publish'd or otherwise, that
past his Care and Emendations: He also presented him
to Cardinal *Barberini*, who at an entertainment of
Music, perform'd at his own expence, look'd for him in
the Croud, and gave him a kind Invitation. To thank
Holstenius for all these Favors, *Milton* wrote afterwards
from *Florence* the ninth of his Familiar Letters. At
Rome he likewise commenc'd a Friendship with the Poet
Giovanni Salsilli, who in the following Tetrastich extols
him for writing so correctly in Latin, Greec, and Italian.

> *Cede Meles, cedat depressa Mincius urna,*
> *Sebetus Tassum desinat usque loqui :*
> *At Thamesis victor cunctis ferat altior undas,*
> *Nam per te, Milto, par tribus unus erit.*

Milton in return sent to *Salsilli*, shortly after lying sick,
those fine Scazons, which may be read among his
Juvenil Poems. And here too did *Selvaggi* adorn him
with this Distich.

> *Græcia Mæonidem, jactet sibi Roma Maronem :*
> *Anglia Miltonum jactat utrique parem.*

Having departed from *Rome* to *Naples*, he was introduc'd by his Fellow-Traveller to *Giovanni Battista*

Manso, Marquiss of *Villa*, a Person most nobly descended, of great Authority, renown'd for his military Atchievments, and a Patron of learned Men. To him the famous *Tasso* inscrib'd his Poem of Friendship, and makes honorable mention of him among the Princes of *Campania* in the twentieth Book of his *Gierusalemme Conquistata*. He went himself to shew him all the remarkable Places of that City, visited him often at his Lodging, and made this Distich in his Commendation, which he addresses to himself.

> *Ut mens, forma, decor, facies, mos ; si pietas sic,*
> *Non Anglus, verum Herclè Angelus ipse fores.*

This exception of his Piety relates to his being a Protestant; and the Marquiss told him, he would have don him several good Offices, had he bin more reserv'd in matters of Religion. But our Author out of Gratitude for all these singular Favors from one of his high Quality, presented him at his departure with an incomparable Latin Eclog, entitul'd *Mansus*, which is extant among his occasional pieces: And that I may mention it by the way, I don't question but it was from *Manso's* Conversation and their Discourses about *Tasso*, that he first form'd his design of writing an Epic Poem, tho he was not so soon determin'd about the Subject.

He was now preparing to pass over into *Sicily* and *Greece*, when he was recal'd by the sad News of a Civil War beginning in *England ;* esteeming it an unworthy thing for him securely to be diverting himself abroad, when his Countrymen were contending at home for their Liberty. Intending therfore to return to *Rome*, he was advis'd by som Merchants to the contrary;

for they had learnt from their Correspondents, that the
English Jesuits were framing Plots against him by
reason of the great Freedom he us'd in his Discourses
of Religion. Notwithstanding, having resolv'd not to
begin any Disputes, but, being ask'd, not to dissemble
his Sentiments whatever might ensue, he went the
second time to *Rome*, and stay'd there two months
longer, neither concealing his Name, nor declining
openly to defend the Truth under the Pope's nose,
when any thought fit to attack him: yet he return'd
safe to his learned and affectionat Friends in *Florence*.
I forgot al this while to mention that he paid a Visit to
Galileo, then an old man, and a Prisoner to the Inquisition for thinking otherwise in Astronomy than
pleas'd the Franciscan Friers. He tarry'd two other
months in *Florence*, and having seen *Lucca*, *Bononia*,
Ferrara, he arriv'd in *Venice*. After spending one
month here, and shipping off all the Books he collected
in his Travels, he came thro *Verona*, *Milan*, cross the
Alps, and along the Lake *Lemanno* to *Geneva*, where he
contracted an intimat Familiarity with *Giovanni Diodati*,
a noted Professor of Divinity, and was known to several
others, particularly to the celebrated Critic and Antiquary *Ezechiel Spanhemius* now alive, to whom he
wrote the 17*th* of his Familiar Letters, and who, together with *Calandrini*, and som more of that City, sent
him intelligence afterwards concerning his Antagonist
Morus, wherof in due order. So leaving this place, and
passing back again thro *France*, he did after one year
and three month's Peregrination return safe into *England*, much about the same time that King *Charles* the
First made his second unsuccessful Expedition against
the *Scots*. As soon as the Complements of Friends or

Acquaintance were over, he hir'd a handsom Lodging in the City, to be a retreat for himself and his Books in such uncertain and troublesom times. But he continu'd a long while inconsolable for the loss of his dearest Friend and Schoolfellow *Charles Diodati*, mention'd before, who dy'd in his absence. He was from *Lucca* originally, but an Englishman born, a Student in Physic, and an excellent Scholar, as I have good reasons to believe, and appears by two Greec Letters of his to *Milton*, very handsomly written, and which I have now in my hands. Our Author in mournful Notes bitterly laments the immature fate of this young Gentleman, whom he denotes by the appellation of *Damon* in an Eclog nothing inferior to the *Maronian Daphnis*, and which is to be still seen among his Latin Miscellanies. By this piece we plainly find that he had already conceiv'd the Plan of an Epic Poem, wherof he then design'd the Subject should be the warlike Actions of the old British Heroes, and particularly of King *Arthur*, as he declares himself in these Verses.

> *Ipse ego Dardanias Rutupina per æquora puppes*
> *Dicam, & Pandrasidos regnum vetus Inogeniæ,*
> *Brennumque, Arviragumque Duces, priscumque Belinum,*
> *Et tandem Armoricos Britonum sub lege Colonos ;*
> *Tum gravidam Arturo fatali fraude Iögernen,*
> *Mendaces vultus assumtaque Gorlois arma,*
> *Merlini Dolus.*

But this particular Subject was reserv'd for the celebrated Pen of Sir *Richard Blackmore*. Som few lines after he declares his Ambition of performing somthing in his native Language that might perpetuat his Name in these Ilands, tho he should be the more obscure and inglorious by it to the rest of the World. His words, because they are wonderfully fine, I shall here insert.

> ——————————————*Mihi satis ampla*
> *Merces, & mihi grande decus (sim ignotus in ævum*
> *Tum licet, externo penitusque inglorius orbi)*
> *Si me flava comas legat Usa, & potor Alauni,*
> *Vorticibusque frequens Abra, & nemus omne Treantae,*
> *Et Thamesis meus ante omnes, & fusca metallis*
> *Tamara, et extremis me discant Orcades undis.*

I said above that it was by his Conversation with the Marquiss of *Villa*, who so nobly honor'd the immortal Memory of *Tasso*, that our *Milton* form'd his vast design. That this was not a mere Conjecture, and that King *Arthur* also was to be the Hero of that piece, let but these Verses of his *Mansus* be consider'd.

> *O mihi si mea sors talem concedat amicum*
> *Phœbæos decorasse viros qui tam bene norit,*
> *Siquando indigenas revocabo in carmina reges,*
> *Arturumque etiam sub Terris bella moventem ;*
> *Aut dicam invictæ sociali fœdere mensae*
> *Magnanimos Heroas, & (O modo spiritus adsit)*
> *Frangam Saxonicas Britonum sub Marte Phalanges.*

But to return to his Lodgings, where we left him, there, both to be eas'd in the reading of the best Authors, and to discharge his Duty to his Sister's Sons that were partly committed to his Tuition, he undertook the care of their Education, and instructed them himself in Latin, Greec, Hebrew and other Oriental Dialects; likewise in several parts of the Mathematics, in Cosmography, History, and some modern Languages, as French and Italian. Some Gentlemen of his intimat Friends, and to whom he could deny nothing, prevail'd

G

with him to impart the same benefits of Learning to their Sons, specially since the trouble was no more with many than a few. He that well knew the greatest Persons in all ages to have bin delighted with teaching others the Principles of Knowlege and Virtue, easily comply'd; nor was his Success unanswerable to the opinion which was generally entertain'd of his Capacity. And not content to acquaint his Disciples with those Books that are commonly read in the Schools, wherof several, no doubt, are excellent in their kind, tho others are as trivial or impertinent; he made them likewise read in Latin the antient Authors concerning Husbandry, as *Cato*, *Varro*, *Columella*, and *Palladius* ; also *Cornelius Celsus* the Physician, *Pliny's* Natural History, the Architecture of *Vitruvius*, the Stratagems of *Frontinus*, and the Philosophical Poets *Lucretius* and *Manilius*. To the usual Greec Books, as *Homer* and *Hesiod*, he added *Aratus*, *Dionysius Periegetes*, *Oppian*, *Quintus Calaber*, *Appollonius Rhodius*, *Plutarch*, *Xenophon*, *Ælians* Tactics, and the Stratagems of *Polyænus*. It was this greatest sign of a good Man in him, and the highest Obligation he could lay on his Friends, without any sordid or mercenary purposes, that gave occasion to his Adversaries with opprobriously terming him a Schoolmaster; tho were this charge as true as it is utterly false, I see not how it should any way tend to his Dishonor, if he had bin necessitated to such a laborious occupation for his living, and discharg'd it with due Honesty and Care. But what's very remarkable is, that the most forward to reproach him in this manner were themselves mean Tutors in the University, and the greatest of 'em only a Professor, which are but nominally distinguishable from Schoolmasters.

He tells us himself in his second Defence, " That on
" his return from Travelling he found all mouths open
" against the Bishops, som complaining of their Vices,
" and others quarrelling at the very Order; and that
" thinking from such beginnings a way might be
" open'd to true Liberty, he heartily engag'd in the
" Dispute, as well to rescue his Fellow-Citizens from
" Slavery, as to help the Puritan Ministers, who were
" inferior to the Bishops in Learning. He first of all
therfore in the year 1641. publish'd two Books of *Reformation*, dedicated to a Friend. In the first of these he
shews, by orderly steps, from *Henry* the Eighth's Reign,
what were all along the real impediments in this Kingdom to a perfect Reformation, which in general he
reduces to two heads, that is, our retaining of Ceremonies, and confining the Power of Ordination to
Diocesan Bishops exclusively of the People. "Our Cere-
" monies, he says, are sensless in themselves, and serve
" for nothing but either to facilitat our return to Popery;
" or to hide the defects of better Knowlege, and to set
" off the Pomp of Prelacy. As for the Bishops, many
of whom he denys not to have bin good Men, tho not
infallible, nor above all human Frailties, he affirms,
" that at the beginning, tho they had renounc'd the
" Pope, they hug'd the Popedom, and shar'd the Author-
" ity among themselves. In King *Edward* the Sixth's
time, he affirms, " they were with their prostitute
" Gravities the common Stales to countenance every
" politic fetch that was then on foot. If a Toleration
" for Mass were to be beg'd of the King for his Sister
" *Mary*, lest *Charles* the Fifth should be angry; who
" but the grave Prelats, *Cranmer* and *Ridley*, should be
" sent to extort it from the young King ? When the

" Lord *Sudley*, Admiral of *England*, and the Protector's
" Brother, was wrongfully to lose his Life, no man
" could be found fitter than *Latimer* to divulge in his
" Sermon the forg'd Accusations laid to his charge,
" therby to defame him with the People. *Cranmer*, one
" of King *Henry's* Executors, and the other Bishops,
" did, to gratify the Ambition of a Traytor, consent
" to exclude from the Succession, not only *Mary*
" the Papist, but also *Elizabeth* the Protestant, tho
" before declar'd by themselves the lawful Issue of their
" late Master.   In Queen *Elizabeth's* Reign he imputes
the Obstructions of further Reformation still. to the
Bishops, and then procedes from Antiquity to prove
that all Ecclesiastical Elections belong'd to the People;
but that if those Ages had favor'd Episcopacy, we
should not be much concern'd, since the best times
were spreadingly infected, the best Men of those times
foully tainted, and the best Writings of those Men
dangerously adulterated; which Propositions he labors
to prove at large.   In the second Book he continues his
Discourse of Prelatical Episcopacy, displays the Politics
of the same; which, according to him, are always
opposit to Liberty: he deduces the History of it down
from its remotest Original, and shews, " that in *England*
particularly it is so far from being, as they commonly
allege, the only Form of Church-Disciplin agreable to
Monarchy, that the mortallest Diseases and Convul-
sions of the Government did ever procede from the
Craft of the Prelats, or was occasion'd by their Pride.
Then he encourages the *English* and *Scots* to pursue their
begun Contest for Liberty by this Exhortation.   " Go
" on both, hand in hand, O Nations, never to be dis-
" united.   Be the Praise and the heroic Song of all

" Posterity. Merit this; but seek only Virtue, not to
" extend your limits: for what need you win a fading
" triumphant Laurel out of the Tears of wretched Men;
" but to settle the pure Worship of God in his Church,
" and Justice in the State ? Then shall the hardest
" Difficulties smooth out themselves before you; Envy
" shall sink to Hell, Craft and Malice be confounded,
" whether it be home-bred Mischief, or outlandish
" Cunning: Yea other Nations will then covet to serve
" you; for Lordship and Victory are but the Pages of
" Justice and Virtue. Commit securely to true Wisdom
" the vanquishing and uncasing of Craft and Subtilty,
" which are but her two Runnagates. Join your invin-
" cible Might to do worthy and Godlike Deeds; and
" then he that seeks to break your Union, a cleaving
" Curse be his Inheritance to all Generations.

After this, certain Ministers having written a Treatise
against Episcopacy, the Title *Smectymnuus* consisting
of the initial Letters of their Names, and a Bishop of no
small Authority having bestow'd an Answer upon it,
Milton, to use his own words, supposing himself not
less able to write for Truth, than others for their Profit
or unjust Power, publish'd his piece of *Prelatical
Episcopacy*. In this Book he proves against the famous
Usher (for he would not readily ingage a meaner Adversary) that Diocesan Episcopacy, or a superior Order to
the common Ministry, cannot be deduc'd from the
Apostolical times by the force of such Testimonies as
are alleg'd to that purpose. Now *Usher's* chief Talent
lying in much reading, and being a great Editor
and Admirer of old Writings, *Milton* shews the Insufficiency, Inconveniency and Impiety of this method
to establish any part of Christianity; and blames those

Persons who cannot think any Doubt resolv'd, or any
Doctrin confirm'd, unless they run to that indigested
heap and fry of Authors which they call Antiquity.
" Whatsoever either Time (says he) or the heedless
" hand of blind Chance, has drawn down to this present
" in her huge Dragnet, whether Fish or Seaweed, Shells
" or Shrubs, unpick'd, unchosen, those are the Fathers.
And so he chides the good Bishop for divulging useless
Treatises, stuft with the specious Names of *Ignatius* and
Polycarpus, with Fragments of old Martyrologies and
Legends, to distract and stagger the multitude of
credulous Readers.

His next performance was *the Reason of Church-
Government urg'd against Prelacy, in two Books*, principally intended against the same *Usher's* account of the
Original of Episcopacy. The Eloquence is masculin,
the Method is natural, the Sentiments are free, and the
whole (God knows) appears to have a very different
force from what the Nonconformist Divines wrote in
those days, or since that time, on the same Subject. In
the beginning of the second Book he mentions his
design of writing an Epic Poem, but continues still
unresolv'd, whether his Hero should be som Prince
before the Conquest, or the Argument be borrow'd
from the Scripture or the antient Heathen History.
But because the account he gives of what the Poet
should propose by such a work is exactly just, and withal
so properly exprest, I shall not grudg to transcribe it in
this place. " These Abilities (says he, speaking of
" Invention and Composition) whersoever they be
" found, are the inspir'd Gift of God; rarely bestow'd,
" but yet to som (tho most abuse them) in every Nation:
" and are of power to breed and cherish in a great

" People the Seeds of Virtue and public Civility, to
" allay the Perturbations of the Mind, and set the
" Affections in a right tune;—or lastly, whatsoever
" is in Religion holy and sublime, in Virtue amiable
" or grave, whatsoever has Passion or Admiration in all
" the changes of that which is call'd Fortune from
" without, or the wily Subtilties and Refluxes of Mans
" Thoughts from within, all these things with a solid
" and treatable Smoothness to paint out and describe.
" Teaching over the whole Book of Sanctity and Virtue,
" thro all the instances of Example, and with such
" delight, to those especially of a soft and delicious
" temper (who will not so much as look upon Truth
" her self, unless they see her elegantly drest) that
" wheras the Paths of Honesty and good Life appear
" now rugged and difficult, tho they be indeed easy and
" pleasant; they would then appear to all Men both
" easy and pleasant, tho they were rugged and difficult
" indeed. And what a Benefit this would be to our
" Youth and Gentry, may be soon guest by what we
" know of the Corruption and Bane which they suck in
" daily from the Writings and Interludes of libidinous
" and ignorant Poetasters; who having scarce ever
" heard of that which is the main consistence of a true
" Poem, the choice of such Persons as they ought to
" introduce, and what is moral and decent to each one,
" do for the most part lap up vitious Principles in sweet
" Pills to be swallow'd down, and make the taste of
" virtuous Documents harsh and sour. But because
" the Spirit of Man cannot demean it self lively in this
" Body without som recreating intermission of labor and
" serious things, it were happy for the Commonwealth
" if our Magistrats, as in those famous Governments

" of old, would take into their care not only the deciding
" of our contentious Law-cases or Brauls, but the
" managing of our public Sports and festival Pastimes;
" that they might not be such as were authoriz'd a while
" since, the Provocations of Drunkenness and Lust, but
" such as may inure and harden our Bodies by martial
" Exercises to all warlike Skill and Performances; and
" may civilize, adorn, and make discrete our Minds by
" the learned and affable meeting of frequent Aca-
" demies, and the procurement of wise and artful
" Recitations, sweeten'd with eloquent and graceful
" Enticements to the love and practice of Justice,
" Temperance and Fortitude, instructing and bettering
" the Nation at all opportunities, that the voice of
" Wisdom and Virtue may be heard every where.
" Whether this may not be don, not only in Pulpits,
" but after another persuasive method, at set and solemn
" Paneguries, in Theaters, Porticos, or what other place
" or way may win most upon the People to receive at
" once both Recreation and Instruction, let them in
" Authority consult.

Another eminent Bishop having written against *Smectymnuus*, our Author publish'd *Animadversions* upon his
Book; and to the Reasons alleg'd from Councils for
substituting a constant form to occasional Prayers in
public, he gives the following Answer. " Set the grave
" Councils, says he, upon their shelves again, and string
" them hard, lest their various and jangling opinions
" put their leaves into a flutter. I shall not intend this
" hot Season to lead you a course thro the wide and
" dusty Champain of the Councils; but shall take coun-
" sel of that which counsel'd them, Reason: And tho
" I know there is an obsolete Reprehension now at your

" Tongues end, yet I shall be bold to say, that Reason
" is the Gift of God in one Man as well as in a thousand.
" By that which we have tasted already of their Cisterns,
" we may find that Reason was the only thing, and not
" any divine Command, that mov'd them to enjoin the
" set forms of a Liturgy. First, lest any thing in
" general might be missaid in their public Prayers, thro
" ignorance or want of care, contrary to the Faith: And
" next, lest the *Arians* and *Pelagians* in particular should
" infect the People by their Hymns and Forms of
" Prayer. But by the good leave of these antient
" Fathers, this was no solid prevention of spreading
" Heresy, to debar the Ministers of God the use of their
" noblest Talent, Prayer in the Congregation; unless
" they had forbid the use of all Sermons and Lectures
" too, but such as were ready made to their hands like
" our Homilies: or else he that was heretically dispos'd
" had as fair an opportunity of infecting in his Dis-
" course, as in his Prayer or Hymn. As insufficiently,
" and, to say truth, as imprudently did they provide by
" their contriv'd Liturgies, lest any thing should be
" pray'd thro ignorance or want of care in the Ministers:
" for if they were careless and ignorant in their Prayers,
" certainly they would be more careless in their preach-
" ing, and still more careless in watching over their
" Flock; and what prescription could reach to bound
" them in both these ? What if Reason, now illustrated
" by the Word of God, shall be able to produce a better
" Prevention than these Councils have left us against
" Heresy, Ignorance, or want of care in the Ministry,
" to wit, that such Wisdom and Diligence be us'd in
" the Education of those that would be Ministers,
" and such a strict and serious Examination to be

" undergon before their admission, as St. *Paul* to
" *Timothy* sets down at large; and then they need not
" carry such an unworthy suspicion over the Preachers
" of God's Word, as to tutor their Unsoundness with
" the a, b, c, of a Liturgy, or to diet their Ignorance and
" want of Care with the limited draught of a Mattin
and Evensong drench. What his opinion was of the
Fathers he further declares when he calls them those
more antient than trusty Fathers, whom Custom and
" fond Opinion, weak Principles, and the neglect of
" sounder Knowlege, has exalted so high, as to have
" gain'd them a blind Reverence; whose Books, in
" bigness and number endless and immeasurable, I
" cannot think that either God or Nature, either divine
" or human Wisdom, did ever mean should be a Rule
" or Reliance to us in the decision of any weighty and
" positive Doctrins: for certainly every Rule and Instru-
" ment of necessary Knowlege that God has given us,
" ought to be so in proportion as may be wielded and
" manag'd by the Life of Man, without penning him
" up from the Duties of human Society. —But he that
" shall bind himself to make Antiquity his Rule, if he
" reads but part (besides the difficulty of choice) his
" Rule is deficient, and utterly unsatisfying; for there
" may be other Writers of another mind, which he has
" not seen: And if he undertakes all, the length of
" Man's Life cannot extend to give him a full and
" requisit knowlege of what was don in Antiquity.
" —Go therfore, and use all your Art, apply your
" Sledges, your Leavers, and your iron Crows, to heave
" and hale your mighty *Polyphemus* of Antiquity to the
" delusion of Novices and unexperienc'd Christians.
The present Ecclesiastical Revenues, he says, were not

at first the effects of just Policy or wholesom Laws,
" but of the superstitious Devotion of Princes and great
" Men that knew no better, or of the base importunity
" of begging Friers, haunting and harassing the Death-
" beds of Men departing this Life in a blind and
" wretched condition of hope to merit Heaven for the
" building of Churches, Cloysters, and Convents; the
" black Revenues of Purgatory, the price of abus'd and
" murder'd Souls, the damn'd Simony of Trentals, and
" the hire of Indulgences to commit mortal Sin.

Milton's next Book was his *Apology* against the Reverend Person who tax'd his Animadversions with being
a scurrilous Libel. This Adversary, as it has always
bin the custom of some People when they can neither
answer well nor defend, had recourse to Defamation
and personal Reflections, which, had they bin true,
could not derogate from the force of his Arguments;
but, being false, must be call'd by their true names of
Lying and Slander. Our Author therfore intreats
those who have found the leisure to read his name
unworthily defam'd, that they would be so good and so
patient as to hear the same Person not unneedfully
defended. Being accus'd of having bin an inordinat
and riotous Youth vomited out of the University, he
makes this reply: " For this commodious Ly I thank
" him; for it has given me an apt occasion to acknow-
" ledge publicly with all grateful mind that more than
" ordinary Favor and Respect which I found above any
" of my Equals at the hands of those courteous and
" learned Men, the Fellows of that College wherin I
" spent som years: who at my parting, after having
" taken two Degrees (as the manner is) signify'd many
" ways how much better it would content them that I

" should stay, as by many Letters full of Kindness and
" loving Respect, both before that time and long after,
" I was assur'd of their singular good Affection towards
" me.   Which being likewise propense to all such as
" were for their studious and civil Life worthy of
" Esteem, I could not wrong their Judgments and
" upright Intentions so much as to think I had that
" regard from them for any other cause than that I
" might be still encourag'd to procede in the honest and
" laudable Course, of which they apprehended I had
" given good proof.   —As for the common Approba-
" tion or Dislike of that place, as now it is, that I should
" esteem or disesteem my self or any other the more for
" that, is too simple and too credulous in the Confuter,
" if he thinks to obtain with me or any right Discerner.
" Of small practice was that Physician who could not
" judg by what both she or her Sister have of a long
" time vomited, that the worse stuff she strongly keeps
" in her Stomach, but the better she is ever kecking at,
" and is queasy.   She vomits now out of Sickness, but
" e're it be well with her she must vomit by strong
" Physic.   —The Suburb wherin I dwell shall be in
" my account a more honorable place than his Univer-
" sity, which, as in the time of her better Health, and
" my own younger Judgment, I never greatly admir'd,
" so now much less.   This is not the only passage of the
Apology wherin he testifys his Contemt of the Universities, for in another place he says, " that what with
" Truanting and Debauchery, what with false Grounds,
" and the weakness of natural Faculties in many of
" them (it being a Maxim with som Men to send
" the simplest of their Sons thither) perhaps there
" would be found among them as many unsolid and

" corrupted Judgments, both in Doctrin and Life, as in
" any other two Corporations of like bigness. This is
" undoubted, that if any Carpenter, Smith, or Weaver,
" were such a bungler in his Trade, as the greater
" number of them are in their Profession, he would
" starve for any Custom. And should he exercise his
" Manufacture as little as they do their Talents, he
" would forget his Art: or should he mistake his
" Tools, as they do theirs, he would mar all the work he
" took in hand. How few among them that know how
" to write or speak in a pure stile, much less to distinguish
" the Ideas and various kinds of Stile! In Latin bar-
" barous, and oft not without Solecisms, declaiming in
" rugged and miscellaneous Gear blown together by the
" four Winds; and in their choice preferring the gay
" rankness of *Apuleius*, *Arnobius*, or any modern *Fus-*
" *tianist*, before the native Latinisms of *Cicero*. In the
" Greec Tongue most of them unletter'd or unenter'd
" to any sound Proficiency in those Attic Masters of
" Wisdom and Eloquence. In the Hebrew Text,
" except it be som few of them, their Lips are utterly
" uncircumcis'd. No less are they out of the way in
" Philosophy, pestring their heads with the sapless
" Dotages of old *Paris* and *Salamanca*. His Antagonist
insinuating a malicious Representation even of his early
rising, he tells him, that his " Morning haunts are,
" where they should be, at home; not sleeping, or
" concocting the Surfeits of an irregular Feast, but up
" and stirring, in Winter often before the Sound of any
" Bell awakens Men to Labor or Devotion; in Summer
" as oft as the Bird that first rouses, or not much tardier,
" to read good Authors, or cause them to be read, till
" the Attention be weary, or the Memory have its full

" fraught.   Then with useful and generous Labors pre-
" serving the Bodys Health and Hardiness, to render
" a lightsom, clear, and not a lumpish Obedience to the
" Mind, for the cause of Religion and our Countries
" Liberty, when it shall require firm Hearts in sound
" Bodies to stand and cover their Stations, rather than
" see the Ruin of our Protestation, and the enforcement
" of a slavish Life.   Passing over his serious and just
Apology for frequenting Playhouses, I shall subjoin the
Reason he gives why som Terms of the Stage might
appear in his Writings without having learnt them in
the Theater; " which was not needful, says he, when
" in the Colleges so many of the young Divines, and
" those in next aptitude to Divinity, have bin seen so
" often on the Stage, writhing and unboning their
" Clergy Lims to all the antic and dishonest Gestures
" of Trinculos, Buffoons, and Bauds: prostituting the
" shame of that Ministry, which either they had or were
" nigh having, to the eys of Courtiers and Court Ladys,
" with their Grooms and Mademoiselles.   There while
" they acted, and overacted, among other young Scholars
" I was a Spectator; they thought themselves gallant
" Men, and I thought them Fools; they made sport,
" and I laugh'd; they mispronounc'd, and I mislik'd;
" and, to make up the Atticism, they were out, and I
" hist.   He was to answer next to the heavy charge of
Leudness with common Prostitutes; and because the
account he gives of himself upon this occasion, and of
that part of his Poetry which regards the affairs of Love,
is not only essential to the History of his Life, but of
good Instruction also to such as read such pleasant and
alluring Books, I suppose none will be offended with
me for laying it here before them.   " I had my time,

" says he, like others that have good Learning bestow'd
" upon them, to be sent to those places where the
" opinion was it might be soonest attain'd; and, as the
" manner is, was not unstudy'd in those Authors which
" are most commended. Of these som were grave
" Orators and Historians, whose matter methought I
" lov'd indeed, but as my Age then was, so I understood
" them; others were the smooth Elegiac Poets, wherof
" the Schools are not scarce, whom both for the pleasing
" Sound of their numerous Writings (which in imita-
" tion I found most easy, and most agreeable to Nature's
" part in me) and for their matter, which what it is
" there be few who know not, I was so allur'd to read,
" that no Recreation came to me more welcom: for
" that it was then those years with me, which are
" excus'd tho they be least severe, I may be sav'd the
" labor to remember you.   Whence having observ'd
" them to account it the chief Glory of their Wit that
" they were ablest to judg, to praise, and by that could
" esteem themselves worthiest to love those high Per-
" fections, which under one or other name they took to
" celebrat; I thought with my self by every Instinct and
" Presage of Nature (which is not wont to be false) that
" what embolden'd them to this task, might with such
" diligence as they us'd embolden me: and that what
" Judgment, Wit, or Elegance, was my share, would
" herein best appear, and best value it self, by
" how much more wisely and with more love of Virtue
" I should chuse the Object of not unlike Praises.   For
" tho these Thoughts to som will seem virtuous and
" commendable, to others only pardonable, to a third sort
" perhaps idle; yet the mentioning of them now will end
" in serious.   Nor blame it, Readers, in those years to pro-

" pose to themselves such a Reward as the noblest Dis-
" positions above other things in this Life have somtimes
" prefer'd: wherof not to be sensible, when good and
" fair in one Person meet, argues both a gross and shal-
" low Judgment, and withal an ungentle and swainish
" Breast. For by the firm settling of these Persuasions
" I became (to my best memory) so much a Proficient,
" that if I found those Authors any where speaking
" unworthy things of themselves, or unchast of those
" Names which before they had extol'd, this effect it
" wrought with me, that from that time forward their
" Art I still applauded, but the Men I deplor'd; and
" above them all prefer'd the two famous Renowners of
" *Beatrice* and *Laura*, who never write but Honor of
" them to whom they devote their Verse, displaying
" sublime and pure Thoughts without transgression.
" And long it was not after, when I was confirm'd in
" the opinion that he, who would not be frustrated of
" his hope to write well hereafter in laudable things,
" ought himself to be a tru Poem; that is, a composition
" and pattern of the best and honorablest things: not
" presuming to sing the high Praises of heroic Men or
" famous Cities, unless he has in himself the Experience
" and the Practice of all that is praiseworthy. These
" Reasonings, together with a certain niceness of
" Nature, an honest Haughtiness and Self-esteem either
" of what I was or what I might be (which let Envy call
" Pride) and lastly, a becoming Modesty, all uniting the
" Supply of their natural aid together, kept me still
" above those low Descents of Mind, beneath which he
" must deject and plunge himself that can agree to
" salable and unlawful Prostitutions. Next I betook
" me among those lofty Fables and Romances which

" recount in solemn Cantos the Deeds of Knighthood
" founded by our victorious Kings, and from hence had
" in renown over all Christendom. There I read it in
" the Oath of every Knight, that he should defend to
" the expence of his best Blood, or of his Life, if it so
" befel him, the Honor and Chastity of Virgin or
" Matron: from whence even then I learnt what a
" noble Virtue Chastity sure must be, to the defence of
" which so many Worthies by such a dear Adventure
" of themselves had sworn; and if I found in the Story
" afterwards any of them by word or deed breaking that
" Oath, I judg'd it the same fault of the Poet, as that
" which is attributed to *Homer*, to have written undecent
" things of the Gods. Only this my mind gave me, that
" every free and gentle Spirit without that Oath ought
" to be born a Knight, nor needed to expect the gilt
" Spur, or the laying of a Sword upon his Shoulder, to
" stir him up both by his Counsil and his Arm, to
" secure and protect the weakness of any attemted
" Chastity. So that even those Books, which to many
" others have bin the fuel of Wantonness and loose
" Living (I cannot think how, unless by divine Indul-
" gence) prov'd to me so many Enticements, as you
" have heard, to the love and stedfast observation of that
" Virtue which abhors the Society of *Bordellos*. Thus
" from the Laureat Fraternity of Poets, riper years, and
" the ceasless round of Study and Reading, led me to
" the shady walks of Philosophy; but chiefly to the
" divine Volumes of *Plato*, and his equal *Xenophon*:
" where if I should tell you what I learnt of Chastity
" and Love (I mean that which is truly so, whose
" charming cup is only Virtue, which she bears in her
" hand to those who are worthy; the rest are cheated

H

" with a thick intoxicating Potion, which a certain
" Sorceress, the Abuser of Love's Names, carries about:
" and if I should tell you too how the first and chiefest
" Office of Love begins and ends in the Soul, producing
" those happy Twins of her divine Generation, Know-
" lege and Virtue) with such abstracted Sublimities as
" these, it might be worth your listening, Readers, as I
" may one day hope to have you in a still time, and
" when there shall be no chiding.   Thus far our
Author, who afterwards made this Character good in
his inimitable Poem of *Paradise Lost*; and before this
time in his *Comus* or Mask presented at *Ludlow* Castle,
like which Piece in the peculiar disposition of the Story,
the sweetness of the Numbers, the justness of the Expression, and the Moral it teaches, there is nothing
extant in any Language.   But to procede with the rest
of the Apology, he's in it very severe upon the Clergy,
not only because in his Judgment he condemn'd several
of their Maxims, but also provok'd by the ill usage he
receiv'd.   Certainly nothing more barbarous and inhuman ever proceded from the mouth of Pope or Mufti,
than this saying of his Antagonist, " You that love
" Christ, and know this miscreant Wretch, stone him
" to death, lest **you** smart for his Impunity.   No
wonder that so many are scandaliz'd when they find
the name of Christ most impudently alleg'd to countenance such devilish Practices, when there is nothing
more evident than that he expresly enjoin'd his Followers to forgive their Enemies, and not to pursue 'em
with the Spirit of Revenge, but rather to reclaim them
from their Errors, and to do 'em all the good they
could.   Our Author, on the other hand, carries his
Resentments, no doubt, too far, when the following

words could drop from his Pen. " There be such in
" the World, and I am among those, who nothing
" admire the Idol of a Bishoprick, and hold that it
" wants so much to be a Blessing, as that I rather deem
" it the merest, the falsest, the most unfortunat Gift of
" Fortune: and were the Punishment and Misery of
" being a Bishop terminated only in the Person, and
" did not extend to the Affliction of the whole Diocess,
" if I would wish anything in the bitterness of my Soul
" to an Enemy, I should wish him the biggest and
" fattest Bishoprick. If *Milton* had bin such a Saint
as never mist of a favorable answer to his Prayers, I
question not but at this rate more would covet to be his
Enemies than his Friends. Another mark of his good
Will to the Prelats is this unpardonable Simile. " A
" Bishop's Foot, says he, that has all its Toes (maugre
" the Gout) and a linnen sock over it, is the aptest
" Emblem of the Prelat himself; who, being a Pluralist,
" may under one Surplice hide four Benefices besides
" the great Metropolitan To which sends a foul stench
" to Heaven. And in another place he calls them,
" the Gulfs and Whirlpools of Benefices, but the dry
" Pits of all sound Doctrin. Agreeable to these
Flowers is his Description of Chaplains somwhere in
*Iconoclastes : * " Bishops or Presbyters we know, says he,
" and Deacons we know; but what are Chaplains ? In
" State perhaps they may be listed among the upper
" Serving men of som great Houshold, and be admitted
" to som such place as may stile them the Sewers or
" Yeomen-Ushers of Devotion, where the Master is
" too resty or too rich to say his own Prayers, or to bless
" his own Table. How much he lov'd to divert himself in this manner, we may perceive by his Apostrophe

to the Presbyterian Ministers, who were heavily branded
by King *Charles* the First, tho after his Death they
would fain be thought his very dutiful and good
Friends.   " O ye Ministers, says *Milton*, read here
" what work he makes among your Gallypots, your
" Balms and your Cordials; and not only your sweet
" Sippets in Widows Houses, but the huge Gobbets
" wherwith he charges you to have devour'd Houses
" and all.   Cry him up for a Saint in your Pulpits,
" while he crys you down for Atheists into Hell.   Nor
is he more merciful to the Liturgy than to the Readers
of it, as appears by this Character.   To contend that
" it is fantastical, if not sensless in som places, were a
" copious Argument, specially in the Responsories.
" For such Alternations as are there us'd must be by
" several Persons; but the Minister and the People
" cannot so sever their Interests as to sustain several
" Persons, he being the only mouth of the whole Body
" which he presents.   And if the People pray, he being
" silent, or they ask one thing and he another, it either
" changes the Property, making the Priest the People,
" and the People the Priest by turns, or else makes two
" Persons and two Bodies Representative where there
" should be but one: which if there were nothing else,
" must be a strange Quaintness in ordinary Prayer.
" The like or worse may be said of the Litany, wherin
" neither Priest nor People speak any entire Sense of
" themselves throout the whole (I know not what to
" name it) only by the timely Contribution of their
" parted stakes, closing up as it were the Schism of a
" slic'd Prayer, they pray not in vain; for by this means
" they keep Life between them in a piece of gasping
" Sense, and keep down the Sawciness of a continual

" rebounding Nonsense. And hence it is that as it has
" bin far from the imitation of any warranted Prayer,
" so we all know it has bin obvious to be the pattern of
" many a Jig. And he who has but read in good Books
" of Devotion, and no more, cannot be so either of Ear
" or Judgment unpractis'd to distinguish what is grave,
" pathetical, devout, and what not; but he will pre-
" sently perceive this Liturgy all over in conception
" lean and dry, of Affections emty and unmoving, of
" Passion, or any heighth wherto the Soul might soar
" upon the wings of Zeal, destitute and barren. Besides
" Errors, Tautologies, Impertinences, as those Thanks
" in the Woman's Churching for her delivery from
" Sunburning and Moonblasting, as if she had bin
" travelling, not in her Bed, but in the Deserts of *Arabia*.
" So that while som men cease not to admire the incom-
" parable Frame of our Liturgy, I cannot but admire as
" fast what they think is becom of Judgment and Taste
" in other men, that they can hope to be heard without
" Laughter. And if this were all, perhaps it were a
" compliable matter. But when we remember this
" our Liturgy, where we found it, whence we had
" it, and yet where we left it, still serving to all the
" Abominations of the Antichristian Temple, it may be
" wonder'd how we can demur whether it should be
" abolish'd or no, and not rather fear we have highly
" offended in using it so long. It has indeed bin pre-
" tended to be more antient than the Mass, but so little
" prov'd, that wheras other corrupt Liturgies have had
" such a seeming Antiquity, that their Publishers have
" ventur'd to ascribe them either to Saint *Peter*, St.
" *James*, St. *Mark*, or at least to *Chrysostom* or *Basil*,
" ours has bin never able to find either Age or Author

" allowable on whom to father those things which " therin are least offensive, except the two Creeds. I shall conclude my account of his Books concerning religious Controversies with this remarkable account of his reading in the Councils and Fathers of the Church. " Som years, says he, I had spent in the Stories of those " *Greec* and *Roman* Exploits, wherin I found many " things both nobly don and worthily spoken: when " coming in the method of time to that age wherin the " Church had obtain'd a *Christian* Emperor, I so pre- " par'd my self as being now to read Examples of " Wisdom and Goodness among those who were fore- " most in the Church, not elswhere to be parellel'd. " But to the amazement of what I expected, Readers, " I found it all quite contrary; excepting in som very " few, nothing but Ambition, Corruption, Contention, " Combustion: insomuch that I could not but love the " Historian *Socrates*, who in the Proem to his fifth Book " professes, he was fain to intermix Affairs of State, for " that it would be else an extreme annoyance to hear in " a continu'd Discourse the endless Brabbles and " Counterplottings of the Bishops. Finding therfore " the most of their Actions in particular to be weak and " yet turbulent, full of Strife and yet flat of Spirit, and " the sum of their best Councils there collected to be " most commonly in Questions either trivial and vain, " or else of short and easy decision, without that great " bustle which they made: I concluded that if their " single Ambition and Ignorance was such, then certainly " united in a Council it would be much more; and if " the compendious recital of what they there did was so " tedious and unprofitable, then surely to fit out the " whole extent of their tattle in a dozen Volumes,

" would be a loss of time irrecoverable. Besides that
" which I had read of St. *Martin*, who for his last sixteen
" years could never be persuaded to be at any Council
" of the Bishops; and *Gregory Nazianzen* betook him
" to the same resolution, affirming to *Procopius* that of
" any Council or Meeting of Bishops he never saw good
" end, nor any remedy therby of evil in the Church, but
" rather an increase: for, says he, their Contentions and
" Desire of Lording no Tongue is able to express.

In the year 1643, he chang'd his condition, and was
marry'd to *Mary* the Daughter of *Richard Powel* of
Forresthill in *Oxfordshire*, a Justice of the Peace, and a
man of good figure in that Country. But whether it
was that this young Woman, accustom'd to a large and
jovial Family, could not live in a Philosophical Retirement; or that she was not perfectly satisfy'd with the
Person of her Husband; or lastly, that, because her
Relations were all addicted to the Royal Interest, his
democratical Principles were disagreable to her Humor
(nor is it impossible that the Father repented of this
match upon the prospect of som Success on the King's
side, who then had his Headquarters at *Oxford*) or
whatever were the reason, 'tis certain that after he
enjoy'd her Company at *London* about a month, she was
invited by her Friends to spend the rest of the Summer
in the Country, to which he consented, on condition of
her return by *Michaelmas*. Yet he saw her not at the
time appointed, and, after receiving several of his
Letters without sending him any answer, she did at
length positively refuse to come, dismissing his Messenger with contemt. This usage incens'd him to that
degree, that he thought it against his Honor and Repose
to own her any longer for his Wife. He made that

time however as easy to himself as he might, somtimes
by keeping a gaudy day with his Friends, and at other
times in conversation with the Lady *Margaret Lee*,
Daughter to the Earl of *Marlborough*, whose sprightly
Wit and good Sense drew frequent Visits from him,
and for whom he had a singular esteem, which he has
left recorded by a Sonnet in her Praise among his other
occasional Poems.   He thought it now high time to
justify by proper Arguments the firm Resolution he had
taken of never receiving his Wife back again, and therfore in the year 1644, he publish'd his *Doctrin and
Disciplin of Divorce*, which he dedicated to the Parlament and to the Assembly of Divines, that as they
were busy then about the general Reformation of
the Kingdom, they might also take this particular case
of domestic Liberty into their consideration: for he
thought all the boasted Freedom of public Judicatures
signify'd little, if in the mean while one must be
oblig'd to indure a kind of Servitude at home below the
Dignity of a Man.   " What thing, says he, is more
" instituted to the Solace and Delight of Man than
" Marriage ?   And yet the misinterpreting of som
" Scriptures, directed mainly against the Abusers of the
" Law for Divorce given by *Moses*, has chang'd the
" Blessing of Matrimony not seldom into a familiar and
" cohabiting Mischief; at least, into a drooping and
" disconsolat houshold Captivity, without Refuge or
" Redemtion.   So ungovern'd and so wild a race dos
" Superstition run us, from one Extreme of abus'd
" Liberty into the other of unmerciful Restraint!   Tho
" God in the first ordaining of Marriage taught us to
" what end he did it (the words expresly implying the
" apt and chearful Conversation of Man with Woman,

" to comfort and refresh him of the evil of a solitary
" Life; not mentioning the purpose of Generation till
" afterwards, as being but a secondary end in Dignity
" tho not in Necessity) yet now if any two be but once
" handed in the Church, and have tasted in any sort the
" nuptial Bed, let them find themselves never so mis-
" taken in their Dispositions thro any Error, Conceal-
" ment, or Misadventure; that thro their different
" Tempers, Thoughts, and Constitutions, they can
" neither be to one another a remedy against Loneliness,
" nor live in any Union or Contentment all their days:
" yet they shall (so they be but found sutably weapon'd
" to the least possibility of sensual Enjoyment) be
" made in spite of Antipathy to fadg together, and
" combine, as they may, to their unspeakable Weari-
" somness, and despair of all sociable Delight, in the
" Ordinance which God establish'd to that very end.
Then he largely shews all the unjust Sanctions concerning Marriage to be owing to the Superstition of
som antient Fathers, and to the design of promoting
the Gain or Authority of the Clergy, as they make a
part of the Canon Law: For the *Greecs*, the *Romans*, and
all civiliz'd Nations, did not only allow of Divorce upon
mutual Aversion or Consent; but in many other cases,
besides the violation of the nuptial Bed, there was a
Separation made on the Petition of one Party, tho the
other should not be willing. His purpose, in short, is
to shew that there are other sufficient Reasons for
Divorce besides Adultery; and that to prohibit any
sort of Divorce, but such as are excepted by *Moses*, is
unjust and against the Reason of the Law: in handling
which Heads he has, besides his Arguments from
Reason, had always a due care to explain those Passages

of Scripture which are thought to contradict his Opinion. The grand Position he maintains is, That *Indisposition, Unfitness, or contrary Humors, proceding from any unchangable cause in Nature, hindring and always likely to hinder the main ends and benefits of conjugal Society* (*that is to say, Peace and Delight*) *are greater Reasons of Divorce than ADULTERY or natural FRI-GIDITY, provided there be a mutual Consent for Separation.* And indeed it seems to be a perfect Tyranny to oblige a Man or Woman beyond the design of their Covenant: nor should they, who never try'd this condition together, be hinder'd from discretely and orderly undoing it, when they find things otherwise than they promis'd themselves; no more than in any other bargain People are punish'd for unwilful Ignorance: since, whenever both Parties are willing, they may draw back their stakes, and leave matters as they were before, or compound for the Damages that may be don. It seems likewise to me very gross, that in Lawmaking (particularly in the Canon Law) a regard should be had to the fit Disposition of the marry'd Couples Bodies, and no consideration of the Agreableness of their Minds, when the Charms of the latter are often the greatest inducements to the conjunction of the former. And since no Man or Woman can be secure of true Information from others, nor infallible in their own Observations upon one another's Humors and Conditions (specially since they are not admitted to a requisit Familiarity for such an inquiry before Marriage) it is the hardest thing in the world that no Clauses should be provided for cases of this nature. As for the common Objection, that Marriage is a Remedy against Fornication and Adultery, I grant it to be most true, if the Parties mutually love; but if it be a forc'd Compact, or afterwards dislik'd, it is so far from producing this good effect, that we clearly see by constant Experience (and Reason may convince us all of it) that such a fatal Knot exposes Men and Women to various Temtations, breaks the Peace of Families, exposes the Reputation of the Children, and disturbs or destroys all the Duties of Society. Nor dos it answer the first Institution which supposes it was not good for Man to be alone, since every body would rather chuse to be alone than be forc'd to keep bad Company. To conclude, Marriage certainly, like all other Contracts, was ordain'd for the benefit of Man, and not Man created for Marriage; wherfore it ought to be suted to his Convenience and Happiness, and not be made a Snare to render him uneasy or miserable. No Pretences can be drawn from this Opinion to favor Libertinism, but on the contrary, the Conduct of the Opposers of it may be terribly hamper'd with infamous Consequences, on which we shall not insist in this place, referring the curious to *Milton's* own Book. As for the Popish and ridiculous practice in certain Spiritual Courts, of separating People from bed and board (which any Couple may agree to do themselves) and refusing 'em the liberty of marrying more for their convenience (if the civil Power dos not interpose for their Relief) I shall have a more proper opportunity to shew the Mischief and Unreasonableness of it.

On the first appearing of this Book, the Clergy did generally declaim against it, and fix'd upon the Author the usual Reproaches of Atheism, Heresy, Leudness, and what not? They daily instigated the Parlament, which little minded their Clamors, to pass their Censure on it; and at last one of them in a Sermon before that august Assembly, on a day of Humiliation, roundly told them that there was a wicked Book abroad which deserv'd to be burnt, and that among their other Sins they ought to repent it had not yet bin branded with a mark of their Displeasure. This man's main accusation being, that *Milton* taught other causes of Divorce than were mention'd by Christ and his Apostles, which was also urg'd against him at the same time by som others, he publish'd the *Tetrachordon*, dedicated to the Parlament, or his Exposition of the four chief Passages of Scripture that treat of Marriage, and the nullifying of the same, namely *Gen. 1. 27, &c. Gen. 2. 18, &c. Deut. 24. 1, &c. Mat. 5. 31, &c.* and *Mat. 29. 3, &c.* Other places out of the Epistles he also occasionally explains; he alleges the Authority of those great Men who favor'd his Opinion, sets down the determination of the Imperial Laws, with more proofs that are usual in such cases. On this Book our Author himself made the following lines:

> I did but promt the Age to quit their Clogs
> > By the known Rules of antient Liberty,
> > When straight a barbarous Noise environs me
> > Of Owls, and Cuckoos, Asses, Apes, and Dogs:
> As when those Hinds that were transform'd to Frogs
> > Rail'd at *Latona's* twinborn Progeny,
> > Which after held the Sun and Moon in fee.
> > But this is got by casting Pearls to Hogs,
> That baul for Freedom in their sensless mood,
> > And still revolt when Truth would set them free.
> > Licence they mean, when they cry Liberty;
> For who loves that, must first be wise and good:
> > But from that mark how far they roave we see,
> > For all this waste of Wealth and loss of Blood.

The next piece he publish'd on this Subject was *the Judgment of the famous Reformer* Martin Bucer *touching Divorce*, extracted out of the second Book of the Kingdom of Christ, dedicated to King *Edward* the Sixth. He exactly agrees with *Milton*, tho the latter had not seen this Book till after the publication of his own. He also shews very fairly, that *Paulus Fagius* the Associat of *Bucer*, that *Peter Martyr*, *Erasmus*, and *Grotius*, did teach the same Doctrin, that he might stop the mouths of such as were determin'd more by these Names than by all the light of Reason or Scripture; and that he might not appear to be call'd an Atheist or Libertin with more reason than these Persons, who notwithstanding they had affirm'd as much as he, were yet generally counted very sober and pious.

The fourth Book he wrote relating to Divorce was his *Colasterion*, being a Reply to one of his Answerers, who, to all the Dulness and Ignorance imaginable, added the highest Bitterness and Malice: so far from tolerably understanding any of the learned Languages (as in som secondhand Quotations he would be thought to do) that he could not rightly spell what he so meanly stole. Yet this rude Invective must be licens'd by Mr. *Carryl*, the same who in his voluminous and sensless Comments did more injury to the memory of *Job*, than the Devil and the *Sabeans* could inflict Torments on him in his life time. But, not content to prefix his *Imprimatur*, he pronounces his Judgment too against *Milton*, which was a most unworthy treatment of him from these men, of whom he deserv'd so well by his former Writings against their Enemies the Bishops; tho, to speak the truth, this was only a service to the Presbyterians by accident: for, as we shall see hereafter, he never intended by humbling the Hierarchy, to set up the Consistorian Tribunal in the room of it. However, the following Reproach was extorted from him by their base Ingratitude. " Mr. Licenser, says " he, you are reputed a man discrete enough, religious " enough, honest enough, that is, to an ordinary com- " petence in all these: But now your turn is to hear " what your own hand has earn'd you, that when you " suffer'd this nameless Hangman to cast into public " such a spiteful Contumely upon a Name and Person " deserving of the Church and State equally to your " self, and one who has don more to the present " advancement of your own Tribe, than you or many " of them have don for themselves; you forgot to be " either honest, religious, or discrete. Whatever the " State might do concerning it, supposing it were a " matter to expect evil from it, I should not doubt to " meet among them with wise, and honorable, and " knowing men. But as to this brute Libel, so much " the more impudent and lawless for the abus'd Author- " ity which it bears, I say again, that I abominat the " Censure of Rascals and their Licensers. These are all the Pieces concerning Divorce written by *Milton*, whose Arguments ought not to be esteem'd the less cogent, because occasion'd by his domestic Uneasiness; when this reason would equally enervat the Apologies exhibited for Christianity under its Persecutors, and frustrat all the noble Treatises of Civil Government, for which we are beholding to the Lawlesness of Tyrants or Usurpers; witness the incomparable and golden Discourses of that Heroic Patron of Liberty, *Algernon Sidney*. And indeed the best Books we have on any Subject, are such as were oppos'd to the prevalency

of the contrary opinion: for as he that was forc'd to
pass som part of his time in the Regions of extreme
Heat or Cold, can best value the Blessings of a temperat
Country; so none can be so well furnish'd with Arguments for a good Cause, like such as were Sufferers
under a bad one; the Writings of unconcern'd and
retir'd Persons being either an Exercise of their Parts,
and the Amusements of idle time, or, what is worse,
pitiful Declamations without any Force, Experience, or
Vivacity.

About this time he wrote a small piece of *Education*
to *Samuel Hartlib*, looking upon the right Institution
of Children to be the Nursery of all true Liberty or
Virtue; and of whatsoever in Government is good and
wise, or in privat practice amiable and worthy.

The next Book he wrote was his *Areopagitica*, or an
Oration to the Parlament of *England* for the liberty of
Unlicens'd Printing, in which he proves that the
Republics of *Greece* and *Italy* never censur'd any but
immoral, defamatory, or atheistical Pieces. Nor was it
by Inferences and Insinuations they were to judg of
Atheism; for they never supprest the Writings of the
Epicureans, nor such other Books denying even the
Doctrins of Providence, and the future State: but it
must have bin a formal doubt or denial of the being of a
Deity. Yet it is beyond contradiction, that those
Nations maintain'd an excellent Government, dis-
tributing public and privat Justice, and abounding in
all Knowlege and Virtue, infinitly above those who have
bin ever since the most rigid Purgers, Corrupters, or
Executioners of Books. The *Roman* Emperors were
Tyrants, and none but such as would imitat them,
should quote their Examples. The Primitive Christians

observ'd no Uniformity of Conduct in this Affair. At
first they were for reading all the Works of the *Gentils*,
but none of those they reckon'd Heretical among themselves; after this they were only for confuting the
Books of the Heretics, and suppressing those of the
Gentils, even such as did not in the least concern
Religion: for about the year 400, in a *Carthaginian*
Council, the very Bishops were prohibited the reading
of Heathen Authors. Had this infamous and barbarous
Resolution bin throly executed (for it had but too much
effect) to what a degree of Ignorance and meanness of
Spirit it would have reduc'd the World, depriving it of
so many inimitable Historians, Orators, Philosophers,
and Poets, the Repositories of inestimable Treasure,
consisting of warlike and heroic Deeds, the best and
wisest Arts of Government, the most perfect Rules and
Examples of Eloquence or Politeness, and such divine
Lectures of Wisdom and Virtue, that the loss of *Cicero's*
Works alone, or those of *Livy*, could not be repair'd by
all the Fathers of the Church. In process of time, when
the Clergy begun to be exalted even above the supreme
Magistrat himself, they burnt and destroy'd every thing
that did not favor their Power or Superstition, and laid
a restraint on Reading as well as Writing, without
excepting the very Bible; and thus they proceded till the
Inquisition reduc'd this abominable practice to the
perfection of an Art by expurgatory Indexes and
Licensing. All the consequences of this Tyranny, as
depriving men of their natural Liberty, stifling their
Parts, introducing of Ignorance, ingrossing all Advantages to one Party, and the like, were perpetually
objected before the Civil Wars by the Presbyterians to
the Bishops; but no sooner were they possest of the

Bishops Pulpits and Power, than they exercis'd the same Authority with more intolerable Rigor and Severity. *Milton*, after shewing the Origin, Progress, and Mischief of this Custom, proves first that we must not read the Bible, the Fathers, nor almost any sort of Books, if we regard the Reasons usually alleg'd to forbid the publishing of others, such as the fear of wresting or mistaking their meaning. Secondly, that the ends propos'd cannot be attain'd after this manner. And, Thirdly, that no man is fit to be a Licenser, not in any one single Faculty, unless he is universally learn'd, or a better Scholar than all the Authors whose Labors he's to license: and that, granting these things possible (tho they are not so) he could neither find strength nor time enough for perusing all Books; and should he use Deputies, he's likeliest to have ignorant, lazy, and mercenary Fellows. Then displaying the Discouragement that must follow hence to all Literature and new Discoveries (with the danger of suppressing Truth, and propagating Error, as it happens in Popish Countries, and the not reprinting of antient Authors in any Language) he proves Licensing to be both unjust in it self, and dishonorable to a free Government. " To " include the whole Nation, says he, and those that " never yet thus offended, under such a diffident and " suspectful Prohibition, what a disparagement it is " may be plainly understood. So much the more, since " Debtors and Delinquents may walk abroad without a " Keeper, but inoffensive Books must not stir forth " without a visible Jailor in their Title. Nor is it to " the common People less than a Reproach; for if we " be so jealous over them, as that we dare not trust them " with an English Pamphlet, what do we but censure

I

" them for a giddy, vitious, and ungrounded People,
" in such a sick and weak state of Faith and Discretion,
" as to be able to take nothing but thro the Glisterpipe
" of a Licenser ? That this is any care or love of them,
" we cannot pretend, since in those Popish Places,
" where the Laity are most hated and despis'd, the same
" strictness is us'd over them. Wisdom we cannot call
" it, because it stops but one breach of License; nor
" that neither, seeing those Corruptions, which it seeks
" to prevent, break in faster at other doors which cannot
" be shut. And it reflects on the Reputation of our
" Ministers also, of whose Labors we should hope
" better, and of the Proficiency which their Flocks reap
" by them, than that after all this light of the Gospel
" which is, and is to be, and after all this continual
" Preaching, they should be still frequented with such
" an unprincipl'd, unedify'd, and Laic Rabble, as that
" the whif of every new Pamphlet should stagger them
" out of their Catechism. This may have much reason
" to discourage the Ministers, when such a low conceit
" is had of all their Exhortations and the benefiting of
" their Hearers, that they are not thought fit to be
" turn'd loose to three Sheets of Paper without a
" Licenser. In another place he says, " A man may
" be a Heretic in the Truth; and if he believes only
" because his Pastor says so, or the Assembly so deter-
" mins, without knowing any other Reason: tho his
" Belief be true, yet the very Truth he holds becoms
" his Heresy. There is not any burden that som would
" gladlier put off to another, than the charge and care
" of their Religion. Who knows not that there be som
" **Protestants who live in as arrant an implicit Faith as**
" **any Lay-Papist of** *Loretto ?* A wealthy man, addicted

" to his Pleasures and his Profit, finds Religion to be a
" Traffic so intangl'd, and of so many pidling accounts,
" that of all Mysteries he cannot endure to keep a
" stock going upon that trade. What dos he therfore,
" but resolves to give over toiling, and to find out som
" Factor to whose care and credit he may commit the
" whole management of his religious Affairs; and that
" must be som Divine of Note and Estimation. To
" him he adheres, resigns the whole Warehouse of his
" Religion with all the Locks and Keys into his custody;
" and indeed makes the very Person of that Man his
" Religion, esteems his associating with him a sufficient
" evidence and commendation of his own Piety. So
" that a man may say his Religion is now no more
" within himself, but is becom a dividual movable, and
" gos and coms near him according as that good man
" frequents the House. He entertains him, gives him
" Gifts, feasts him, lodges him; his Religion coms
" home at night, prays, is liberally sup'd, and sum-
" tuously laid to sleep; rises, is saluted, and (after the
" Malmsy or som well-spic'd Brewage, and better
" breakfasted than he whose Morning-appetite would
" have gladly fed on green Figs between *Bethany* and
" *Jerusalem*) his Religion walks abroad at eight, and
" leaves his kind Entertainer in the Shop trading all
" day without his Religion. Another sort there be,
" who, when they hear that all things shall be order'd,
" all things regulated and settled, nothing written
" but what passes thro the Customhouse of certain
" Publicans that have the tunnaging and poundaging
" of all freespoken Truth, will straight give themselves
" up into your hands, make 'em and cut 'em out what
" Religion you please; there be Delights, there be

" Recreations, and jolly Pastimes that will fetch the day
" about from Sun to Sun, and rock the tedious year as
" in a delightful dream.   What need they torture their
" heads with that which others have taken so strictly
" and so unalterably into their own purveying ?   These
" are the Fruits which a dull Ease and Cessation of our
" Knowlege will bring forth among the People.   Nor
" much better will be the consequence among the
" Clergy themselves.   It is no new thing never heard
" of before for a Parochial Minister, who has his
" Reward, and is at his *Hercules* Pillars in a warm
" Benefice, to be easily inclinable (if he has nothing
" else that may rouse up his Studies) to finish his Circuit
" in an English Concordance and Topic Folio, the
" Gatherings and Sayings of a sober Graduatship, a
" Harmony and a Catena, treading the constant round
" of certain common doctrinal Heads, attended with
" their Uses, Motives, Marks, and Means;   out of
" which, as out of an Alphabet or sol fa mi, by forming
" and transforming, joining and disjoining variously a
" little Bookcraft, and two hours Meditation, he might
" furnish himself unspeakably to the performance of
" more than a weekly charge of Sermoning: not to
" reckon up the infinit helps of Interlineries, Brevi-
" aries, Synopses, and other loitring gear.   But, as for
" the multitude of Sermons already printed on every
" Text that is not difficult, he need never fear penury of
" Pulpit Provision;   yet if his Rear and Flanks be not
" impal'd, if his backdoor be not secur'd by the rigid
" Licenser, but that a bold Book may now and then
" issue forth and give the assault to som of his old
" Collections in their trenches, it will concern him to
" keep waking, to stand in watch, to set good Guards

" and Sentinels about his receiv'd Opinions, to walk the
" round and counterround with his Fellow-Inspectors,
" fearing lest any of his Flock be seduc'd, who also then
" would be better instructed, better exercis'd and dis-
" ciplin'd. And God send that the fear of this Dili-
" gence, which must then be us'd, do not make us
" affect the laziness of a licensing Church. Such was
the effect of our Author's *Areopagitica*, that the following
year *Mabol*, a Licenser, offer'd Reasons against Licensing; and, at his own request, was discharg'd that
Office. And certainly there's nothing deserves more
wonder, than that any wise People should suffer a small
number of injudicious Fellows, always ready to suppress whatever is not relish'd by their own Sect or the
Magistrat, to be the sole Masters and Judges of what
should or should not be printed; that is, of what the
Nation is to know, speak, or understand : and I need not
hesitat to affirm that such a Power in the hands of any
Prince (the Licensers being always his Creatures) is more
dangerous even than a standing Army to Civil Liberty;
nor in point of Religion is it inferior to the Inquisition.

But to return to his privat Affairs, lest he might seem
by his several Treatises of Divorce not to act from an
intire Conviction, but out of sudden Resentment, or to
shew his Parts in maintaining a Paradox, he was
seriously treating a Marriage with a young Lady of
great Wit and Beauty, when one day as he was at a
Relations house whom he often visited, he was extremely
surpriz'd to find his Wife (whom he thought never to
have seen more) acknowleging her fault at his feet, and
begging Forgiveness with tears. At first he seem'd inexorable, but his own Generosity, and the intercession
of Friends, soon procur'd a perfect Reconciliation,

with an act of Oblivion for all that was past. The first fruit of her return was a Girl, born within a year after: And so far was he from remembring former Provocations, that the King's Interest in every place visibly declining, he receiv'd his Wives Father and Mother, several of her Sisters and Brothers into his own House, where they had Protection and free Entertainment till their Affairs were in a better condition. And now both his own Father dying, and his Wives Relations returning to their several Habitations, he reviv'd his Academic Institution of som young Gentlemen, with a design, perhaps, of putting in practice the model of Education lately publish'd by himself. Yet this course was of no long continuance; for he was to be made Adjutant General to Sir *William Waller*, but that the new modelling of the Army soon following, and Sir *William* turning cat in pan, this design was frustrated.

A little after *Fairfax* and *Cromwell* had march'd thro the City with the whole Army to quell the Insurrection of *Brown* and *Massy*, now grown discontented likewise with the Parlament, our Author chang'd his great House for one more accomodated to his Circumstances, where in the midst of all the noise and confusion of Arms, he led a quiet and privat Life, wholly delighted with the Muses, and prosecuting his indefatigable search after useful and solid Knowlege.

Having occasionally mention'd that Great man General *Fairfax*, I shall subjoin here, because it is not printed among his other Poems, a Sonnet our Author sent him:

> *Fairfax*, whose Name in Arms thro *Europe* rings,
> And fills all mouths with Envy or with Praise,
> And all her jealous Monarchs with Amaze,
> And Rumors loud which daunt remotest things:

Thy firm unshaken Valor ever brings
    Victory home, while new Rebellions raise
    Their *Hydra* Heads, and the false *North* displays
    Her broken League to imp her Serpent Wings.
O yet a nobler task awaits thy hand,
    For what can War but Acts of War still breed,
    Till injur'd Truth from Violence be freed,
And public Faith be rescu'd from the brand
    Of public Fraud ? In vain dos Valor bleed,
    While Avarice and Rapine share the Land.

The following lines, never likewise publish'd among
his Poems, he wrote on Sir *Henry Vane* the Younger:

Vane, young in years, but in sage Counsils old,
    Than whom a better Senator ne'er held
    The Helm of *Rome* (when Gowns not Arms repel'd
    The fierce *Epirot*, and the *African* bold)
Whether to settle Peace, or to unfold
    The drift of hollow States, hard to be spel'd.
    Then, to advise how War may best b'upheld,
    Man'd by her two main Nerves, Iron and Gold,
In all her Equipage: Besides to know
    Both spiritual and civil, what each means,
    What serves each thou hast learn'd, which few have don.
The bounds of either Sword to thee we ow;
    Therfore on thy right hand Religion leans,
    And reckons thee in chief her eldest Son.

But after *Charles* the First (somtime before judg'd
an Enemy by the Parlament) was made a Prisoner by
their victorious Army, afterwards judicially try'd and
condemn'd, and the form of the Government was
chang'd into a Democracy or Free State, the Presbyterian Ministers, who from the beginning were the
King's mortal Enemies, but now inrag'd that the
Independents and other Sects should enjoy either

Liberty or Life (not angry at the Fact but the Faction)
did tragically declaim in their Pulpits, that the King's
Usage was very hard, that his Person was sacred and
inviolable, and that any Violence offer'd to him in the
field (much less by the hands of an Executioner) was
contrary to the Doctrin of the Reform'd Churches.
This oblig'd *Milton* in the year 49, to write his *Tenure
of Kings and Magistrats*, wherin he labors to prove that
it is not only in it self a most equitable thing, but that
it has also bin so esteem'd by the free and considering
part of Mankind in all ages, that such as had the Power
might call a Tyrant to account for his Maladministration, and after due Conviction to depose or put him to
death, according to the nature of his Crimes: And
further shews, that if the ordinary Magistrats of any
Nation refuse to do 'em this justice, that then the duty
of Self-preservation, and the good of the whole (which
is the supreme Law) impowers the People to deliver
themselves from Slavery by the safest and most effectual
methods they can. As for the Presbyterians, who were
then grown so tender of Majesty (and that only because
they could not, absolutely and exclusively of others,
govern all mens Persons and Consciences) he evidently
shews that they were the most zealous to take arms
against the King, to devest and disanoint him of his
Dignity, nay to curse him in all their Sermons and
Pamphlets over the Kingdom (wherof there remain
numerous Monuments still to be produc'd) that, in a
word, after they had join'd with others to a degree from
which Men of Honor or Prudence could not retreat,
they were louder than the Cavaliers themselves to cry
Disloyalty and Treason. After proving at large that
they broke their Allegiance to him, obey'd another

Authority, and had often given Commission to slay
where they knew his Person could not be exempt from
danger; and where, if chance or flight had not sav'd
him like others, he must be infallibly kil'd, he shews
how ridiculously it became them to pretend a tenderness
for his Person or Character; whereas indeed it was
neither Persuasion nor Remorse, but their aversion to
civil and religious Liberty that hurry'd 'em to these
extremes. But because I hope the bulk of those now
cal'd *Presbyterians* in *England*, som few leading Men
excepted, are no such Enemies to a Toleration, and
that they understand no more of the Consistorian,
Classical, or Synodical Judicatories, than they allow of
the Inquisition or a Hierarchy, I shall in this place to
disabuse 'em, and to let 'em see how much better others
foresaw their Fate than Passion would suffer themselves
at that time, insert the following Passage: " As for the
" Party cal'd *Presbyterian*, says *Milton*, of whom I
" believe very many to be good and faithful Christians,
" tho misled by some of turbulent Spirit, I wish them
" earnestly and calmly not to fall off from their first
" Principles, nor to affect Rigor and Superiority over
" Men not under them; not to compel unforcible
" things in Religion especially, which if not voluntary,
" becomes a Sin; nor to assist the Clamor and malicious
" Drifts of those whom they themselves have judg'd to
" be the worst of Men, the obdurate Enemies of God
" and his Church: nor to dart against the Actions of
" their Brethren, for want of other Argument, those
" wrested Laws and Scriptures thrown by Prelats and
" Malignants against their own sides, which tho they
" hurt not otherwise, yet taken up by them to the Con-
" demnation of their own doings, give scandal to all

" Men, and discover in themselves either extreme
" Passion or Apostacy. Let them not oppose their best
" Friends and Associats who molest 'em not at all,
" infringe not the least of their Liberties, unless they
" call it their Liberty to bind other Mens Consciences,
" but are still seeking to live at peace with them, and
" brotherly Accord. Let them beware an old and per-
" fect Enemy, who tho he hopes by sowing Discord to
" make them his Instruments, yet cannot forbear a
" minute the open threatning of his destin'd Revenge
" upon them, when they have serv'd his Purposes. Let
" them fear therfore, if they be wise, rather what they
" have don already, than what remains to do; and be
" warn'd in time that they put no confidence in Princes
" whom they have provok'd, lest they be added to the
" Examples of those that miserably have tasted of the
" Event. —I have something also to the Divines, tho
" brief to what were needful, not to be Disturbers of the
" Civil Affairs, being in hands better able, and to whom
" it more belongs to manage them; but to study harder,
" and to attend the Office of good Pastors, not per-
" form'd by mounting twice into the Chair with a
" formal Preachment huddl'd up at the odd hours of a
" whole lazy Week, but by incessant pains and watch-
" ing—which if they well consider'd, how little leisure
" would they find to be the most pragmatical Sidesmen
" of every popular Tumult and Sedition ? And all this
" while they are to learn what the true end and reason
" is of the Gospel which they teach, and what a world
" it differs from the censorious and supercilious lording
" over Conscience. It would be good also they liv'd so
" as might persuade the People they hated Covetous-
" ness, which, worse than Heresy, is Idolatry; hated

" Pluralities and all kind of Simony; left rambling
" from Benefice to Benefice, like ravenous Wolves,
" seeking where they may devour the biggest.   Let
" them be sorry that, being cal'd to assemble about
" reforming the Church, they fell to progging and
" solliciting the Parlament (tho they had renounc'd the
" name of Priests) for a new settling of their Tithes
" and Oblations, and doublelin'd themselves with
" spiritual places of Commodity beyond the possible
" discharge of their Duty.   Let them assemble in
" Consistory with their Elders and Deacons to the
" preserving of Church-Disciplin each in his several
" charge, and not a pack of Clergymen by themselves
" to bellychear in their presumptuous *Sion* ; or to pro-
" mote designs to abuse and gull the simple Laity, to
" stir up Tumults, as the Prelats did before them, for
" the Maintenance of their Pride and Avarice.   On
this occasion I must remark, that by reason of the
Presbyterians warmly joining with others the last Parliament to promote Penal Laws against the *Socinians*, I
find few People will believe that those in *England* differ
from their Brethren in *Scotland* about Persecution, nor
that their own Sufferings of late have made 'em more
tender to the Consciences of others.   This naturally
leads Men to think that they have not repented of their
Rigor in the Civil Wars; and that should the Dissenters
once more get the Secular Sword into their hands, they
would press Uniformity of Sentiments in Religion as
far as any other Protestants or Papists ever yet have
don: witness their inhuman Treatment of *Daniel
Williams* (a sober man and a judicious Divine) for no
cause that I can discern, but that he made Christianity
plainer than som of his Collegues in the Ministry,

and that, it may be, he takes a greater latitude
than such as thro their ignorance cannot, or will not
from design.   But what renders them most suspected
of affecting Dominion, is the Project of Comprehension
now on foot, whereof som men of figure among 'em
seem to be so fond, whereby the rest are easily deceiv'd,
and like to be left in the lurch by certain Persons who
for several years past made the Hierarchy and Liturgy
such strange Bugbears: tho, if the Church will please
to becom a kind Mother to themselves, and shew a
little complaisance for their old Friends, they are ready
to pronounce her Orders, her Prayers, and her Ceremonies to be very innocent and harmless things; but
mistaken formerly for the Pillars of Antichrist, the
Symbols of Idolatry, the Dregs of Popery, the Rags of
Superstition, and Protestant Paint to hide the Defor-
mities of the old *Babylonish* Whore.   And after all,
whatever ours may be, Comprehension in all other
places of the World has never bin any thing else but
the Combination of a few Parties to fortify themselves,
and to oppress all others by their united Force, or by
an absolute Exclusion from Preferment, and other
Advantages to which by Nature or personal Merit they
had an equal claim with the rest of their Fellow-
Citizens.   Tho to be persecuted in their turn is the just
Judgment of God upon Persecutors, yet Vengeance
must be left to Heaven: and the Wishes of all good
Men are that the National Church, being secur'd in her
Worship and Emoluments, may not be allow'd to force
others to her Communion; and that all Dissenters from
it, being secur'd in their Liberty of Conscience, may
not be permitted to meddle with the Riches or Power of
the National Church.

After these things our Author thinking to have leisure enough for such an undertaking, apply'd himself intirely to the History of the *English* Nation, which he intended from the remotest traditional beginning to continue down to his own time, and had already finish'd four Books of the same, when neither courting nor expecting any such Preferment, he was taken into the Service of the New Commonwealth. Hitherto he gratuitously lent his Country the aid of his Pen, content with the esteem of good Men, and the internal Satisfaction of having perform'd his Duty; while others, that deserv'd it not so well, were variously rewarded, som with Riches, som with Honors, and all with Liberty. But the Publication of the *Tenure of Kings and Magistrats* reviving the fame of his other Books, and as well shewing the Excellency of his Stile and Capacity, as his Affection to the good old Cause, he was made Secretary to the Council of State for all foren Affairs: for the Republic scorn'd to acknowlege that sort of Tribute to any Prince in the World which is now paid to the *French* King, of managing their Matters only in his Language; and took up a noble Resolution, to which they firmly adher'd, that they would neither write to others, nor receive their Answers, except in the *Latin* Tongue, as being common to them all, and the properest in it self to contain great things, or the Subject of future Pens. But this Proceding could not be acceptable to those whose Transactions were asham'd or afraid to see the light, and whose Names will not be transmitted to Posterity, unless for dextrously cheating their own People, and laying the Springs of their Tyranny or Neglect in the dark, tho the Effects are sufficiently felt by their deluded Subjects, and the

Injustice visibly expos'd to all discerning eys. None could be found more fitted for such a Post than *Milton*, who quickly gain'd no less Reputation to himself than Credit to the State that imploy'd so able a Person. Of this the Letters he wrote under that and the succeeding Administrations (for he serv'd *Oliver*, *Richard*, and the *Rump*) are abundant evidence, being for different Reasons admir'd by Critics and Statesmen, as they are certain and authentic Materials for such as may hereafter write the History of those times.

But it was not only in foren Dispatches that the Government made use of his Pen; for just after the King's Death appear'd a Book under his Name, intitul'd, *Eikon Basilike*, wherin he vindicats himself in so many distinct Chapters from the chief Heads of those Tyrannies charg'd upon him by the People, either as occasions of the Civil War, or as Inhumanities committed during the same. This piece, like *Cesar*'s last Will, doing more execution upon the Enemy than its Author when alive, *Milton* was commanded to prevent by an Answer those ill effects the *Eikon Basilike* might produce. Having undertaken this task, he observes that Kings indeed have gain'd glorious Titles from their Flatterers or Favorers for writing against privat men, as our *Henry* the Eighth was stil'd *Defender of the Faith* for ingaging *Luther ;* yet that no man can expect much Honor by writing against a King, as not usually meeting with that force of Argument in such courtly Antagonists, which to confute might add to his fame. " Kings, says he, tho strong in Legions, are most " commonly but weak at Arguments. As they who " ever have accustom'd from the Cradle to use their " Will only as their right hand, their Reason always as

" their left: whence unexpectedly constrain'd to that
" kind of Combat, they prove but weak and puny
" Adversaries. Nevertheless, continues he, for their
" sakes, who thro Custom, Simplicity, or want of better
" teaching, have not more seriously consider'd Kings
" than in the gaudy name of Majesty, and admire them
" and their doings, as if they breath'd not the same
" Breath with other mortal men, I shall make no scruple
" to take up this Gauntlet, tho a Kings, in the behalf of
" Liberty and the Commonwealth. Having thus
accepted the Challenge, he fairly measures Weapons,
and answers all the Allegations of that Book beyond the
possibility of a Reply. But every Chapter of it ending
with Devotion, model'd into the form of a privat
Psalter, he once for all gives his judgment of it in these
words. " They, who so much admire the Archbishops
" late Breviary, and many other as good Manuals and
" Handmaids of Devotion, the Lipwork of every pre-
" latical Liturgist, clapt this together, and quilted it out
" of Scripture Phrase, with as much ease, and as little
" need of Christian Diligence or Judgment, as belongs
" to the compiling of any ordinary and salable piece of
" English Divinity that the Shops value. But he who
" from such a kind of Psalmistry, or any other verbal
" Devotion, without the pledg and earnest of sutable
" Deeds, can be persuaded of a Zeal and true Righteous-
" ness in the Person, has much yet to learn; and knows
" not that the deepest Policy of a Tyrant has bin ever to
" counterfeit Religion: and *Aristotle* in his Politics has
" mention'd that special Craft among twelve other
" tyrannical Sophisms. Neither want we Examples.
" *Andronicus Comnenus* the *Byzantin* Emperor, tho a
" most cruel Tyrant, is reported by *Nicetas* to have bin

" a constant Reader of St. *Paul*'s Epistles; and by
" continual Study had so incorporated the Phrase and
" Stile of that Apostle into all his familiar Letters, that
" the Imitation seem'd to vy with the Original. Then
having instanced our *Richard* the Third, to whom he
might have added *Tarquin* who built the stately
Temple of *Jupiter Capitolinus*, and the *Russian Basilo-
witz* that pray'd seven times a day, he discovers a piece
of Royal Plagiarism, or (to be more charitable) of his
Chaplains Priestcraft; for one of King *Charles*'s
Prayers, stil'd *a Prayer in the time of Captivity*, deliver'd
by himself to Dr. *Juxon*, and twice printed among his
Works in Folio, is plainly stolen and taken without any
considerable Variation from the mouth of *Pamela*, an
imaginary Lady, to a Heathen Deity in Sir *Philip
Sidney*'s *Arcadia*. This has bin mention'd by others
after *Milton*, and those Prayers laid parallel together on
divers occasions. One of *Milton*'s Sagacity could not
but perceive by the Composition, Stile, and timing of
this Book, that it was rather the production of som idle
Clergyman, than the Work of a distrest Prince, either
in perpetual hurry at the head of a flying Army, or
remov'd from one Prison to another during his unfortunat Captivity till his Death. Besides the Theological
Phrases frequently interspers'd, there are such fanciful
Allusions and bold Comments in it upon the secret
Judgments of God, as smell rankly of a System or the
Pulpit. When he mentions the fate of the *Hothams*, by
whom he was repuls'd at *Hull*, he says of the Father,
*That his Head was divided from his Body, because his
Heart was divided from the King ; and that two Heads
were cut off in one Family for affronting the Head of the
Commonwealth ; the eldest Son being infected with the Sin*

of the Father, against the Father of his Country. These and such Arguments drawn only from the Book it self, without any further light, induc'd a great many at that time to suspect the Imposture; and that because *Cromwel* got such a Reputation among the People for his suppos'd Piety, the Royalists would represent the King to be a wiser Man and better Christian. But in the year 1686, Mr. *Millington* happening to sell the late Lord *Anglesey's* Library by Auction, put up an *Eikon Basilike* ; and a few bidding very low for it, he had leisure to turn over the Leaves, when to his great Surprize he perceiv'd written with the same noble Lords own hand the following *Memorandum :*

King Charles *the Second, and the Duke of* York, *did both (in the last Sessions of Parlament,* 1675. *when I shew'd them in the Lords House the written Copy of this Book, wherin are som Corrections and Alterations written with the late King* Charles *the First's own hand) assure me, that this was none of the said King's compiling, but made by Dr.* Gauden *Bishop of* Exeter: *which I here insert for the undeceiving of others in this point, by attesting so much under my own hand.*

ANGLESEY.

This occasion'd the World to talk; and several knowing the Relation which the late Dr. *Anthony Walker* an *Essex*-Divine had to Bishop *Gauden*, they inquir'd of him what he knew concerning this Subject, which he then verbally communicated to them: but being afterwards highly provok'd by Dr. *Hollingworth's* harsh and injurious Reflections, he was oblig'd in his own defence to print an account of that Book, wherin are sufficient Answers to all the Scruples or Objections that can be made, and wherof I here insert an exact Epitome. He tells us in the first place that Dr. *Gauden* was pleas'd to

K

acquaint him with the whole design, and shew'd him
the Heads of divers Chapters, with som others that were
quite finish'd: and that Dr. *Gauden* asking his opinion
of the thing, and he declaring his Dissatisfaction that
the World should be so impos'd upon, *Gauden* bid him
look on the Title, which was *the King's Portraiture ;* for
that no man is suppos'd to draw his own Picture. A
very nice Evasion! He further acquaints us, that som
time after this, being both in *London*, and having din'd
together, Dr. *Gauden* took him along with him to Dr.
Duppa the Bishop of *Salisbury* (whom he made also
privy to his design) to fetch what Papers he had left
before for his Perusal, or to shew him what he had since
written: and that upon their return from that place,
after *Gauden* and *Duppa* were a while in privat together,
the former told him the Bishop of *Salisbury* wish'd he
had thought upon two other Heads, the Ordinance
against the Common-Prayer-Book, and the denying his
Majesty the attendance of his Chaplains; but that
Duppa desir'd him to finish the rest, and he would take
upon him to write two Chapters on those Subjects,
which accordingly he did. The reason, it seems, why
Dr. *Gauden* himself would not perform this, was, first,
that during the Troubles he had forborn the use of the
Liturgy, which he did not extraordinarily admire; and,
Secondly, that he had never bin the King's Chaplain,
wheras Dr. *Duppa* was both his Chaplain, his Tutor,
and a Bishop, which made him more concern'd about
these Particulars. Thirdly, Dr. *Walker* informs us that
Dr. *Gauden* told him he had sent a Copy of *Eikon
Basilike* by the Marquiss of *Hartford* to the King in the
Ile of Wight ; where it was, we may be sure, that he
made those Corrections and Alterations with his own

Pen, mention'd in my Lord *Anglesey's Memorandum :* and which gave occasion to som then about him that had accidentally seen, or to whom he had shown the Book, to believe the whole was his own. Fourthly, Dr. *Gauden*, after the Restoration, told Dr. *Walker*, that the Duke of *York* knew of his being the real Author, and had own'd it to be a great service; in consideration of which, it may be, the Bishoprick of *Winchester*, tho he was afterwards put off with that of *Worcester*, was promis'd him. And, notwithstanding it was then a Secret, we now know that in expectation of this Translation, the great House on *Clapham*-Common was built indeed in the name of his Brother Sir *Denis*, but really to be a Mansionhouse for the Bishops of *Winchester*. Fifthly, Dr. *Walker* says, that Mr. *Gauden* the Doctor's Son, his Wife, himself, and Mr. *Gifford* who transcrib'd it, did believe it as firmly as any fact don in the place where they were; and that in that Family they always spoke of it among themselves (whether in Dr. *Gauden's* Presence or Absence) as undoubtedly written by him, which he never contradicted. We learn, Sixthly, that Dr. *Gauden*, after part of it was printed, gave to Dr. *Walker* with his own hand what was last sent to *London;* and after shewing him what it was, seal'd it, giving him cautionary Directions how to deliver it, which he did on Saturday the 23d of *December*, 1648. for Mr. *Royston* the Printer, to Mr. *Peacock* Brother to Dr. *Gauden's* Steward, who, after the Impression was finish'd, gave him, for his trouble, six Books, wherof he always kept one by him. To these Particulars Dr. *Walker* adds that the Reason why the Covenant is more favorably mention'd in *Eikon Basilike*, than the King or any other of his Party would do, was because Dr. *Gauden* himself

had taken it; That in the devotional part of this
Book there occur several Expressions which were
habitual to Dr. *Gauden* in his Prayers, which always in
privat and public were conceiv'd or extemporary: and
that to his knowlege it was Dr. *Gauden*, being best
acquainted with the Beauty of his own Sayings, who
made that Collection of Sentences out of *Eikon Basilike*,
entitul'd, *Apophthegmata Caroliniana*. These and som
Observations about the same individual Persons variation of Stile on different Subjects, with the facility and
frequency of personating others, may be further consider'd in Dr. *Walker's* original account. In this condition stood the Reputation of this Book, till the last and
finishing discovery of the Imposture was made after
this manner. Mr. *Arthur North*, a Merchant now living
on *Towerhill*, *London*, a man of good Credit, and a
Member of the Church of *England*, marry'd the Sister
of her that was Wife to the Doctor's Son *Charles Gauden*,
who dying left som Papers with his Widow, among
which Mr. *North*, being concern'd about his Sister in
Law's Affairs, found a whole bundle relating to *Eikon
Basilike* : These Papers old Mrs. *Gauden* left to her
darling Son *John*, and he to his Brother *Charles*. There
is first a Letter from Secretary *Nicholas* to Dr. *Gauden*.
2. The Copy of a Letter from Bishop *Gauden* to Chancellor *Hyde*, where, among his other Deserts, he pleads
that what was don like a King, should have a Kinglike
Retribution, and that his design in it was to comfort and
incourage the King's Friends, to expose his Enemies,
and to convert, *&c*. There is, 3. The Copy of a Letter
from the Bishop to the Duke of *York*, wherin he strongly
urges his Services. 4. A Letter under Chancellor
Hyde's own hand, dated the 13*th* of *March*, 1661.

wherin he expresses his uneasiness under the Bishop's
importunity, and excuses his inability yet to serve him:
but towards the Conclusion it contains these remarkable
words; *The Particular you mention has indeed bin im-*
parted to me as a Secret ; I am sorry I ever knew it : and
when it ceases to be a Secret, it will please none but Mr.
Milton. There are other Papers in this bundle, but
particularly a long Narrative of Mrs. *Gauden's* own
Writing, irrefragably shewing her Husband to be
Author of *Eikon Basilike*. It entirely confirms Dr.
Walker's account, and contains most of the facts we
have hitherto related, with many other curious Circumstances too long to be here inserted, yet too extraordinary not to be known; wherfore I refer the Reader
to the original Papers, or to the faithful extract made
out of it before several learned and worthy Persons, and
which is printed in a Paper intitul'd, *Truth brought to*
light. Thus came all the World to be convinc'd of this
notorious Imposture; but which as it was dexterously
contriv'd, and most cunningly improv'd by a Party
whose Interest oblig'd 'em to keep the Secret, so it
happen'd to be discover'd by very nice and unforeseen
Accidents. Had not *Gauden* bin disappointed of *Win-*
chester, he had never pleaded his Merit in this affair;
nor would his Wife have written her Narrative, had
King *Charles* the Second bestow'd one half years Rent
upon her after her Husband's decease, which upon her
Petition, and considering her numerous Family, none
could imagin should be refus'd. It was a slighter
accident that begot a Confession from two Kings, and
Charles's own Sons: and I doubt if any other than one
of Mr. *Millington's* great Curiosity, and no Bigotry, had
the disposal of my Lord *Anglesey's* Books, we should

never have heard of the *Memorandum*. Had not *Holling-worth*'s indiscrete Zeal provok'd the only Man then alive who had any personal knowledge of this business, Dr. *Walker* had never publish'd his Account; nor could the whole discovery be so complete, without the least intricacy or question, without Mr. *North*'s Papers. When I seriously consider how all this happen'd among our selves within the compass of forty years, in a time of great Learning and Politeness, when both Parties so narrowly watch'd over one another's Actions, and what a great Revolution in Civil and Religious Affairs was partly occasion'd by the Credit of that Book, I cease to wonder any longer how so many supposititious pieces under the name of Christ, his Apostles, and other great Persons, should be publish'd and approv'd in those primitive times, when it was of so much importance to have 'em believ'd; when the Cheats were too many on all sides for them to reproach one another, which yet they often did; when Commerce was not near so general, and the whole Earth intirely overspread with the darkness of Superstition. I doubt rather the Spuriousness of several more such Books is yet undiscover'd, thro the remoteness of those Ages, the death of the Persons concern'd, and the decay of other Monuments which might give us true Information; especially when we consider how dangerous it was always for the weaker side to lay open the tricks of their Adversaries, tho never so gross: and that the prevailing Party did strictly order all those Books which offended them to be burnt, or otherwise supprest, which was accordingly perform'd, as well in obedience to the Laws by som, as out of conscientious Obligations by others, which made the execution more effectual than

usually happens in cases of an ordinary Nature. Of
this we are furnish'd with numberless Examples by
Church-Historians, who have preserv'd intire several of
the Laws and Orders enacted to this purpose. From
these general Remarks I must observe in particular,
that it's likely when *Charles* the Second knew the forgery
of this Book, he was fully confirm'd in the Popish
Religion, which in his Childhood he learnt of his
Mother, and in his Exile by his Foren Conversation.
The Author of *Eikon Basilike* desires him to adhere to
the Church of *England*, as necessary both for his Soul's
peace, and that of the Kingdom. This and the like
Exhortations of Respect for the Liturgy and Clergy,
might shew, at least, the Judgment of his dying Father;
but from Dr. *Gauden* it was mere Interest and Imposture. *Charles* therfore, who knew *Morley*, *Duppa*, and
others, to approve of this Fraud to which they were
privy, and for whose Advantage the belief of it was
serviceable, must either suspect the Forgeries laid by
Protestants to the charge of Popery, when he actually
knew the Protestants to play the same Game: or not
being able to deny the Popish Cheats,'tis most probable
the Opinion which his intimat Friends had of him was
too true, that he was really of neither Church, but
believed the Pretences of both to be Credulity or
Craft; and that the transactions of his last Minutes
were only the effects of a weak Mind in a distemper'd
Body.

Milton wrote also in the year 48. *Observations* upon
the Representation of the Presbytery of *Belfast* in *Ireland*, concerning the King's Death, the breaking of the
Covenant, and the Toleration of different Persuasions,
to which these Priestlings, as he calls them, were mortal

Enemies; while they call'd their own Presbyterian
Government the Hedg and Bulwark of Religion, which
is exactly the language of the Popish Inquisition.   In
the same *Observations* he examins the Duke of *Ormond's* Letter to Colonel *Jones* Governor of *Dublin*, persuading him to revolt from the Parlament. *Milton* is
very angry that *Ormond* made a contemtuous mention
of General *Cromwel*, " who, according to him, had don
" in a few years more eminent and remarkable Deeds
" wheron to found Nobility in his House tho it were
" wanting, and perpetual Renown to Posterity, than
" *Ormond* and all his Ancestors put together could shew
" from any Record of their *Irish* Exploits, the widest
" Scene of their Glory.   But his chiefest Remarks are
upon the Articles of Peace which *Ormond* concluded in
the King's Name, and by his Authority, with the Popish
Irish Rebels, wherin they are pardon'd for the Massacre
and Depredation of the *English* Protestants; acknowledg'd to be dutiful and loyal Subjects; are discharg'd
from taking the Oath of Supremacy, principally fram'd
on the account of Papists; and, in a word, such Free-
doms and Privileges were granted to those inhuman
Butchers, as were never injoy'd by their *English* Con-
querors.   The Second Article empowers the *Irish* Parlament to repeal or suspend (as they think fit) *Poyning's*
Act, the only security of their dependence on *England*.
They are intrusted by him with the Militia; and so
indulgent was he to these his choice Favorits, as
ridiculously to promise them the repealing of those Acts
which prohibited their plowing with Horses by the
Tail, or burning of Oats in the Straw, marks of their
sottish and indocil Barbarity.

And now we com to his Master-piece, his chief and

favorit Work in Prose, for Argument the noblest, as being the Defence of a whole free Nation, the People of *England*; for stile and disposition the most eloquent and elaborat, equalling the old *Romans* in the purity of their own Language, and their highest Notions of Liberty; as universally spread over the learned World as any of their Compositions; and certain to endure while Oratory, Politics, or History, bear any esteem among Men. *It cannot be deny'd*, says that excellent Critic *Monsieur Baile*, *that* Milton's *Latin stile is easy, brisk and elegant; nor that he defended the Republican Cause with a world of Address and Wit*: Agreable to which Judgment is the unanimous Suffrage of Foreners, not excepting the most zealous Assertors of Monarchy. It was written upon this occasion. *Charles* eldest Son to the King of the same name living in Exile, and wanting som body to paint the Death of his Father in the blackest Colors, either to render the Authors of it odious, the better to bring about his own return; or, if that effect did not answer, to move the Compassion of Foren Potentats to procure his Restoration, was told of *Salmasius* a Professor of the University of *Leyden* in *Holland*, as the fittest person for his purpose. This Man had got such a mighty Name from his *Plinian Exercitations*, and his critical Notes on several *Latin* and *Greec* Authors, that none was thought so knowing to equal, or so hardy to incounter him. This Man therfore *Charles* the Second hir'd for a hundred *Jacobuses* to write that bulky Volume, which in the year 49 appear'd under the Title of *Defensio Regia*, or a Defence of *Charles* the First to *Charles* the Second. *Salmasius* being better verst in the Writings of Grammarians, and Lexicographers (which sort of Men were his chief

Admirers) than in those of Legislators and Politicians, gave a true Demonstration that mere Scholars, when they meddle with anything that requires Reasoning or Thought, are but mere Asses: For being wholly occupy'd about frivolous Etymologies, or the bare sound of words, and living most of their time excluded from Conversation, bury'd in dust among Worms and mouldy Records, they have no exact Knowlege of things, and are perfect strangers to all the useful business of the World.   Accordingly the Royal Defence was destitute of Eloquence or Art, being nothing else but a huge heap of Rubbish, consisting of injudicious Quotations, very disorderly piec'd together, seldom making for his purpose; and, when they seem'd to favor him, quite spoil'd again by his own impertinent Comments.   But what's worse than all the rest, he appear'd on this occasion such an absolute stranger and bungler in his own Province, as to open a large Field for *Milton* to divert himself with his barbarous Phrases and Sole-cisms.   Nor had he more Wit likewise than to publish his *Defence* of Monarchy in *Holland*, at the same time that he had a Pension from that Free State, and was actually entertain'd in their Service; for tho the *Dutch* were then no good Friends to the *English*, being jealous of their growing Power, yet they could not be pleas'd with any Writing oppos'd to the common Cause of Liberty, and accordingly they blam'd *Salmasius*, and order'd the *Defence* to be supprest.   No sooner did this Book appear in *England*, but *Milton* being then present, was unanimously nam'd by every Member of the Coun-cil of State to answer it; so good an opinion they had of his Capacity, neither did he fail their Expectations: for within a very short time he publish'd his *Defensio pro*

Populo Anglicano, or the Defence of the People of *England ;* wherin, to speak no more of his admirable Stile than we have don already, nor of his handsomly exposing the Ignorance or Fury of *Salmasius,* he defended the Procedings of the People of *England* from the beginning of the Civil War to that time, with such Force of Arguments and Authority of Examples, that since there could be no dispute about the Victory he obtain'd over his Adversary, the only doubt remaining with his Readers was, which should be counted superior, his own great Reading, Politeness, or Judgment. The Subject is too nice for me to make any extract of it according to the Method I observ'd in some of his other Books; and besides it deserves so much to be consider'd at length in the Original, or in the *English* Version by Mr. *Washington* of the *Temple,* that I will not deprive any body of that pleasure. It's true indeed, that some have blam'd *Milton* for his rough usage of *Salmasius,* nor herein will I pretend wholly to excuse him: But when I consider how basely the whole *English* Nation was abus'd by *Salmasius,* as so many Barbarians or Euthusiasts, fiercer than their own Mastifs and yet sillier than *Athenian* Owls, it gos a great way with me towards *Milton's* Justification; and if we add to this, that he speaks not in his own Person, but as the Mouth of a potent State traduc'd by a pitiful Professor, there be those in the World that will positively commend him. Two passages only I shall insert here out of his Book; wherof the first shall be an Epigram he made to ridicule his Adversary for medling with Affairs to which he was a stranger, having all his intelligence from inrag'd and partial Exiles; but particularly for his mistaking of *English*

Names, and his mentioning of the County Court, and
Hundred.

> *Quis expedivit Salmasio suam Hundredam ?*
> *Picamque docuit verba nostra conari ?*
> *Magister artis venter, & Jacobæi*
> *Centum, exulantis viscera Marsupii regis.*
> *Quod si dolosi spes refulserit nummi,*
> *Ipse, Antichristi modo qui primatum Papæ*
> *Minatus uno est dissipare sufflatu,*
> *Cantabit ultro Cardinalitium Melos.*

> *English'd,*
> Who taught *Salmasius,* that *French* chattring Py,
> To aim at *English,* and *Hundreda* cry ?
> The starving Rascal, flusht with just a hundred
> English *Jacobusses, Hundreda* blunder'd;
> An outlaw'd King's last Stock. A hundred more
> Would make him pimp for th' Antichristian Whore;
> And in *Rome's* Praise imploy his poison'd Breath,
> Who threaten'd once to stink the Pope to death.

In these Verses he reflects on *Salmasius* for declaring
himself against any sort of Hierarchy in his Book *de
Primatu Papæ*, and yet being a mighty stickler for
Bishops in his Defence of the King. The other Passage
shall be the Epilogue or Conclusion of *Milton's* Book.
" And now I think, says he, that by God's Assistance I
" have finish'd the Work I undertook, namely, to
" defend the noble Actions of my Countrymen at home
" and abroad, against the raging and envious madness
" of this distracted Sophister; and to assert the com-
" mon Rights of the People against the unjust domina-
" tion of Kings, not out of any hatred to Kings, but
" Tyrants: nor have I purposely left unanswer'd any
" one Argument alledg'd by my Adversary, nor any

" Example or Authority quoted by him, that seem'd to
" have any force in it, or the least colour of a proof;
" perhaps I have bin guilty rather of the other extreme,
" of replying to som of his Fooleries and Trifles as if
" they were solid Arguments, and therby may seem to
" have attributed more to them than they deserv'd. One
" thing yet remains to be don, which perhaps is of the
" greatest concern of all, and that is, that you my
" Countrymen confute this Adversary of yours your
" selves; which I do not see any other means of your
" effecting than by a constant indeavour to outdo all
" Mens bad words by your own good Deeds. When
" you labor'd under more sorts of Oppression than one,
" you betook your selves to God for Refuge, and he was
" graciously pleas'd to hear your most earnest Prayers
" and Desires. He gloriously deliver'd you, the first of
" Nations, from the two greatest Mischiefs of this
" Life, and the most pernicious to Virtue, Tyranny and
" Superstition; he indu'd you with that Greatness of
" Soul to be the first of Mankind, who, after having
" conquer'd and captivated their own King, have not
" scrupl'd to condemn him judicially, and, according to
" that just Sentence, to put him to death. After per-
" forming so illustrious an Action as this, you ought to
" do nothing that's mean and little, not even to think,
" much less to do any thing but what is great and
" sublime. To attain which Praise there is only this one
" way, that as you have subdu'd your Enemies in the
" field, so to make it appear that unarm'd and in full
" Peace you of all Mankind are ablest to conquer
" Ambition, Avarice, the love of Riches, and can best
" avoid those Corruptions of Prosperity which are apt
" to get the better of other Nations; to shew as great

" Justice, Temperance, and Moderation, in preserving
" your Liberty, as you have don Courage in freeing
" your selves from Slavery. These are the only Argu-
" ments and Authorities by which you will be able to
" evince that you are not such Persons as this Fellow
" represents you, Traitors, Robbers, Murderers, Par-
" ricides, Madmen; that you did not put your King to
" death out of any ambitious design or a desire of
" invading the Rights of others, not out of any seditious
" Principles or sinister Ends, not agitated by Fury or
" Madness; but that it was wholly out of love to your
" Liberty, Religion, Justice, Virtue, and inflam'd with
" an Affection for your Country, that you punish'd a
" Tyrant. But if it should happen otherwise (which I
" pray God mercifully to forbid) if as you have bin
" valiant in War, you should grow debauch'd in Peace,
" you that have had such visible Demonstrations of the
" Goodness of God to your selves, and his Wrath against
" your Enemies, and that you should not learn by so
" eminent and memorable an Example before your
" eys, to fear God and work Righteousness, for my
" part, I shall easily grant and confess (for I cannot deny
" it) all the ill that Liers and Slanderers now think or
" speak of you to be true. And you will find in a little
" time that God's Displeasure against you will be greater
" than it has bin against your Adversaries, greater
" than his benign Favor and paternal Care which you
" have experienc'd above all the Nations under Heaven.
Milton was rewarded with a thousand Pounds for this
performance; and how differently his Defence of the
People, and that of *Salmasius* for the King were entertain'd by the curious, we may learn from the Mouth of
him that next appear'd for the Royal Cause. " What

" the most accomplish'd *Salmasius*, says he, has dis-
" cretely written in defence of the Right and Honor of
" *Charles* the *British* Monarch, murder'd by wicked
" Men, has born but one Impression, and saw the
" Light with great difficulty; with so much hatred
" dos the World persecute Truth in these latter times:
" but of what the most execrable *Milton* has spitefully
" elaborated to ruin the Reputation of the deceas'd
" King, and to destroy the hereditary Succession
" of the Crown, there are so many Editions, that I am
" uncertain to which of them I should refer my Reader;
" so passionatly fond are Men grown now of Lies and
" Calumnies! On this Book our Author did not think
it worth his while to animadvert, but delegated that
easy task to his younger Nephew *John Philips*, now
alive, who soon wrote a sufficient Answer to Bishop
Bramhal; for so this new Antagonist was suppos'd to
be cal'd.

Salmasius made a huge figure at this time in the
Swedish Court, whither Queen *Christina* invited all the
Men of Letters in *Europe*, so that her whole Train was
compos'd in a manner of Grammarians, Rhetoricians,
Philosophers, Astrologers, and Critics: nor was her
Administration unanswerable to her Attendents; for
besides a total neglect of good Laws for the public
Benefit, and her imprudent preferring of Strangers
before the Natives of the Country, she led a mere
romantic Life, somtimes frolicsomly disguising her self
in Mens Clothes, and then gravely disputing with her
Doctors, till at last she was forc'd to a shameful Abdi-
cation of the Government; and the end of all her
Learning was to turn Papist for a Pension from the
Pope, or to have an old meager Frier to pardon her Sins,

and a brawny Cardinal for her Stallion. Now no sooner had the Defence of the *English* Nation reach'd *Sweden*, and was read to the Queen at her own desire, but *Salmasius*, who till then had bin as it were her prime Minister, and who, when he first saw the Book, foolishly swore he would destroy *Milton* and the whole Parlament, decreas'd so much in her esteem, and dwindled to such a degree in the opinion of all others, that he thought it not for his Interest to continue longer there, and was dismist with extraordinary Coldness and Contemt. And not expecting to be better receiv'd in *Holland*, or any where else, he left an imperfect posthumous Reply, and had recourse to Death, the last refuge of the Miserable, and the safest shelter to cover them from Infamy and Disgrace. *Milton*, on the other hand, was, on the first appearance of his Book, visited or invited by all the Ambassadors at *London*, not excepting those of Crown'd Heads, and particularly esteem'd by *Adrian Paw* the Ambassador of the flourishing Republic of *Holland*. His Book indeed was burnt at *Paris*, not by order of the Parlament, but, at the instigation of the Priests, by the Lieutenant Civil, and likewise at *Tholouse*, which serv'd only to procure it more Readers: for he was highly extol'd at the same time, or complemented by Letters from the most ingenious Persons in *Germany* or *France* ; and, as if the old *Grecian* Republics had reviv'd to decree the accustom'd Honors to the Assertors of Liberty, *Leonardus Philaras*, an *Athenian* born, and Ambassador from the Duke of *Parma* to the *French* King, wrote a fine Commendation of his Defence, and sent him his Picture, together with a personal Elogium. From these undeniable Matters of Fact (without deciding the merit

of the cause on either side) it is plain that in the judgment of all *Europe*, *Milton* got infinitly the better of
Salmasius; for it could not be Partiality to a Free
Government, but the resistless Light of Truth, that
obtain's such a Confession from the Ministers or Subjects of absolute Princes.

Now he had som leisure again to follow his other
Studies of a more delightful and peaceable nature than
these Controversies, and had also a Son born to him,
who dy'd in his Infancy. In the year 52, he remov'd
for his Health from his Lodgings at *Whitehal* to a
House opening into St. *James*'s Park, which shall be the
Scene of all his Actions till the Restoration of the Royal
Family. In this place his first Wife dying in Childbed,
he, after a convenient space, marry'd a second, *Catharine*
the Daughter of Captain *Woodcock* of *Hackney*, who
within a year dy'd also in the same condition, and was
about a month after follow'd by her Child, which was a
Girl. His Sight was quite gon before this Match; for
by reason of his continual Studies, and the Headach,
to which he was subject from his Youth, his Eys were
decaying for a dozen years before: but we shall have
an occasion by and by to give a further account of this
matter.

The same year appear'd a bitter Invective from
abroad against the Parlamentarians. The Title of it
was, *The Cry of the King's Blood for Vengeance to Heaven* *Clamor Reg*
against the English Parricides*. In this Book *Milton* is *Sanguinis a*
Coelum, &c
particularly traduc'd, and accus'd to have bin expel'd
out of the University of *Cambridg* for som Misde-
meanors, wherupon he retir'd into *Italy*: but the falsity
of this Story is already prov'd. Several other frivolous
things are laid to his charge, which he on the other hand

L

denies; nor do his Adversaries insist upon them in their Answers: now there cannot be a clearer proof of his Innocence, than that being accus'd he publicly denies the fact, and his Enemies can't contradict him. But Envy and Malice often carry such as have got the worse to affirm most absurd and ridiculous things: So *Salmasius* in his dying Reply foolishly reports that *Milton* wrote not the Defence himself, but lent his Name to the Hand of a little *French* Schoolmaster at *London*. But, as it always happens in such cases, he got nothing by this silly figment, but gave *Milton* an opportunity of making his own Ability, and the Weakness of *Salmasius*, further known to the World. Thus som People think to gratify an offended Person with telling him a hundred ilnatur'd Stories of his Antagonist to which his Passion makes him give credit without due Examination, and then becoms a Fool by asserting them. The true Author of the *Clamor Regii Sanguinis* was *Peter du Moulin* the younger, a Prebendary of *Canterbury ;* but *Alexander Morus* a *French* Minister being the Publisher of it, and having prefix'd a Dedication in the Printer's Name to *Charles* II, he was generally thought to be the Writer of the whole. This *Morus* was the Son of a learned *Scot*, who was Principal of the Protestant College formerly at *Castres* in *Languedoc*. His insufferable Haughtiness, immoderat Inclination for Women, and Contemt of his Collegues, made him odious and uneasy wherever he liv'd. He was hasty, ambitious, satyrical, and could never commend any thing but his own Works, or those of his Admirers. He was cry'd up for a Seraphic Preacher; but, as *Baile* judiciously says, his Talent must have consisted in the Gracefulness of his Pronunciation and Gesture, or in those Flourishes and Puns wherof his Sermons are full: for 'tis certain that they retain not those Charms now on Paper which they were said to have formerly in the Pulpit. Against him therfore *Milton* by public Command publishes a second Defence for the People of *England*, which, besides what the Title promises, contains a bloody Satyr upon *Morus*, nor dos he deny himself to have bin the occasion of *Salmasius*'s Death. I shall not rake into the Ashes of the Dead, but content my self with inserting here two pieces of *Milton*'s Wit. The first is a Distich made upon *Morus* for getting *Pontia* the Maid of his Friend *Salmasius* with Child.

> *Galli ex Concubitu gravidam te, Pontia, Mori,*
> *Quis bene moratam, morigeramque neget ?*

The other shall be an Epigram wherin *Milton* laughs at *Morus* for threatning him with a second Edition of *Salmasius*'s Defence of the King, augmented with Animadversions on his Defence of the People.

> *Gaudete Scombri, & quicquid est piscium Salo,*
> *Qui frigida Hyeme incolitis algentes freta,*
> *Vestrûm misertus ille Salmasius Eques*
> *Bonus amicire nuditatem cogitat ;*
> *Chartæque largus apparat papyrinos*
> *Vobis cucullos præferentes Claudii*
> *Insignia, nomenque, & Decus Salmasii :*
> *Gestetis ut per omne cetarium forum*
> *Equitis clientes, scriniis mungentium*
> *Cubito virorum, & capsulis gratissimos.*

The Author of the *Clamor Regii Sanguinis* having barbarously objected to *Milton* his Blindness, and that he was meager and pale, he gives him an Answer in these words: " I was never counted deform'd, as I know, by

" any that ever saw me; but whether to be counted
" handsom or not is none of my concern. My Stature,
" I confess, is not extraordinary tall, yet I am rather a
" middlesiz'd than little Man.   But what if little I
" were ?   Have not many Persons eminent in the Arts
" of War and Peace bin so before me ?   tho I see no
" reason why that should be cal'd little which in
" Courage is sufficiently great.   Neither am I so slender;
" for I was strong and capable enough in my Youth to
" handle my Weapons, and to exercise daily Fencing;
" so that wearing a Sword by my side, as became a
" Gentleman, I thought my self a match for those that
" were much stronger, and was not afraid of receiving
" an affront from any body.   I have still the same Soul
" and Vigor, but not the same Eyes; yet to all outward
" appearance so sound, so clear, and free from the
" least spot, as theirs who see furthest: and herein only,
" in spite of my self, I am a Deceiver.   My Counten-
" ance, than which he says there's nothing paler, is still
" of a Color so contrary to wan and bloodless, that tho
" I am above forty, any body would think me ten years
" younger, being neither contracted in Body or Skin.
" If in any of these Particulars I told a Ly, I should be
" deservedly ridiculous to many thousands of my own
" Countrymen, and to several Strangers that personally
" know me.   As for his Blindness, he says that such
a condition is not miserable, but not to be able
to bear it; and then quotes the Examples of valiant,
learned, wise, and holy Men of all times that have bin
blind.   But the loss of his Eys being objected to him
as an effect of divine Vengeance, after solemnly pro-
testing that he's not conscious of any thing for which he
should deserve that punishment more than other Men,

he adds, " As for what I wrote at any time (since the
" Royalists think I now suffer on that account, and
" triumph over me) I call God to witness that I did not
" write any thing but what I then thought, and am
" still persuaded to be right, and true, and acceptable
" to God; not led by any sort of Ambition, Profit, or
" Vainglory; but have don all from a sense of Duty and
" Honor, out of piety to my Country, and for the
" Liberty of Church and State. On the contrary, when
" that Task of answering the King's Defence was
" injoin'd me by public Authority, being both in an ill
" state of Health, and the Sight of one Ey almost gon
" already, the Physicians openly predicting the loss of
" both if I undertook this Labor; yet nothing terrify'd
" by their Premonition, I did not long balance whether
" any Duty should be prefer'd to my Eys. And what
he really thought of his Blindness, and how he bore
it, may be further perceiv'd by this Sonnet to his
Friend *Cyriac Skinner*, never printed with his other
Poems.

Cyriac, this three years day, these Eys, tho clear
    To outward view of blemish or of spot,
    Bereft of sight, their seeing have forgot.
    Nor to their idle Orbs dos Day appear,
Or Sun, or Moon, or Star, throout the year;
    Or Man, or Woman. Yet I argue not
    Against Heaven's hand, or will, nor bate one jot
    Of Heart or Hope ; but still bear up, and steer
Right onward. What supports me, dost thou ask ?
    The Conscience, Friend, t'have lost them overply'd
    In Liberty's Defence, my noble Task,
Wherof all *Europe* rings from side to side.
    This Thought might lead me thro this World's vain Mask,
    Content, tho blind, had I no other Guide.

Morus publisht his *Fides publica* in answer to *Milton*'s
Defensio second Defence, to which the latter oppos'd a *Defence of*
pro se *himself;* and by Original Letters, or the like Authentic
Pieces, made good all his Assertions against his Adversary: wherupon *Morus* vanquisht and baffled, quitted
the Field.   Our Author was now *Latin* Secretary to the
Protector *Oliver Cromwel*, who, he confidently hop'd,
would imploy his Trust and Power to extinguish the
numerous Factions of the State, and to settle such a
perfect Form of a Free Government, wherin no single
Person should injoy any Power above or beside the
Laws: but he particularly expected his establishing an
impartial Liberty of Conscience, to which he incourages
him by these Lines, never printed among his Poems.

> *Cromwel*, our chief of Men, that thro a croud
> Not of War only, but Distractions rude,
> (Guided by Faith and matchless Fortitude)
> To Peace and Truth thy glorious Way hast plow'd,
> And fought God's Battles, and his Work pursu'd,
> While *Darwent* streams with Blood of *Scots* imbru'd,
> And *Dunbar* Field resound thy Praises loud,
> And *Worc'sters* Laureat Wreath.   Yet much remains
> To conquer still;   Peace has her Victories,
> No less than those of War.   New Foes arise
> Threatning to bind our Souls in secular Chains:
> Help us to save free Conscience from the Paw
> Of Hireling Wolves, whose Gospel is their Maw.

He had leisure enough now from his Imployment in
the State (no Adversary daring to appear any more) to
pursue his *History of Britain*, and his new *Thesaurus*
Linguæ Latinæ : but what took up most of his time
was the Epic Poem he had so long design'd, and which
is since printed under the Title of *Paradise Lost*, wherof

in due order.   But the next Book he publisht was *a Treatise*, dedicated to the Parlament, *of Civil Power in Ecclesiastical Causes*, shewing that it is not lawful for any Power on Earth to compel in Matters of Religion, whether Speculative or Practical; or in any thing except Immorality, or what evidently subverts the Foundations of Civil Society: for which reason he justly excludes Popery from this Toleration, for being not so much a Religion, as a Politic Faction wherof the Members, whersoever they are, own the Pope for their Superior, to the prejudice of the Allegiance due to their Natural Soverains.   Besides, that they never tolerat others where they have the mastery;   and that their Doctrin of Dispensations, or keeping no Faith with such as they count Heretics, renders 'em worse than Atheists, and the declar'd Enemies of all Mankind besides those of their own Communion.

After this he addrest to the Parlament, *Considerations touching the likeliest means to remove Hirelings out of the Church ;*   not that he was against all sort of Maintenance for the public ministry of Religion, which he acknow- leges due by the Light of Reason, as well as the Examples of all Ages;   but he proves that Tithes were inconven- ient, and not of Divine Right, which was then strongly asserted even by the Presbyterians and Independents. He observes, that two things do mainly corrupt Religion, and hinder the advancement of Truth, Force on the one side restraining the Professors, and Hire on the other side corrupting the Teachers of it.   " The " latter of these, says he, is by much the more dangerous: " for under Force, tho no thanks to the Forcers, true " Religion oftimes best thrives and flourishes;   but the " corruption of Teachers, most commonly the effect of

" Hire, is the very bane of Truth in them who are so
" corrupted.   There is much curious History in this
Book concerning Church Revenues, to which I refer
those who have not read Father *Paul* of Beneficiary
Matters, nor Father *Simon* who wrote after him.
Speaking of the Ministers, " They pretend, says he,
" that their Education, either at School or the Univer-
" sity, has bin very chargeable, and therfore ought to
" be repair'd afterwards by a fruitful Maintenance:
" wheras it is well known that the better half of them
" (and ofttimes poor and pitiful Boys, of no merit or
" promising hopes that might intitle them to the public
" Provision, but their poverty and the unjust favor of
" Friends) have had the most of their breeding, both
" at School and University, by Scholarships, Exhibi-
" tions, and Fellowships, at the public Cost, which
" might ingage them the rather to give freely as they
" freely receiv'd.   Or if they have miss'd of these Helps
" at the latter place, they have after two or three years
" left the course of their Studies there (if they ever well
" began them) and undertaken, tho furnisht with little
" else but ignorance, boldness, and ambition, if with no
" worse Vices, a Chaplainship in som Gentleman's
" House, to the frequent imbasing of his Sons with
" illiterat and narrow Principles.   Or if they have liv'd
" there upon their own, who knows not that seven
" years charge of living there, to them who fly not from
" the Government of their Parents to the License of a
" University, but com seriously to study, is no more
" than may be well defray'd and reimburst by one
" year's Revenue of an ordinary good Benefice ?   If
" they had then Means of breeding from their Parents,
" 'tis likely they have more now; and if they have, it

" must needs be mechanic and disingenuous in them to
" bring a Bill of Charges for the learning those liberal
" Arts and Sciences which they have learnt (if they have
" indeed learnt them, as they seldom have) to their own
" benefit and accomplishment. Towards the conclusion he has these words; " I have thus at large
" examin'd the usual Pretences of Hirelings, color'd
" over most commonly with the Cause of Learning and
" Universities; as if with Divines Learning stood and
" fell, wherin for the most part their Pittance is so
" small; and, to speak freely, it were much better there
" were not one Divine in the University, nor no School
" Divinity known, the idle Sophistry of Monks, the
" Canker of Religion; and that they who intended to
" be Ministers, were train'd up in the Church only by
" the Scripture, and in the Original Languages therof
" at School, without fetching the compass of other Arts
" and Sciences more than what they can well learn at
" secondary leisure, and at home. Neither speak I this
" in contemt of Learning, or the Ministry, but hating
" the common cheats of both; hating that they who
" have preacht out Bishops, Prelats, and Canonists,
" should, in what serves their own ends, retain their
" false Opinions, their pharisaical Leven, their Avarice,
" and closely their Ambition, their Pluralities, their
" Nonresidences, their odious Fees, and use their Legal
" and Popish Arguments for Tithes: That Indepen-
" dents should take that name, and seek to be Depen-
" dents on the Magistrat for their Maintenance; which
" two things, Independence and Statehire in Religion,
" can never consist long or certainly together. For
" Magistrats at one time or other, not like these
" at present our Patrons of Christian Liberty, will pay

" none but such whom by their Committees of Exam-
" ination, they find conformable to their Interest and
" Opinions: And Hirelings will soon frame themselves
" to that Interest and those Opinions which they see
" best pleasing to their Paymasters; and, to seem right
" themselves, will force others as to the Truth.   After
proving the Christian Religion not to be more difficult
than any other Art or Science, nay, and that the knowlege of it may be much sooner attain'd; " We may
" conclude, says he, that if Men be not all their lifetime
" under a Teacher to learn Logic, Natural Philosophy,
" Ethics, or Mathematics, which are more difficult;
" that certainly it is not necessary to the attainment of
" Christian Knowlege, that Men should sit all their life
" long at the feet of a pulpited Divine, while he, a
" Lollard indeed over his elbow Cushion, in almost the
" seventh part of forty or fifty years, teaches them scarce
" half the Principles of Religion: And his Sheep oft-
" times sit all the while to as little purpose of benefiting,
" as the Sheep in their pews at *Smithfield*, and for the
" most part are by som Simony or other bought and
" sold like them; or, if this Comparison be too low,
" like those Women, mention'd by St. *Paul*, ever
" learning and never attaining; yet not so much thro
" their own Fault, as thro the unskilful and immethodi-
" cal Teaching of their Pastor, preaching here and there
" at random out of this or that Text, as his ease or
" fancy, and ofttimes as his health guides him.
    Cromwel being dead, *Richard* depos'd, and the Army
having restor'd the old famous Parlament, but almost
as soon dissolv'd it, *Milton* wrote a Letter to som
Statesman, with whom he had a serious discourse about
the lamentable Confusions of that time.   It is in a very

pathetic Stile, and contains a true Representation of
what the Soldiers had don; to whom he tells, that it is
scarce to be exampled, even among Barbarians, that an
Army duly paid should, for no cause at all, subdue the
Supreme Power that set them up. "This, says he,
"other Nations will judg to the sad dishonor of that
"Army, lately renown'd for the civilest and best
"order'd in the Universe, and by us here at home for
"the most conscientious. Now, if an Army deserving
this Character was capable of inslaving their Country,
what may be expected from any other, as most are, of
a worse disposition? In this Letter he delivers the
Model of a Commonwealth; not such as he thought
the best, but what might be readiest settled at that time
to prevent the restitution of Kingship and Domestic
Disorders, till a more favorable Season, or better Dispositions for erecting a perfect Democracy. This and
another small Piece to the same purpose, addrest I
suppose to *Monk*, were communicated to me by a
worthy Friend, who, a little after the Author's Death,
had them from his Nephew; and I imparted them to
the Publishers of the new Edition of his Works in
Folio.

His last Piece before the Restoration of the Royal
Family, except the *brief Notes* he publisht on Dr.
Griffith's Sermon, was intitul'd, *The ready and easy Way
to establish a Free Commonwealth, and the Excellence
therof compar'd with the Inconveniences and Dangers of
readmitting Kingship in this Nation.* This Book appear'd
in Sixty, when he perceiv'd that noxious humor of
returning to Bondage, as he calls it, to prevail, which
was instil'd by som Deceivers, and nourisht by the bad
Principles or false Apprehensions of the People. "If

" their absolute Determination be to enthral us, says
" he, before so long a *Lent* of Servitude, they may per-
" mit us a little Shroving time first, wherin to speak
" freely and take our leaves of Liberty.   He indeavors
to set before the Eys of the Nation the folly and unreasonableness of all they had so valiantly don for
several years, if they at last readmitted Kingship; that
they would be the shame of all free Countrys, and the
Laughingstock of all Monarchies.   " Where is this
" goodly Tower of a Commonwealth, will Foreners say,
" which the *English* boasted they would build to over-
" shadow Kings, and be another *Rome* in the West ?
" The Foundation indeed they laid gallantly, but fell
" into a worse Confusion, not of Tongues but of Fac-
" tions, than those at the Tower of *Babel* ; and have
" left no Memorial of their Work behind them remain-
" ing, but in the common laughter of *Europe*.   Which
" must needs redound the more to our shame, if we but
" look on our Neighbors the *United Provinces*, to us
" inferior in all outward Advantages; who notwith-
" standing, in the midst of greater Difficulties, cour-
" agiously, wisely, constantly went thro with the same
" Work, and are settled in all the happy injoyments of
" a potent and flourishing Republic to this day.   Be-
" sides this, if we return to Kingship, and soon repent
" (as undoubtedly we shall when we find the old
" Incroachments coming by little and little upon our
" Consciences, which must necessarily procede from
" King and Bishop united inseparably in one Interest)
" we may be forc'd perhaps to fight over again
" all that we have fought.   —A Free Commonwealth
" was not only held by wisest Men in all Ages, the
" noblest, the manliest, the equallest, the justest Govern-

" ment, the most agreable to due Liberty, and pro-
" portion'd Equality, both Human, Civil, and Christian,
" most cherishing to Virtue and true Religion, but also
" plainly commended, or rather injoin'd by our Savior
" himself to all Christians, not without a remarkable
" disallowance, and the brand of Gentilism upon King-
" ship. God in much displeasure gave a King to the
" *Israelits*, and imputed it a Sin to them that they
" sought one: but Christ apparently forbids his Dis-
" ciples to admit of any such Heathenish Government.
" *The Kings of the* Gentils, says he, *exercise Lordship over*
" *them, and they that exercise Authority upon them are*
" *cal'd Benefactors : But you shall not do so, but he that is*
" *greatest among you, let him be as the younger ; and he*
" *that is chief, as he that serves.* The occasion of these
" words was the ambitious desire of *Zebedees* two Sons
" to be exalted above their Brethren in the Kingdom,
" which they thought was to be er'e long upon Earth.
" That he speaks of Civil Government is manifest by
" the former part of the Comparison, which infers the
" other part to be always of the same kind. And what
" Government coms nearer to this Precept of Christ,
" than a Free Commonwealth ? Wherin they who are
" greatest are perpetual Servants and Drudges to the
" Public at their own cost and charges, neglecting their
" own Affairs, yet are not elevated above their Brethren,
" live soberly in their Families, walk the Streets as other
" Men, may be spoken to freely, familiarly, friendly,
" without Adoration. Wheras a King must be ador'd
" like a Demigod, with a dissolute and haughty Court
" about him, of vast Expence and Luxury, Masks and
" Revels, to the debauching of our prime Gentry both
" Male and Female, not in their Pastimes only, but in

" earnest by the loose Imployments of Court-Service,
" which will be then thought honorable.   There will be
" a Queen of no less charge; in most likelihood out-
" landish and a Papist, besides a Queenmother such
" already, together with both their Courts and numerous
" Train.   Then a Royal Issue, and e're long severally
" their sumtuous Courts, to the multiplying of a servil
" Crew, not of Servants only, but of Nobility and
" Gentry bred up then, not to the hopes of Public, but
" of Court Offices; to be Stewards, Chamberlains,
" Ushers, Grooms, even of the Closestool: And the
" lower their Minds are debas'd with Court opinions
" contrary to all Virtue and Reformation, the haughtier
" will be their Pride and Profuseness.   As to the burden
" of Expence, we shall soon know it to our cost; for
" any good to us, deserving to be term'd no better than
" the vast and lavish price of our Subjection, and their
" Debauchery, which we are now so greedily cheapen-
" ing, and would so fain be paying most inconsideratly
" to a single Person, who, for any thing wherin the
" Public really needs him, will have little else to do but
" to bestow the eating and drinking of excessive
" Dainties, to set a pompous face upon the superficial
" actings of State, to pageant himself up and down in
" progress among the perpetual Bowings and Cringings
" of an abject People, on either side deifying and adoring
" him for nothing don that can deserve it.   In this Book
he delivers the Model of a Commonwealth, well suted
perhaps to the Circumstances of that time, but inferior
in all respects to *Harrington's Oceana*, which for the
Practicableness, Equality, and Completeness of it, is
the most perfect form of such a Government that was
ever delineated by any antient or modern Pen.

And now, the King being ready to land, our Author was discharg'd from his Office of Latin Secretary, and oblig'd for the Safety of his Person to leave his House near St. *James*'s Park, where for eight years before he was visited by all Foreners of Note, by several Persons of Quality, and by the Ingenious of every Persuasion or Party. *Andrew Marvel*, who by his Parts and Probity made himself so much known since that time in *England*, us'd to frequent him the oftenest of any body; and whether it was he or *Milton* (for both are nam'd for it) that made the Verses sent with *Cromwel*'s Picture to the Queen of *Sweden*, I am uncertain: but whoever was the Author, they deserve a room in this place.

Cromwel speaks:

Bellipotens virgo, septem Regina Trionum
Christina, Arctoi lucida stella poli ;
Cernis quas merui dura sub Casside rugas,
Utque senex armis impiger ora tero :
Invia fatorum dum per vestigia nitor,
Exequor & populi fortia jussa manu.
Ast tibi submittit frontem reverentior umbra,
Nec sunt hi vultus regibus usque truces.

English'd.

Bright martial Maid, Queen of the frozen Zone,
The Northern Pole supports thy shining Throne;
Behold what Furrows Age and Steel can plow,
The Helmet's weight opprest this wrinkled Brow.
Thro Fate's untrodden Paths I move, my Hands
Still act my freeborn Peoples bold Commands:
Yet this stern shade to you submits his Frowns,
Nor are these looks always severe to Crowns.

From the year 52, to that of 60, he corresponded much with learned Foreners, as appears by his Letters to *Millius, Oldenburg, Heimbachius, DeBrass, Leo ab Aizema,* and *Emeric Bigot.* His Admirer *Leonardus Philaras* coming upon som occasions to *London,* went to see *Milton,* who, tho he could not see him again, was extremely pleas'd with his Conversation. He afterwards acquainted *Milton* by a Letter, that there was a Physician who perform'd Wonders on blind People at *Paris,* and requests him to send in writing the state and progress of his Distemper, which to gratify his Friend our Author perform'd, yet without expressing any hopes of a cure. *Cyriac Skinner* was one of his constant Visiters, which Honor he not seldom receiv'd also from the pious and virtuous Lady *Ranelagh,* whose Son, the present Earl of *Ranelagh,* he instructed for som time, and sent him several Letters of Advice during his Travels abroad; but in one directed to him at the University, he uses these words: " As for what you " write to me, that you are so much pleas'd with *Oxford,* " you cannot persuade me the more that you receiv'd " any Improvement there, or art becom a bit the wiser, " unless you shew me som other Reasons for it. Those " Victories of Princes which you extol, and such other " things, wherin Force has the greatest share, I would " not have you too much admire, especially now being " a Hearer of Philosophers: where's the wonder if in " the Country of Rams there grow strong Horns, which " are able to batter Towns and Cities with such " violence ? But learn thou from thy Childhood to ' discern and judg of great Examples, not from Violence " and Force, but by Justice and Temperance.

But, as I said before, he was now oblig'd to abscond till the Act of Oblivion was publish'd, wherin he and *John Goodwin* (the great spreader of Arminianism, and

who in writing also justify'd the Death of *Charles* the
First) were only excepted from bearing any Office in the
Nation. Our Author had many good Friends to inter-
cede for him both in the Privy Council and in the
House of Commons; nor was *Charles* the Second such
an Enemy to the Muses as to require his Destruction,
tho som are of opinion that he was more oblig'd to that
Prince's Forgetfulness than to his Clemency.

As soon as his Pardon was past the Seals, he appear'd
again, and marry'd his third Wife *Elizabeth*, the
Daughter of Mr. *Minshal* of *Cheshire*, recommended to
him by his Friend Dr. *Paget*. He had no Children by
this last Wife, nor any living by his second; but of his
three Daughters by the first, he made two very serviceable to himself, and, in so doing, to the rest of the
World. For tho many sent their Sons to read for him,
and several grown Persons were ambitious of obliging
him that way for their own Improvement; yet he
taught these young Women to read and pronounce
with great exactness the *English*, *Italian*, *Spanish*,
French, *Hebrew*, *Greec*, and *Latin* Languages. So that
whatever Book he had occasion to use, one of 'em was
forc'd to read it to him, tho neither of 'em understood
a word of those Writings, except *English* their Mother
Tongue. This Drudgery could not but render them
in time very uneasy; and accordingly, when he understood their Murmurs, he dispens'd with their Duty in
this case, and sent them out to learn other things more
becoming their Sex and Condition.

What imploy'd a good part of his Thoughts for many
years before, and was at first only design'd to be a
Tragedy, I mean his incomparable Epic Poem, intitul'd
Paradise Lost, he now had sufficient leisure to

M

prosecute and finish. It is a great wonder that this piece should ever be brought to perfection, considering the many Interruptions that obstructed it. His Youth was spent in Study, Travelling, and religious Controversy; his Manhood was imploy'd in Affairs of State, or those of his Family; and in his latter years, to speak nothing of a decaying Fancy, nor of his personal Troubles, he was by reason of his Blindness oblig'd to write by whatsoever hand came next, ten, or twenty, or thirty Verses at a time; and consequently must trust the judgment of others at least for the Pointing and Orthography. But another difficulty that stopt its passage to the World was very singular: for his Vein never happily flow'd but from the Autumnal to the Vernal Equinox, as his Nephew *Edward Philips* affirms, who says he was told this particular by *Milton* himself; and yet I fancy he might be mistaken as to the time, because our Author in his *Latin* Elegy on the approach of Spring seems to say just the contrary, as if he could not make any Verses to his satisfaction till the Spring begun, according to these lines:

> *Fallor ?   An & nobis redeunt in carmina vires,*
> *Ingeniumque mihi munere veris adest ?*
> *Munere veris adest, iterumque vigescit ab illo,*
> *(Quis putet) atque aliquod jam sibi poscit opus.*

A more judicious Friend of his informs me, that he could never compose well but in the Spring and Autumn: And let it be which way you will, it follows that this Piece was compos'd in half the time he was thought to be about it. As to the choice of his Subject, or the Particulars of his Story, I shall say nothing in defence of them against those People who brand 'em with Heresy and Impiety: for to incur the Displeasure of certain ignorant and supercilious Critics, argues free thinking, accurat Writing, and a generous Profession of Truth. I'm sure if *Hesiod*, or such other fabulous Authors in the rude ages of the World, had given so intelligible, coherent, and delightful an account of the Creation of the Universe, and the Origin of Mankind their System had past for Divine Inspiration; and the Unbelievers of it would appear to be so few, that any of 'em might well be shewn for a Monster rather than be thought worthy of Punishment or Confutation. As to the regularity of the Poem, I never knew it question'd by any but such as would build themselves a Reputation on the flaws and mistakes they discover in other Mens Labors. But the unparallel'd Sublimity and Force of the Expression, with the delicacy of his Thoughts, and the copiousness of his Invention, are unanimously own'd by all ranks of Writers. He has incontestably exceded the fecundity of *Homer*, whose two Poems he could almost repeat without book: nor did he com much short of the correctness of *Virgil*; which is affirm'd by one whose judgment in this Province will be acknowleg'd by every man that is not willing to expose the defect of his own. I mean the famous *John Dryden*, the best *English* Poet alive, the present Glory of our Stage, and the Model of the same to future Ages; for he (having absolutely master'd these three Originals by framing a Tragedy out of *Paradise Lost*, making the Charms of *Virgil* appear in the *English* Tongue, and studying *Homer* for the same purpose) pronounces his Judgment in favor of *Milton* by this incomparable and envy'd Epigram.

> Three Poets in three distant Ages born,
> *Greece*, *Italy*, and *England* did adorn:

The first in Loftiness of Thought surpast;
The next in Majesty; in both the last.
The Force of Nature could no further go:
To make a Third, she join'd the other Two.

The first edition of *Paradise Lost* was publish'd in the
year 1666, in ten Books; but afterwards, amended and
inlarg'd by himself, it was dispos'd according to his
Direction into twelve Books, as it is read at present.   I
must not forget that we had like to be eternally depriv'd
of this Treasure by the Ignorance or Malice of the
Licenser; who, among other frivolous Exceptions,
would needs suppress the whole Poem for imaginary
Treason in the following lines.

—As, when the Sun new risen
Looks thro the Horizontal misty Air
Shorn of his Beams, or from behind the Moon
In dim Eclipse disastrous Twilight sheds
On half the Nations, and with fear of change
Perplexes Monarchs.

Milton, taking an occasion from *Satan's* ascending out
of infernal Darkness towards the Light of this World
then newly created, perpetuats the History of his own
Blindness in this admirable Passage.

Hail, holy Light; Ofspring of Heaven Firstborn,
Or of th' eternal coeternal Beam,
May I express thee unblam'd ?   Since God is Light,
And never but in unapproached Light
Dwelt from Eternity, dwelt then in thee
Bright Effluence of bright Essence increate.
Or hearst thou rather pure ethereal Stream,
Whose Fountain who shall tell ?   Before the Sun,
Before the Heavens thou wert; and at the Voice
Of God, as with a Mantle, didst invest

The rising World of Waters dark and deep,
Won from the void and formless Infinite.
Thee I revisit now with bolder Wing,
Escap'd the *Stygian* Pool, tho long detain'd
In that obscure Sojourn; while in my flight
(Thro utter and thro middle Darkness born)
I sung of *Chaos* and eternal Night,
Taught by the heavenly Muse to venture down
The dark Descent, and up to reascend
Tho hard and rare. Thee I revisit safe,
And feel thy sovrain vital Lamp; but thou
Revisit'st not these Eys that roll in vain
To find thy piercing Ray, and find no dawn:
So thick a Drop serene has quench'd their Orbs
Or dim Suffusion veil'd! Yet not the more
Cease I to wander where the Muses haunt
Clear Spring, or shady Grove, or sunny Hill,
Smit with the Love of sacred Song; but chief,
Thee, *Sion*, and thy flowry Brooks beneath
That wash thy hallowed Feet, and warbling flow,
Nightly I visit. Nor somtimes forget
Those other two equal'd with me in Fate
(So were I equal'd with them in Renown)
Blind *Thamyris* and blind *Mæonides*,
And *Tyresias* and *Phineus*, Prophets old.
Then feed on Thoughts that voluntary move
Harmonious Numbers; as the wakeful Bird
Sings darkling, and, in shadyest Coverts hid,
Tunes her nocturnal Note. Thus with the Year
Seasons return, but not to me returns
Day, or the sweet approach of Ev'n, or Morn,
Or sight of vernal Bloom, or Summers Rose,
Or Flocks, or Herds, or human Face divine:
But Cloud instead, and everduring Dark
Surrounds me, from the chearful ways of Men
Cut off; and, for the Book of Knowlege fair,
Presented with an universal Blank

Of Nature's Works to me expung'd and raz'd,
And Wisdom at one entrance quite shut out.
So much the rather, thou Celestial Light,
Shine inward, and the Mind thro all her Powers
Irradiat: there plant Eys, all Mist from thence
Purge and disperse, that I may see and tell
Of things invisible to mortal sight.

An Epic Poem is not a bare History delightfully
related in harmonious Numbers, and artfully dispos'd;
but it always contains, besides a general representation
of Passions and Affections, Virtues and Vices, som
peculiar Allegory or Moral. *Homer* therfore, according
to *Dionysius Halicarnassæus*, expresses strength of Body
in his *Iliad* by the Wars of the *Greecs* and *Trojans*, but
particularly by the valiant Deeds of *Achilles :* and in his
Odysseus he describes generosity of Mind by the
Adventures and Wandrings of *Ulysses* in his return
from *Troy*. Thus *Torquato Tasso* has prefixt an Explica-
tion to his *Gierusalemme Liberata :* Nor was *Milton*
behind any body in the choice or dignity of his Instruction; for to display the different Effects of Liberty and
Tyranny, is the chief design of his *Paradise Lost*. This
in the conclusion of his second Book of *Reformation*,
publish'd in 41, he tells us was his Intention at that
time; and he afterwards made this promise good. His
own words being part of a Prayer to God, deserve
serious consideration. "Then, says he, amidst the
" Hymns and Hallelujahs of Saints, som one may per-
" haps be heard offring at high strains in new and lofty
" measures, to sing and celebrat thy divine Mercies, and
" marvellous Judgments in this Land throut all Ages,
" wherby this great and warlike Nation (instructed
" and inur'd to the fervent and continual practice of

" Truth and Righteousness, and casting far from it
" the Rags of its old Vices) may press on hard to that
" high and happy Emulation to be found the soberest,
" wisest, and most Christian People at that day, when
" Thou, the eternal and shortly expected King, shalt
" open the Clouds to judg the several Kingdoms of the
" World; and, distributing national Honors and
" Rewards to religious and just *Commonwealths*, shalt
" put an end to all earthly *Tyrannies*, proclaiming thy
" universal and mild Monarchy thro Heaven and Earth.
" Where they undoubtedly, that by their Labors,
" Counsels, and Prayers, have bin earnest for the com-
" mon Good of Religion and their Country, shall
" receive (above the inferior Orders of the Blessed) the
" regal addition of Principalities, Legions, and Thrones
" into their glorious Titles; and in supereminence of
" beatific Vision, progressing the dateless and irrevol-
" uble Circle of Eternity, shall clap inseparable hands
" with joy and bliss in overmeasure for ever. But they
" on the contrary, that by the impairing and diminution
" of the true Faith, by the Distresses and Servitude of
" their Country, aspire to high Dignity, Rule, and
" Promotion here, after a shameful end in this life
" (which God grant them) shall be thrown down eter-
" nally into the darkest and deepest Gulf of Hell: where
" under the despitful controul, the trample, and spurn
" of all the other Damn'd, that in the anguish of their
" torture shall have no other ease than to exercise a
" raving and bestial Tyranny over them as their Slaves
" and Negros, they shall remain in that plight for ever,
" the basest, the lowermost, the most dejected, most
" underfoot, and downtrodden Vassals of Perdition.
I shall end my account of this Divine Poem with a Copy

of *Latin* Verses made upon it by *Samuel Barrow,* a
Doctor of Physic.

Qui Legis amissam Paradisum, grandia magni
  Carmina Miltoni, quid nisi cuncta Legis ?
Res cunctas, & cunctarum primordia rerum,
  Et fata, & fines, continet iste Liber.
Intima panduntur magni penetralia mundi,
  Scribitur & toto quicquid in orbe latet.
Terrqæue tractusque maris, cœlumque profundum,
  Sulphureumque Erebi flammivomumque specus.
Quæque colunt terras, pontumque, & tartara cæca,
  Quæque colunt summi lucida regna poli.
Et quodcunque ullis conclusum est finibus usquam,
  Et sine fine Chaos, & sine fine Deus :
Et sine fine magis (siquid magis est sine fine)
  In Christo erga homines conciliatus amor.
Hæc qui speraret, quis crederet esse futurum ?
  Et tamen hæc hodie Terra Britanna Legit.
O quantus in bella duces ! quæ protulit arma !
  Quæ canit, et quanta prælia dira tuba !
Cœlestes acies ! atque in certamine cœlum !
  Et quæ cœlestes pugna deceret agros !
Quantus in ætheriis tollit se Lucifer armis !
  Atque ipso graditur vix Michaele minor !
Quantis ac quam funestis concurritur iris !
  Dum ferus hic stellas protegit, ille rapit !
Dum vulsos montes, ceu tela reciproca, torquent ;
  Et non mortali desuper igne pluunt :
Stat dubius cui se parti concedat Olympus,
  Et metuit pugnæ non superesse suæ.
At simul in cœlis Messiæ insignia fulgent,
  Et currus animes, armaque digna Deo,
Horrendumque rotæ strident, & sæva rotarum
  Erumpunt torvis fulgura luminibus,
Et flammæ vibrant & vera tonitrua rauco
  Admistis flammis insonuere polo :

Excidit attonitis mens omnis, & impetus omnis,
  Et cassis dextris irrita tela cadunt.
Ad pœnas fugiunt, &, ceu foret Orcus Asylum,
  Infernis certant condere se tenebris.
Cedite Romani scriptores, Cedite Graii,
  Et quot recens fama, vel celebravit anus.
Hæc quicunque leget tantum cecinisse putabit
  Mæonidem ranas, Virgilium Culices.

In the year 1670 he publish'd his *Paradise Regain'd*, consisting of four Books; but generally esteem'd much inferior to *Paradise Lost*, which he could not endure to hear, being quite of another mind: yet this occasion'd som body to say wittily enough that *Milton* might be seen in *Paradise Lost*, but not in *Paradise Regain'd*. With this last Book he publisht his *Samson Agonistes*, an admirable Tragedy, not a ridiculous mixture of Gravity and Farce according to most of the Modern, but after the Example of the yet unequal'd Antients, as they are justly cal'd, *Æschylus*, *Sophocles*, and *Euripides*.

In the year 70 also came abroad his *History of Britain*, wherof we had occasion to speak before. He deduc'd it only to the *Norman* Conquest, and yet we have it not as it came out of his hands; for the Licensers, those sworn Officers to destroy Learning, Liberty and good Sense, expung'd several passages of it wherin he expos'd the Superstition, Pride, and Cunning of the Popish Monks in the *Saxon* Times, but apply'd by the sagacious Licensers to *Charles* the Second's Bishops. This puts me in mind of a *Reply* to a certain Person by Sir *Robert Howard* lately deceast, a Gentleman of great Generosity, a Patron of Letters, and a hearty Friend to the Liberty of his Country. Being told that he was charg'd in a Book with whipping the Protestant Clergy on the back of the

Heathen and Popish Priests, he presently ask'd what they had to do there? He was a great admirer of *Milton* to his dying day; and, being his particular Acquaintance, would tell many pleasant Stories of him, as that he himself having demanded of him once what made him side with the *Republicans*? Milton answer'd, among other Reasons, because theirs was the most frugal Government; for that the Trappings of a Monarchy might set up an ordinary Commonwealth. But not to digress too far, our Author bestow'd a Copy of the unlicens'd Papers of his History on the Earl of *Anglesey*, who, as well as several of the Nobility and Gentry, was his constant Visitor. Nor was he less frequented by Foreners to the last, than in the time of his flourishing condition before the Restoration. It is an irreparable loss to this most potent Nation, that *Milton* did not find leisure to bring down his History to his own times: For (as the noblest Ornament of all Politeness and Litera-ture Sir *William Temple* justly complains) " tho the " *English* are so renown'd by the Fame of their Arms " and Exploits abroad, so applauded and envy'd for " their wise and happy Institutions at home, so flourish-" ing in Arts and Learning, and so adorn'd by excellent " Writers in other Kinds, yet none of 'em has produc'd " one good or approv'd general History of *England*. " But our Histories (continues he) have bin written by " such mean and vulgar Authors, so tedious in their " Relations, or rather Collections; so injudicious in the " choice of what was fit to be told or to be let alone; " with so little order, and in so wretched a Stile; that " as it is a shame to be ignorant in the Affairs of our " own Country, so 'tis hardly worth the time or pains " to be inform'd, since for that end a Man must read

" over a Library, rather than a Book: and after all,
" must be content to forget more than he remembers.
This Charge is too true, and yet it's very strange it
should be so, seeing no Country.in the World has
afforded a greater diversity or a better choice of Actions,
nor is furnisht with more ample or authentic Materials
for framing a just and full body of History. Would
Sir *William* be pleas'd to continue so useful a Work,
according to the inimitable Specimen he has publisht
for encouraging som other to pursue this Attemt,
England might boldly compare with *Rome*, and himself
be reckon'd equal with *Livy*. But tho he gos no further
than the *Norman* Conquest, which is the period of
Milton, yet we expect a larger Account from *James
Tyrrel*, the worthy Grandson of Archbishop *Usher*.
This learned Gentleman, to supply the Defects wherof
Sir *William Temple* complains, has undertaken to write
a General History of *England*, from the remotest
traditional Beginnings to this time. The first Volume
of it is already abroad, which reaches likewise to
William the First; the Second is now finisht; and I
hope he'l meet with sufficient encouragement to make
a speedy publication of the rest. For tho his Work may
not perfectly reach Sir *William*'s Plan in the nicest
exactness of Order, Stile, and Composition; yet it must
be confest by all true Judges to be the most impartial
and complete, the faithfullest, the most methodical, and
in all respects the best Collection that was ever made
in *England*. All our Manuscript historical Records,
and the numerous company of our particular Historians, can serve for little more to posterity than
to verify the Contents of this Book; nor will any
body be at the trouble to preserve 'em for this pur-

pose, that is not a stranger to Mr. *Tyrrel's* Diligence and Integrity.

Milton wrote som Miscellaneous Pieces much inferior to his other Works, as a *Grammar* for learning the *Latin* Tongue; a *Logic* after the method of *Petrus Ramus ;* a brief History of *Muscovy*, and of other less known Countries lying eastward of it as far as *Cathay*, collected from the Relations of several Travellers: he translated out of *Latin* into *English* the Declaration of the *Poles* concerning the Election of their King *John* the Third, containing an Account of the Virtues and Merits of the said Prince; he publisht Sir *Walter Raleigh's Prince*, or his *Maxims* and *Aphorisms of State ;* and he also printed his *Cabinet Council*. More pieces of this rarely accomplisht, tho unfortunat Gentleman, were made public by other persons; and I daily expect som more from *James Tyrrel*, who has the Manuscript Copies in his hands, and, I dare affirm, will not envy such a blessing to the Nation.

Our Author's Juvenil and Occasional Poems, both in *English* and *Latin*, were printed in one small Volume. I took notice of the best of 'em in many places of this Discourse; but the Monody wherin he bewails his Learned Friend Mr. *King* drown'd in the *Irish* Seas, is one of the finest he ever wrote.

The *Danish* Resident prevail'd with *Milton* to get the Letters of State (formerly mention'd) transcrib'd, and which were publisht after his death; as were also his *Familiar Letters* in 74, wherin, to use the words of *Morhof*, there are many Characters of Antient and Modern, of Domestic and Foren Authors, very fit to be read and understood. The last thing he wrote, and that was publisht a little before his Death, is his *Treatise*

of true Religion, Heresy, Schism, Toleration, and the best
means that may be us'd to prevent the growth of Popery.
He observ'd (as all discerning Men must have don at
that time) the prodigious increase of the *Romish* Superstition, occasion'd partly by the Persecution against
Dissenting *Protestants*, but more by the incouragement
it receiv'd from the Royal Brothers *Charles* and the
Duke of *York*. From the Principles which our Author
lays in his Book (and which, I think, are those of the
first Reformers) he infers that no true *Protestant* can
persecute any persons for speculative Points of Conscience, much less not tolerat his fellow *Protestant*, tho
in som things dissenting from his own Judgment.
After shewing that false Religion consists in the corrupt
Traditions of Men, and their arbitrary Additions to the
divine Rule or Standard of all Truth, he was at no
great labor to prove the Members of the *Roman* Church
to be the greatest Heretics in the World. As for
Schism, or the division of Congregations from their
difference in Opinions, he shews it may happen in
the true Church as well as in the false; but that in the
first it need not break Communion or brotherly Love,
no more than among the *Pharises* and *Sadduces*, who
amicably met at their common Worship in *Jerusalem*.
" It is human frailty to err, says he, and no Man is
" infallible here on Earth. But so long as the *Lutherans*,
" *Calvinists, Anabaptists, Socinians*, and *Arminians*, pro-
" fess to set the Word of God only before them as the
" Rule of their Faith and Obedience; and use all
" diligence and sincerity of heart by reading, by learn-
" ing, by study, by prayer for illumination of the Holy
" Spirit, to understand this Rule and obey it, they have
" don whatever Man can do. God will assuredly

" pardon them, as he did the Friends of *Job*, good
" and pious Men, tho much mistaken (as there it
" appears) in som points of Doctrin. But som will say,
" with *Christians* it is otherwise, whom God has
" promis'd by his Spirit to teach all things. True, all
" things absolutely necessary to Salvation: But the
" hottest Disputes among *Protestants*, calmly and charit-
" ably examin'd, will be found less than such. The
" *Lutheran* holds Consubstantiation; an error indeed,
" but not mortal. The *Calvinist* is tax'd with Pre-
" destination, and to make God the Author of Sin; not
" with any dishonorable thoughts of God, but, it may
" be, overzealously asserting his absolute Power, not
" without plea from Scripture. The *Anabaptist* is
" accus'd of denying Infants their right to Baptism;
" they say again, that they deny nothing but what the
" Scripture denys them. The *Arian* and *Socinian* are
" charg'd to dispute against the Trinity; yet they
" affirm to believe the Father, Son, and Holy Ghost,
" according to Scripture and the Apostolic Creed. As
" for the terms of Trinity, Trinunity, Coessentiality,
" Tripersonality, and the like, they reject them as
" Scholastic Notions not to be found in Scripture, which,
" by a general *Protestant* Maxim, is plain and perspic-
" uous abundantly to explain its own meaning in the
" properest words belonging to so high a matter, and so
" necessary to be known; a mystery indeed in their
" Sophistic Subtilties, but in Scripture a plain Doctrin.
" The *Arminian* lastly is condemned for setting up Free
" Will against Free Grace; but that imputation he
" disclaims in all his Writings, and grounds himself
" largely upon Scripture only. It cannot be deny'd
" that the Authors or late Revivers of all these Sects or

" Opinions were learned, worthy, zealous, and religious
" Men, as appears by their Lives written, and the Fame
" of their many eminent and learned Followers, perfect
" and powerful in the Scriptures, holy and unblamable
" in their Actions: And it cannot be imagin'd that God
" would desert such painful and zealous Laborers in
" his Church, and ofttimes great sufferers for their
" Conscience, to damnable Errors and a reprobat Sense,
" who had so often implor'd the assistance of his Spirit;
" but rather, having made no Man infallible, that he
" has pardon'd their Errors, and accepts their pious
" Endeavors, sincerely searching all things according
" to the Rule of Scripture, with such guidance and
" direction as they can obtain of God by Prayer. What
" *Protestant* then, who himself maintains the same
" Principles, and disavows all implicit Faith, would
" persecute, and not rather charitably tolerat such men
" as these, unless he means to abjure the Principles of
" his own Religion ? If it be ask'd how far they should
" be tolerated ? I answer, doutless equally, as being
" all *Protestants* ; that is, on all occasions to be per-
" mitted to give an account of their Faith, either by
" arguing, preaching in their several Assemblies, by
" public writing, and the freedom of printing. Nothing
can be imagin'd more reasonable, honest, or pious, than
this passage; and I don't remember ever to have met
with any person who spoke with such disinterestedness
and impartiality of our various Sects in Religion except
Thomas Firmin, whose Charity was as much extended
to men of different Opinions, as it was to the Poor of all
Sorts in good Works; but in this last respect he was
never yet equal'd, nor likely to be easily exceded by any
hereafter: tho his excellent Example is admir'd by

several, and deserves to be imitated by all. In the last place, *Milton* shews that *Popery* (not as it is a Religion, but as a tyrannical Faction oppressing all others) is intolerable, and that the best method of keeping it from ever increasing in this Nation, is by the toleration of all kinds of *Protestants* or any others whose Principles do not necessarily lead 'em to Sedition or Vice. But this Subject is since perfectly exhausted, and treated with greater clearness and brevity than ever before in a Letter concerning *Toleration* by *John Lock*, who in his Book of *Human Understanding* must be confest to be the greatest Philosopher after *Cicero* in the World; for he's perfectly acquainted with human Nature, well vers'd in the useful Affairs of the World, a great Master of Eloquence (Qualities in which the *Roman* Consul excel'd) and like him also a hearty lover of his Country, as appears by his Treatises of *Government* and *Education*, not inferior in their kind to the divinest Pieces of *Tully*. *Milton's Thesaurus Linguæ Latinæ*, design'd as a Supplement to *Stephanus*, was never publisht, and has bin of great use to Dr. *Littleton* in compiling his Dictionary. He wrote likewise a *System of Divinity*, but whether intended for public view, or collected merely for his own use, I cannot determin. It was in the hands of his Friend *Cyriac Skinner*; and where at present is uncertain.

This is a full and true account of his genuin Works and Sentiments, not putting the Directions or Assistance, which he frequently gave other Writers, to his account. Towards the latter part of his time he contracted his Library, both because the Heirs he left could not make a right use of it, and that he thought he might sell it more to their advantage than they could be able to do themselves. His Enemies reported that Poverty constrain'd him thus to part with his Books: and were this true, it would be indeed a great disgrace, not to him (for Persons of the highest Merits have bin often reduc'd to that condition) but to any Country that should have no more regard to Probity or Learning: this Story however is so false, that he dy'd worth fifteen hundred Pounds, besides all his Goods. The House wherin he was born, and which Strangers us'd to visit before the Fire, was part of his Estate as long as it stood. He put two thousand Pounds into the Excise, which he lost when that Bank fail'd; not to mention another great Sum which was gon for want of management and good advice. He was never very healthy, nor too sickly; and the Distemper that troubled him most of any other was the Gout, of which he dy'd without much pain in the year from the birth of Christ 1674, and in the six and sixtieth of his own Age. All his learned and great Friends in *London*, not without a friendly concourse of the Vulgar, accompany'd his Body to the Church of S. *Giles* near *Cripplegate*, where he lies buried in the Chancel, and where the Piety of his Admirers will shortly erect a Monument becoming his worth, and the incouragement of Letters in King *William's* Reign.

Thus liv'd and dy'd *JOHN MILTON*, a Person of the best Accomplishments, the happiest Genius, and the vastest Learning which this Nation, so renown'd for producing excellent Writers, could ever yet shew: esteem'd indeed at home, but much more honor'd abroad, where almost in his very Childhood he made a considerable figure, and continues to be still reputed one of the brightest Luminaries of the Sciences. He

N

was middlesiz'd and well proportion'd, his Deportment erect and manly, his Hair of a light brown, his Features exactly regular, his Complexion wonderfully fair when a Youth, and ruddy to the very last. He was affable in Conversation, of an equal and chearful Temper, and highly delighted with all sorts of Music, in which he was himself not meanly skil'd. He was extraordinary temperat in his Diet, which was any thing most in season or the easiest procur'd, and was no Friend to sharp or strong Liquors. His Recreations, before his Sight was gon, consisted much in feats of Activity, particularly in the exercise of his Arms, which he could handle with dexterity: but when Blindness and Age confin'd him, he play'd much upon an Organ he kept in the House; and had a Pully to swing and keep him in motion. But the love of Books exceded all his other Passions. In Summer he would be stirring at four in the Morning, and in Winter at five; but at Night he us'd to go to bed by nine, attributing the loss of his Eys to his late watching when he was a Student, and looking on this custom as very pernicious to Health at any time: but when he was not dispos'd to rise at his usual hours, he always had one to read to him by his bedside. As he look'd upon true and absolute Freedom to be the greatest Happiness of this Life, whether to Societies or single Persons, so he thought Constraint of any sort to be the utmost Misery: for which Reason he us'd frequently to tell those about him the intire Satisfaction of his Mind, that he had constantly imploy'd his Strength and Faculties in the defence of Liberty, and in a direct opposition to Slavery. He ever exprest the profoundest Reverence to the Deity as well in Deeds as Words; and would say to his Friends, that the divine

Properties of Goodness, Justice, and Mercy, were the adequat Rule of human Actions, nor less the Object of Imitation for privat Advantages, than of Admiration or Respect for their own Excellence and Perfection. In his early days he was a Favorer of those Protestants then opprobriously cal'd by the name of *Puritans :* In his middle years he was best pleas'd with the *Independents* and *Anabaptists*, as allowing of more Liberty than others, and coming nearest in his opinion to the primitive practice: but in the latter part of his Life, he was not a profest Member of any particular Sect among Christians, he frequented none of their Assemblies, nor made use of their peculiar Rites in his Family. Whether this proceded from a dislike of their uncharitable and endless Disputes, and that Love of Dominion, or Inclination to Persecution, which, he said, was a piece of Popery inseparable from all Churches; or whether he thought one might be a good Man, without subscribing to any Party; and that they had all in som things corrupted the Institutions of Jesus Christ, I will by no means adventure to determin: for Conjectures on such occasions are very uncertain, and I never met with any of his Acquaintance who could be positive in assigning the true Reasons of his Conduct.

I shall now conclude this Discourse with a Character given of him by a Man of unparallel'd Diligence and Industry, who has disoblig'd all sides merely for telling the Truth either intirely, or without disguise; and who, since most Men have the frailty of ingaging in Factions, cannot be suspected of Partiality in favor of *Milton*. He was a Person, says *Anthony Wood* in the first Volume of his *Athenæ Oxonienses*, of wonderful Parts, of a very sharp, biting, and satyrical Wit; he was a good Philosopher and Historian; an excellent Poet, Latinist, Grecian, and Hebrician; a good Mathematician and Musician; and so rarely endow'd by Nature, that had he bin but honestly principled, he might have bin highly useful to that Party, against which he all along appear'd with much Malice and Bitterness.

AND now, *Sir*, I end with you, with whom I begun, not doubting but this small Present, both from the dignity of the Subject and your Favor to the Writer, will be kindly accepted. It may indeed be the more plain and unpolish'd, but not the less useful or sincere for coming out of a Country Retirement. The most knowing Persons acknowlege that Divine Philosophy her self was begot in the Woods, where agreably passing her Infancy, and growing up in the neighboring Fields, she became gentle in time, and so ventur'd to com into Towns and Cities; but being quickly weary'd there with the Tumult of Business or Faction, and longing for her former Tranquillity, she straight retir'd into Gardens or Groves, to her Fields and Woods again. 'Tis probable that you (as well as I or any other) may disapprove of *Milton*'s Sentiments in several cases, but, I'm sure, you are far from being displeas'd to find 'em particulariz'd in the History of his Life; for we should have no true Account of things, if Authors related nothing but what they lik'd themselves: one Party would never suffer the Lives of *Tarquin*, or *Phalaris*, or *Sylla*, or *Cæsar*, to appear; while another would be as ready to suppress those of *Cicero*, of *Cato*, of *Trajan*, or *Brutus*. But a Historian ought to conceal or disguise nothing, and the Reader is to be left Judg of the Virtues he should imitate, or the Vices he ought to detest and avoid, without ever loving his Book the less: for (as the Lord *Bacon* truly said) *a forbidden Writing is thought to be a certain Spark of Truth that flies up in the faces of them who seek to tread it out.* But your extraordinary Judgment and Candor, join'd to the best Learning, and an exact Knowlege of Men and Affairs, render my further inculcating of these Maxims very needless; and therfore I shall only put you in mind, *Sir*, that my desire of gratifying your Curiosity conquer'd my Aversion to write any thing during this pleasantest Season of the Year.

I. T.

Sept. 3. 1698.

FINIS.

EXPLANATORY NOTES

and

REMARKS

on

MILTON's

𝔓𝔞𝔯𝔞𝔡𝔦𝔰𝔢 𝔏𝔬𝔰𝔱.

BY

J. RICHARDSON, Father and Son.

With the LIFE of the AUTHOR, and a Difcourfe on the POEM. By J. R. Sen.

LONDON:

Printed for JAMES, JOHN, and PAUL KNAPTON, at the *Crown* in *Ludgate-ftréet*, near the Weft-End of St. *Paul's.*

M.DCC.XXXIV.

IF I can give a more Exact, and a more Just Idea of *Milton*, and of *Paradise Lost* than the Publick has yet had of Either, I am Assur'd it will be Acceptable to all Honest and Ingenuous Minds of What Party Soever. This is All I Intend; not a Panegyrick, not to give my Own Sense of What a Man should be, but what This Man Really was. Not to Plead for the Poet, or the Poem, but for Truth, by giving Light into What hath Hitherto lain in Obscurity, and by Dispelling Mistakes which have Injur'd the Memory of a Deserving Man, Debas'd a Work Worthy of the Highest Estimation, and Robb'd the World of the Pleasure and Advantage it Might have Receiv'd, and I presume to Hope Will Hereafter Receive. This is My Aim in the Present Undertaking. Whoever Reads without being the Better for My Labour in Some Degree, 'tis Their Own Fault; though that they are not More Benefitted may be Mine; not for any Defect in my Will, but Capacity. Concerning *Milton*, I will First of All, as well as I am Able, Show you his Person; Then his Mind; Afterwards You shall be Acquainted with the Principal Occurrences of his Life ; his Provision for Maintenance; and Lastly, I will Consider the General Character of his Life, as to Happiness, by Comparing in very few Words his Sufferings and Enjoyments.

He was rather a Middle Siz'd than a Little Man, and Well Proportion'd; Latterly he was———No; Not Short and Thick, but he would have been So, had he been Somthing Shorter and Thicker than he Was. His Deportment was Manly and Resolute, but with a

Gentlemanly Affability. in his Habit Plain, Clean, and
Neat. his Voice was Musically Agreeable. When
Young he was Esteem'd Handsom, Chiefly I believe
because he had a Fine Skin, and a Fresh Complexion.
his Hair was a Light Brown, which he wore Parted a-
top, and Somwhat Flat, Long, and Waving, a little
Curl'd. the Print Prefix'd shows the Face of him who
Wrote Paradise Lost, the Face We Chiefly desire to be
Acquainted with, 'tis done from a Picture which I have
reason to believe he Sate for not long before his Death,
I have therefore given a little more Vigour to the Print,
and but a Little. the Complexion must be Imagin'd as
of One who had been Fair and Fresh Colour'd. *Toland*
says he was Ruddy to the Last, My Picture and other
Information does not tell us That, but that he might
have been So not long before. the Colour of his Eyes
inclin'd to Blue, not Deep; and though Sightless, they
were as he says Himself, *Clear to Outward View of
Blemish or of Spot*; he was Told So, and 'tis Certain the
Gutta Serena (which was His Case) does not appear to
Common Eyes, and at a little Distance; but Blindness,
even of That Kind is Visible, in the Colour, Motion,
and Look of the Eye which has the sad Unhappiness
of being Extinguish'd by it. 'tis Wonderfully Exprest
in the Picture from Whence this Print was made, as
well as the Sett of the Mouth, and the rest of the Air.
I have Imitated it as well as I could in a Way of Working which I Never Practic'd but on a Few Plates, and
Those in my Youth, except an Attempt on One or Two
near 20 Years ago. the Laurel is not in the Picture,
the two Lines under it are my Reason for putting it
There, not what Otherwise would have been Imagin'd.
All the World has given it him long since.

One that had Often seen him, told me he us'd to come to a House where He Liv'd, and he has also Met him in the Street, Led by *Millington*, the same who was so Famous an Auctioneer of Books about the time of the Revolution, and Since. This Man was then a Seller of Old Books in *Little Britain*, and *Milton* lodg'd at his house. This was 3 or 4 Years before he Dy'd. he then wore no Sword that My Informer remembers, though Probably he did, at least 'twas his Custom not long before to wear one with a Small Silver-Hilt, and in Cold Weather a Grey Camblet Coat. his Band was Usually not of the Sort as That in the Print I have given, That is, as my Original is, but like What are in the Common Prints of him, the Band usually wore at That time; to have a more Exact Idea of his Figure, let it be remembered that the Fashion of the Coat Then was not Much Unlike what the Quakers Wear Now.

I have heard many Years Since that he Us'd to Sit in a Grey Coarse Cloath Coat at the Door of his House, near *Bun-hill* Fields Without *Moor-gate*, in Warm Sunny Weather to Enjoy the Fresh Air, and So, as well as in his Room, received the Visits of People of Distinguish'd Parts, as well as Quality. and very Lately I had the Good Fortune to have Another Picture of him from an Ancient Clergy-man in *Dorsetshire*, Dr. *Wright*; He found him in a Small House, he thinks but One Room on a Floor; in That, up One pair of Stairs, which was hung with a Rusty Green, he found *John Milton*, Sitting in an Elbow Chair, Black Cloaths, and Neat enough, Pale, but not Cadaverous, his Hands and Fingers Gouty, and with Chalk Stones. among Other Discourse He exprest Himself to This Purpose; that was he Free from the Pain This gave him, his Blindness would be Tolerable.

Sufficient Care had not been taken of This Body, he had a Partiality for his Mind; but All that Temperance, Chastity, and every Wholesom Vertue could do, was done; Nor did he forbear Sometimes to Walk and Use Exercise, as himself says, *Eleg.* I. 50. VII. 51. and in a Passage in his *Apol.* for *Smectymnuus* which will be Quoted Anon on Another Occasion. but This was not Enough to Support him Under that Intense Study and Application which he took to be his Portion *in This* Life. He lov'd the Country, but was little There. nor do we hear any thing of his Riding, Hunting, Dancing, *&c.* When he was Young he learnt to Fence, probably as a Gentlemanly Accomplishment, and that he might be Able to do Himself Right in Case of an Affront, which he wanted not Courage nor Will for, as Himself intimates, though it does not appear he ever made This Use of his Skill. after he was Blind he us'd a Swing for Exercise.

Musick he Lov'd Extreamly, and Understood Well. 'tis said he Compos'd, though nothing of That has been brought down to Us. he diverted Himself with Performing, which they say he did Well on the Organ and Bas-Viol. and This was a great Relief to him after he had lost his Sight.

in relation to his Love of Musick, and the Effect it had upon his Mind, I remember a Story I had from a Friend I was Happy in for many Years, and who lov'd to talk of *Milton*, as he Often Did. *Milton* hearing a Lady Sing Finely, *now will I Swear*" (says he) *This Lady is Handsom.*" his Ears Now were Eyes to Him.

This little Hint puts me in Mind to Consider Him as a Lover, which might have been Overlook'd for any thing that is Said of Him in the Accounts we have; Only that he Marry'd Three times; And (as he says Himself somewhere) he had a particular Fancy, for which however I don't remember he gives any Reason, he would never think of taking a Widow; 'tis certain he did not, none of the Three Wedded by him were Such. Nor is it Observ'd he was in Love (as the Phrase is) with any of These; on the Other Hand nothing is said to his Disadvantage with regard to Tenderness as a Husband. Once indeed it appears by a Latin Poem of his (*Eleg*. VII. written when he was about 19) he fell in Love for the First time; He met the Lady upon Some Walks at *London*, Lost Sight of her, Never knew who she was, nor Saw her More, but Resolv'd Love should Thenceforward give him no farther Trouble.

but he was Mistaken, as appears by three fine Latin Copies of Verses to *Leonora*, a Young Lady who Sung Admirably at *Rome;* and five *Italian* Sonnets, and a *Canzona* that seem to be for the same Lady. He was not Insensible of Beauty; See his First Latin Elegy. but let it be remember'd This was when he was a Young Man. We hear nothing of This After his return from *Italy*.

When he was a Youth he Sometimes read Romances; and, as Good Minds Naturally will, turn'd All to his Advantage——*So that even Those Books, which to Many Others have been the Fuel of Wantonness, and Loose Living, I cannot think how, Unless by Divine Indulgence, prov'd to Me so many Incitements, as you have heard, to the Love and steadfast Observation of That Vertue which abhors the Society of Bordelloes.*" *Apol. for Smectymnuus.*

in This Spring of Life he also Sometimes saw a Play, and visited Publick Walks, and Such Kind of Diversions. He was a Chearfull Companion; but no Joker: his Conversation was Lively, but with Dignity. and as he was whilst Young, he Continu'd to be in his more Advanc'd Age. in a Latin Letter (his 21st, in the Year 1656) he thus Writes to *Emeric Bigot*.

It was extreamly Gratefull to Me that you thought Me Worthy to be visited preferably to Others when you came into England, *and 'tis still more gratefull that you now Salute me with Letters : for you came to me perhaps only led by the Opinion of the World, but your Returning by Letter is the result of your Own Judgment, or at least Benevolence. of which I find that I have great reason to Congratulate my Self ; for Many that have been very Considerable in their Writings, have had nothing but what was Low and Vulgar in their Private Conversation. for Me, if I can obtain, that having Written Somthing perhaps Tolerable, I may not appear to be Unequal in my Mind and Manners, I shall add a Weight to my Writings, and shall gain still more Honour and Praise from Them, (if indeed they do Deserve Any,) when it shall be seen that it has been drawn, not more from the Most Celebrated Authors, than, Pure, and Sincere from the Intimate Sense of my Own Mind, and very Soul.*

He had a Competent Knowledge in the Mathematicks; but doubtless he never design'd to persue That Science through All its Branches, nor to their Utmost Extent.

Whatever he Undertook was Dispatch'd as soon as possible. He was Always in Hast. *Cosa Fatta Capo hà* is an old *Florentine* Proverb. a thing Done has a Head; the Finishing Stroke is the principal One, the

Work is Nothing without it. *For Me* (says he in a Letter to *Diodatus*, Ep. 6. 1637) *Such is the Impetuosity of My Temper, that no Delay, no Quiet, no Different Care and Thought of Almost Any thing Else, can stop me 'till I come to my Journey's End, and Finish the Present Study to the Utmost I am Able.* This Last Clause shows also his Exactness and Care, without Which That Eagerness to have Done is a Vice.

Temperance was with Him a Favourite Vertue; See *Parad. Lost* V. 5. XI. 472, 515, 530, *&c.* and when he was Young (21) he Writes Finely on this Subject to his Friend *Diodatus Eleg.* vi. Here, after he had been Praising several of the Ancient Poets on Account of This Vertue, he says,

Diis etenim Sacer, &c.
Such Bards belong to Heav'n, by Heav'n are Blest,
They breathe Great Jove who dwells within their Breast.

Milton was not Nice, but took what was Set before him. All kinds of Strong Liquors he Hated. Let Those Ask Help from Them who want such Assistance. His Muse needed them not. His Celestial Patroness deign'd her Nightly Visitation Unimplor'd, and Dictated to him Slumb'ring, or Inspired *Easy his Unpremeditated Verse.* as *Parad. Lost* IX. 21. And he Slept but because he Must.

He set out in Life with a Disregard to Riches, or Advancement in the World. the Enriching and Adorning of his Mind; the Acquiring, Accumulating and Storing Up Great, Lovely, and Usefull Ideas, and that not for Himself Only, but for the Publick Good, was His Scheme, the Business He Conceiv'd was Appointed for Him in This Life; That he in Fact Executed This Project with Great Fervour will be seen

in its Place. Here I shall give you Some of his
Thoughts on That Matter, as I find them in his Anim-
adversions upon the Remonstrant's Defence against
Smectymnuus, Written soon after he came from Travel.
He had resolv'd to apply Himself to Learning, but not
for Gain.——*Doe they thinke then that all these Meaner
and Superfluous things come from God, and the Divine
Gift of Learning from the Den of* Plutus, *or the Cave of*
Mammon ? *Certainly never any Clear Spirit, Nurst up
in Brighter Influences, with a Soul inlarg'd to the Dimen-
sions of Spacious Art and High Knowledge, ever enter'd
There but with Scorn, and thought it ever Foul Disdain to
make Pelf or Ambition the Reward of his Studies, it being
the Greatest Honour, the Greatest Fruit and Proficiency of
Learned Studies to Despise These things*——and a little
after——*which Poor and Low-pitch'd Desires, if they do
but mix with those other Heavenly Intentions that draw
a Man to this Study, it is justly expected that they should
bring forth a Base-born Issue of Divinity,* (That is the
Subject he is upon in particular) *like that of those imperfect and Putrid Creatures that receive a Crawling Life
from Two Most Unlike Procreants, the Sun and Mudd.*
and not only in these his Younger Years, but All his
Life after, he shew'd he bore *a Generous Mind above the
Peasantly Regard of Wages and Hire.* if he had Recom-
pences of That kind for his Services to the Publick,
they were not the End he propos'd in Serving, for he
was *a Contemner of Filthy Lucre. For This,* (saith he in
his Apology for *Smectymnuus*) *I cannot omit without Ingratitude to that Providence Above, who hath ever bred
me up in Plenty, although my Life hath not been Unexpen-
sive in Learning and Voyaging About ; so long as it shall
Please Him to lend me what he hath Hitherto thought*

good, which is enough to serve me in all Honest and Liberal Occasions, and Somthing Over besides, I were unthankful to that highest Bounty, if I should make my self so Poor as to sollicit Needily any such kind of Rich Hopes as this *Fortune-teller dreams of.* It is to be Noted he was Yet Unmarried.

His Early Application to Study, and Success in it, Himself gives Us an Account of in his Introductory Discourse to his Second Book of *the Reason of Church Government,* after having *Petition'd to the Gentler Sort that it might not be Envy to him, Venturing to Divulge Unusual things of Himself,* he says,————*After I had from my First Years, by the Ceaseless Diligence and Care of my Father (whom God Recompence) been Exercis'd to the Tongues, and Some Sciences, as my Age would suffer, by Sundry Masters and Teachers both at Home and at the Schools, it was found that whether Ought was Impos'd me by Them that had the Overlooking, or betaken to of my Own Choice in English, or other Tongue, Prosing or Versing, but Chiefly This Latter, the Style by certain Vital Signs it had, was likely to Live.* Much to the same Purpose he says in his Apology for *Smectymnuus,* Sect. 6.————*For This good hap I had from a Carefull Education, to be Inur'd and Season'd Betimes with the Best and Elegantest Authors of the Learned Tongues, and thereto brought an Ear that could measure a just Cadence, and Scan without Articulating; rather Nice and Humorous in what was Tolerable than Patient to read every Drawling Versifier.*

He Acquir'd Betimes an Uncommon Stock of Learning, and all Those Languages in which the Variety and Sublimity of Humane Knowledge is Treasur'd up for Those who can Unlock the Cabinet, and know how to Judge, and make Use of what they find.

o

He understood French, Spanish, Italian, Latin, Greek and Hebrew; their Prose, and Poetick Dialects, for in all Languages These are Different. His Own Tongue, as Us'd by Him is Poetick English, 'tis Enrich'd and Strengthen'd with *Attick* and *Roman* Spoils, in Words, Phrases, and Idiom; nor has he Forgot to Restore Some Beauties which had been Long Neglected; So that His English is Worthy to be Learnt, and has been Endeavour'd to be Imitated, but His is Still his Own. Nor had he only Learnt these Languages So as to Construe them, and as a Scholar, but as a Master; and such a One as perceiv'd the Force, the Beauty, and Extent of a Word or Phrase, so as to take from Thence Ideas which Lexicographers and Grammarians are often Strangers to; his Latin in Particular is on all hands Allow'd to be like That of the *Augustan* Age: and So remarkable was he for his Knowledge in the *Italian* Tongue that the *Crusca* (an Academy Set up for the Reducing, and keeping the *Florentine* Language to its First Purity) made no Scruple to Consult Him, Whom they had receiv'd an Academician, on Difficult and Controverted Points. and indeed he had most Diligently read All their Ancient as well as their Modern Classick Poets, Historians, and Orators. See *Francini's* fine Panegyrick Ode in Honour of *Milton* Prefix'd to the Juvenile Latin Poems, and *Milton's* Own Letter to *Buonmatteo*, the 8th of his Latin Epistles. 'twas Written from *Florence*, in 1638. I will give a small Part of it.——*for my Part I can say that my Lips are not only Moisten'd with those two Languages* [Greek and Latin] *but As much as my Age Allow'd, have drank as Large Cups of it as any One; Yet notwithstanding I come with Joy and Delight to your* Dante *and* Petrarch:

nor has even Attic Athens *itself so held me upon the Shoar of her clear* Ilyssus, *nor That Dear Old* Rome *upon the banks of* Tyber, *but that I often love to Visit your* Arno, *and the Hills of* Fesole.

See also his Latin Letter to his Father.

But no Quality of Mind is More Conspicuous in Him, not even Piety and the Love of Civil and Ecclesiastical Liberty, than his Passionate Fondness for the Muses. I said This was as *Conspicuous*; and indeed he does Now, and has Long Since Shone in the Eyes of the Generality of the World, rather as a Great Poet, than as a Good Man, though even Poetry was Long Suspended whilst he was, as He thought, Combating in the Cause of God, and his Country's Liberty. but he was a Poet Early, and Always in his Soul. and Excell'd All Ancients and Moderns. (I take leave to Say so upon Many Good Authorities; I Pretend not to be Any in This Case) he Excell'd in Lyrick, Pastoral, Dramatick, Epic, and a Kind Purely Original, Such is his *Masque*. Comedy indeed he never attempted that we know of, nor Dogrel. Much Less any thing in the Least Profane, or Indecent.

He had Read and Studied all the Greatest Poets, and had made All his Own: *Homer* he could Almost repeat without Book; and above All he found Divine Nourishment for his Muse Where 'tis Superlatively Rich, that is, in the Holy Scriptures. He, if Ever Man was, *was Smit with the Love of Sacred Song*. and he was Every way Qualify'd to Sustain the Celestial Impulse; for, besides his general Great Reading, and Thorough Knowledge of Words, he had an Elevated Mind, and an Imagination, and That Lively and Strong, Most Eminently so. Imagination is Essential to Poetry; 'tis

Manifest He Conceiv'd Greatly, and Beautifully; and what he Thus Saw he Communicated as far as Words can. No Man ever Painted like Him in That way, though, (which I have Often wonder 'd at) He does not appear to have Much Regarded what was done with the Pencil; no not even when in *Italy*, in *Rome*, in the *Vatican*. Neither does it seem Sculpture was Much Esteem'd by him.

He had a Gravity in his Temper, Not Melancholly, or not 'till the Latter Part of his Life, not Sour, Morose, or Ill-Natur'd; but a Certain Severity of Mind, a Mind not Condescending to Little things. his *Juvenile* Poems are So no Otherwise than as they were Wrote in his Younger Years, for their Dignity and Excellence they are sufficient to have set him among the most Celebrated of the Poets, even of the Ancients themselves; his *Mask* and *Lycidas* are perhaps Superior to all in their Several Kinds. of the First of These, Sir *Henry Wootton* in his Letter to *Milton*, gives a great Encomium, and *Toland* says, " that for the peculiar Disposition of the Story, the Sweetness of the Numbers, the Justness of the Expression, and the Moral it teaches, there is Nothing like it extant in any Language." As great an Encomium have I heard of *Lycidas* as a Pastoral, and That when *Theocritus* was not forgot; *Theocritus*, of whom *Virgil* was but an Imitator in his Pastorals, as he was of *Homer* in his *Æneis*. the *Allegro* and *Penseroso* are Exquisite Pictures. his Latin Poems have the Same Gravity and Dignity, and Most of them remarkably Excellent, though All Written while he was a Young Man, or *Almost* Before. even his Few Love Poems have a Sort of Dignity and Gravity in them. I will present the English Reader with the

Concluding Stanza's of One of Those in Italian. Speaking of his Heart, he says,

'tis Honest, Steddy, and not soon Afraid,
*   Genteel of Thought but knows no Cunning Art :*
*   When the Deep World roars, and the blue Lightnings dart,*
Self-Adamantine-Arm'd, 'tis not Dismay'd.

As much of Envy Careless, and of Chance,
*   and Hopes, and Fears that Vulgar Minds Abuse,*
*   as in Lov'd Vertue Ardent to advance,*
and Win the Tuneful Lyre and Gentle Muse.
*   There only you will find it Less Secure*
*   Where* Love *hath fixt a Wound no Time can Cure.*

nor does he fail to tell his Mistress what he Loves her for; what should Excite even That Passion in a Wise and Good Breast.

Some of his most Particular and Distinguish'd Good Qualities I have Noted, but a General Love of Vertue appears throughout the whole Course of his Life. Thus he writes to *Diodatus*, Ep. VII. 1637.——*It is impossible for Me not to Love and Cherish Such as You, for, what God has Otherwise Decreed of Me I know not, This I am Sure of, He hath Instill'd into Me, if into Any One on Earth, a most Severe Love of Vertue. never did* Ceres *seek with Half so much Labour Her* Proserpine *as I persue This same Idea of Beauty, as Some most Amiable Object, through all the Forms and Faces of things, (for the Gods have many Forms;) Searching through Day and Night, and Eye her often Leading before me, and Distinguish'd by certain Undoubted Footsteps. 'tis for This, My* Diodatus, *that when I meet with Any one who despises the Vulgar, and Dares to Think, and Speak, and Be Her, to Him I bind my Self, my Friend, and Cling to the Utmost of my Power. for if I, whether by a Poorness of Nature, or by Some Fate, am So Made that I can not be ever Able, with all my Contention and Ardent Labour to Emerge to that Dear Splendour and Height of Glory, yet Sure both God and Men will Allow me the Humble Praise of Loving and Admiring Those who have Gain'd it, or Aspire to it with Success.*

What *Milton* meant by Vertue is what All should mean by it, a Constant, Uniform, Universal Regularity of Manners. *Vertue that Wavers is not Vertue, but Vice revolted from it self, and after a While returning.* These are his own Words. but of This More hereafter. for I fear it will be to little Purpose if I proceed on *Milton's* Moral or Religious, 'till I have quenched or abated the Prejudices of Most of my Readers with Regard to his Political Character. 'tis Certain he was a Republican: So was *Cato*, So was *Brutus*, So was *Phocion*, *Aristides*. ——Such were by Much the Most of the Greatest Names of Roman and Greek Antiquity. We have none of These Prejudices against Them, but Admire, and are Delighted with their Abilities and Vertues; and, if we are Wise and Good Our Selves, will become Wiser and Better by their Example notwithstanding they were Republicans, and Did, or Encourag'd the Doing, what We who happen to possess Other Notions of Government would Abhor to Think of. in Judging of a particular Man, let us Consider him as an Individual of the Species, as a Rational Creature, not as of any Particular Country, or as having had his small Portion of Being in whatsoever Point of the Vast Circle of Eternity. We all judge Thus when we Read *Plutarch*; Reading Mee alters not the Case in That; or if we cannot Intirely divest our Selves of all Kind of Prejudices; if we find a Byas towards a Greek or Roman upon Account of the

Great Idea we have of Those People, let our own Country-man have a Share of our Partiality; and Consider *Milton* as a *Briton, and a Brave One too*, and One who sacrific'd More than Most of us will Care to do, and Ventur'd Still More in the Cause of Civil and Religious Liberty, as He thought, though upon Principles, and in a Manner, as You and I are Far from Approving. be That to God and his Own Conscience.

and *Who art Thou that Judgest Another?* That Other has an Equal Right to Return the Reproach; and if he has not more Wit, Good Manners or Charity will do so, and with Apellations Equally Opprobrious. Whenever we differ in Our Opinions, Each Disputant Alike Thinks the Other in the Wrong: Which is So must be left to Him, whose *Thoughts are not as Our Thoughts*, but who is a Common, and an Indulgent Father to Both Parties, How much soever they are Imbitter'd against Each Other. Difference in Opinion will Always be, but All should agree in Mutual Good Will, Forbearance and Charity. *Humanum est Errare.*

Not only his Political Principles have been Censur'd, but his Behaviour under them as Virulent, and Dishonest.

Milton appears to have had a Natural Greatness, Warmth and Vigour of Mind, together with an Openness and Generosity, all which is True Magnanimity. This Blazes wherever he goes from One End of his Life to the Other. Such Minds are apt to take Strong and Deep Impressions; and as He was Fully persuaded he was Engag'd in the Cause of God, and of Liberty, he exerted every Nerve. if *Hercules* Grapples with *Anteus*, Ceremony is Forgotten, the Bones must Crash.

When He was a Young Man, Setting out to Travel, Sir *Henry Wootton* recommended to him that Wise Maxim, *I Pensieri Stretti, e il Viso Sciolto.* (Close Thoughts, and an Open Countenance.) he disdain'd to be the Tyrant of his own Sentiments, They were Free as Himself desir'd to be; he could not Stoop to Dissimulation. He sacrific'd his Prudence to his Zeal. at *Rome* he Talk'd as Occasion offer'd, not as a Traveller, but rather as an Apostle. and when Afterward at *Naples* he was Advis'd by no means to return home That Way, he Despis'd the Danger he was told Threat'n'd him, and went Thither, hast'ning back to his Country from all his New Acquir'd Friends, Men the Most Remarkable for Wit and Learning in *Italy* at That time, and whom he Much Lov'd, and who Equally Lov'd Him, Young as he was, and Notwith-standing his Known Difference in Opinion, and though they had seen but a Few of his Italian and Latin Poems, nor the Best of These Neither as not being Yet written. he came, Denying Himself the Pleasure he had Resolv'd on of Visiting *Sicily*, and Chiefly *Greece*, *Athens* in Particular; a Nation and City he was Always Enamour'd of as the Great Fountain from whence flow'd those Streams which Gladded his Heart, for he was more a Greek than a Roman; he Forsook all These Endearments to come Hither, where War was Kindling apace, to Assist with the Utmost of his Abilities on the Side where He judg'd Truth was. if any had said to him as the Elder Brother of *David* said to that *Stripling.* 1 Sam. xvii. 28, 29. *Why camest thou down Hither ? and with Whom hast thou left those few Sheep in the Wilderness ? I know thy Pride, and the Naughtiness of thine Heart, for thou art come down that thou mightst see the Battle.* he would have Answer'd as *David*; *What have I now done ? is there not a Cause ?*

Who Now would Expect he should *Dawb with Untemper'd Mortar ?* he Writes in all his Controversial Works with the same Ardour his Soul Felt, let Men call it Virulence, or Zeal as they happen to be Inclin'd.

but his Fervour was not Unrestrainable When 'twas Evident it could be to no Purpose; for after the Restoration, he no more Engag'd in the Old Disputes; he had given Sufficient Proofs of his Courage in Former times: but even Now he Scorn'd to Flatter Power, as Many did; the Same Openness and Honesty was seen in him, his Old Principles were well known to continue, they are seen even in *Paradise Lost.*

if it be Suggested, that he had Base and Unworthy Ends in View, Applause, Gain, Revenge, in short, Any Passion that was not Honest; Besides what I am just come from saying concerning the Greatness and Undisguis'd Openness of Heart which seems to have been Natural to him, 'tis Certain by All the Accounts we have, that he Engag'd in the Quarrel, and Long continu'd to Write, without any Recompence more than the Ease he found in Undertaking what his Monitor Within call'd upon him to do, and a Consciousness of having done what He Conceiv'd was his Duty. This he did though Otherwise the Work was his Aversion. for This he ceas'd *to Wander where the Muses haunt,* the Flowry Fields of *Parnassus,* to tread the Thorny, Rough, Miry, Gloomy Ways of Disputation; for This he Sacrific'd his Health, and Repose, his Eyes, and Probably Some Years of Life, not without Some Hazard of doing So in a manner very Ignominious. I am not Justifying his Principles, but his Sincerity,

That is what I am pleading for, and for your Indulgence
to the Ashes of a Man, to Whom I owe Much of the
Happiness of my Life, of a Man who Meant Well to
Us all, and to our Posterity; and that You, Looking
on his Urn might Incense it with your Kind Sentiments
and Benedictions, as I shall to my Latest Breath. But
behold Here he is, he will Speak for Himself, and he
has a Right to be Believ'd in a Case which Himself can
only Know, and when His Testimony is Supported by
all the Other Parts of his Character, and by the Other
Circumstances of his Life.

*I Invoke the Immortal Deity, Revealer and Judge of
Secrets, that wherever I have in This Book Plainly and
Roundly (though Worthily, and Truly) laid open the Faults
and Blemishes of Fathers, Martyrs, or Christian Emper-
ours, or have Otherwise inveighed against Error and
Superstition with Vehement Expressions, I have done it
neither out of Malice, nor list to speak Evil, nor any Vain
Glory, but of meer Necessity to Vindicate the Spotless Truth
from an Ignominious Bondage, whose Native Worth is
Now become of Such a Low esteem that She is like to find
Small Credit with Us for what She can say.* See his
Treatise of *Reformation ; Toland's* Edit. of his Prose
Works p. 252. and This was Publish'd when he first
Set out on this Unpleasing Task. in Another Dis-
course of about the same Date (*Reason of Church
Government*) Prose Works p. 220. he Thus Opens his
Heart at Large.

*For Surely to every Good and Peaceable Man it must in
nature needs be a Hatefull thing to be the Displeaser and
Molester of Thousands ; much better would it like him
doubtless to be the Messenger of Gladness and Contentment,
Which is his chief intended business, to all Mankind, but*

that they Resist and Oppose their own true Happiness. but when God commands to take the Trumpet, and blow a Dolorous or a Jarring Blast, it lies not in Man's Will what he shall Say, or what he shall Conceal. If he shall think to be Silent, as Jeremiah *did, because of the Reproach and Derision he met with daily, and* all his familiar Friends watcht for his Halting, *to be Reveng'd on him for Speaking the Truth, he would be forc'd to confess, as he confest ;* his Word was in my Heart as a burning Fire shut up in my Bones, I was weary with Forbearing, and could not Stay. *Which might teach these times not Suddenly to condemn all things that are Sharply Spoken, or Vehemently Written, as proceeding out of Stomach, Virulence, and Ill Nature ; but to consider rather that if the Prelats have leave to Say the worst that can be said, and Do the worst that can be Don, while they strive to keep to Themselves, to their great pleasure and commodity, those things which they ought to Render up, no man can be justly Offended with him that shall endeavour to Impart and Restore without any Gain to Himself those Sharp, but Saving words which would be a Terror and a Torment in him to keep back. For me I have determined to lay up as the best Treasure, and Solace of a good Old Age, if God voutsafe it me, the Honest Liberty of Free Speech from my Youth, where I shall think it Available in So dear a Concernment as the Churches good. For if I be either by Disposition, or what Other Cause, too Inquisitive, or Suspicious of my Self and mine Own doings, who can help it ? but this I Foresee, that should the Church be brought under heavy Oppression, and God have given me Ability the while to Reason against that Man that should be the Author of so Foul a deed ; or should She, by Blessing from Above on the Industry and Courage of Faithfull Men*

*change this her Distracted estate into Better daies without
the least Furtherance or Contribution of those few Talents
which God at that present had lent Me, I foresee what
Stories I should hear within my self, all my life after, of
Discourage and Reproach.   Timorous and Ingratefull, the
Church of God is now again at the foot of her Insulting
Enemies : and Thou Bewailst, What matters it for Thee,
or Thy Bewailing ?   When time was, thou couldst not find
a Syllable of all thou hadst Read, or Studied, to utter in
Her Behalf.   Yet Ease and Leasure was given thee for
thy retired Thoughts out of the Sweat of other Men.   Thou
hadst the Diligence, the Parts, the Language of a Man, if
a vain Subject were to be Adorn'd or Beautifi'd, but when
the Cause of God and his Church was to be pleaded, for
which purpose that Tongue was given thee which thou
hast, God Listen'd if he could hear thy Voice among his
Zealous Servants, but thou wert Dumb as a Beast ; from
hence forward Be That which thine own Brutish Silence
hath made thee.   or Else I should have heard on the other
Ear ;   Slothfull, and Ever to be Set light by ;   the Church
hath Now overcom her late Distresses after the Unwearied
Labours of Many her true Servants that stood up in her
Defence ;   Thou also wouldst take upon Thee to Share
amongst Them of Their Joy :   but Wherefore Thou ?
Where canst thou Shew any Word or Deed of Thine which
might have hastned her Peace ? whatever Thou dost Now
Talk, or Write, or Look is the Almes of Other Mens Active
Prudence and Zeale.   Dare not now to Say, or Do any
thing better than thy former Sloath and Infancy ; or if
thou darst, thou dost Impudently to make a thrifty purchase of Boldness to thy Self out of the Painfull Merits of
other Men : what Before was thy Sin, is Now thy Duty
to be, Abject and Worthlesse.   These and Such like Lessons*

*as These, I know would have been my Matins duly, and
my Even-Song. but Now by this little Diligence, mark
what a Privilege I have gain'd ; with Good Men and
Saints to claim my right of Lamenting the Tribulations of
the Church, if She should Suffer, when Others that have
Ventur'd Nothing for her Sake, have not the honour to be
admitted Mourners. But if She lift up her Drooping
Head and Prosper, among those that have Something
More than Wisht her Wellfare, I have my Charter and
Freehold of Rejoycing to Me and my Heirs. Concerning
therefore this wayward Subject against Prelaty, the touching whereof is so distastful and disquietous to a number of
men, as by what hath been said I may deserve of charitable
Readers to be Credited, that neither Envy nor Gall hath
enter'd me upon this Controversy, but the enforcement of
Conscience only, and a preventive fear least the Omitting of
this Duty should be against me when I would Store up to
my self the good provision of Peacefull hours : So lest it
should be still imputed to me, as I have found it hath bin,
that Some Self-pleasing humor of vain-glory hath incited
me to contest with Men of high estimation, now while
Green years are upon my head, from this Needlesse Sur-
misal I shall hope to Disswade the Intelligent and Equal
Auditor, if I can but say Successfully that which in this
Exigent behoovs me, although I would be heard only, if it
might be, by the Elegant and Learned Reader, to whom
Principally for a while I shall beg leave I may address my
Self. To him it will be no new thing though I tell him
that if I hunted after praise by the ostentation of Wit and
Learning, I Should not write thus out of mine own Season,
when I have neither yet compleated to my minde the full
Circle of my Private Studies, although I complain not of
any Insufficiency to the Matter in hand, or were I ready to*

my wishes, it were a folly to commit any thing Elaborately compos'd to the Carelesse and Interrupted listening of these Tumultuous times.   Next if I were wise only to mine Own ends, I would certainly take Such a Subject as of it self might catch Applause, whereas This hath all the Disadvantages on the Contrary, and Such a Subject as the Publishing whereof might be Delayd at pleasure, and time enough to Pencill it over with all the curious Touches of Art, even to the perfection of a Faultlesse Picture; when as in This Argument the Not deferring is of great Moment to the good Speeding, that if Solidity have leisure to do her office, Art cannot have much.   Lastly, I should not chuse this manner of Writing, wherein knowing my self Inferior to my Self, led by the Genial Power of Nature to Another Task, I have the use, as I may account it, but of my Left hand.

I will subjoyn two Other Passages, Much Shorter than This.   They are in his *Defensio* 2da *pro Pop. Anglican.*   Written Many Years after, though the Passages I am going to produce, refer to a Point of Time Somwhat Earlier; that is, before he was made Latin Secretary.   the First of These is in *p.* 91.   *Tol.* Edit. in *English* Thus.

———*nor do I Complain of the very Small Part that hath come to Me of Reward and Advantage for My Service to the Commonwealth, and of the very Great One of Ignominy and Reproach; Contented that I have been a Zealous Asserter of what was Right, for it Self Alone, and* Gratis ; *let Others look to That.   and be it known to You that Those Conveniencies, and That Wealth You Reproach me with I have never touch'd; and that, on the Account of what You Chiefly Accuse me of, I am not made a Penny the Richer.*   the Other is in *p.* 98.

I have thus, from my private Study, given my Time and Labour, somtimes to the Church, somtimes to the Commonwealth, though neither This nor That hath given Me any thing in return but Security ; What I have done hath, of it Self, given Me a Good Conscience within, a Good Esteem amongst the Good, and, withall, This Just and Honest Liberty of Speaking ; Others were Busy in the mean time in accommodating Themselves with Honours and Profits ; Me No Man hath seen Solliciting ; None seen Making under-Interest by my Friends ; None Posted up in the Lobby with my Petitioning Countenance, or Assiduous at the Doors and in the Entrys of the Great. I was generally at Home, Living Frugally upon my Own, though often considerably Shorten'd by these Civil Broils, and Tax'd to the Rigour, sometimes almost Unjustly.

Another Noble Passage, wherein there is a Bright Character of a Mind Truly Pious and Honest, and what is in particular to the Present Purpose, I reserve for a yet more Proper Place, and shall proceed, Now that I am upon This Sort of Work, to Brush off more Dirt; not indeed So Black as What I have been upon, nor so Inveterate, but which, if he knows I have Undertaken to endeavour to do him Right, he Expects I should Clear him of as well as I Can, and the rather, because he has no where done it Himself that I know of, perhaps as being a Domestick Affair, or perhaps he Never Suspected his Garment Had, or would have any Such Spot upon it.

I don't remember to have Ever heard he was Sour, Ill-natur'd, or Morose in General, and in Common Life, but the Contrary: the Warmth, the Vigour which is seen Somtimes in his Writings, Especially when Defending Himself from Cruel, and Base Calumny,

Charity and Honesty will impute to Other Causes. or Admitting he had been Commonly Peevish; at Some times, who is not So, in Some degree? his Many Provocations, Disappointments, Misfortunes, Pains, &c. would have Excus'd even a Philosopher. but in all Appearance he was too much So to have been Remarkably Blameable on This Article, or rather that Affability and Good Nature was his General Character. The Charge I am Now to Speak to is, that Whatever he was Elsewhere, How Patiently soever he bore the Provocations Two of his Wives gave him (One liv'd but a few Months after their Marriage, and we know Nothing of Her Behaviour) Yet, That he was too Rigid a Master of his Family; but more Especially, That he was a Severe and Cruel Father.

a Man that Practises Severity on Himself in an Exact Observation of Vertue's Commands, finds himself Obliged by those very Laws to Exact a like Obedience from All under his Care. I have Heard, and do Believe, and Allow, *Milton's* Family was a Well Order'd Government; Licentiousness was not Permitted by Him: he could be a Rigid Monarch Here with a good Grace; he could require Vertue, Frugality, and Strict Discipline (which Women and Children fail not to call Severity) as he Bravely Led the Way, by being an Example, and Able moreover to Stand a Retrospect into his Own Behaviour when Young, and through all the Stages of Life. and Happy would it be if in these little Patriarchal Monarchies the Subjects would Obey Such Laws, Rigid though they may Seem to be to Green Years, or Green Minds; it would be Happiness to Themselves More than to their Governors, Otherwise than as *Rejoycing in Their Joy.*

'tis however very Natural for an Old Man, Enur'd to Strict Vertue, and One whose Passions are Weakened with Continual Assaults and Repulses, to Expect Too much from his Dependants in Such Different Circumstances; He should Practise that Superiority of Wisdom He pretends to, in making Allowances as Reason Dictates, and remember This Sort of Prudence is also Vertue; He should Thus as it were Set up Another Person within Himself, and let Him make Proper Abatements to his Own Laws of Perfection. These New Laws would Then be Such, Relatively Consider'd, (which Surely is the Right way of Considering All things) as the Other are Abstractedly; and Thus save Himself a great deal of Uneasiness, Anger, and Sorrow, and Preserve Love and Peace, and Joy in his Own Mind. and all This *Milton* did for Ought We, or Any that Accuse him know to the Contrary. his Behaviour to his First Wife on a Most remarkable Occasion, (as shall Appear in its Place) makes it exceeding Probable he Conducted Himself by These Kind Reasonings; that he Exacted not from Others what Himself would have done, but what He ought to Suppose They were Capable of doing.

but there is One very Particular Instance of Severity he is Charg'd with. the Fact is Certain, the Severity is Apparent; but Whether 'tis a Fault or no is the Question. what I mean, is his Compelling Two of his Daughters to Learn to Read, without Understanding One Word, Several Languages, and to Read To, and Write For him Continually. I speak here of Two Thus Employ'd, though Some say but One, She that dy'd a few Years Since, and was so much Spoke of, and Visited and So Nobly Reliev'd for His Sake. An

P

Accident Prevented My Seeing her, but I was not Un-
mindful of what was Due to the Memory of her Father.
'tis One of the Unhappinesses of Age to be Blam'd as
Morose and Severe, when the Person is not Guilty of
it, or not to the Degree he is Charged with, and that
Partly because 'tis Probable, and therefore Expected.
the World is what we are not tempted to be Better
pleas'd with by Long Knowing it; Disappointments,
Ingratitude, Baseness, Villany, &c. put us Somtimes
out of Humour in spite of all our Philosophy; to say
nothing of Other Disagreeable Circumstances from
Within, Incident to Old Age. Younger People should
make Allowances to Us, as They Expect We should
Indulge Them in Their Weaknesses; but they are not
Usually Arriv'd to That Degree of Wisdom till Themselves become of Our Number, and cease to Reproach
Us. When Things are Wrong, as Both Parties are
Somtimes in Fault, Both are Blam'd; because, though
it may be One Only is justly Blameable, the World
knows not Which That is, and therefore, always in-
clin'd to Judge Unkindly, they spread Censure as
Wide as they Can. This Doubles the Injury on the
Guiltless Person; and This is Many Times the Case
in Family Disputes, particularly betwixt Parents and
Children; and Such is the Byas towards the Young
People, for what Reasons I will not Stay to Enquire,
(I should have said Prejudices, for Reason directs
rather to the Other Side) if Any thing is Amiss, and
the Question is Whether the Father or the Children
are to Blame, All, or the Greater Part falls to the Share
of the Old Man. Would to God I could produce
Milton, his Own Advocate on the Present, as on Other
Occasions ! He would do Himself Right, whether by

Owning, or Denying the Justice of the Charge; He would Clear his Own Honour by Acquiring the Greatest, That of Scrupulously Adhering to Truth; but as for Ought we can learn, This Reflection on his Mind is Posthumous, I beg Leave to appear in His Stead, and hope to be heard with Patience and Candour defending an Orphan-Reputation, by Imagining, as well as I can, what He would have said; though far Otherwise than if he was Dictating to Me. Perhaps He would not have Condescended to have Answer'd These Cavillers, Unless by Roughly Asking them what Business they had to Concern themselves with, much less to Censure His Conduct in his Domestick Affairs; there being Secrets in All Families which no Body has a Right to Enquire into, and yet without Knowing These Throughly, and in Every Particular, no Solid Judgment can be made? He Probably would have put These Busy-Bodies in Mind of the Spanish Proverb, *A Fool is Wiser in his Own House, than a Wise Man in that of his Neighbour.* and then have Appeal'd to the rest of his Character, Recommending them to the Great Rule of Charity, the Sum of Moral and Evangelical Vertue.

but if he had Condescended to give them Explicit Satisfaction, we may Imagine him telling them that these Daughters were born about the time his Sight first fail'd him, that is, about the Year 50. it cannot be Suppos'd they were capable of having Learnt before they were 12 years Old, till When they might as well be Thus employ'd as any how Else, not being kept to it too Strictly, which is not Pretended. We are Now therefore in the Year 62. Then, and Soon after we are Assur'd he had Plenty of Other Assistance, and in a few Years after, by that time they were about 20 Years of Age, their Father, Partly from Their Complaints, Partly from his Own Reflections, Acquitted them of This Duty. What is there in All This Much more than what is done very Commonly, That of requiring a Child to read what He or She as little Understands, or takes Pleasure in as these Girls did his Latin, Greek, Hebrew, &c? 'tis true, they were kept from what was More Delightful. and Happy would it be were Young People kept, even Thus, from What Most Nowadays are Educated in; Happy to Themselves, as well as to Those who in Reality Love them Best; and That, not Only for the Present, but Throughout every Stage of their Future Life.

but Admitting it was a Hardship; let the Father be taken into the Account, let Some regard be had to Him. Here was an Old Man, Blind, Infirm, near Ruin'd, Afflicted; Standing in great Need therefore of Assistance from Those of Whom he had reason to Expect it, and of what Consolation They could Afford; One of the Principal Branches of which was Reading, and Writing for him. he was not in a Condition to Hire a Proper Person Always to Attend as his Own Children, or, if he would have done That, he must have Lessen'd his Provision for his Family. They were Then at Work for Themselves. and was it Nothing (think ye) no Hardship upon Him to Teach Girls as These were Taught? Consider His Distress, Either way; and Pity Him you have been Blaming, and Who was by Much the Greater Sufferer, whether They Assisted Him or did not; and Consider Withall that They Deserv'd the Uneasiness in Proportion as they Felt and Complain'd of it, as He Felt His the More, the More he found Theirs Was.

As we are at a Loss as to the Particulars of the Affair, What I have Suggested will I hope be Sufficient, Only let Me add, that That Daughter, who was Certainly One (if there was really more than One) that was Thus Serviceable to her Excellent Father in his Distress, Express'd no Uneasiness, that I ever heard of, when she gave Accounts of *Milton*'s Affairs to the Many Enquirers Lately; but on the Contrary, spoke of him with Great Tenderness; particularly I have been told She said He was Delightful Company, the Life of the Conversation, and That on Account of a Flow of Subject, and an Unaffected Chearfulness and Civility. One Instance of her Tender Rememberance of him I cannot forbear relating. the Picture in Crayons I have of him was shown her After several Others, or which were Pretended to be His; when Those were shown, and She was Ask'd if She could recollect if She had ever seen Such a Face. No, No. but when This was Produc'd, in a Transport,——'tis My Father, 'tis my Dear Father ! I see him ! 'tis Him ! and then She put her Hands to several Parts of Her Face, 'tis the very Man ! Here, Here——

it has been said, This Daughter not only withdrew her Assistance in Reading, &c. but went away to *Ireland*, where She Married, all, not only without her Father's Consent, but even his Knowledge. but I never heard 'twas upon Occasion of any Unkindness of His, Unless as having Married; That This Mother-in-Law was as Mothers-in-Law frequently are, has been Suggested to be the Cause;——There is no End

of going into Family Affairs, in which 'tis Impossible
to come At Materials to be Sufficiently Instructed, and
He must be very Impertinent, and Negligent of his
Own Business that should go about it. We will have
done; Leaving the General Character of my Client,
his Vertue, Piety, Good Disposition; his Good Sense,
Prudence, &c. to Finish My Plea, in This Cause Commenc'd against Him by the Pretended Friends of his
Children, but in Reality by People, Malicious to His
Name, or Such Who with an Affectation of Goodness
which Costs Them Nothing, care not if they Wound
One Already Injur'd. Let These Sort of Creatures
remember how Natural it is for Offenders to Justify
Themselves with Falsities and Unjust Reproaches,
which the Injur'd Father rather Chooses to Bear, than
to Wipe them Off by Irrecoverably Losing, or Ruin-
ing the Rebel; and Then, that, a Father's Love is
Another Sort of a Feeling than that Counterfeit Good
Nature, Pity, or whatever Other Name they affect to
give to the Passion they are under the Influence of on
Such Occasions, and which perhaps is Oftener Self-
Love, Ill-Nature, or Malice, than they would willingly
have it thought to be, or perhaps than they Imagine
Themselves.

but *Milton* (So every Wise and Good Man) as

————————————*those Elect*
Angels, Contented with their Fame in Heav'n,
Sought not the Praise of Men :

Par. Lost. VI. 374.

and what Delight to be by Such Extoll'd,
to Live upon their Tongues, and be their Talk,
of whom to be Disprais'd were no small Praise ?
His Lot, who dares be Singularly Good.

th'Intelligent among them and the Wise
are Few, and Glory scarce of Few is rais'd.
This is true Glory and Renown, when God
Looking on the Earth, with Approbation marks
the Just Man, and Divulges him through Heav'n
to all his Angels, who with true Applause
Recount his Praises.

                            Par. Reg. III. 54.

'tis Now high time to proceed to *Milton's* Religious Character. if in That there are Prejudices against him, let what Wee, (Himself and I) have Already said be remembred and Consider'd, without a Feeble Narrowness of Mind, and with that Generous, Christian, and Philosophical Charity Himself so Strongly Recommends, or rather which is not Only Recommended, but Commanded by the Highest Example and Authority.

As in making a Portrait, the Complexion and each particular Feature may have been Carefully enough Observ'd and Imitated, but still what is Most Important remains; the Air, the Mind, the Grace, the Dignity, the Capacity, the Vertue, Goodness, *&c.* These must be Express'd as found in the Subject, 'tis Else an Insipid, a Bad Picture. to finish the Portrait of *Milton's* Mind, I must Now say What he was with regard to Religion, Much more Important than Any of his Other Qualities. Thus to Finish in Painting, None but a Great Master Can, which, by the way, is the reason there are so Few Good Pictures. I will continue the same Faithfulness I have us'd Hitherto, in what I am upon, and hope to give at least as Just a Resemblance in what Remains, whether Beautyful or Not, and as Conspicuous to Good Eyes; which All have not who yet Fancy they See very Clearly.

that *Milton* Believ'd in God, that he was a Christian, and a Protestant is Certain, but of what Denomination of all the Several Sub-divisions of These, or if of Any, Known and Profess'd, is not Clear; but he Ever was a Dissenter from Our Church as by Law Established. that he had a Religious Turn of Mind, an Early Tincture of Piety is evident from what he Wrote when Young, and by all the Accounts we have of him. This has been seen Already. However I will add a Fine Passage to this Purpose; for I am always Glad to bring him, Giving his Own Account of Himself, and I doubt not, but my Reader is no less pleas'd, that he Should for Another Reason than that it comes with such Authentick Evidence; besides his Prose Works are but too little known. Thus he says, entring upon a Theological Subject. *if I have done Well either to be Confident of the Truth, whose Force is Best seen against the Ablest Resistance, or to be jealous and Tender of the Hurt that might be done among the Weaker by the intrapping Authority of Great Names titl'd to False Opinions ; or that it be lawful to attribute somewhat to Gifts of God's imparting, which I Boast not, but Thankfully Acknowledge, and fear also least at my certain Account they be reckon'd to Me Many rather than Few ; or if lastly it be but Justice not to defraud of due Esteem the Wearisome Labours and Studious Watchings, wherein I have spent and tir'd out almost a Whole Youth, I shall not distrust to be acquitted of Presumption: knowing, that if Heretofore All Ages have receiv'd with Favour and good Acceptance the Earliest Industry of Him that hath been Hopeful, it were but hard Measure Now, if the Freedom of any Timely Spirit should be opprest merely by the Big and Blunted Fame of his Elder Adversary ; and that His Sufficiency must be Now Sentenc'd not by Pondering the Reason he shews, but by calculating the Years he brings.* See his Preface to his Apology for *Smectymnuus.* in That to his *Reason of Church Government,* he tells Us he was *destin'd of a Child* to the Service of the Church by his Parents and Friends and his Own Resolutions. and, as he had an Early Religious Turn of Mind, that he persisted in it throughout the Whole Course of his Life is Apparent by his Writings, and Otherwise.

His Rule was the Holy Scripture. This was his Guide in Faith and Practice; but Interpreted by his Own Judgment Ultimately. What Better, what Other can Any of Us Have, Desire or Pretend to? How This led Him is not our present Business. This was his Sole Rule, not Humane Authority, as is Remarkably declar'd in the Beginning of his Discourse on *Prelatical Episcopacy,* where he says, *not contented with the Plentiful and Wholsom Fountains of the Gospel, they began after their Own Lusts to heap to Themselves Teachers ; and as if the Divine Scripture wanted a Supplement, and were to be eek't out, they cannot think any Doubt resolv'd, and any Doctrine confirm'd, unless they run to that Indigested heap and frie of Authors which they call Antiquity. Whatsoever Time, or the Heedless Hand of Blind Chance, hath drawn down from of Old to this Present, in her huge Drag-net, whether Fish, or Sea-Weed, or Shells, or Shrubbs, Unpick'd, Unchosen, those are the Fathers.*——Thus he goes on till a little after he concludes this Point by saying that *he thought he could do Religion and his Country no better Service for the time, then doing his Utmost Endeavour to recall the People of God from this vain Forraging after Straw, and to reduce them to their Firm Stations under the Standard of the*

Gospel; by making appear to them, First the Insufficiency, Next the Inconveniency; and Lastly, the Impiety of these Gay Testimonies, that their great Doctors would bring them to dote on. Concerning the Scripture, he Writes Thus in his Preface to the *Reason of Church-Government.*——*God having to this End Ordain'd his Gospel to be the Revelation of his Power and Wisdom in Christ Jesus. and This is One Depth of his Wisdom, that he could so plainly Reveal so great a Measure of it to the Gross, Distorted Apprehensions of Decay'd Mankind. Let Others therefore Dread and Shun the Scriptures for their Darkness, I shall Wish I may deserve to be reckon'd among Those who Admire and Dwell upon them for their Clearness. and This seems to be the Cause, why in those places of Holy Writ, wherein is Treated of Church-Government, the Reasons thereof are not Formally, and Profestly set down, because to Him that Heeds attentively the Drift and Scope of Christian Profession, they easily imply Themselves.*

This then was *Milton's* Only Rule, or if you please, his own Reason Inform'd and Govern'd by it. but whatever it led him to, that he had Charity for all Others, Honestly Endeavouring, as He, *to Worship God Aright,* is seen by a Fine Passage in One of the Last of his Works [*of True Relig. &c. fol.* 808,] where he says, *It is a Human Frailty to Err, and no Man is Infallible here on Earth. but so long as all These,* (he was speaking of Lutherans, Calvinists, Anabaptists, Socinians, Arminians,) *profess to set the Word of God Only before them as the Rule of their Faith and Obedience; and use all Diligence and Sincerity of Heart by Reading, by Learning, by Study, by Prayer for the Illumination of the Holy Spirit to Understand This Rule and Obey it, they have done whatever Men can do. God will Assuredly*

Pardon them, as he did the Friends of Job, *Good and Pious Men, though Much Mistaken, as there it appears, in some Points of Doctrine.*

His Contempt for a Lazy Adherence to What Men Implicitely Receive, and his Approbation of an Honest and Free Exercise of the Understanding in Finding Out, and making Use of what Helps are to be Had from Without, or the Dictates of Internal Reason, is seen in what he says, Addressing Himself to the Parliament and Assembly, with his Treatise on *Divorce* (printed 1644.)

If it were Seriously ask'd, and it would be no Untimely Question, Renowned Parliament, Select Assembly, who of all Teachers and Masters that have ever taught, hath drawn the Most Disciples after him, both in Religion and in Manners, it might be not Untruly Answer'd, Custome. though Vertue be commended for the most Persuasive in Theory, *and Conscience in the plain Demonstration of the Spirit, finds most Evincing, yet whether it be the Secret of Divine Will, or the Original Blindness we are born in, So it happens, for the Most part, that Custome still is Silently receiv'd for the Best Instructor, Except it be, because her Method is so Glib and Easy in some manner like to that Vision of* Ezekiel, *rowling up her Sudden Book of Implicit Knowledge, for Him that Will, to Take and Swallow down at Pleasure ; which proving but of Bad Nourishment in the Concoction, as it was Heedless in the Devouring, Puffs up Unhealthily, a certain Big Face of pretended Learning, Mistaken among Credulous Men, for the Wholesom Habit of a Soundness and good Constitution ; but is indeed no other than the Swol'n Visage of Counterfeit Knowledge and Literature, which not only in Private Marrs our Education, but also in Publick is the Common Climer into every Chair, where either Religion is Preach'd, or Law Reported :*

filling each Estate of Life and Profession, with Abject and Servile Principles ; Depressing the High and Heaven-born Spirit of Man, Far beneath the Condition wherein either God Created him, or Sin hath Sunk him.   To persue the Allegory, Custom being but a meer Face, as Eccho is a meer Voice, rests not in her Unaccomplishment, until by a Secret Inclination, She Accorporate herself with Error, who being a Blind and Serpentine Body without a Head, willingly Accepts what He Wants, and Supplies what Her Uncompleatnesse went Seeking.   Hence it is that Error Supports Custome, Custome Count'nances Error. and these Two between them would Persecute, and Chase away all Truth and Solid Wisdome out of Humane Life, were it not that God, rather then Man, Once in many Ages cals together the Prudent and Religious Counsels of Men deputed to represse the Encroachments, and to worke off the Inveterate Blots and Obscurities wrought upon our Mindes by Suttle Insinuating of Error and Custome :   Who with the Numerous and Vulgar Train of Their Followers make it Their Chiefe Designe to Envie and Cry-Down the Industry of Free Reasoning under the terms of Humor and Innovation ; as if the Womb of Teeming Truth were to be Clos'd up if She Presume to bring forth ought, that Sorts not with Their Unchew'd Notions and Suppositions.   Against which Notorious Injury and Abuse of Mans Free Soule, to Testifie and Oppose the Utmost that Study and true Labour can attaine, Heretofore the Incitement of Men reputed Grave hath led Me among Others : and Now the Duty and the Right of an Instructed Christian cals Me through the Chance of Good and Evil Report to be the Sole Advocate of a Discount'nanc't Truth ; a High Enterprise Lords and Commons, a High Enterprise, and a Hard, and Such as Every Seventh Son of a Seventh Son does not Venture on.

*Nor have I amidst the Clamor of So much Envie and Im-
pertinence, Whether to Appeal but to the Concourse of So
much Piety and Wisdom here Assembled. bringing in my
hands an Ancient and most Necessary, most Charitable, and
yet most Injur'd, Statute of* Moses : *not Repeal'd ever by
Him who Only had the Authority, but thrown Aside with
much Inconsiderate Neglect, under the Rubbish of Canonical
Ignorance ; as once the Whole Law was by some such like
Conveyance in* Josiah's *time. And He who shall endeavour
the Amendment of any Old Neglected Grievance in Church
or State, or in the Daily Course of Life, if he be Gifted with
Abilities of Mind that may raise him to so High an Undertaking, I grant he hath Already Much whereof Not to
Repent him ; yet let me areed him not to be Fore-man of any
Misjudg'd Opinion, unless his Resolutions be Firmly Seated
in a Square and Constant Mind, not Conscious to itself of
any Deserved Blame, and Regardless of Ungrounded
Suspicions.*

For Himself, he seems to have had little Regard to
the Exteriour of Religion; We hear of Nothing of
That even in his Last hours; and whatever he did in
the Former Parts of his Life, he frequented no Publick
Worship in his Latter years, nor used any Religious
Rite in his Own Little Family. it seems very Probable
that as he was Always very Anti-Episcopal, and no
Lover of Our Establish'd Church, neither could he
bear with the Tolerated Preachers after the Restoration; Those of whom he speaks, when he says, that
they were seen *under Subtle Hypocrisy to have Preached
their Own Follies, most of them not the Gospel, Time-
servers, Covetous, Illiterate Persecutors, not Lovers of the
Truth, Like in all things whereof they accused their Pre-
decessors :* This Passage I have from a Fragment that

was not Printed till several Years after *Milton's* Death,
Anno 1681. 'twas a Part of his History of England,
and Expung'd, it being but a Sort of Digression, and
to avoid giving Offence to a Party quite Subdu'd, and
whose Faults the Government was then Willing to
Have Forgotten. there is a great deal more to This
Purpose, as also on the Villanous Abuse of Power in
Mony-Matters of These People, and of That Party
which Himself notwithstanding his great Merits with
them had Tasted of Severely.

his Aversion to, and Contempt of These Pretended
Divines, I am the more persuaded of from a Story I
well remember to have heard Many Years Since, in
Such a manner, as to make it Credible, though Other-
wise, and without what we learn from the little Tract
just now Cited, I should still wish it was not true.
Milton had a Servant, who was a very Honest, Silly
Fellow, and a Zealous and Constant Follower of these
Teachers; when he came from the Meeting, his
Master would frequently Ask him What he had heard,
and Divert Himself with Ridiculing Their Fooleries,
or (it may be) the Poor Fellow's Understanding; both
One and t'other Probably; However This was so
Grievous to the Good Creature, that he left his Service
upon it.

Now that I am Conjecturing, I will go on a little
farther. Possibly *Milton* thought All National Churches
or Publick Religions had Somthing in them Political,
Somthing *Corrupted from the Simplicity that is in Christ,*
2 *Cor.* xi. 3. This is what he seems More than to
Intimate, when in that Florid Discourse, his *Areopagitica,* (and which by the way, he wrote as a Specimen
of the Oratorian Style) he says, *Truth indeed came Once*

into the World with her Divine Master, and was a Perfect Shape most Glorious to look on ; but when He ascended, and his Apostles after him were laid Asleep, then strait arose a Wicked Race of Deceivers, who as that Story goes of the Egyptian Typhon *with his Conspirators, how they dealt with the good* Osiris, *took the Virgin Truth, hew'd her Lovely Form into a thousand Pieces, and scatter'd them to the four Winds. from That time ever Since, the Sad Friends of Truth, such as durst appear Imitating the Careful Search that* Isis *made for the Mangl'd Body of* Osiris, *went up and down gathering up Limb by Limb still as they could find them. Wee have not yet found them All, Lords and Commons* (this was Written Anno 1644) *nor ever shall do till her Master's Second Coming ; Hee shall bring together every Joynt and Member, and shall Mould them into an immortal Feature of Loveliness and Perfection.*

the Sincerity I have Profest in Drawing This Picture, and which as I resolve to Practice, will not permit me to Pass over in Silence Another Conjecture which Some have made; I mean that *Milton* was an *Arian*; and This is built on Certain Passages in *Par. Lost.* Some of Those I am pretty Well Assur'd are very Capable of an Orthodox Construction, as All of them are for Ought I know. But as I neither Care to Meddle with a Dispute which I am not well acquainted with; and as 'tis no Other than a Conjecture, which lies against him, and seems to be Over-rul'd by So many Pious and Learned Divines (Sound in This Fundamental Article) having Approv'd and Encourag'd the Book; and as Two have very Lately Expressly Acquitted him of That Charge; and as Moreover 'tis Certain, that in his Middle-Age he has shown he was Right as to This Point, I wave it, and claim in his

Behalf that he be Esteem'd as Continuing So to the Last. the Passage I mention'd is in his Discourse of *Reformation*, just at the Close of it; 'tis Thus. *Thou therefore that sitst in Light and Glory Unapproachable, Parent of Angels and Men! Next thee I implore, Omnipotent King, Redeemer of that Lost Remnant whose Nature Thou didst Assume, Ineffable and Everlasting Love! and Thou the Third Subsistance of Divine Infinitude* Illuminating Spirit, *the Joy and Solace of Created things!* One Tri-Personal GODHEAD! *Look upon,* &c.

Milton had Always a Firm Belief of the Being of a God, and a Mind which could not fail from his Existence to Infer his Government of the Universe, and all This in such a One must Produce True Piety, Veneration, Submission, Dependance, Love mix'd with Filial Awe, Joy, *&c.* This Appears Perpetually to every Observing Reader of his Works, Verse or Prose. His Other Speculative Religious Opinions whereby he is Distinguish'd, are rather Political than Religious, Such as relate to the Circumstantials rather than to the Essentials or Substance of Religion; Church-Government, Church-Communion, Ceremonies, the Millennium, *&c.* on which 'tis not necessary to Enlarge, and I am Glad it is not.

What is Practical comes Next to be Consider'd. I will Select a Few Remarkable Passages of This Sort, and from his Prose Works as Those are not so commonly known, though not less Excellent in their Kind for Great and Noble Thoughts and Expressions; his Poetical Works Abound with Morality, as well as Piety, and in Particular *Paradise Lost*. One of Those Passages I am Now upon is cited in our Note on v.583 of the XIIth Book of That Poem, to which I not only

Refer you, but Recommend it to your Consideration: Here let me add what he says in p. 321 *Tol.* Edit.——— *Let him not open his Lips against the Providence of Heaven, or tax the Ways of God and his Divine Truth, for they are Equal, Easy, and not Burthensome ; nor do they ever Cross the Just and Reasonable Desires of Men, nor involve this our Portion of Mortal life into a Necessity of Sadness and Malecontent, by Laws commanding over the Unreducible Antipathies of Nature Sooner or Later found, but allow us to Remedy and shake off Those Evils into which Human Error hath led us through the Midst of our Best Intentions, and to Support our Incident Extremities by the Authentick Precept of Soveraign Charity, whose Grand Commission is to Do and to Dispose over all the Ordinances of God to Man, that Love and Truth may Advance each other to Everlasting ; while Wee, Literally Superstitious through Customary Faintness of Heart, not Venturing to pierce with our Free thoughts into the Full Latitude of Nature and Religion, Abandon our Selves to serve under the Tyranny of Usurp'd Opinions, suffering Those Ordinances which were Allotted to Our Solace and Reviving, to Trample over Us, and Hale Us into a Multitude of Sorrows which God never Meant Us. and Where he sets us in a fair Allowance of Way, with Honest Liberty and Prudence to our Guard, we never leave Subtilizing and Casuisting till we have Straitned and Pared that Liberal Path into a Razor's Edge to walk on, between a Precipice of Unnecessary Mischief on either side ; and starting at every False Alarm, we do not know which way to set a foot forward with Manly Confidence and Christian Resolution, through the Confused ringing in our Ears of Panick Scruples and Amazements.*

in p. 351.———*What can be more Opposite and Disparaging to the Cov'nant of Love, of Freedom, and of our*

Q

*Manhood in Grace, than to be made the Yoking Pedagogue
of New Severities, the Scribe of Syllables and Rigid Letters,
not only Grevious to the Best of Men, but Different and
Strange from the Light of Reason in them, save only as they
are fain to Stretch and Distort their Apprehensions, for fear
of Displeasing the Verbal Straitness of a Text, which our
Own Servil Fear gives us not the leisure to understand
Aright ?*

p. 290.———*there is a Certain Scale of Duties, there is
a certain Hierarchy of Upper and Lower Commands, which
for want of Studying in right Order, all the World is in
Confusion.*

This Strict Interpretation of Texts without having a
Prudential and Conscientious Regard to the Great
Scope and Design of Things he Somwhere calls an
Alphabetical Servility, tending to Antichristian Cruelty.

p. 369.———*what can This be but Weak and Shallow
Apprehension, to forsake the Standard Principles of Institution, Faith and Charity ; then to be Blank, and Various at
every Occurrence in Scripture, and in a Cold Spasm of
Scruple, to rear Peculiar Doctrines upon the Place that
shall bid the Gray Autority of most Unchangeable and
Sovran Rules to stand by and be Contradicted ?*

p. 364.———*for This is a Confest Oracle in Law, that
He who looks not at the Intention of a Precept, the More
Superstitious he is of the Letter, the More he Misinterprets.*

p. 368.———*that his Disciples, and all Good Men might
learn to Expound him in this Place, as in all other his
Precepts, not by the Written Letter, but by that Unerring
Paraphrase of Christian Love and Charity, which is the
Sum of All Commands, and the Perfection.*

p. 326.———*Last of all, to Those whose Mind is still to
maintain Textual Restriction, whereof the bare Sound cannot*

*consist Sometimes with Humanity, much less with Charity, I
would ever Answer by putting them in Remembrance of a
Command above All Commands, which they seem to have
forgot, and Who spake it ; in Comparison whereof This
which they so exalt is but a Petty and Subordinate Precept.*
Let them go *therefore with Whom I am loath to Couple
them, yet they will needs run into the same Blindness with
the Pharisees ;* let them go therefore *and consider well
what this Lesson means,* I will have Mercy and not
Sacrifice; *for on That Saying* all the Law and Prophets
depend, *much more the Gospel, whose End and Excellence
is Mercy and Peace : or if they cannot learn That, how
will they learn This ? which yet I shall not doubt to leave
with them as a Conclusion, that God the Son hath put all
Other things under his Own feet, but his Commandmants
he hath left all under the feet, of Charity.*

Who that Cries out These Notions Savour of Libertin-
isin, of Licentiousness; let him Shut his Lips again,
till he has considered on What these Masculine Sentiments are Built; and for the Present what is said by
S. *Paul,* 2 Cor. v. 13. *Whether we be Besides our Selves
it is to God ; or whether we be Sober, it is for Your Cause.*

Let the Tree be judg'd by its Fruit. We know of no
Immoralities of any Kind. how should he be Guilty of
Any ? A Mind So Employ'd, So Fortify'd as His was,
left no Place for an Attack; Temptation had no Inor-
dinate Passion to work upon. However, as Some
Aspersions have been cast at him, Chiefly with relation
to his Moral Behaviour in his Younger Years, he shall
Answer for Himself. he will be forc'd to say Somthing
in his Own Praise, as 'tis Often Necessary for the most
Modest Men to do, Hear him therefore first of all
Excusing himself for That. though Supposing those

Overflowings of Comfort and Self-Approbation, which
is One of the Great Rewards of a Good Mind, appear to
have Somtimes a Mixture of Ostentation, or Folly, 'tis
not without Excuse, and the Best Examples; What
think you of St. *Paul*, 2 Cor. xi. 16. &c ? Here is
Milton, he Offers to speak; Attend with Candour. *p.*
174. *Tol.* Edit.———*Not caring to burthen me with those
Vices, whereof, among whom my Conversation hath been,
I have been ever least Suspected ; perhaps not without
some Suttlety to cast me into Envie by bringing on Me a
Necessity to enter into Mine Own Praises. in which Argument I know every Wise Man is more Unwillingly drawn to
Speak, than the most Repining Eare can be Averse to Heare.
Neverthelesse since I dare not wish to passe this Life Unper-
secuted of Slandrous Tongues, for God hath told us that to
be Generally Prais'd is Wofull, I shall relye on His
Promise to free the Innocent from Causelesse Aspersions :
whereof nothing Sooner can Assure me then if I shall feele
Him Now Assisting me in the just Vindication of My Selfe,
which yet I could Deferre, it being more meet that to those
Other matters of Publick Debatement in This Book, I
should give Attendance First, but that I feare it would but
Harme the Truth for Me to Reason in Her behalf so long as
I should suffer my Honest Estimation to lye Unpurg'd from
These Insolent Suspicions. And if I shall be Large, or
Unwonted in Justifying my Selfe to Those who know me not,
for Else it would be Needlesse, let them consider that a Short
Slander will oft-times reach farder than a Long Apology ;
and that He who will do Justly to All Men, must begin
from knowing How, if it so happen, to be not Unjust to
Himself. I must be thought, if this Libeller (for Now he
shews himself to be So) can find Beliefe, after an Inordinat
and Riotous Youth spent at* the University, *to have been at*

length Vomited out thence. *for which Commodious Lye, that he may be encourag'd in the Trade another time, I Thank him, for it hath given Me an Apt Occasion to Acknowledge Publickly with all Gratefull Minde, that more then Ordinary Favour and Respect which I found above Any of my Equals at the hands of those Curteous and Learned Men, the Fellowes of that Colledge wherein I spent some Yeares : who at my Parting, after I had taken two Degrees, as the manner is, signif'd many Ways, how much better it would Content Them that I would Stay; as by many Letters full of Kindnesse and Loving Respect, both Before That time and Long After, I was Assur'd of their Singular good Affection towards Me.——*

I beg that none will interpret it Invidiously that this Man has Oblig'd me to say of My Self More than I would have said. for it is absolutely Necessary, and That, for more Reasons than One. First, That So many Good and Learned Men who now Read these my Writings in all our Neighb'ring Nations may not be induc'd by His slanders to Repent themselves of the Good Will which I am Sure they bear me, but that they may Still be persuaded that I am not One who Stains his Honest Writings with Dishonest Manners, nor What He hath Spoken as a Freeman with Actions which denote a Slave ; and that My Life, by God's Goodness has ever been Far remote from Turpitude and Crime ; Then, that Those Illustrious and truely Laudable Men whom I have Undertaken to Praise may Know, That I esteem Nothing more Shamefull than to come to Their Praises, My Self Vile, and Only worthy of Blame. Lastly, let the People of England *know, whom either my Fate, or Duty, Certainly their Own Vertue has oblig'd Me to Defend, that if I have Liv'd Always with Modesty and Honour, My Defence of Them, I dont know whether an*

*Honour and an Ornament, Certainly Shall Not be a Shame
or Reproach to Them.   Who then I am, and Whence, I
will Now tell you*——he goes on to give a History of
his Life.   Def. 2da p. 95. *against* Alexander Morus.
Tol.

Let us Now proceed to the Particular Vindications
of himself in Answer to his Calumniating Enemies.
p. 178. Tol.——*That Care was Ever had of Me, with
my Earliest Capacity, not to be Negligently train'd in the
Precepts of Christian Religion : This that I have hitherto
related hath been to show that though Christianity had bin
but Slightly taught Me, yet a certain Reserv'dnesse of
Natural Disposition, and Moral Discipline learnt out of the
Noblest Philosophy was Enough to keep Me in Disdain of
Farre Lesse Incontinences than This of the* Bordello.——
*Nor did I Slumber over That place, expressing such High
Rewards of Ever accompanying the Lamb, with those
Celestial Songs, to Others Inapprehensible, but Not to
Those who were not Defil'd with Women, which doubtless
Meanes Fornication, for Marriage must not be calld a
Defilement.   Thus large I have purposely bin, that if I have
bin Justly Taxt with This Crime it may come upon me after
all this Confession with a Tenne-fold Shame : but if I have
hitherto deserv'd no such Opprobrious word, or Suspicion,
I may hereby Ingage my Selfe now Openly to the faithfull
Observation of what I have profest.*   Again in the same
Discourse (his *Apol.* for *Smectymnuus*) *p.* 175.   *Those
Morning haunts are where they Should be, at Home ; not
Sleeping, or Concocting the Surfeits of an Irregular Feast,
but Up, and Stirring, in Winter Often before the Sound of
any Bell awakens Men to Labour or Devotion, in Summer
as Oft as the Bird that First Rouses, or not Much Tardyer,
to Read Good Authors, or cause them to be Read, till the*

Attention be Weary, or the Memory have its full Fraught :
Then with Usefull, and Generous Labors Preserving the
Body's Health and Hardiness, to render a Lightsom, Clear,
and not a Lumpish Obedience to the Mind for the Cause of
Religion and our Country's Liberty when it shall require
Firm Hearts in Sound Bodies to Stand, and Cover their
Stations, rather than see the Ruin of our Protestation and the
inforcement of a Slavish Life. and a while after——*I*
was confirm'd in the Opinion that He who would not be
frustrated of his hope to write Well hereafter in Laudable
things ought Himself to be a true Poem, that is, a Com-
position and Pattern of the Best and Honourablest things,
not presuming to Sing the High Praises of Heroic Men, or
Famous Cities unless he has in Himself the Experience, and
the Practice of all that is Praise-worthy. These Reasonings,
together with a certain Niceness of Nature, an Honest
Haughtyness and Self-Esteem, either of what I Was, or
what I Might be, (which let Envy call Pride) and Lastly, a
Becoming Modesty, all Uniting the Supply of their Natural
Aid together, kept me still above those Low Descents of
Mind, beneath Which He must Deject and Plunge himself
that can agree to Salable and Unlawfull Prostitutions.

if I have Accumulated Passages of This Kind it has
not been Meerly to Delineate the Mind of *Milton*, or to
Vindicate His Character, it has been done with Yet a
Nobler and a More Extensive View, it has been done
not without Hopes that Others may be Excited to be
Enamour'd, as Hee, with the *Beauty of Holiness*. but
on This Occasion also See this Eloquent Man saying
to You as to the late Lord *Ranelagh* when at the University, and in Some Measure under His Care. he Thus
writes to Him. (See *Tol.* in *Milton's* Life, p. 176.)
Learn Thou from thy Childhood to Discern and Judge of

Great Examples, not from Violence and Force [from the *Cæsars* and *Alexanders*] *but by Justice and Temperance.*

in his *Reason of Church-Government* (writing when he was between 30 and 40) B. II. Chap. 3. he gives a fine Image of a Pious and Vertuous Mind, which also Attend to; it Concerns Us All. *But He that holds himself in Reverence and due Esteem, both for the Dignity of God's Image upon him, and for the Price of his Redemption, which he thinks is Visibly markt upon his Forehead, accounts himself both a Fit Person to do the Noblest and Goodliest Deeds, and Much better worth than to Deject and Defile with Such a Debasement and Such a Pollution as Sin is, Himself so highly Ransom'd and Enobled to a New Friendship and Filial Relation with God. Nor can he fear so much the Offence and Reproach of Others, as he dreads, and would blush at the Reflection of his Own Severe and Modest Eye upon Himself, if it should see him Doing, or Imagining that which is Sinful, though in the Deepest Secrecy.*

though 'tis Somwhat Long, you will Thank me for Subjoyning a Passage, which could not come but from a Mind truly Christian, and the Pen of One who had the Soul of an Ancient Philosopher and Poet; 'tis a noble Instance of his good Heart, particularly in That Branch of True Philosophy, the Submitting Chearfully to the Divine Will, and making the Right Use of Afflictions, and amongst Others, of the Malice and Wickedness of Men. 'tis in the Second Defence *pro Pop. Angl.* and is a Sort of a Collection of what has been Seen in the Several Fine Passages I have given. Thus in English.

As for what relates to Me, I call Thee, O God! to Witness, Thee the Searcher of my most Inward Mind, and of all my Thoughts, that I am Conscious to My self of Nothing (though I have, as much as was in Me, Often and Seriously Thought This with My Self, and Sifted all the most Private Passages of my Life) of Nothing, either of Late, or Long Since Committed, whose Hainousness might deservedly draw on me This Calamity. [his Blindness] *And as for what I have Written at any Time (since the Royalists pretend I suffer This as a Judgment, and triumph on that Account) I in like Manner call God to Witness, that I have never Written any thing on that Subject, that I was not Then Persuaded was, and am Now Persuaded is Acceptable to God ; And also that So I did, not Mov'd by any Ambition, Gain, or Glory, but from a Sence Alone of my Duty, of what was Honest, and of Piety to my Country ; and that I did it too, not only to Restore the Liberty of the State, but also chiefly to recover that of the Church, Insomuch that when It was Enjoyn'd Me by the Publick Voice of my Country to Answer that* Defence of the King, *and I at the same time Labour'd under a very Ill State of Health, and withal was upon the Point of Loosing one of my Eyes ; and my Physicians assur'd Me peremptorily, that if I undertook this Task, I must unavoidably loose Both in a little Time ; Not at all Dismay'd by their Sentence, I thought I Heard the Voice, not of a Phisician, no nor of* Epidaurian Æsculapius *himself from his Secret Oracle, but that of Some more Divine Monitor Within ; That I had Now Two Lots at the same time propos'd to Me by a certain fatal Necessity of the Divine Pleasure, Here Blindness, There My Duty ; so that I must either voluntarily resign my Sight, or Desert what God Impos'd upon me. Wherefore I consider'd with my Self, that Many had bought a Lesser Good with a Greater Loss, glory with Death ; To Me on the contrary, there was propos'd a Greater good for a Lesser Loss ; An*

Opportunity of Acheiving the most noble and Usefull duty,
with the bare Loss of my Eyes ; Which Duty, as it is more
Solid in it self than any Glory, so it ought sure to be far
more Desirable and Preferable. I determin'd then to make
Use of the short Remains of Light I had Decree'd My Self,
as much as might be for the Publick Profit. You see what
I Chose, what I Rejected, and by what Reason induc'd.
Let then those that Calumniate me with Divine Judgements
cease to Revile, and to Reproach me with their own
Dreams ; Let them Know that I neither am Sorry for, nor
Repent me of my Lot ; that I remain Unmov'd and Steddy
in my Purpose ; That I neither Feel God Almighty Angry,
nor Is He, but rather in the Greatest things I experience his
Clemency and Fatherly Goodness towards Me ; but in
Nothing more than in This, that from his Confirmations and
Comfortings I Chearfully acquiesce in his Divine Will ;
thinking oftner what He hath Given Me, than what He
hath Denied Me ; and lastly, that I would not Exchange
for any other of his greatest Benefits, the Consciousness of
this Action that they Reproach Me with, nor Lay down the
Remembrance of it, which is a perpetual Fund to Me of
Tranquillity and Joy. To End, As for my Blindness, I
prefer It, if I Must have One either to that of Salmasius,
or Your's. Your's is Sunk into your Deepest Senses,
Blinding your Minds, so that You can See nothing that is
Sound and Solid ; Mine, Takes from Me only the Colour
and Surface of Things, but does Not Take away from the
Mind's Contemplation, What is in Those Things of True
and Constant. Moreover, how many Things are there
which I would Not See ? How many which I can be
Debar'd the Sight of without Repining ? How Few Left
which I Much Desire to See ? But neither am I Dis-
heartend that I am Now become the Companion of the

Blind, of the Afflicted, of Those that Sorrow, and of the Weak ; Since I Comfort my Self with the Hope, that These Things do, as it were, make Me Belong *still more to the Mercy and Protection of the Supream Father. There is, according to the Apostle, a Way through Weakness to the greatest Strength ; Let me be the Most Weak, Provided that in my Weakness that Immortal and Better Strength Exert it Self with more Efficacy ; Provided that in my Darkness the Light of the Face of God Shine the Clearer ; So shall I prove at the same time the Most Weak and the Most Strong ; Dark-Blind and at the same time Clear-Sighted ; O Let Me be Consummate in this Weakness ! in This, Perfected ! Let Me be Thus Enlighten'd in This Darkness ! And sure, We that are Blind are not the Last Care of God, who hath been in This Clement above All, and Bountifull to Us, that He will have Us See Nothing but Himself. Vile Men that Mock Us ! Injure Us ! and that endeavour to raise us Enemies ! The high Dispensation of God, his Favour hath given Us a Protection from the Injuries of Men, and render'd Us allmost Sacred ; Nor doth He indeed seem to have brought this Darkness upon Us, so much by the Dimness of our Eyes, as by the Shadow of his Protecting Wings. To This I Impute, that my Friends are more Ready and Officious to Serve Me than Before, and more frequently Visit Me, some of which are not less True and Faithfull than those of Old,* Pylades *and* Theseus: *For They do not Think that by This Accident I am become altogether Nothing, or that the only Worth of an Honest and Upright Man is plac'd in his Eyes. Far from it, the Greatest Men in the Commonwealth do not Desert Me, since, if My Eyes have Deserted Me, it hath not been for Idly Withering in Laziness, but in Facing the Greatest Dangers, with Activity, and among the First, for Liberty ; But, Reflecting*

*on Humane Sort, they Now Favour Me, and Spare Me as
One that hath Finish'd his Warfare, Indulging Me Now,
and Granting Me Vacation and Leisure. If I have any
Trophys, they Take them not down ; Publick Office, they
do not Deprive Me of it ; If Profit from Thence, They do
not Lessen it, and although not equally Usefull to Them
Now, yet they continue no less Bountifull to Me ; Doing Me
that same Honour as the* Athenians *of Old did to Those
that they Decreed should be Kept at the Publick Expense.*

*Whilst then I can thus Comfort my Self, both toward
God and towards Man, for my Blindness, for Eyes that have
been Lay'd Down in the Cause of What is* Honest, *Let
None Mourn for Them, or Pity Me ; Far be it also that I
should Grive for Them My Self, or that I should want
Resentment to Despise with Ease Such as Rebuke my
Darkness, or Charity, with more Ease, to Forgive Them.*

I will deny Self the Pleasure of Transcribing More
to This Purpose. All his Writings have Intersperst an
Odour of Sanctity, not that Cant which was the Character and the Blemish of the Times in which he Liv'd, but
a Manly Eloquence flowing from a Heart in which
shone the Divine Grace. 'tis seen Breaking forth in his
most Furious Disputes, 'tis seen even There; as I once
saw the Sunbeams Wreathing amongst the Flames and
Smoak and Horror of a House on Fire; but his Other
Works, if partly mistaken, are Fragrant with Piety and
Vertue; Above All, *Paradise Lost* is *a Spring of Fragrance ;* That from End to End

Impurpled with Celestial Roses smiles.

I know not how to Conclude my Account of *Milton's*
Religion better than by recommending you to That
given by Himself of *Adam's* in his Regenerate State;

'tis in the XII Book of his Poem, beginning at *v.* 561. Here our Progenitor professes his Faith in One God, and that 'tis his Duty to Obey, Love, and Fear him; to consider Him as Always Present, to Depend upon his Providence, Ever Merciful and Omnipotent. and moreover that Suffering for the Sake of a Good Conscience, is the Noblest Fortitude; and then Crowns All these Articles of his Faith with an Acknowledgement of his Redemption by the Son of God. All This an Angel Approves, but with the Addition of Good Works. Integrity, Vertue, Patience, Temperance, Love, All Comprehended in One Word CHARITY. This no doubt the Poet intended as a Delineation of True Religion; and Probably 'twas Copy'd from What he found Engraven on his Own Heart; at least *Charity*, which *Hopeth, Believeth, Endureth, is Kind ; Charity* Directs, Commands Us to think so. This is what he Professes to be His Sense in a Discourse Dedicated to the Parliament just before Their Dominion was at an End, That of *Civil Power in Ecclesiastical Causes——— What Evangelical Religion is, is told in Two Words,* Faith *and* Charity, *or* Belief *and* Practice. *That Both These Flow, either the One from the Understanding, the Other from the Will, or Both jointly from Both ; Once indeed Naturally Free, but Now only as they are Regenerate and wrought on by Divine Grace, is in Part evident to Common Sense and Principles Unquestion'd, the rest by Scripture.*

this Last Clause is Rich in Comfort and Glory to Restor'd Mankind, and seems to Import Much the Same Idea as that of S. *Paul, Coloss.* iii. 3.—*Your Life is Hid with Christ in God.* Mix'd with that Immense Ocean of Eternal Being by vertue of our Relation to the Mediator.

Now that we have seen This Picture of the Mind of *Milton*, Drawn by Himself Chiefly, though I have put it together; not Quite So Well perhaps as it might have been; but as 'tis too Large for the Eye to take it In Clearly at One View, I will Contract it. and Thus he appears to be Studious, Grave, Chaste, Temperate, to be void of Covetousness, Ambition, or Ostentation; to have a Warm Zeal for Liberty, Civil and Religious, not for Interest, but as his Duty; to be Irreproachable as to any Wilful and Corrupt Deviations, However he may have been Mistaken; though Otherwise he has not been destitute of a Masculine Judgment. Above all, his Mind Shines with Noble Sentiments of Religion, and Piety: Lastly, it is Truly Poetical. Great, Strong, Elegant, and Sublime; it Raises and Beautifies all its Objects as much as Humanity Can, and Where That Fails, has gone Farther than Any Other Humane Intellect Ever Attain'd to.

the Man is Now before you, his Person, and his Mind; if the Latter is not without Blemishes, the Case is very Different from That of his Corporeal Blindness, These are Spots, Motes, he is Bright All over Else. nor are his Blemishes Offensive to Charity, Who will Consider Him as a Man, Subject Therefore to Error. View him So, and Those Defects may be no more Dishonour to him than his Extinguish'd Eyes were. in fine, He was an Ancient Greek and Roman. a Philosopher, a Divine, a Christian, a Poet.——but there are Readers, who from the Materials I have brought together, will form a Nobler Idea of him than any Words of Mine can give, and Such a One as will Appear in Lustre, though at the same time they Review the Brightest Names of Antiquity.

You will Now be Desirous to know What Kind of
Life was Allotted to This Extraordinary Man; How
His Portion of Being in This Mortal State was Em-
ploy'd.

He was Born in *Bread-street* in *London*, 9 *December*
1608. his Father having been Disinherited for being
a Protestant, for his Ancestors (Gentlemen) were Hot
Papists, got his Bread by the Profession of a Scrivener.
This Son, the Eldest of Two, was Educated Partly at
Home, and Partly at *Paul's* School, and was Fit for the
University at 15, when he went to *Christ's* in *Cambridge*,
where he continu'd 7 Years. he was a hard Student
from his Childhood, Sate up Reading till Midnight;
but Whether That, or a Natural Indisposition, or Both,
Occasion'd it, he was much Subject to Head-Achs,
which also hurt his Eyes; or perhaps the same Cause
produc'd Both those Effects: he Then Chose to rise
Early in the Morning, and went to Bed at 9, and was
Thus Secure from the Importunities of Less Temperate
Friends. His Father design'd him for the Church;
That he Avoided, upon Account of the Subscription,
which he Scrupled. (See his Introduction to the second
Part of *Church-Government*.) and by his Poetical Latin
Letter to his Father it seems as if he Then would have
persuaded him to the Law; Somthing was thought
Necessary whereby Mony might be got. That too the
Poet Avoided, and Probably the more Easily, his
Father having (as by that Letter it appears) a Taste for
Politeness, Scrivener though he was. 'tis Evident he
Intended to Give himself to the Muses Intirely, and his
Parents, who were Both very Fond of him, Indulg'd
his Genius. his Father had by This time acquir'd a

Moderate Estate by his Profession, and having but Three Children, was Content with it, and Retir'd into the Country, to *Horton* near *Colebrook* in *Buckingham-shire :* Here Young *Milton* continu'd 5 Years, Labouring at his Books. He Then Travell'd into *Italy* by the way of *France ;* the French he Never lik'd, the Mercurial Temper of That Nation was very Different from his Solidity; he Hasten'd Thence; Stopt Some time at *Florence ;* Then away to *Rome,* where he also Stay'd; then On till he reached *Naples.* He design'd for *Greece,* but the Distractions at Home brought him back, after having spent about 15 Months Abroad: but he Em-ploy'd That time very Diligently, in the Conversation of Men, the Most Esteem'd for their Wit and Learning, and who Much Esteem'd Him. the Verses Wrote by Some of them in his Praise, and which are Printed with his Juvenile Works, and Some of his Own Latin Poems and Letters, are Proofs of This, as well as Beautiful in Themselves; particularly his *Mansus.* They had seen but Little of him Then. How was he Ador'd Afterward! and Is!

Some One or More Mistakes there must be in the Accounts of Time I have given, and I have given them as I found them; by These we are got but into the Year 1636, the 28th of *Milton's* Age, whereas 'tis certain he came from his Travels in the Year 39 or 40. we must Therefore Allow him to have Spent More time in some of the Places where we have hitherto seen him. but not Abroad, for Himself (Defen. 2da) says, That was 15 Months. *Bayle* was therefore Misinform'd, who says 'twas 3 Years.

Soon after, or upon his Return to *England,* he Settled in *London,* in St. *Bride's* Church-Yard near *Fleet-street ;*

though his Father was Yet Alive, and for About 7 Years after. He undertook to Educate the Sons of his Sister, for That 'tis not Probable he had Any Other, than the Recompence Such Near Relations are Suppos'd to make; he at the Same time did the Same Good Office to Some Other Young Gentlemen, Whether he receiv'd any Pecuniary Reward for That is the Question; 'tis said Not; but what if he Did?

This did not Employ All his Time and Thoughts; as it was not his Intention it should. And Now for Some Years Poetry must be Suspended, and all the Delights of the *Greek* and *Roman* Ideas Exchang'd for Modern Janglings; his Aversion, but as his Zeal represented them to be his Duty, and Somthing Within, which He Interpreted to be the Voice of God and his Country, call'd him into the Lists of Controversy, while the Country Gentlemen, Citizens, Artificers, and Peasants became Men of the Sword, Polluting our Delightful Fields with the Blood of Relations, Friends and Neighbours.

I know not if we are to Regret the Loss of So many years in which this Fine Genius would have Busied it Self on More Delightful Subjects, Since what they Did produce, has a Kind of Excellence in Writing which is not Elsewhere to be found. the Poet is Seen, however Disguis'd by Polemical Accoutrements. Let not Us Now Consider him Whether in the Right or Not, That Point is Settled by our Superiours; Nor let us lose the Pleasure he gives us as a Writer, by Amusing our Selves with his Faults in Opinion; Whatever Allowances Divines Permit us to think God Will, or Will Not make to an Erroneous Conscience, Sure We who know our Selves so Subject to Mistake, should for our Own

R

Interest Stretch Indulgence towards One Another as far as it Can go.

Another Change happen'd to him a little after he had been Engag'd in this New Course; in the Year 1643, the 35th of his Age, he Marry'd the Daughter of a Gentleman of *Oxfordshire*. but Whether from Difference of Party, for Her Father was a Warm Royalist, or that She coming from a House of Luxury, great Plenty, at least, and Gaity, to One where Severity of Manners was Only found, or whatever Else was the Reason, She Forsook him, about a Month after Marriage, and Refug'd in her Former Home. at Parting She Pretended only to go for the Air, he Consented for a Certain time, but after several Frivolous Excuses in Answer to his Kind Invitations to Return, She at last, not only Absolutely Refus'd him, but dismiss'd his Messenger with Scorn. This Engag'd *Milton* in Another Intestine War, a Controversy in Another Kind, and Produc'd those Treatises of His in favour of Divorce. that he believ'd his Arguments were Solid, this Conscientious Man gave good Proof, by making his Addresses to Another, who it seems was also Convinc'd by them, a Lady of great Wit and Beauty; This was not however till he had born the Obstinacy of his Wife for about 4 Years. but when this New Affair was in full Career, all was Stopt on a Sudden. he was at a Friend's house upon a Visit; his Wife Surpriz'd him; she came into the Room and all in Tears flung her Self at his Feet. at first he seem'd Inexorable, but the Submission of a few Minutes drove away the Provocations of So Long a Continu'd Crime. He Melted, Receiv'd her, and was Reconcil'd; Probably not only mov'd by Good Nature, and his Unextinguish'd Former Love, but as not at Liberty Now in Conscience, as when She seem'd Irreclaimable. a Like Scene between *Adam* and *Eve* in *Parad. Lost.* X. 937. seems to have been Copy'd from This.

> *She ended Weeping, and her Lowlie plight,*
> *Immoveable till Peace obtain'd from Fault*
> *Acknowledg'd and Deplor'd, in* Adam *wrought*
> *Commiseration ; Soon his heart relented*
> *towards her, his Life so Late, and Sole Delight,*
> *Now at his Feet Submissive in Distress,*
> *Creature so Fair his Reconcilement seeking,*
> *his Councel whom she had Displeas'd, his Aide ;*
> *as One Disarm'd, his Anger all he lost,*
> *and thus with Peacefull Words Uprais'd her soon.*

Thus ended This Uncommon Misfortune; and perhaps the more Effectually by his having Shown the World his Opinion concerning Divorce; This was a Rod held over her, Exacting her Good Behaviour. but his Generosity and Goodness, together with this great Proof of his Conjugal Love, even to the Sacrificing a New Passion, and very Probably the Quiet and Honour of a New Lover, were Nobler Engagements; yet not Content with These, Her Family, upon the Turn of the Times to the Disadvantage of the Royal Cause, found in the Man they had Horribly Ill Used, a Protector and Friend; to That Degree, as to be taken, Father and Mother and Brothers and Sisters, to his Own house, and There Entertain'd till their Affairs were in a Better Condition; to which No doubt *Milton's* Assistance and Interest did not a Little Contribute. a Noble Example of Generosity, Good-Nature, Forgiveness, and doing Good for Evil, and That, Notwithstanding Difference of Party, and His Own Flaming

Zeal. I have often Wonder'd that in a Dispute on which he Wrote Several Treatises, was of Long Continuance, and made much Noise, and Especially when He Fortify'd his Arguments by the Concurrent Opinions of Several Famous Divines, that he knew not of a Case, the Same as His, only that 'twas not Quite so Justifyable, 'twas that of *Galeazzo Caraccioli* Marquis of *Vico*, who was Allow'd to take Another Wife by the most Famous Protestant Divines after a Solemn Deliberation. See *Moreri*.

Still he was Unhappily Engag'd in the Other War against Popery, Prelacy, and Monarchy, a Pure Volunteer; but after Serving Thus Several Years he was taken into Pay, by the Infant Common-Wealth; Afterwards he was Employ'd (as Latin Secretary still) by *Oliver*, *Richard* and the *Rump*. When Monarchy rose again, and They were all Sunk, *Milton's* Publick Employment Sunk too; but That gave him an Opportunity of being Much more Serviceable to the World than in that Narrow Sphere, and in the Service of a Usurpation. for Now he Wrote for Mankind, for True Religion and Vertue, and for the Delight, together with the Instruction and Edification of his Fellow-Creatures; of his Own Country more Especially; for Now *Paradise Lost* was to Break Forth.

In the time of his being Secretary, his Health greatly Abated, but whether Otherwise than by the Gout is not Certain; nor When That begun. in This time too he Intirely lost his Sight, which had been Decaying Many Years, while he too Closely Persu'd his Studies; Himself imputes this Total Extinction of Light to his Writing in the Defence of that Strange Action of his Country (as He Supposes, We say of an Up-start

Faction) but That Only Demolish'd What was Totter-
ing Before, 'twas to Learning, 'twas to the Muses he
Sacrificed his Good Eyes, his Weak Ones only were
Offered up in his Controversy with *Salmasius.* Though
I resolv'd to be Expeditious in the Part of his Picture
I am now upon, and Have been, and Shall be So in the
Main, There are Some Particulars of it, which will
require a little more Finishing; This of his Blindness
is One of These; I will therefore produce the Letter
Milton wrote to his Friend *Leonardus Philara,* an
Athenian by Birth, but Envoy of the Duke of *Parma* to
the French King. 'tis Dated 28 Sep. 1654.

*As I have been from my Childhood, if Any ever was, an
Admirer of all the* Greek *Name, and particularly of your*
Athens, *I have Always believ'd that One time or other that
Gratefull City would make me Some Returns of Benevolence.
nor hath the Ancient Genius of your most Noble Countrey
Deceiv'd my Augury, having given me You, a Genuine*
Athenian *and True Friend.*———

*Since You advise Me not to fling away All Hopes of
Recovering my Sight, for that You have a Friend at* Paris,
Thevenot *the Physician, Particularly Famous for the Eyes,
whom you offer to Consult in my behalf if you receive from
Me an Account by which he may Judge of the Causes and
Symptons of my Disease, I will do what You Advise me
to, that I may not seem to Refuse any Assistance that is
Offer'd, perhaps from God.*

*I think 'tis about Ten Yeares, more or less, since I began
to perceive that my Eye-sight grew Weak and Dimm, and
at the same time my Spleen and Bowels to be Opprest and
troubled with* Flatus; *and in the Morning when I began
to Read, according to Custom, my Eyes grew Painfull
immediatly, and to refuse Reading, but were Refresh'd after*

a Moderate Exercise of the Body. a Certain Iris *began to Surround the Light of the Candle if I look'd at it ; Soon after which, on the Left Part of the Left Eye (for That was Some Years Sooner Clouded) a Mist arose which hid everything on That side ; and looking Forward if I Shut my Right Eye, Objects appear'd Smaller. My Other Eye also, for these Last Three Yeares Failing by degrees, Some Months before all Sight was Abolish'd Things which I look'd upon seem'd to Swim to the Right and Left ; Certain Inveterate Vapours seem to Possess my Forehead and Temples, which After Meat especially, quite to Evening, Generally, Urge and Depress my Eyes with a Sleepy Heaviness. nor would I omit that whilst there was as yet Some Remainder of Sight, I no sooner lay down in my Bed, and turn'd on my Side, but a Copious Light Dazzled out of my Shut Eyes ; and as my Sight Diminish'd every day Colours Gradually more Obscure Flash'd out with Vehemence ; but now that the Lucid is in a manner Wholly Extinct, a direct Blackness, or else spotted, and, as it were, woven with Ash-Colour, is us'd to pour it Self in. Nevertheless the Constant and Settled Darkness that is before Me as well by Night as by Day, seems nearer to the Whitish than the Blackish ; and the Eye, rolling itself a little, seems to admit I know not what little Smallness of Light as through a Chink.*

Another Remarkable Circumstance of *Milton's* Life must not be Slightly pass'd over. 'tis what He calls his *Defence of the People of England* against *Salmasius*, who had wrote a *Defence* of King *Charles* I. after his Death. This Work was not *Milton's* Choice, he was Appointed to it by the Unanimous Voice of the Council of State, the Then Publick Authority; not but that He most Willingly Undertook it as soon as he enjoy'd such a measure of Health as would endure the Fatigue of Writing; and Such was his Ardour to Write on This *Great Subject* that he Enter'd upon it *being yet Weak in Body, forced to write by Piece-Meal, and break off almost every hour*, as he says in his Introduction to that famous Work; though, as he says Elsewhere, it was with the most Apparent Hazard of his Sight, and which in Effect was Totally Extinguish'd on This Occasion; nor could he be Unaware of the Possible, and not very Improbable Chance of being put to Death for what he did.

This Dispute continu'd four or five Years, not with *Salmasius* only, whose Heart 'tis thought *Milton* broke; that he Dy'd whilst he was preparing a Laborious Reply to the *Defence of the People of England*, is Certain; Others Abroad took up the Quarrel. These too felt the Severity of their Antagonist. the Chief of These was *Morus*, the Next, if not Equal, to *Salmasius* in Fame; Both were Esteem'd as the Principal of the Learned Men of That Age till This War with *Milton ;* and These Alone He condescended to Combat with. This Controversy and Victory Rais'd the Reputation of *Milton* both at Home and Abroad; He was Visited and Invited by the Foreign Ambassadors at *London*, not Excepting Those of Crown'd Heads, and Honour'd and Esteem'd by All of Whatever Party that had a True Taste of Learning, Language, Stile, Spirit, Wit, *&c.* though (let it be Observ'd) *Paradise Lost* was Yet Uncreated.

I will not wholly Justify His Pleasantry and Personal Reflections, all Foreign to the Argument, and Unworthy the Importance of the Subject, and Love of Truth. Somthing must however be Allow'd to the

Time and Custom.   The Ancients in their Wars were
Barbarous Compar'd to the Moderns, at present War is
a Polite Amusement to what it was an Age or two ago;
'tis much the Same in Controversy.   if *Milton* was in
Fault Here his Adversaries were no less So; I hope
More, for they Loaded him with Lyes.   After all (as
Bayle observes on This Occasion) " 'tis of Use to get
the Laughers on One's Side "; 'tis not the Serious and
the Reasonable who are to Determine, if the Majority
are to be the Judges.

the Famous Serjeant *Maynard* heard One just call'd
to the Bar Plead Admirably.   " Young Gentleman,
(says he) You have Talk'd Well to the Wise; but learn
to please the Fools, Among Them you will find Most
Clients."   but not to Borrow an Excuse for This Practice in Controversy from *Bayle*, or any one Else, *Milton*
furnished One for Himself on a like Occasion, when he
was Scurrilously Attack'd by an Unknown Author upon
his Doctrine of *Divorce*.   'tis in his Treatise, call'd
Colasterion, just at the End of it.   *I have Now done That
Which for Many Causes I might have thought could not
Likely be My fortune, to be put to this Under-work of
Scouring, and Unrubbishing the low and sordid Ignorance
of Such a Presumptuous Lozel.   Yet* Hercules *had the
Labour once impos'd upon him to carry Dung out of the*
Augean *Stable.   At any Hand I would be Rid of him :
for I had rather, since the Life of Man is likened to a Scene,
that all my Entrances and Exits might mix with Such
Persons only whose Worth Erects Them and their Actions
to a Grave and Tragick Deportment, and not to have to do
with Clowns and Vices.   But if a Man cannot Peaceably
Walk in the World, but must be Infested ; Somtimes at
his Face with Dorrs and Horse-flies, Somtimes beneath*

with Bawling Whippets and Shin-Barkers, and Those to be set on by Plot and Consultation with a Junto of Clergy-men and Licencers, Commended also and Rejoyc'd in by Those whose Partiality cannot Yet forgo Old Papistical Principles ; have I not cause to be in Such a Manner Defensive, as may procure me Freedom to Pass more Un-molested Hereafter by Those Incumbrances, not so much regarded for Themselves, as for Those who Incite them ? and what Defence can Properly be used in Such a Despicable Encounter as This, but either the Slap or the Spurn ? if they can Afford me None but a Ridiculous Adversary, the Blame belongs not to Me, though the whole Dispute be Strew'd and Scatter'd with Ridiculous ?——a little after Thus——*Since my Fate extorts from me a Talent of Sport, which I had Thought to hide in a Napkin, He shall be my* Batrachomuomachia, *my* Bavius, *my* Calandrino, *the Common Adagy of Ignorance and Over-weening.* I with the more Pleasure apply These Passages to the Dis-putants *Milton* had Now to deal with, *Salmasius* and *Morus*, as that the Character Here given of an Antagon-ist so well fits These Gentlemen; Contemptible in the Affair in which they were Engag'd, and with Regard to any Other Merit than as Scholars, Grammarians or Jokers. but *Milton* chose much rather to Grapple with Another sort of Adversary, and with other Weapons, for Thus he Concludes.——*If any Man Equal to the Matter, shall think it Appertains him to take in Hand This Controversy,*——*if his Intents be Sincere to the Publick, and shall carry him on without Bitterness to the Opinion, or the Person Dissenting, let him not, I intreat him, guess by the Handling, which Meritoriously hath been bestowed on this Object of Contempt and Laughter, that I account it any Displeasure don me to be Contradicted in Print : But as it*

*leads to the Attainment of any thing more True, shall
esteem it a Benefit, and shall know how to Return his
Civility and Fair Argument in Such a Sort as He shall
Confess that to do So is my Choice ; and to have don Thus
was my Chance.* This was Written about six Years
before the *Salmasian* Controversy.

One would be tempted to Wonder what was become
of the English, Especially the Great Names among the
Clergy of That time, Such Zealous Preachers for the
Church and Monarchy, that the Poor Banish'd King
was put to the Great Expence (to Him Then) of a
Hundred Jacobus's to *Salmasius*, for Writing against
Those who had put his Father to Death, in a Manner
So Amazing to the Whole World: and how came it to
pass, that as the Dispute Spread we hear of None of
them; only that *Bramhall* was Suppos'd to be the
Author of an Inconsiderable Piece, which *Milton* made
his Younger Nephew Answer ? Who would not have
thought to have found Numbers of Great Writers of
our Own, Men of Piety, Learning, Judgment, and Wit,
Engaging as Volunteers in Such a Cause ? No, All are
Quiet. the Work is left to a Mercenary Foreigner,
and at That time a Professor of a Republican University, and a Pensioner to that State; a Man of Learning
indeed, and a Great Etymologist, but a Meer Scholar,
without Genius, Judgment, or Knowledge of the World;
Morus was also a Worded Man; and he was a Cele-
brated Preacher, but That Fame was Owing to his
Grace of Action as an Orator, or rather to that False
Wit which produces Puns, Jokes, Conceits, *&c.*
Always Odious, but Abominable in the Pulpit; for
Such Qualities as These, Insolence, Self-Conceit, Lying,
Pride and Ill-Nature, not to say worse, it has been

Milton's Fate to have had his Enemies Remarkable. Thus it was in This Dispute, and it ended Accordingly; in Their Confusion, and in his Glory.

> a haughty Wave Whelming on Ocean's back,
> Insults the Navy, and Derides the Wrack;
> but Pouring On Triumphant to'ard the Shoar
> Assaults a Rock; the Rock disdains the Roar,
> Receives the Stroak; 'tis but a Boasting Sound,
> nor more than Dash, and Foam, and Froth is found.

From the Year 52, to the time of the Restoration, *Milton* liv'd in a House, which look'd into the Park, Whither he had remov'd from his Lodgings in *Whitehall* for the Benefit of the Air, his Health being much Impair'd, as well as his Sight gone. He was Allow'd a Substitute, and his Salary as Secretary was Continu'd.

Soon after his coming to This House, his Wife Dy'd, in Childbed. 'twas not long e'er he Marry'd Again, Blind and Ill as he was; This Second Wife dy'd also in Childbed within a Year, and the Child soon after. he continu'd a Widower 'till after the Great Change of Government, and seems to have past his Time after his *Salmasian* Controversy was ended, which was in the Year 1655, as an Infirm, Blind Man could, but One who Lost both Health and Sight in the Pursuit of Knowledge, in Conversing with the Beauties of the Ancient Writings, and Applying All he could Attain in the Service (as he was Fully Persuaded) of Religion and National Liberty. a Great Part of This time he also had the Pleasure of seeing what he conceiv'd a National Happiness, which Himself had Largely Contributed to, though he also, in the Latter part of These Years must be Suppos'd to Observe the Tottering Condition of that Fabrick with Grief and Terror. He

Publish'd three or four small Treatises on Religion and Government.

Probably in This Period he went on with what he had Began Before, the English History from the Earliest times in which Any Accounts of it are Extant; he Discontinued it when he had brought it down to the *Norman* Conquest. he also set himself to Collect out of all the Classicks in Verse and Prose, a Latin *Thesaurus*, in Emendation of That done by *Stephanus*, and to the Framing a Body of Divinity out of the Bible. the History was Publish'd, but not 'till the Year 1670. the Other two were Never Printed, though said to have been finish'd. but the *Thesaurus* is not Lost to the World, as appears by the Preface to *Littleton*'s Dictionary.

He was still preparing Himself for his Great Work; *Wood* says 'twas Begun in This time, but it does not appear he had gone in Earnest about it; not but that it seems to have been in View when he Wrote to *Henry Oldenburgh*, Minister of *Bremen* to the Senate of *England*, Anno 1654. This Letter gives an Idea of Him at That time; in It he says to this Effect. *Now that I have done with these Disputes I prepare for Other things, I know not whether more Noble or more Usefull than Asserting Liberty, if I can do it for my Ill Health, and this want of Sight more Grevous than any Old Age, if, in fine, for these Clamours and Evil Tongues which perpetually Surround Me, for an Idle Leisure never pleas'd Me, and Those Unforeseen Controversies with the Adversaries of Liberty Dragg'd me Unwillingly, Intent upon very Different, and Much more Delightfull Subjects ; Yet So that I do not Repent me at all of having Undertaken them since 'twas Necessary, for I am very far from thinking that That*

Controversy was Vain and Trifling, as You seem to Intimate.

it has been said *Milton* was put upon Translating *Homer*; he was Certainly the Best Fitted for it of any Man on Some Accounts, on Others not at All. for as he says in the P.S. to the Judgment of *Bucer* concerning Divorce——*Me, who never could delight in long Citations, much Less in whole Traductions ; whether it be Natural Disposition, or Education in Me, or that my Mother bore me a Speaker of what God made mine Own, and not a Translator.* A good Reason for Declining it, as he did.

the Year 1660, as all the World knows, Open'd a New Scene in *England ;* it did so to *Milton* to be sure in Particular.

'twas Necessary for him to Abscond. he Quitted his House where he had Liv'd in great Honour and Convenience Eight Years, and was thick Envellop'd in the Cloud which, amidst the Glaring Sun-shine of That time, rose on Some Few, whose Active Zeal or Crimes had put a Mark upon them for Ruin.

That *Milton* escap'd is well known, but not How. by the Accounts we Have 'twas by the Act of Indemnity; only Incapacitated for any Publick Employment. This is a Notorious Mistake, though *Toland*, the Bishop of *Sarum, Fenton*, &c. have gone into it, Confounding Him with *Goodwin*, their Cases were very different, as I found upon Enquiry.

Not to take a Matter of this Importance upon Trust, I had first of all Recourse to the Act itself; *Milton* is not Among the Excepted. if he was so Conditionally Pardon'd, it must Then be by a Particular Instrument; That could not be after he had been Purify'd Intirely by the General Indemnity; nor was it Likely the King, who had Declar'd from *Breda* he would Pardon All but whom the Parliament should judge Unworthy of it, and had Thus Lodg'd the Matter with Them, should Before They had come to a Determination bestow a Private Act of Indulgence, and to One so Notorious as *Milton*. 'tis true *Rapin* says several Principal Republicans apply'd for Mercy whilst the Act was Yet depending; but quotes no Authority; and upon Search, no Such Pardon appears on Record, though Many are two or three Years after, but then they are without Restrictions; Some people are willing to have a Particular, as well as the General Pardon. but whatever was the Case of Others, there is a Reason besides what has been already noted, to believe no Such Favour would Now be shewn to *Milton ;* the House of Commons (16 *June*, 1660) Vote the King be mov'd to call In *Milton's* two Books, and That of *John Goodwin* Written in Justification of the Murther of the King, in Order to be Burnt. and that the Attorney-General do proceed against them by Indictment or Otherwise. *June* 27. An Order of Council, Reciting that Vote of the 16th, and that the Persons were not to be found, Directs a Proclamation for calling In *Milton's* two Books, which are here Explain'd to be that against *Salmasius (the Defence)* and his Answer to *Eicon Basilike;* as also *Goodwin's* Book; and a Proclamation was Issu'd accordingly, and Another to the Same Purpose 13th *August*. as for *Goodwin* he Narrowly Escap'd with Life, but he was Voted to be Excepted out of the Act of Indemnity amongst the Twenty design'd to have Penalties Inflicted short of Death. and *August* 27, those Books of *Milton* and *Goodwin* were burnt by the Hangman. the Act of Oblivion was pass'd the 29th.

[*Kennet's* Regist.] 'tis seen by This account, that *Milton's* Person and *Goodwin's* are Separated, though their Books are Blended together.

As the King's Intention Appear'd to be to Pardon All but Actual Regicides, as Bishop *Burnet* says (p. 163.) 'tis Odd he should say in the Same Breath almost all People were surpriz'd that *Goodwin* and *Milton* Escap'd all Censure (Neither is That True as has been seen) Why should it be so Strange, They not being Concern'd in the King's Blood? That he was Forgot, as *Toland* says Some people Imagin'd, was very Unlikely; however 'tis Certain by what has been shewn from Bishop *Kennet* he was Not. That He should be Distinguish'd from *Goodwin* with Advantage will justly appear Strange; for his Vast Merit as an Honest Man, a Great Scholar, and a most Excellent Writer, and his Fame on That Account, will hardly be thought the Causes, Especially when 'tis Remembred *Paradise Lost* was not yet produc'd, and the Writings on which his Vast Reputation Stood were Now Accounted Criminal, Every One of them, and Those Most which were the Main Pillars of his Fame; *Goodwin* was an Inconsiderable Offender Compar'd with Him.

Some Secret Cause must be recurr'd to in Accounting for This Indulgence. I have heard that Secretary *Morrice* and Sir *Thomas Clargis* were his Friends, and manag'd Matters Artfully in his Favour; Doubtless They, or Sombody Else did, and They very Probably, as being very Powerful Friends at That time. but still How came They to put their Interest on Such a Stretch in Favour of a Man So Notoriously Obnoxious? Perplex'd and Inquisitive as I was, I at length found the Secret, which He from Whom I had it Thought he

had Communicated to Me Long Ago, and Wondred, he had not. I will no Longer keep You in Expectation; 'twas Sir *William Davenant* obtain'd his Remission in Return for his Own Life procur'd by *Milton's* Interest when Himself was under Condemnation, *Anno* 1650. A Life was owing to *Milton*, (*Davenant's*) and 'twas Paid Nobly, *Milton's* for *Davenant's* at *Davenant's* Intercession. the Management of the Affair in the House of Commons, whether by Signifying the King's Desire, or Otherwise was Perhaps by Those Gentlemen Nam'd. It will Now be expected I should declare What Authority I have for This Story. My first Answer is Mr. *Pope* told it to me. Whence had He it? from Mr. *Betterton.* Sir *William* was His Patron. to obtain full Credit to This piece of Secret History, 'twill be Necessary to Digress a little, if indeed it be a Digression. *Betterton* was 'Prentice to a Bookseller, *John Holden*, the same who Printed *Davenant's Gondibert.* There Sir *William* Saw him, and persuading his Master to Part with him, brought him first on the Stage. *Betterton* then may be Well Allow'd to know This Transaction from the Fountain Head. that Sir *William* was under Condemnation, as has been said, his Postscript to that Book, shews; 'twas Printed in 51. for the Great Curiosity of it, I will present the Reader with That part which relates to This Affair. 'tis Dated from *Cow's Castle in the Isle of Wight*, October 22, 1650. " I am here
" arriv'd at the Middle of the 3d Book, which makes an
" Equal Half of the Poem; and I was Now by Degrees
" to present you (as I promis'd in my Preface) the
" Several Keys of the Main Building, which should
" convey you through Such Short Walks as give an
" Easy View of the whole Frame. But 'tis high time

" to Strike Sail, and Cast Anchor (though I have run
" but Half my Course) when at the Helm I am threatned
" with Death, who though he can Visit us but Once,
" seems Troublesome; and even in the Innocent may
" beget such a Gravity, as diverts the Musick of Verse.
" And I beseech Thee (if thou art so Civil as to be
" pleas'd with what is Written) not to take it Ill that I
" run not on 'till my Last Gasp. for though I intended
" in this Poem to Strip Nature Naked, and Cloath her
" again in the Perfect Shape of Vertue; yet even in so
" Worthy a Design, I shall ask Leave to desist when I
" am interrupted by so great an Experiment as Dying:
" and 'tis an Experiment to the most Experienc'd; for
" None (though his Mortification may be Much Greater
" than Mine) can say, *he has Already Dy'd*."

After all it is to be Observ'd, that the Pardon which
Secur'd *Milton* to us, was That of the Parliament, into
whose Hands the King had Committed the Affair, and
Who did as they thought fit; in Some Points, no doubt,
Complying with the Royal Intimations, in Other Osten-
tatious of their Zeal, and, Then most Remarkably
Fashionable Loyalty. Though the King had Express'd
his Desire, that the Indemnity should Extend to All
who were not Immediately Guilty of the Murder of his
Father, and had said it Mainly in his Speech of 27th
July; Yet That Restriction was far from being Punc-
tually Observ'd. the Interest that Sav'd *Milton* was
Therefore Made To, and was Effectual with the
Parliament, or rather the Legislature; the Nation For-
gave him, though they Little Knew how Well he would
Reward their Clemency by his Future Writings,
Chiefly *Paradise Lost.* and what made This Clemency
the More Remarkable, is, that This very Year whilst

s

his Fate was in Suspense, the Old Controversy was Rais'd up with Bitter Invectives. *Salmasius* Dy'd Some Years before, whilst he was Preparing a Furious Reply. This Work, though Imperfect, was Now Printed; but *Milton's* Fortune and Merit withstood this Malicious Attack.

'Twas Enough that *Milton* was Screen'd from being Excepted in the General Pardon, his Life and Person were Then Safe, his Two most Obnoxious Books being Sacrific'd in his Stead, was the most that his Friends could Hope for. Bishop *Burnet's* Conclusion of what he says on This Head I will add. " *Milton* had appear'd " so Boldly, though with Much Wit and great Purity " and Elegancy of Style, against *Salmasius* and Others, " upon that Argument of the putting the King to Death, " and had discover'd Such Violence against the late " King and all the Royal Family, and against Monarchy, " that it was thought a Strange Omission if He was " forgot, and an odd Strain of Clemency if it was " Intended he should be Forgiven. He was not " Excepted out of the Act of Indemnity. and After- " wards he came out of his Concealment, and lived " many Years Much Visited by All Strangers, and " much Admir'd by All at Home for the Poems he " Writ, though he was then Blind, chiefly That of " *Paradise Lost*, in which there is a Nobleness both of " Contrivance and Execution, that, though he Affected " to Write in Blank Verse, without Rhyme, and made " many New and Rough Words, yet it was esteem'd " the Beautifullest and Perfectest Poem that ever was " Writ, at least in Our Language." This Passage is put in This place Intire, though the Latter part of it refers to what comes after. I will only further Observe, that had the Bishop known This Story of Sir *William Davenant*, he would not have been One of the Wonderers at *Milton's* Escape.   How many things appear Unaccountable, meerly because Our Selves cannot Account for them.   the Wisest Men fall into This Folly in Some degree every Day of their Lives.

Secur'd by Pardon, *Milton* Appear'd again in Publick, and in a short time Marry'd his Third Wife.   He was Now Blind, Infirm, and 52 Years Old.   He had several Dwellings in the remaining part of his Life. One in *Jewen-street* [Elwood 156.]   This was in 1662, and about 1670 I have been told by One who Then knew him, that he Lodg'd Some time at the House of *Millington* the Famous Auctioneer Some Years ago, who Then Sold Old Books in *Little Britain*, and who us'd to Lead him by the Hand when he went Abroad. He Afterwards had a Small House near *Bunhill-Fields*, where he Dy'd, about 14 Years after he was out of Publick Affairs.   Besides Those Dwellings *Elwood* says in his Own Life, (p. 246.)   " Himself took a Pretty Box for him in *Giles-Chalfont*, [*Bucks*] for the Safety of Himself and Family, the Pestilence Then growing Hot in *London*."

His Time was Now Employ'd in Writing and Publishing, particularly *Paradise Lost*.   and after That, *Paradise Regain'd*, and *Samson Agonistes*.   the Last of These is Worthy of Him, the Other of any One else. if it be True that he preferr'd This to the First of the Three, What shall we say ?——

Well it was for Him that he had So Fine an Amusement, and a Mind Stor'd with Rich Ideas of the Sublimest Kinds: for besides what Affliction he Must have from his Disappointment on the Change of the

Times, and from his Own Private Losses, and probably Cares for Subsistence, and for his Family ; he was in Perpetual Terror of being Assassinated, though he had Escap'd the Talons of the Law, he knew he had Made Himself Enemies in Abundance. he was So Dejected he would lie Awake whole Nights. He then kept Himself as Private as he could. This Dr. *Tancred Robinson* had from a Relation of *Milton's*, Mr. *Walker* of the Temple. and This is what is Intimated by Himself, VII. 26.

> *On Evil Daies though fall'n and Evil Tongues,*
> *in Darkness, and with Dangers compast round,*
> *and Solitude;*

His Melancholy Circumstances at This time are describ'd by an Enemy, in what my Son found written in the Spare Leaf before the Answer to *Eicon Basilike*.

" Upon *John Milton's* not Suffering for His Traiterous Book
" when the Tryers were Executed 1660.

" That thou Escapd'st that Vengeance which o'ertook,
" *Milton*, thy Regicides, and thy Own Book,
" was Clemency in *Charles* beyond compare,
" And yet thy Doom doth prove more Grevious farr.
" Old, Sickly, Poor, Stark Blind, thou Writ'st for Bread,
" So for to Live thou'dst call *Salmasius* from the Dead.

if This Writer had known of the Terrors mention'd Above, he would have been glad to have Added to his Other Miseries This which was Equal to All the rest put together. if He can be said to be Miserable who Could write *Paradise Lost*.

But He is at Rest, and has Enrich'd the World with what is Inestimable. and his Name, as Party Malice Dies, or Fades with Time, will Bloom; it has Bloom'd

Long Since, 'twill Open and Spread Beauty and Fragrance More and More, if not Nippt by a Deprav'd Taste. *Thou shalt hide* [him] *in the Secret of thy Presence from the Pride of Man : Thou shalt keep* [him] *Secretly in a Pavilion from the Strife of Tongues*, Ps. xxx. 20. He Dy'd *Nov.* 10, 1674. of the Gout, but with So Little Pain, that Those in the Room knew not when he Expired.

I cannot find what Children he had at his Death. three Daughters his First Wife brought him, and then a Son who Dy'd an Infant. Another Daughter his Second Wife Dy'd in Childbed of, the Child soon follow'd. by his Last he had None. What became of One of Those Daughters, even Long before his Death, is Uncertain. *Toland* says Two were Assistant to him, 'till it growing Intolerable to them, they were sent to Learn what was More Proper for Young Women than Hebrew, Greek, &c. *Wood* says but One; *Deborah* the Youngest, was his Amanuensis. This then must be She who was So Visited and Reliev'd a few Years Since.

When just before his Death *Socrates* was ask'd How he would be Bury'd, his Answer was to This Effect; have I been talking to you all this while to so little Purpose ? [on the Soul's Immortality] *Socrates* will be gone far out of your reach; as for the Body of *Socrates* Dispose of it with Decency, and as the Laws direct. what was call'd *Milton*, has Long been Mouldring under the Pavement of the Church of *S. Giles Cripplegate*, close by his Indulgent Father. the Circumstances of his Family Excus'd a Monument, nor was any Such Necessary.

I have heard however that One was a few Years ago

Intended to have been Set up for him in *Westminster-Abby* ; by Whom I know not; but it was not permitted upon Account of his Political Principles. a Case not much Unlike That of poor *Ophelia* in *Shakespear*, who was suppos'd to have had Wrong Notions concerning Self-Murther.   What her Brother *Horatio* says is Admirable,

> ——————*I tell thee, Churlish Priest,*
> *a Minist'ring Angel shall my Sister be*
> *when Thou ly'st Howling.*

I have shewn you *Milton's* Face, his Person, his Mind. I have then told How he pass'd through Life. Let us Now Enquire what were his Circumstances with regard to his Fortune, his Means of Subsistence. Which I have Chosen to make a Distant Article, that, as in a Composition in Painting there Ought to be Certain Groups or Masses, that the Eye may not be Perplex'd and Confounded; in This Picture of this Extraordinary Man there should be the Like Art used to Assist the Reader to View and Comprehend the Whole, Clearly and at Ease.

How Long *Milton's* Father Subsisted him is not said; he had no Employment whereby to Get Any thing, if 'tis true he was not Paid for his Trouble in the Education of Young Gentlemen, which I confess I don't very throughly Believe; for his Father's Estate was not Large, nor had he Design'd him for a Gentleman, without an Employment for his Maintenance; and besides 'tis said he not only Instructed his two Nephews, and the Sons of a particular Friend or two, but when he had Discontinu'd That for a while, he Undertook it again in a Larger House, hired for That Purpose; tho' That also was laid Aside in a short time, and Himself

Engag'd in an Employment of Honour and Advantage
for about 12 years. I have been told he had 200 *l.* per
Ann. *Salmasius* in his *Responsio,* p. 16. says the Parliament allow'd him 4000 Livres Annually for Writing
for them. about a Year or two before This Alteration
in his Affairs his Father Dy'd, and He became possess'd
of an Elder Brother's Share of his Estate. 1000 *l.* 'tis
said was besides given him for Writing his *Defence of
the People of England* ; So that Now he was in Plentiful
Circumstances, though he made no Use of them in
Luxury or Ostentation. but not only upon the Change
of the Government he Lost his Employment, he was
Otherwise a Great Sufferer in his Fortune. he had put
2000 *l.* in a Fund of Those Days, the Excise, That was
all Lost; Another Large Sum went for want of Management in Money-Matters, which People of *Milton's*
Turn of Head are rarely Expert at; and in the Fire of
London the House in which he was Born, (all that was
remaining of his Paternal Estate) was Burnt. Nevertheless, what by Money he had Sav'd, what by the
Sale of his Library a little before his Death, and perhaps
by Presents, for So I have heard it Intimated, he Left
at his Death 1500 *l.* besides his Goods. So that he was
in no Difficulties Considering His Temper and Manner
of Life, Austere and Frugal. That Daughter, who a
few years since was So much Visited and Reliev'd for
her Father's Sake, and for the Share She had in Producing the *Paradise Lost*, Reading and Writing for him,
Satisfy'd Us in That particular.

But how Easy soever *Milton* was on That Article,
'tis More than Probable his Wife, who was not a
Philosopher and Poet as He, nor consequently So
Amus'd and Delighted with what Such a Mind, and

So Stor'd as His, was, 'tis Exceeding Probable She
Disturb'd him Somtimes for his Carelessness, or want
of Skill of This Sort.   Especially if She was, as I have
heard, a Termagant.   What Fortune She, or Either of
his Other Wives brought him is not said, only that All
were the Daughters of Gentlemen, but be That as it
will, She cannot be Blam'd if She Wish'd for a Better
Maintenance at Present, and a More Promising View of
the Future than She had.   This is Natural to think, but
the Story with which I shall conclude this Branch of the
Account of the Author of *Paradise Lost*, Confirms what
I have Suggested, but what is More Important, it
Alone gives us an Amiable Picture of that Beloved Man.

My Authority is *Henry Bendish* Esq: a Descendant
by his Mother's side, from the Protector *Oliver Cromwell ;* Their Family and *Milton's* were in Great Intimacy Before and After His Death, and the thing was
known among them; Mr. *Bendish* has heard the Widow
or Daughter or Both say it, that Soon after the Restauration the King Offer'd to Employ this Pardon'd Man
as his Latin Secretary, the Post in which he Serv'd
Cromwell with So much Integrity and Ability; (that a
like Offer was made to *Thurlow* is not Disputed as ever
I heard) *Milton* Withstood the Offer; the Wife press'd
his Compliance.   *Thou art in the Right* (says he) *You,
as Other Women, would ride in your Coach ; for Me, My
Aim is to Live and Dye an Honest Man.*

Upon the whole Matter, as he never made Riches
or Show his Aim, he was not Troubled with Either;
nor on the Other hand with the Want of the Necessities,
or Conveniences, or, as far as he Desir'd, of the Ele-
gancies of Life.   but from his Cradle to his Grave he
Liv'd in Honour and Content; and Such a Man is

Truly Great and Rich, and Such Only. Above all, whatever Mistaken Notions may be Imputed to him, he Appears to have been Rich, and Splendid in a Consciousness of his Own Integrity, and upon That Foundation with a Noble Contempt for the Tongue of Ignorance, Malice, and Detraction.

Pleasure, I mean not what is Sensual, and as it is Oppos'd to Vertue, but That which is Consistent with, and Often the Effect of Religion and Philosophy, This Pleasure, as 'tis what makes Existence Valuable, is the Main Affair of Life. to form an Idea Therefore of the Life of any Particular Man, the Way must be to Balance his Enjoyments and Sufferings One against the Other, and then to Observe How the Account Stands. I have long thought Men are Nearly Equal in This Great Circumstance, how Vastly soever they may Differ in the Subordinate Ones. 'tis not my Intention to Pursue This Thread of Speculation at This time, as being Improper, but I should not Compleat what I Undertook, which was to Show you the Author of *Paradise Lost*, as well as I was Able, if I Omitted to Consider him in This Light, to View him with regard to Pain and Pleasure.

it has been Seen that he was Tormented with Head-Achs, Gout, Blindness; and that though he was a Gentleman, and had Always Enough for a Philosopher, he made no Show, nor had the Affluences of Fortune, Perhaps was Somtimes a little Streightned, at least his Family was not Easy, how much Soever Himself was, Only on Their Accounts. he had Other Domestick Vexations, particularly that Uncommon and Severe One of the Affront and Scorn of a Wife he Lov'd, and the

Continuance of it for some Years. and This without Allowing him time to know what Conjugal Happiness was. Many of his Choicest Years of Life were Employ'd in Wrangling, and Receiving and Racquetting Back Reproach, Accusation, and Sarcasm. Which though he had an Arm and Dexterity fitted for, 'twas an Exercise of his Abilities very Disagreeable to Him: as it must needs be to One Accustom'd to Praise, as He was in his Younger Years, to One Ever Labouring to Deserve Esteem and Love, to find Himself Laden with Obloquy and Hatred by a Great Part of Mankind, and even by Many of Those from whom he had a Right to Expect and Demand the Contrary. And when he return'd to those Employments of his Faculties he Chiefly Delighted in, Especially Poetry, it must Grieve him to find Them So little Regarded, as in the Case of *Paradise Lost*, of which More in its Place. Add to All This, that Latterly when Publick Affairs ran in a Channel he had All his Life before been Labouring to Dam up, it must give Him no Small Affliction; Considering withal his Own Particular Sufferings. and Danger of Worse. All which must have an Additional Weight as Age and Infirmities, and perhaps their Unusual Concomitant, Lowness of Spirits, Gain'd Ground upon Him. What Now of Pleasure had He to Balance against This? if his Fortune and Appearance were not Considerable, Neither did he Desire they Should; nor did he Wish the Applauses of Other than Wise and Good Men, that is, Those he Judg'd to be So; the Praises of the Rest he Well knew were not to be had in behalf of the Most Uncommon Merit. and that This Rest is Always the Majority: but he was Greatly Honour'd by Those whose Approbation is True Glory.

the Gratifications of Sense, Otherwise than as Nature, and Temperance had given them a Pure, and Wholesom Relish, he knew little of. Only Musick he Enjoy'd. Whilst he had Sight, the Source of Perpetual Pleasure to Refin'd Eyes, he seems to have Little by Their Means, at least Little from the Labours of Art. though that he saw Nature Beautifully, I am Sure by the Pictures of That Kind he has Enrich'd our Collections with. He, (in a Word) was All Mind, an Intellectual Man. and Such were his Pleasures. A Strong Tide of Knowledge which his Soul Thirsted after was Ever Flowing. With his Learning Came in the Noblest Ideas, Philosophical, Divine and Poetical; nor were Such Wanting Perpetually Suggested from Within, Equal, or Superiour to the Best of his Wellcom Acquisitions; These Sweetned and Improv'd All the Incidents of Life; All Such a Man Sees, Tastes, Touches, All that is Common, and Un-Notic'd to Vulgar, or not Exalted Minds, to Such as His becomes Joyous. Above All, He had Vertue and Piety; not only an Unmolested Conscience, Unpolluted, but a strong Sense of having Done his Duty, What He Conceiv'd to be So; the very Utmost the Best of Us Can do, and which Whoever Has, will believe he finds *the Spirit it Self bearing Witness with His Spirit that He is a Child of God*. This was His Rejoycing. Whether he was in the Right or Not, Alters not the Case as to the Approbation and Exultation of his Own Mind. Mr. *Locke* wrote a Letter to a Friend, (Mr. *Collins*) not to be deliver'd to him till After Himself was Dead. I have seen the Original, it has These Words, as near as I can remember, 'tis Many Years ago that I saw it.——" May You Continue to " Enjoy Plenty, and Health, which Providence has

" Bestow'd on You, and which your Vertue Intitles you
" to. I know you Lov'd me while I was Living, and
" will Honour my Memory now that I am Dead; the
" best Use to be made of it, is to Believe there is no
" Happiness Equal to a Consciousness of having done
" Well; This I have found, and This You will find
" when you come to make up the Account."   A Man
always Busied as *Milton* was, Possess'd of Such Sublime
Ideas and Sentiments, and of Such a Consciousness——
I enquire not what were the Other Circumstances of
his Life, and will admit (as it must happen to the Wisest
and Best of Men, and of the most Poetical Genius)
Nature Somtimes broke in upon the Strongest Ram-
parts the Muse, Philosophy, and Religion could Provide; Yet Surely *John Milton* was in the Main, and
upon the foot of the Account, a Happy Man.   to What
Degree Who can tell ?

> ——————————*though fall'n on Evil Dayes,*
> *on Evil Dayes though fall'n, and Evil Tongues ;*
> *in Darkness, and with Dangers compasst round,*
> *and Solitude ; Yet not Alone while Thou*
> *Visit'st my Slumbers Nightly, or when Morn*
> *Purples the East :*————Parad. Lost. VII. 25.

in the Muse was His *Joy and Crown of Rejoycing*, and
in the Testimony of a Good Conscience;

> ——————————this Sensual World was not
> a Paradise to Him, but he Possest
> a Paradise Within Him, Happier far!

We have been Entertain'd (Greatly I may say,
Speaking of My Self) with the Picture of a Man, of a
Mind, as well Worthy our Consideration and Esteem,
as Most of Those whose Lives are Written by any

Ancient or Modern; More than far the Greater Number; and the rather as being within the reach in Some degree, I mean his Piety and Vertue, of our Imitation. Whatever Spots, or Blemishes appear upon his Judgment in certain Points, let the Charitable Eye look beyond Those on his Immaculate Integrity. Such who have not Hitherto done This, but have Suffer'd what They have been Taught, or Chosen to Dislike in Him, to Eclipse him, so as that, though they See him to be a Great Poet, they look on him as Shining with a Sort of *Disastrous* Light, will, if they possess Good Minds, Rejoice in finding a Character Amiably Bright, where they Expected no Such; and will perhaps Read Him with More Delight, and Enrich their Own Minds the More by So doing, than if Themselves had continu'd Labouring under their Old Prejudices. Had he liv'd in Ancient *Rome* or *Athens*, what a Lustre would his Name have been Cloath'd with! Yes, and Here too, and Now, had our Publick Affairs Continu'd in the Channel in which He had Help'd to put them.

My Other Delightful Task remains; 'tis to give the History of *Paradise Lost*, and Some Idea of it.

As *Milton* intended Some Such Work, tho' the Subject was not Resolv'd on, We must Date its Original from That Intention, Especially as it Answers to the Main Scope of what was Then invelop'd in a General Idea. This was So Early as his Acquaintance and Friendship with *Giov. Batta. Manso*, Marquiss of *Villa* at *Naples ;* as appears by that admirable Latin Poem address'd to that Nobleman, and which must have been Written about the Year 1639. the Subject first thought on, was the Story of King *Arthur*. This is seen by his

Latin Elegy on *Damon*, written upon his Return from *Italy*, a little after the Other.

the Same Resolution continu'd, and the Same Subject was in View, though far from being Resolv'd on, after he was Engag'd in the Controversies of the Times. in his Preface to the 2d Part of *the Reason of Church Government*, printed in 1641, he discourses Largely on what was his Design in a More Seasonable time. See *Toland's* Edit. of his Prose-Works, *p.* 221. I will quote Two or Three Passages.——*I began Thus far to Assent both to Them* [his Italian Friends] *and divers of my Friends Here at Home ; and not less to an Inward Prompting which Now grew daily upon Me, that by Labour and Intent Study, (which I take to be my Portion in This Life) joyn'd with the strong Propensity of Nature, I might perhaps leave Somthing So Written to After times, as that they should not Willingly let it die.* and presently after——*there ought no regard be Sooner had than to God's Glory by the Honour and Instruction of my Countrey. For Which Cause, and not Only for that I knew it would be hard to Arrive at the Second Rank among the Latins, I apply'd my Self to that Resolution which* Ariosto *follow'd against the Perswasions of* Bembo, *to fix all the Industry and Art I could Unite in the Adorning of my Native Tongue ; not to make Verbal Curiosities the End, That were a Toylsom Vanity, but to be an Interpreter and Relater of the Best and Sagest things among mine own Citizens throughout this Iland in the Mother Dialect, that what the Greatest and Choicest Wits of* Athens, Rome, *or Modern* Italy, *and those Hebrews of Old did for Their Country ; I in my proportion, with This, Over and Above, of being a Christian, might do for Mine.*——He then proceeds upon the Undetermin'd Situation of his Mind, as to the

Story, and Manner of Treating it; but expatiates on the Great Advantage Poetry might be to a Nation, and then thus. *the thing which I had to say, and those Intentions which have Liv'd within Me ever since I could conceive my Self any thing Worth to my Countrey, I return to crave Excuse that Urgent Reason hath pluckt from me by an Abortive and Foredated Discovery; and the Accomplishment of them lyes not but in a Power Above Man's to Promise; but that None hath by more Studious ways Endeavour'd, and with more Unwearied Spirit that None shall, That I dare almost Aver of my Self as far as Life and free Leisure will extend.——Neither do I think it Shame to Covenant with any knowing Reader, that for some few Years I may go on Trust with him towards the Payment of what I am Now Indebted, as being a Work not to be rais'd from the Heat of Youth, or the Vapours of Wine, like That which flows at Wast from the Pen of some Vulgar Amorist, or the Trencher-Fury of a Riming Parasite; nor to be obtain'd by the Invocation of Dame Memory, and her Siren Daughters, but by Devout Prayer to that Eternal Spirit who can enrich with all Utterance and Knowledge, and sends out his Seraphim with the hallow'd Fire of his Altar to Touch and Purify the Lips of whom he pleases: to This must be added Industrious and Select Reading, Steady Observation, Insight into all Seemly and Generous Arts and Affairs; till which in some measure be compast, at mine Own Peril and Cost I refuse not to sustain this Expectation from as many as are not loth to Hazard so much Credulity upon the Best Pledges that I Can give them.*——Such he had already given in Those of his Juvenile Poems as were Known, particularly the *Mask*, &c. and in What of Him were already publish'd, More were given afterwards even in his Controversial Works, for in These

were seen the Fire and Spirit, and often the Flights of a
Poet, as well as the Characters of a Scholar, an Orator
and a Disputant. but the Promise was not Fulfill'd
'till near 30 Years after 'twas made; and though the
poem Intirely and most Remarkably Answers the
Description here given of it, except as to the Subject,
the World Easily Forgives That (which indeed was not
Promis'd) 'tis not *Arthur*, or any Other Story of *Roman*,
Greek, or *Jewish* Antiquity, but of the Ancestor of
Human Kind of which he Treats. And it came at a
Time such as He Promis'd it.——*With such Abstracted
Sublimities as These it might be worth your Listning,
Readers, as I may One day hope to have Ye in a Still time,
when there shall be no Chiding ; not in these Noises, the
Adversary, as ye know, Barking at the Door.*——See in
his Apology for *Smectymnuus*, at *p.* 177 of his Prose-
Works, where are also Abundance of Fine Thoughts
concerning Himself, with relation to such a Work as he
Always had in his View to be produc'd One day, how
Remote soever.

When he wrote that Letter to *Henry Oldenburgh* in
1654, quoted Already (*p.* 268) he Seems to be Entring
upon his Long Projected Work, as was Then Observ'd,
but This is Uncertain; as it is whether he had even
Yet resolv'd on the Form of his Poem.   'tis said he had
Once thoughts of a Tragedy, and that Some of the
Sketching of it is in his Own Hand amongst the MSS.
of *Trinity* College in *Cambridge*.

Whatever Preparations he had made, it seems Probable, he set not about the Work in good Earnest 'till
after the Restauration. the Beginning of the IXth Book
gives Grounds for This Conjecture. the Subject he was
Long Choosing and Beginning Late : he Apprehends

his Vigour is Decay'd by Years, or that the Cold
Climate may Affect him too much, So Entring on his
VIIth Book, he Complains he is *fall'n on Evil Dayes and
Evil Tongues, compast round with Dangers,* &c. an Exact
Description of This time according to Him, though
So Gay and Happy to the Nation in General. But
Whenever it was Wrote 'twas Shewn, as Done, to
Elwood in the Year 1665, at *Chalfont St. Giles,* Whither
Milton was then retir'd upon Account of the Plague, as
has been seen. *Elwood* says he left it with him, desiring
his Opinion of it. Which I have often Thought was a
great Argument of his Modesty. See *p.* 246 of that
Honest Quaker's Life.

How had that Man, *Milton,* the Courage to Undertake, and the Resolution to Persist in Such a Work with
the Load of Such Difficulties upon his Shoulders! Ill
Health, Blindness; Uneasy in his Mind, no doubt, on
Occasion of the publick Affairs, and of his Own; not
in Circumstances to maintain an Amanuensis, but Him-
self Oblig'd to teach a Couple of Girls (or as Some say
One) to Read Several Languages, and to Pronounce
them, so as not to be Grievous to an Ear as Delicate as
His, or even to be Intelligible. to be perpetually Asking
One Friend or Another who Visited him to Write a
Quantity of Verses he had ready in his Mind, or what
should Then occur.—This Reflection brings to my
Remembrance what Himself says on Another Occasion
(*Address to the Parliament,* Prose Works, *p.* 390.)
*God it seems Intended to Prove me whether I Durst Alone
take up a Rightfull Cause against a World of Disesteem,
and found I Durst.* He was Now to be Try'd if he
Durst Under all his Discouragements *Assert Eternal
Providence, and Justifye the Wayes of God to Men* in an

T

Epic Poem (said to be the Utmost Stretch the Human Mind is Capable of.) He Undertook the Work, and was Equal to it.

For the truth is, though he was in Some respects in a Disadvantageous Situation for Such an Enterprize, in Others he had Peculiar Encouragements. That Inexhaustible Fund of Learning in all the Languages in which Science is deposited, particularly what relates to Poetry; a most Intimate Knowledge of All the Poets worthy his Notice, Ancient or Modern; Chiefly the Best, and above All *Homer ;* nor will I forbear to say the Scripture, Infinitely Superiour to *Homer,* as in Other respects, so in its being a Treasure of the Sublimest Poetry. More even than All This, and without Which All his Other Great Talents had been of no Avail on This Occasion, he Possess'd the Soul of Poetry, the Soul of a Poet of the First and Purest Ages, with the Additional Advantages of Later Times; Chiefly of Christianity. Add yet to All This the vast Amusement and Pleasure it must be to Him Amidst his Difficulties and Distresses to have the Noblest Ideas continually making his Imagination a Scene of Happiness; the Hope of Fame, in the Accomplishment of what had been from his Youth Resolv'd on as the Great Work of his Whole Life, the Great Fruit of all his Laborious Studies; which Work Compar'd with all that he did Else, all Those however Esteem'd by All Men of Taste at Home and Abroad, were but as if done with his *Left hand;* 'tis his own Expression.

the Coldness of the Climate being mention'd as One of the Disadvantages he was Under in Writing this Poem, gives Countenance to what has been said, that he Wrote it only in Spring and Summer. that Sweet part of the Year he certainly Lov'd, Everybody does, Those of a Poetical Turn are Remarkable for it, and He in Particular, See his Latin Poem on Spring; his Muse was us'd to Revive as the Vegetable World does at That Season, it did So when he was Young, as well as in his Advanc'd Years. *Toland* says he had been inform'd he wrote only in the Winter, but he does not believe it, to be Sure 'twas a Mistake. for My Own part I cannot Comprehend that Either is Exactly True; that a Man with Such a Work in his Head can Suspend it for Six Months together, or but One; though it may go on more Slowly, but it must go On. This laying it Aside is contrary to that Eagerness to Finish what was Begun, which he says was his Temper. You have had the Passage, *p.* 207. Other Stories I have heard concerning the Posture he was Usually in when he Dictated, that he Sat leaning Backward Obliquely in an Easy Chair, with his Leg flung over the Elbow of it. that he frequently Compos'd lying in Bed in a Morning ('twas Winter Sure Then) I have been Well inform'd, that when he could not Sleep, but lay Awake whole Nights, he Try'd; not One Verse could he make; at Other times flow'd *Easy his Unpremeditated Verse*, with a certain *Impetus* and *Æstro*, as Himself seem'd to Believe. Then, at what Hour soever, he rung for his Daughter to Secure what Came. I have been also told he would Dictate many, perhaps 40 Lines as it were in a Breath, and then reduce them to half the Number.— I would not Omit the least Circumstance; These indeed are Trifles, but even Such contract a Sort of Greatness when related to What is Great.

After all Difficulties were Overcome, and Advantages Employ'd, the Book was in Danger of lying Buried in

Manuscript, by the Impertinence, Folly, Malice, or whatever Else, of the Licencer, who besides Other Objections fancy'd there was Treason in that Noble Double Simile. *As when the Sun new ris'n* &c. I. 594.

the Price for which *Milton* sold his Copy is Astonishing. and Here we were in Another Danger of Losing This Poem. Happy was it for the World that *Milton* was Poor and Depress'd, Certainly he must be so at This time. the Price this Great Man Condescended to take for such a Work; Such a Work! was Ten Pounds, and if a Certain Number went off, then it was to be made up Fifteen. the Contract was in being a few Years since; I need not tell you I have Try'd to get a Sight of it; they say 'tis Lost.

What is also Wonderful, there was great Appearance of Danger that *Milton* should have had but the Lesser Sum. the Man so Qualify'd by Nature and Education, who had made So *Eclatant* a Figure in the Learned World, who had been So Employ'd and Honour'd by the most Potent Republick upon Earth, and by Her Rewarded with 1000 *l.* for a Work however Great, Much Inferiour to This as to the Requisite Abilities for its Production, and its Use, and Duration; for This Man to be Recompenc'd so Contemptibly for Such a Work! what could be the Meaning of it? Unless Party-Malice, and Folly; or that the Gay Beginning of the Reign of *Charles* II. diverted the Taste of the Publick from what was of So Sublime a Nature. or was it not That Very Sublimity that Dazzled too Strongly Eyes Unacquainted with any thing that bore the least proportion with it?

the Contract just Now mention'd, was dated 27 *April* 1667. So says *Fenton* in his Short Account of

Milton prefix'd to his Edition of the Poem, in which he Aim'd at Pointing it Better. He assures us of the Substance of the Bargain concerning the Price; I have more Reasons to believe the thing is as he says. but *Fenton* tells us that the Book was First Publish'd 1669. Others have thought so too; and 'tis true there are of the First Quarto Editions with That Year in the Title-page. the Case is Thus; there are Three several Titles with a little Variation in Each, besides That of the Date; there are of 67, and 68, as well as of 1669. the Same Sheets, only a Word and a Point or two alter'd, the Sheet Otherwise the Same, not Cancell'd, but the Alteration made as 'twas Printing; So that Part of the Impression was So far different from the Other part. and not only there were Three Several Title-pages but a Short Advertisement to the Reader, the Arguments to the Several Books, and an Errata is Added, with a little Discourse concerning the Kind of Verse. but These little Additions were not Exactly the Same in Every Year, as neither were the Names of the Book-sellers, through whose Hands it pass'd. the First Title, That of 67 was immediately follow'd by the Poem, Naked of Advertisement, Errata, &c.

in 74 (the Year in which the Author Dy'd) he put out Another, the 2d Edition, with Some few Alterations, Additions Chiefly; and Now the Poem was divided into Twelve Books, which at First was in Ten. the VIIth and Xth Books are each Divided into Two. This is the Only Authentic Edition of the *Paradise Lost* as Thus Perfected; and 'tis very scarce. Another Octavo came out in 78. Ten Years after 'twas Printed in Folio, with Cuts by Subscription. In 95 Mr. *Tonson* gave us All our Author's Poetical Works, with the

same Cuts as to the Former Folio Edition, together
with Copious Notes by P. H. (I have been told, This
was *Philip Humes*) on *Paradise Lost*.   This is its 6th
Edition.   Since then it has been Reprinted in Several
Sizes, the Last in 1732, the 15th, if That of 1730 was,
as its Title-page says, the 14th, for the Last says not
what Edition it is.   We have Endeavour'd, but never
could see the 5th, nor the 11th or 12th, for That of the
Year 20 is One of them, but which, it does not say.

It has been a Current Opinion that the late Lord
Sommers first gave this Poem a Reputation.   is it not a
sufficient Reproach to our Country that *Paradise Lost*
lay Neglected for Two or Three Years ?   though even
for Those it may be Pleaded that Party-Partiality, and
the Then Gay Taste of Wit are answerable for a great
Share of the Guilt; 'Twas not Altogether Stupidity;
Hudibras about the same time had its due Regard; and
Deserv'd what it had, if it did not (as of late the *Beggar's
Opera* did by That where were heard *Senesino, Cuzzoni,*
&c.) draw away the Juice from a Much Nobler Plant.
Paradise Lost was known and Esteem'd Long before
there was Such a Man as Lord *Sommers*.   the Pompous
Folio Edition of it with Cuts by Subscription in the
Revolution-Year, is a Proof of what I Assert.   Lord
Dorset, Waller, Dryden, Sir *Robert Howard, Duke,
Creech, Flatman,* Dr. *Aldrich, Atterbury,* (since Bishop
of *Rochester*) Sir *Roger L'Estrange ;* and I will take
Leave on This Occasion, to remember Mr. *Riley*
(whose Disciple I was in Painting, and who Convers'd
with the Greatest Men of his Time, and was justly
Esteem'd by them not only as a Painter, but as a
Gentleman) These were Subscribers; Lord *Sommers*
was So too, but He was Then *John Sommers,* Esq; No

doubt, when he was So conspicuous Himself as He Afterwards was, His Applause and Encouragement Spread and Brightned its Lustre. but it had Beam'd Out Long before. I, even I, while a Youth, and not having ever Honour'd Other Names in Modern Poetry than *Shakespear*, *Cowley*, *Dryden*, &c. and whom, especially the two first, I was fond of (as I always was of the Muses) but *Milton* I had never heard of; I happening to find the First Quarto in Mr. *Riley's* Painting-Room was Dazzled with it, and from that Hour all the rest (*Shakespear* excepted) Faded in my Estimation, or Vanish'd. I immediately began to Store up in my Mind Passages to Regale and Nourish my Mind with at All times. Such a Work could not fail of reaching Better Eyes; as it did Soon, from whatever Cause it First Rose *Shorn of its Beams*. Sir *George Hungerford*, an Ancient Member of Parliament, told me, many Years ago, that Sir *John Denham* came into the House one Morning with a Sheet, Wet from the Press, in his Hand. What have you there, Sir *John* ? Part of the Noblest Poem that ever was Wrote in Any Language, or in Any Age. This was *Paradise Lost*. However 'tis Certain the Book was Unknown 'till about two Years after, when the Earl of *Dorset* produc'd it. Dr. *Tancred Robinson* has given Permission to Use his Name, and what I am going to relate He had from *Fleet Shephard*, at the *Grecian* Coffee-House, and who often told the Story. My Lord was in *Little-Britain*, Beating about for Books to his Taste; There was *Paradise Lost*; He was Surpriz'd with Some Passages he Struck upon Dipping Here and There, and Bought it; the Bookseller Begg'd him to speak in its Favour if he Lik'd it, for that they lay on his Hands as *Wast Paper*. Jesus!

——*Shephard* was present. My Lord took it Home, Read it, and sent it to *Dryden*, who in a short time return'd it: *This Man* (says *Dryden*) *Cuts us All Out, and the Ancients too.* Much the Same Character he gave of it to a North-Country Gentleman to whom I mention'd the Book, he being a Great Reader, but not in a Right Train, coming to Town Seldom, and keeping Little Company. *Dryden* Amaz'd him with speaking So Loftily of it. Why Mr. *Dryden*, says he, (Sir *W. L.* told me the thing Himself) 'tis not in Rime. *No. nor would I have done my* Virgil *in Rime if I was to begin it again.* 'twas when That Work was in Hand. and yet *Dryden* had some Years before *Rim'd Milton* in his *State of Innocence, Tagg'd his Lines*, as *Milton* said. the Fashion was in those days to wear much Ribbon, which Some Adorn'd with Taggs of Metal at the Ends.

the Book was Now fallen into Good Hands, and Poor *Milton* was Secure of his Full Pay, the Whole 15*l.* Thus Encourag'd, This Man set forth Another Improv'd Edition, as was said just now, but Liv'd not to see the Success of That; He Dy'd As soon as he had Thus Perfected the Work Providence Seems Chiefly to have Appointed for him.

Himself Intended it for his Native Country, Other Nations were to Enjoy it as much as Translations could Bestow it on them. *Hog* put it into Latin Anno 1690. It has had Several *French, High* and *Low Dutch* Translations. Half of it has been done in *Italian*, by *Rolli*, and we hope for the Other six Books. the Famous, Learned Abbè *Salvini*, the same who Translated *Addison's Cato* into Italian, shew'd my Son at *Florence* an Intire Translation of it, and said he Intended to Print it. 'tis not yet done that we know of. And now I take the

Liberty Once more to mention my Self on This Occasion, though I will not do it without setting *Milton's* Example to Plead in my behalf. He having spoken already in a Sort of Praise of Himself [*Reason of Church-Government*, B. 2.] goes on Thus. *and though I shall be Foolish in saying More to this Purpose, yet since it will be Such a Folly as Wisest Men going about to Commit, have only Confest and so Committed, I may Trust with more Reason, because with more Folly, to have Courteous Pardon.* What I would say is, that Our Books of Painting having been Translated into French and Dispers'd all over *Europe* by That Means, Especially where any Store of Good Pictures are, and These having Abundance of Quotations from *Milton* as from a Classic, Those being the First Books that have So Consider'd him: This has given a Specimen of the Whole, which has at least done Some Service to the Name of *Milton*, how much More Soever the Translation of Mr. *Addison's* Spectators on the Subject, and the Passages He has given may have done.

Thus, what by One means, what by Another, and Those Complicated and Manag'd as Providence well Can, This Poem, this *Waste Paper*, (like an Acorn Hid and Lost) has, by its Inherent Life, and a Little Cultivation, Sprung Out of the Earth, Lifted up its Head and Spread its Branches, a Noble Oak; has become a Richer Treasure to the World than it has receiv'd from Most of Those Names which Glitter in the Records of Time.

Who would have Imagin'd Now that *Milton's Paradise Lost* was not Yet Safe! 'tis in our Possession indeed in Many Editions, but *Milton's* Blindness and Other Disadvantages has Occasion'd Suggestions and

Assertions that we have it not as the Author *gave* it, but as Corrupted by Presumption, Folly, Carelessness, and I know not What. Presumption, Folly, or Somthing Worse, has been at Work, in Suggesting, or Believing Such things, which is the more Dangerous because founded on a Specious Probability, which Commonly Cheats Us, Few having the Opportunity, or the Skill to Distinguish between Probability and Truth; and Fewer yet that are not too Lazy to Examine with that Degree of Care and Pains which Truth will Demand. Persuasion is Cheaper come at by Probability.

Some may perhaps Imagine the Poem had been more Perfect if the Author had not been depriv'd of his Sight. I will Consider This in the First place.

and 'tis Such a Compliment to the Abilities of *Milton* that I confess I cannot come up to; how Poetical soever My Imagination may be thought to be in That Instance; I rather think that we owe some of the most Sublime Beauties of the Poem to That Circumstance; his Mind being not Depress'd with it, but Richly Arm'd against the most Calamitous Dispensations of the Divine Will by an Humble and Devout Resigna- tion, and a Philosophical, a Christian Resolution, with a Competent Measure of Supernatural Assistance En- abling him to lay hold of the Advantages which are to be found Accompanying Every Accident, or Provi- dential Event that Can possibly happen in Human Life; as there is No Good, how Bright Soever in Appearance, but carries with it Some Alloy. Blindness (God knows) is Terrible; I, who take In More Pleasure at my Eyes than Most Men, for I Perpetually find my Self Surrounded with what I see Abounds with Beauty; I conceive Strongly of That Calamitous Disease; but

at the Same time know that in That Case the Thoughts
may be More Collected, Intense and Fixt than when a
Multiplicity and Variety of Objects call them off, or
Divide their Powers. 'tis a Common Observation, that
a Loss or Defect in One Faculty is Compensated with
Advantages to the rest. Nor is it Unnatural to a Good
Mind, call'd off from Worldly Enjoyments by Some
Disastrous Circumstance, to Raise it Self, with More
Vigour than Otherwise it would Ever have Exerted,
Thither where are hid the Treasures of Wisdom, Un-
attainable in This Atmosphere, the Cares and Joys of
Sense in which the Generality of Us are Envelop'd.
That *Milton* was Thus *Rapt above the Pole* when he
Wrote *Paradise Lost* Seems to Me Apparent whenever
I open the Book, or recur to that Treasury of Fine
Passages of it laid up in my Mind. the Poem it Self
does *More than Whisper* it lost Nothing by its Author's
Blindness. but I love as often as I can, to bring Him
to tell my Reader what I would Say if I were able. be
pleas'd then to turn back to pag. 250; to which add
what he says in a Letter (Ep. 21.) to *Emeric Bigot* Anno
1656——*I rejoyce then that you have a just Sense of the
Tranquillity of my Mind in This so Great a Loss of my
Sight——as for the being bereav'd of my Sight wherefore
should I not bear it with Patience since I hope 'tis not so
much Lost, as call'd Inward, and Added to the Vigour of
my Mental Sight.* as II 51.

> *So much the rather thou Celestial Light*
> *Shine Inward, and the Mind through all her Powers*
> *Irradiate, There plant Eyes, all Mist from Thence*
> *Purge and Disperse,*————

As little did his Book Suffer by This Misfortune in
regard to the Correctness of the Impression, how much

Soever the Contrary may at First Sight seem Probable.
the Work is Compleat, and Pure.

Milton's Blindness, and Suppose Poverty, hindred
not his being Agreeable to Such Kind of Friends Who
Alone are Worthy of the Name, and Who Alone were
like to be Serviceable to him on This Occasion; Others
indeed Fled him; So much the better for Us, and Him.
and may Such Abject Minds keep far away from every
Good Man! Providence has Kindly taken Care for
That, and Did also take Care that *Milton* should not be
Destitute of Abundant Assistance to Supply his Want
of Sight. I have Already given a Noble Passage from
his *Defensio* 2ᵈᵃ. at Length, and Recommended it just
now, a Small Part of it is Full to my Present Purpose,
This I will give my Self the Pleasure of Transcribing
that the Reader should not be at the Trouble of Turning
to it again.———*My Friends are more Ready and Officious
to Serve me than Before, and more Frequently Visit me,
Some of which are not less True and Faithfull than those of
Old,* Pylades *and* Theseus. *For They did not think that
by This Accident I am become Altogether Nothing, or that
the Only Worth of an Honest and Upright Man is plac'd
in the Eyes. Far from it, the Greatest Men in the Commonwealth do not Desert me, since if my Eyes have Deserted
me it hath not been for Idly Withering in Lazyness, but in
Facing the Greatest Dangers with Activity, and among the
First for Liberty.*

But it may be said This was in 54, the Case was
Alter'd after the Restoration when 'tis Exceeding
Probable, or rather Certain, *Paradise Lost* was what he
was Mostly Employ'd upon. the Friends of a Good
Man are Usually Good Men; He had Doubtless
Always Such who Still Lov'd him for What he had Not

Lost, however his Fortune and Figure in the World might be Chang'd; and who Lov'd him the More as he More stood in Need of their Assistance. That Party, whatever their Guilt was, was never Charg'd with Sordid Self-Interestedness. But suppose they had been Base, As well as Rebels and Republicans, he was Otherwise Assisted in relation to what we are Upon. Thus we are Assur'd from *T. Elwood*, p. 154. " This Person " [*Milton*] having filled a Publick Station in the Former " Times, lived Now a Private and Retired Life in " *London :* and having Wholly lost his Sight, kept " Always a Man to Read to him; which Usually was " the Son of Some Gentleman of his Acquaintance, " whom, in Kindness, he took to Improve in his " Learning." This was in 1662.

Elwood Himself was One of Those who So Assisted him; Nor was it Easy for Such to get Admittance on Those Terms, So many were Glad of the Office for their Own Sakes, as this Honest Writer goes on to say. Himself was forc'd to wait Some time e'er he could have the Privilege to be receiv'd to This Service; and This (let it be Observ'd) was in Those years in which *Paradise Lost* was Wrote and Publish'd; for his Acquaintance with *Milton*, which Began in 62, Improv'd into a Continu'd Friendship; and no Wonder, *Elwood* was a Most Honest Sincere Man, had Learning, and Lov'd it, and Try'd also to be a Poet. He, or Some Other of These Young Gentlemen were Able by *Milton's* Direction to do all that is said to be Wanting, and Would Gladly, as well as Write for him. Nor can it be Suppos'd in a Work, which he had almost All his Life consider'd as One of the Chief Businesses of it, *Milton* would fail to take Care, in All that was Material to its Perfection, as the Correct Pointing and Printing most Certainly is, as well as the Writing. One that Writes for the Publick Good, or Fame, has done but Half what he Intended if This is not taken Sufficient Care of, Rather if his Work is Noble, he Thus Exposes a Beautiful Offspring on the Mountains to be Mangled by Savage Beasts; or Chang'd into a Monster by the *Circæan* Wand of Some Accursed *Comus*. *Milton* would no doubt provide against This as far as Human Wisdom could Then Forsee.

He spar'd not his Pains; as he wanted not Ability to do what I am saying. He Did much the Same for Others. *Elwood*, a Most Honest Creature, and a Hearty Admirer and Lover of his Master (as he calls him) says that——" having a Curious Ear, he understood by my Tone when I Understood what I Read, " and when I did not: and accordingly would stop me, " and Examine me, and open the most Difficult Pas- " sages to me."

but what we learn from *Milton* Himself sets us at Perfect Ease on This Article. Thus he Writes, concluding a Latin Letter to *Heimbachius*, Counsellor of the Elector of *Brandenburg*, 'twas in the year 1666——*I will finish, but must first beg you to Excuse it if you find any thing Wrong Written, or not Rightly Pointed, because I have only a Boy which I Dictate to, who knows nothing of Latin, and to whom I was forc'd with Great Uneasyness and Pain to Count every Letter.* by the way, *Paradise Lost* was Finished the Year before This, and Printed the Year after; This appears to have been an Accident, he did not Use to be Thus Destitute; but it shows *Milton's* Exactness even in the Pointing of a Familiar Letter. That Such Accidents must needs have been very Rare is Manifest by what has been said just Now; but what is This to *Paradise Lost* ? That was of Another Sort of Concernment, and might be taken Care of when the time was Proper, and all the Necessary Helps Ready.

What has been alledg'd as Probabilities, appears in Fact to be Certain. That the Original MS. was of the Hand-Writing of Several is Agreed, but does That appear by the Printed Book ? Nothing Less; 'tis Uniform Throughout: it must have Then been Revis'd and Corrected by Some one, Directed at least. and that This was *Milton* himself is Evident by its Exact Conformity with his Spelling and Pointing in What he Publish'd when he had his Sight; as also with his Other Works after That was gone. for full Satisfaction, Those that please may have recourse to Those Works, the Original Editions, for They are to be had. in the Mean time if they will give Me Credit, they will be Assured, that not only the Printing is Equally Accurate with what is to be found in Any of them, but 'tis rather More So than in most of the rest. as indeed 'tis of more Importance, that it should be Just Here than in Any of his Other Works, as 'tis his Principal One, and That in which even the Points Direct and Determine the Sense most Often and most Remarkably. We have found, in Several Instances, that what seem'd at first Sight to be the True One, was far Inferiour to what was indeed So, but would not have been Discover'd, unless by following Those Guides, Almost Universally Faithful.

There are Some Peculiarities in the Spelling of certain Words in *Paradise Lost*, not by Accident, but from One End to the Other; the Same is in what he Wrote with his Own Hand Years before. to go into

a Detail of These would be Dry to the Reader, nor is it
Agreeable to Me; but One remarkable Instance I will
give: the Word *Their* in This Poem, as in Many of his
Writings, is *Thir*.   What led him to This way of
Spelling this Word I know not, but he began it long
After he was a Publisher, though long Before *Paradise
Lost*.   'tis not an Ancient Way of Writing, it was
Always *Their* or *Theyr*.

Several Other Particularities of This Kind are to be
found in *Milton's* Works, Which let any One peruse,
they will be Convinc'd that there is Such a Similitude
of Spelling between Those Published when he was
Blind, and Those Before, that shows they *were All under
the same Direction*.   Had we not known it Otherwise
the Author would not have been suspected to be Blind
by Any want of Exactness in This.

In *Paradise Lost* Care has been taken of the Orthography where the Sense was in no Danger, and meerly
for the sake of Accuracy; as in the Word *Scent* Thus
Always Spelt, to distinguish it from *Sent*.   to Smell is
Sentir (Fr.) *Sentire* (It.) Thence we have *Scent*, but as
no *c* is in the Word we borrow from, *Milton* rejects it.
So the Word *Rhime* being deriv'd from *Rhythmos* (Gr.)
signifying (as *Milton* Himself has explain'd it) *Apt
Numbers, fit Quantity of Syllables, and the Sense Variously
drawn out from One Verse into Another ;* and we having
Made the same Word to stand for *the jingling Sound of
Like Endings*, He has Distinguish'd the Different Ideas
by Spelling the Latter without the *h*.   This is of Consequence, the Sense of the place not being Always
Sufficient to keep the Reader from Confounding those
Ideas.   This Difference in the Spelling of these Words
is seen in the short Discourse concerning the Verse in

the first Quarto Edition, That of 68 or 69, and the
Octavo of 74, I.16. the Neglect of This in the Edition
of 78, the First after the Author's Death, was the First
Corruption that crept into the Copies of this Poem, and
which has been follow'd by More, particularly in the
Pointing, which consequently has also Somtimes Cor-
rupted, Somtimes Perplexed the Sense; not but that
Words also have been Chang'd, though indeed but
Rarely, the Spelling Frequently; *Sent, Thir, Perfet,*
Then, (when a Comparative) *Soule, Eeven, Minde, Don,*
Burden, &c. All Moderniz'd and Spelt as Now.

in *Paradise Lost* there is a Remarkable Proof of Care
which we have not Observ'd in any of our Author's
Other Works, or Those of any Other Writer, and that
is, the Words *He, we, me, ye,* are with a Double or a
Single *e,* as the Emphasis lies upon them, or does not.
We could produce a great Number of Instances of This.
Take only Two, II. 1021-2-3. VI. 286, 288. Nay, a
Neglect of This kind is put into the Errata of the First
Edition, the Fault is in II. 414. but the Second Edition
has happen'd to Overlook it, though Otherwise Exceed-
ingly Correct.

There is Still Another Uncommon Instance of Care
in the Printing: in the First Edition. Faults were
discover'd when Part of the Impression was wrought
off; 'twas not thought worth while to Cancel the Leaf,
but the Correction was made, and the Sheet gone On
with So Corrected, and for the Sake of Those that were
already Printed, Notice was taken in the Errata, by
which means Those who happen'd to have the Perfect
Sheet, if they compar'd the Text with the Errata, must
be at a loss to know what was the Occasion. One of the
Instances I am speaking of, is III. 760, *with* is chang'd

U

to *in*. This Fault was Probably discover'd early; we have Six of the First Edition, and but One of them has *with*. I must observe further of This Leaf, the Numbers of the Verses were Wrong mark'd, and Alter'd, but not with due Care. the true Number of the Lines of this Third Book is 743. Another Instance of the Same Nature I have been giving is in V. 257. the Leaf is Evidently the Same, but the Sheets Printed off began a new Paragraph with this Line, and had no Comma after Cloud; a Comma was put, and the Line went on with the rest without beginning a Paragraph.

From hence, no Cloud, or, to obstruct his Sight, and so it is in the Second Edition, and as it Ought to be. but This Fault was not Seen so Early as the Other; Three of my Six of the First Edition have it, the Other Three are Corrected.

These kind of Niceties must be Tedious to a Reader, they are to Me, and would not have taken up so much of my Time and His, but that the producing them are Important to the Book. I will however give but One Proof more of the great reason we have to Depend upon the Two First Editions of *Paradise Lost*.

Milton was Always Careful in the Printing; Little Tracts had an Errata, if wanted, as well as Larger Works, and This After He was Blind as well as Before; though Generally what he publish'd needed them as Little as any I have Observ'd, and he was particularly Scrupulous herein; Faults are put into His Errata's, which Few, or None but Himself, would have taken Notice of, but he knew of what Importance to the Sense, the Misplacing or Omission even of a Comma Oftentimes is. He complains of the Dutch Reprinter of his *Second Defence* for his Carelessness or Malice in

This Particular. He shows the like Concern in his Letter to *Heimbachius*, mention'd lately. Accordingly though at the First Publication of *Paradise Lost*, it had no Errata, as in truth it scarce Needed Any, but at the Reprinting of the Title-page One was Added, tho' it consisted of what None but a Most Exact Writer would have Notify'd. Such as are above mention'd. the Second Edition, that of 1674, never had Any, Those of the Other are There Corrected, All but a Trifle or two, but by Much Comparing One with the Other, as we have had Occasion, and by very Often Reading over that Second Edition (for That we have made our Standard Book, Undoubtedly we Ought) we have found it had no New Faults to make an Errata Necessary, a Word or Two, and perhaps Here and There, Rarely, a Point. So That Agreeing So nearly with the First Edition, and That having been so Throughly Sifted for Faults and Corrected, we have reason to Assure our Selves, especially if we take Both These Authentick Editions together, that we are in Possession of the Genuine Work of the Author As much as in Any Printed Book whatsoever.

and I dare Appeal to Any Intelligent Reader for the Truth of This, Provided he Presumes Not on his Own Sense of a Passage, and Then Blames the Words or Points as not Expressive of That. Let him come Honestly to receive *Milton's* Sense, as Wee have done, and you will rarely hear him Complain of the Printer, or the Editor.

And not only we have the Genuine Work as much as can be Hop'd for from Printing, Why not as from Any Manuscript can be Expected ? since such a Number of Verses, Written and Corrected by a very Careful

Man, with his own Hand, will go off with Some Faults, and I think Rarely without as Many, and as Material as in the Edition I am speaking of; I know of None, but Here and There a Point, and perhaps I am Somtimes Mistaken in Those I think are Wrong, for Words I Know of, or Remember but Three, Nor is it quite Certain One of These is not what *Milton* Intended; That is *Smelling*, instead of *Swelling*, VII. 321. another is in the same Book, and just by v. 451, *Fowl* instead of *Soule*, nor is the Intire Word Mistaken, for *Milton* spells *Fowle* v. 389, as I have done here, So *Soule* with an *e*. the Other is *Me*, instead of *we*, IX. 1019. how Easily These Faults might be Committed by the Printer, and the most Exact Authors with *Lynxes* Eyes, I leave the Reader to judge; and then Whether This Book affords any Pretence or Excuse to a New Editor, who shall Dare to Change though it were with the Utmost Deliberation, and Taste. He may indeed Honestly Say Thus and Thus the Author Should have Thought or Said, but let him not Palm Himself upon us as a Genuine *Milton*.

Concerning This Kind of Licentiousness, our Divine Author Speaks like Himself in his *Areopag.* I shall with Pleasure Transcribe two or three Passages——*as good almost kill a Man as kill a good Book : who kills a Man kills a reasonable Creature, God's Image ; but he who Destroys a Good Book, kills Reason it Self, Kills the Image of God, as it were in the Eye. Many a Man lives a Burthen to the Earth, but a Good Book is the Pretious Life-Blood of a* Master-Spirit, *Imbalm'd and Treasur'd up on Purpose to a Life beyond Life*——*Revolutions of Ages do not oft Recover the Loss of a Rejected Truth, for the Want of Which whole Nations fare the Worse*——

Which Course Leo *the* 10th, *and his Successors follow'd,
until the Council of* Trent, *and the Spanish Inquisition
Engendring together, brought forth, or perfected those
Catalogues, and Expurging Indexes that rake through the
Entrals of Many an Old Good Author with a Violation
Wors than Any could be offer'd to his Tomb*————*Yet if
These Things be not Resented Seriously and Timely by
Them who have the Remedy in thir Power, but that such*
Iron-Moulds *as These shall have Authority to knaw out the
Choicest Periods of Exquisite Books, and to commit Such a
Treacherous Fraud against the Orphan remainders of
Worthiest Men after Death, the more Sorrow will belong to
that Haples Race of Men, whose Misfortune it is to have
Understanding. Henceforth let no Man care to learn, or
care to be more than Worldly Wise ; for Certainly in
Higher Matters to be Ignorant and Slothful, to be a Com-
mon Stedfast Dunce, will be the Only Pleasant Life, and
only in request.*

Every Author has a Right to say What a Lady said
to a Painter (not to Me upon my Word) when She
Observ'd him, under Pretence of Complimenting her,
making a Face for her which She had not been Acquainted with. *Sir,* (says She) *I see what you are about,
You don't like my Face, and are for giving me a Better in
the Stead of it. I'd have you to know My Face is as Good as
Any You will make, let me have That if you Can, but I
will have no Other, nor Other do my Friends Desire.* If
any Author could put his Head out of his Grave, and
say Thus to an Editor, *Milton* might, and he may say it
as justly as the most Beautiful Woman Alive, were She
Sitting for her Picture to the Best Painter in the World.
But when Conceited Daubers, though they have seen
All that *Italy* is Adorn'd with, when Such as have

neither *Pittoresque* Eyes, nor Hands, Pretending to Excel Beauty, show us a Monster instead of an Angel, who can have Patience ? if a Like Attempt is made upon an Admir'd Poetical Work, Who can forbear saying, *Pray you Sir, no more of your Patches in a Poem quite Elevated above your Reach and Imitation ?* Such Kind of People as These were in Ancient times as Now, and are well Describ'd by Him who says, *As a Madman who casteth Firebrands, Arrows, and Death, So is the Man that Deceiveth his Neighbour, and saith, Am I not in Sport ?*

in a word, as *Milton's* Care in This Matter is not to be doubted, nor his Ability and Opportunity to Prevent the Corruption Pretended, or to Detect any Such, had it been Attempted (for Fact, as well as Probability is on Our Side) Whatsoever Suggestion or Assertion, in Jest or in Earnest, concerning Some Unknown, Pragmatical, or Rascally Editor has been flung out, 'tis spilt on the Ground, and Stinks in the Nostrils of all who have a right Sense of the Veneration Due to the Ashes of an Excellent Writer and a Good Man, and to Good Nature, Good Manners, Truth and Justice. but they shall not hurt the Book, That, and its Author are safe. So—*Go thy Ways, the Flour and Quintessence of all Editors.* the Edition of 1674 is the Finish'd, the Genuine, the Uncorrupted Work of *John Milton.*

the Subsequent Editions are not very Faulty, Some of them Especially, but This ought to be the Model of Some Future Edition, and follow'd Letter for Letter and Point for Point, with very few Exceptions, and Those should Methinks be taken no Notice of in the Text but the Margin, or by way of Errata. I mention a Future Edition, and hope to See Such a One as I have mention'd, That of 74 being Exceeding Rare.

I proceed to Other Particularities of *Paradise Lost*. There is Musick in all Language; the Meanest Peasant Varies the Sound as he Speaks, though in That he is Easily known from a Gentleman. Sound is abundantly more Expressive of the Sense than is Commonly Imagin'd; Animals who have not the Use of Words, that We understand at least, Express their Minds by Sounds as well as by Gestures, Looks and Actions; and we know Their Meaning as we know That of a Man whose Language we are Absolute Strangers to. Verse and Prose have Each their Peculiar Musick, and whether One, or the Other 'tis Different according to the Subject. All kinds of Verses have Sounds of their Own; Blank Verse comes nearest to Prose, and as the Prose of Some Writers Approaches Verse, *Milton's* Blank Verse, That of *Paradise Lost*, has the Beauty of Both; it has the Sweetness of Measure, without stopping the Voice at the end of the Line, or Any where else but as the Sense requires; One Verse runs into Another, and the Period concludes in any part of a Line Indifferently, and as if 'twas his Choice 'tis very often Not at the End of One or of a Couplet, as is too Frequent with Those who write in Rime. He has frequently Eleven Syllables in a Verse, but 'tis rarely So unless Those are no more in Quantity than the Ten of Another.

> *Fall'n Cherube, to be Weak is Miserable*
> *Doing or Suffering: but of This be Sure,*

the *e* in the Middle of the Word *Suff'ring* must be Melted in the Pronunciation, as if written Without it as here; and the two Syllables made by that Vowel, and the *a* that follows in *Miserable* are so Short as to be Equal to but One in any part of the Line.　So

Assur'd me and still Assure.　though what thou tell'st

here *Me* and *and* are both so Short as to be no more in Quantity than if they were but One Syllable.　to read right requires Some Judgment, and some Experience in *Milton's* Manner who Abounds More with These Instances than most English Poets; but, well Read, the Musick of His Verse is Exceeding Delicate and Noble, though Somwhat Peculiar to Himself; for He, (as in his Language) has Profited Himself of the Greeks and Latins; His *Ictus*, or *Cadence*, or Musick bears towards Them, as he has form'd himself Upon Their Examples into Somthing of his Own, by his Own Ear, and which was a very Musical, Experienc'd and Judicious One. See further concerning his Versification in his Short Discourse before the Poem.

It will seem Strange to Those who do Me the Honour to Entertain themselves with what I Offer them, when they find Me remarking on the Greek and Latin Writers, whose Language I have Acknowledg'd my Self not to Understand.　My Time of Learning was Employ'd in Business.　but after All, I Have the Greek and Latin Tongues, I have them because a Part of Me Possesses them to Whom I can recur at Pleasure, just as I have a Hand when I would Write or Paint, Feet to Walk, and Eyes to See.　My Son is my Learning, as I am That to Him which He has Not; We make One Man; and Such a Compound Man (what Sort of One Soever He is whom We make) May Probably, produce what no Single Man Can.　When therefore I, in my

Own Person talk of Things which in my Separate Capacity I am known to be a Stranger to, let Me be Understood as the Complicated *Richardson*. 'Twas Necessary to Say This as having Engag'd in a Work I am, Singly, as Unqualify'd for as the Ear is to Write; but when I want to do That I make use of my Hand; so if I would see the Satellites of *Jupiter*, or those of *Saturn*, or the Belts of One, or the Ring of the Other, I know well enough my Naked Eye is as no Eye at all on This Occasion; I then apply to my Telescope: In what depends on the Knowledge of the Learned Languages my Son is my Telescope. 'tis by the help of This I have seen That in *Milton* which to Me Otherwise had been Invisible; though before I had my Instrument I saw a Sky of shining Stars, How much more Throng'd and Bright soever That Sky Now appears.

Milton's Language is English, but 'tis *Milton's* English; 'tis Latin, 'tis Greek English; not only the Words, the Phraseology, the Transpositions, but the Ancient Idiom is seen in All he Writes, So that a Learned Foreigner will think *Milton* the Easiest to be Understood of All the English Writers. This Peculiar English is most Conspicuously seen in *Paradise Lost*, for This is the Work which he Long before Intended should Enrich and Adorn his Native Tongue———*not caring to be once Nam'd Abroad though Perhaps I could Attaine to That, but Content with these British Ilands as My World, whose Fortune hath Hitherto bin, that if the* Athenians, *as Some say, made their Small Deeds Great and Renown'd by their Eloquent Writers,* England *hath had her Noble Atchievements made Small by the Unskillfull Handling of Monks and Mechanicks.* See

More to the Present Purpose in the Preface (Cited more than Once already) to his second Book *of Church-Government.*

to this *Miltonick* English may be apply'd what Himself Says of the New-Testament-Greek——*He therefore who thinks to* Scholiaze *upon the Gospel, though Greek, according to his Greek* Analogies, *and hath not been Auditor to the Oriental Dialects, shall want in the heat of his Analysis no Accommodation to Stumble.* Tetrachord. *Tol.* Ed. 365.

Poetry pretends to a Language of its Own. That of the Italian Poetry is so remarkably peculiar that a Man may Well understand a Prose Writer, and not a Poet. Words, Tours of Expression, the Order of them, All has Somthing not Prosaic. This is Observable particularly in *Shakespear.* *Milton* has Apply'd it to that Sublimity of Subject in which he perpetually Engages his Readers, above what *Shakespear* ever Aim'd at and where This is Peculiarly Necessary.

Nor does he want Abundant Instances of what All Good Poets Have. the Sound of the Words, their Harshness, Smoothness, or Other Properties, and the Ranging, and Mixing them, all help to Express as well as their Signification. We have Noted This Occasionally, in Particular on VII. 303.

As his Mind was Rich in Ideas, and in Words of Various Languages to Cloathe them with, and as he had a Vast Fire, Vigour and Zeal of Imagination, his Style must Necessarily Distinguish it Self; it Did So; and even in his Younger days, his Juvenile Poems, English, Latin, and Italian, have a Brilliant not Easily found Elsewhere; Nor is it not seen in his Controversial Prose Works; *Paradise Lost* wants it not, in which

there are Specimens of All his Kinds of Styles, the
Tender, the Fierce, the Narrative, the Reasoning, the
Lofty, *&c.* So Early as when he Wrote for Divorce,
though he Conceal'd his Name his Hand was known
——*My Name I did not Publish* (says He) *as not willing
it should Sway the Reader either For me or Against me, but
when I was told that the Style, which what it Ails to be so
soon distinguishable, I cannot tell, was known by most Men*
——There is Somthing in Every Man's whereby he is
Known, as by his Voice, Face, Gait *&c.* in *Milton* there
is a certain Vigour, whether *Versing or Prosing*, which
will Awaken Attention be She never so Drowsy, and
then Persuade her to be Thankful though She was
Disturb'd.

a Reader of *Milton* must be Always upon Duty; he is
Surrounded with Sense, it rises in every Line, every
Word is to the Purpose; There are no Lazy Intervals,
All has been Consider'd, and Demands, and Merits
Observation. Even in the Best Writers you Somtimes
find Words and Sentences which hang on so Loosely
you may Blow 'em off; *Milton's* are all Substance and
Weight; Fewer would not have Serv'd the Turn, and
More would have been Superflous.

His Silence has the Same Effect, not only that he
leaves Work for the Imagination when he has Entertain'd it, and Furnish'd it with Noble Materials; but
he Expresses himself So Concisely, Employs Words
So Sparingly, that whoever will Possess His Ideas
must Dig for them, and Oftentimes pretty far below the
Surface. if This is call'd Obscurity let it be remembred
'tis Such a One as is Complaisant to the Reader, not
Mistrusting his Ability, Care, Diligence, or the Candid-
ness of his Temper; not That Vicious Obscurity which

proceeds from a Muddled Inaccurate Head, not Accustomed to Clear, Well Separated and Regularly Order'd Ideas, or from want of Words and Method and Skill to Convey them to Another, from whence Always Arises Uncertainty, Ambiguity, and a Sort of a Moon-Light Prospect over a Landscape at Best not Beautiful; whereas if a Good Writer is not Understood 'tis because his Reader is Unacquainted with, or Incapable of the Subject, or will not Submit to do the Duty of a Reader, which is to Attend Carefully to what he Reads.

What *Macrobius* says of *Virgil* is Applicable to Milton. " He keeps his Eye Fix'd and Intent upon *Homer*, " and emulates Alike his Greatness and Simplicity; his " Readiness of Speech and Silent Majesty." by *Silent Majesty*, he seems to Mean with *Longinus :* " His " Leaving more to the Imagination than is Express'd."

and Now 'tis of no great Importance whether this be call'd an Heroic or a Divine Poem, or only, as the Author himself has call'd it in his Title-page, a Poem. What if it were a Composition Intirely New, and not reducible under any Known Denomination ? but 'tis Properly and Strictly Heroic, and Such *Milton* intended it, as he has Intimated in his Short Discourse concerning the Kind of Verse, and which is prefix'd to it; as also in his Entrance on the Ninth Book; and 'tis not His Fault if there have been Those, who have not found a Hero, or Who he is. 'tis *Adam*, *Adam*, the First, the Representative of Human Race; He is the Hero in This Poem, though as in Other Heroic Poems, Superiour Beings are Introduc'd. the Business of it is to conduct Man through Variety of Conditions of Happiness and Distress, All Terminating in the Utmost Good. from a State of Precarious Innocence, through Temptation, Sin, Repentance, and finally a Secure Recumbency Upon, and Interest In the Supream Good by the Mediation of his Son. He is not Such a Hero as *Achilles, Ulysses, Æneas, Orlando, Godfrey,* &c. all Romantic Worthies, and Incredible Performers of Fortunate, Savage Cruelties; He is one of a nobler Kind, Such as *Milton* Chose to Write of, and found he had a Genius for the Purpose. he is not Such a Conqueror as Subdu'd Armies or Nations, or Enemies in Single Combat, but his Conquest was What Justly *gave Heroic Name to Person, and to Poem* ; His Hero was *More than a Conqueror through Him that Loved us.* as Rom. viii. 37.

This was declar'd to be the Subject of the Poem at the Entrance on it, Man's First Disobedience and Misery 'till our Restoration to a More Happy State. the Design of it is also Declar'd; 'twas to Justify Providence, All which is Done. the Moral we are also Directed to, and This the Poet has put into the Mouth of an Angel. Many Moral Reflections are excited throughout the Whole Work, but the Great One is Mark'd Strongly XII. 745. &c. PIETY AND VERTUE, ALL COMPRIZ'D IN ONE WORD CHARITY, IS THE ONLY WAY TO HAPPINESS.

if the Sublimity and Peculiarity of the Matter of this Poem, if its Superiority in That Respect has rais'd it above Some of the Rules given by *Aristotle,* or Whatever Other Criticks, and Gather'd From, or Founded on the *Iliad, Odyssey,* or *Æneid,* it has Distinguish'd it to its greater Glory; 'tis not only an Heroic Poem, but the Most So that Ever was Wrote. *Milton* did not despise Rules, Such as were Built upon Reason, So far as those Establish'd Reach'd; but as his Free and Exalted Genius Aspir'd Beyond what had Yet been Attempted in the Choice of his Subject, Himself was his Own Rule when in Heights where None had gone before, and Higher than Which None Can Ever go.

Milton's true Character as a Writer is that he is an Ancient, but born two Thousand Years after his Time. his Language indeed is Modern, but the Best, next to Greek, and Latin, to Convey those Images Himself Conceiv'd; and That moreover Greek'd and Latiniz'd and made as Uncommon and Expressive as our Tongue could be, and yet Intelligible to us for whom he Wrote. But All his Images are Pure Antique. So that We read *Homer* and *Virgil* in reading Him. We hear Them in our Own Tongue, as we See What They Conceiv'd when *Milton* Speaks; Yes, and We find Our Selves amongst Persons and Things of a more Exalted Character. *Connoisseurs* in Painting and Sculpture can Best tell what is the Difference of Taste in Ancient and Modern Work, and can therefore Best Understand what I am Now Saying; it must Suffice that I tell Others that there is a Certain Grace, Majesty and Simplicity in the Antique which is its Distinguishing Character. the Same Kind of Taste is Seen in Writing; and *Milton* has it, I think, to a Degree beyond what We have ever found in Any Modern Painter or Sculptor, not Excepting *Rafaelle* Himself.

Those who are unaccustom'd to this Train of Thinking, may only please to Dip into *Chaucer*, *Spencer*, *Ariosto*, even *Tasso* or any of the Moderns, and observe what *Gothick* Figures and Things present Themselves to their Imagination, or what are Comparatively Mean. let them read even the Ancients, the Best of Them (always excepting the Most Ancient of all, the *Pentateuch*, *Job*, and Some Other of the Sacred Books) and they will find even These Fill not, nor Inrich the Mind as *Milton* does; His *Eden*, His Chaos, Hell, Heaven; His Human Figures, His Angels, Good and Evil, His Mediator, His God, all is Superiour to what is Elsewhere to be found, All are with regard to the rest like what *Rafaelle's* Pictures Exhibit, Compar'd with what we See in Those of any Other Master; Or, (to Speak more Familiarly to Common Observation) they are as *Westminster* Abbey, or even St. *Paul's*, Compar'd with the *Pantheon*, the *Coliseum*, the Temple of *Theseus*, or Other Remains of Architecture of the Purest Antiquity; even the Prints of them, Those I mean done by the Best Hands, and which are not very Rare, will Explain, and Prove what I Advance.

in the *Parnassus*, (One of the Famous Pictures of *Rafaelle* in the *Vatican*) *Dante* is represented as having his Eye upon *Homer;* had *Milton* been put there, *Homer* and He ought to have been Embracing Each other. he Knew him Perfectly; it should not be said he Copy'd, he Imitated him, but that they both Wrote by the Self-same Poetical Genius. what is Purely *Milton's* Own is Equal at least to the Best of that Prince of Poets, and when he Profits himself of What He has done, 'tis with Equal Beauty and Propriety. a Simile, for Instance, in *Paradise Lost*, Shines no less than in the *Iliad* or the *Odyssey*, and Some of *Milton's* have the Same Peculiarity as we find in Some of *Homer*, they Strike firmly on the Point they are directed to, and the Main Business being done, the Poet gives the rein a little to Fancy, Entertaining his Reader with what is not Otherwise to the Purpose. This by the way. *Virgil* has also Borrow'd from *Homer*, and Much more than *Milton*. but even *Virgil* has not Always done it with

Equal Success. it has been said 'twas as Easy to take
the Club out of the Hand of *Hercules*, as a Simile from
Homer. *Virgil* has made use of That in Od. VI. 102,
where *Nausicaa* Daughter of King *Alcinous* is said to be
Distinguish'd amongst her Maids as *Diana*, Taller than
her Nymphs about her; This Simile *Æn*. I. 502 is
apply'd to *Dido*, surrounded by, not Maids or Women,
but Men whom the Reader will imagine to be Soldiers,
Guards. Who sees not the Simile Now has not only
Lost its Beauty, but, as a Flower cropt from its Native
Stalk, 'tis Faded, 'tis Offensive. You will find No
Such Instances in *Milton*. And not only Similes, whatever Other Passages He Transplants they rear their
Flourish'd heads, are as Gay and as Fragrant as whence
they were taken. and what Glory the Invention has not
in Such Occasions is fully recompenc'd to the Genius
and Judgment; What is Inserted Fits as well as in the
Original Work; or if That is not Equal to *Milton's*
Own, He makes it So by Raising its Native Character.
to call Large Fields, or a far Extended Plain, an Ocean,
is Beautifully Poetical, Some of the Ancients have done
so; the same Bold Allusion Offends the Imagination
when it strikes upon it Unprepar'd; as in *Spencer*,
B. II Can. II St. 22, where a Bear and Tyger are
introduc'd as Fighting on the *Lybick* Ocean. *Milton's*
Boldest Borrow'd Figures, as his Own, when they
Awaken the Mind do it not with a Sudden Crash, but
as with Musick; if they Surprize, they don't Startle
Us. You will not find a Single Instance of Such
Improprieties in Him.

　　the Earliest Antiquity had the Best Writers; whether
from the Natural Vigour, Greatness and Simplicity of
Mind in that Youth of the World, or that Those Writers

having had their Choice, took the finest Thoughts, which Their Followers must either Borrow, or Copy, or if they affected to be Originals, must be Content with Worse, or give Those a Sort of Novelty by departing from the Original Simplicity. *Milton* has Profited Himself of what All, whether Ancients of One or the Other Class, have done, and of All that is to be found of Excellent among the Moderns, Little however in Comparison of the Other, but all He touches becomes as if 'twas the Pure Gold of the Best Antiquity.

My Son has a very Copious Collection of These, and as they Often Assisted Us in Our Understanding Our Author's true Meaning, they would (if inserted) have been Our Vouchers in Those Cases. to have added All These Fine Passages would have been Improper in our Present Undertaking, though perhaps they may be seen Together Hereafter.

But whatever *Milton* has Woven into his Poem of Others, still his Sublimest Passages are More So than could enter the Heart of *Orpheus, Hesiod, Homer, Pindar, Callimachus,* &c. Such as the Heathen World were Incapable of by Infinite Degrees, Such as None but the Noblest Genius could attain to, and That Assisted by a Religion Reveal'd by God Himself. We have then in *Paradise Lost* a Collection, the Quintessence of All that is Excellent in Writing; Frequently Improv'd and Explain'd Better than by the Best of their Profess'd Commentators, but Never Debas'd; and a Sublimity which all other Human Writings put Together have not. to Compleat All, He has made Use of All These, so as to be subservient to the Great End of Poetry, which is to Please and Inrich the Imagination, and to Mend the Heart, and make the Man Happy.

x

that This was His Idea of the Use of Poetry, and his
Intention in This his Principal Work; This, for the
Production of Which All his Study, Learning, Capacity, and Genius; his Whole Life was Mainly given to,
will appear by what he Says, though Much more, by
what he has Done.

in his Preface to the second Book concerning *Church-
Government,* So often mention'd, he Writes Thus——
*These Abilities, wheresoever they be found, are the Inspired
gift of God rarely bestow'd, but yet to Some (though Most
Abuse) in every Nation : and are of power, beside the
Office of a Pulpit, to Inbreed and Cherish in a Great People
the seeds of Vertu, and Publick Civility, to Allay the Per-
turbations of the Mind, and set the Affections in Right Tune ;
to celebrate in Glorious and Lofty Hymns the Throne and
Equipage of God's Almightiness, and what he Works, and
what he suffers to be Wrought with high Providence in his
Church; to sing the Victorious Agonies of Martyrs and
Saints, the Deeds and Triumphs of Just and Pious Nations,
doing Valiantly through Faith against the Enemies of
Christ ; to Deplore the General Relapses of Kingdoms and
States from Justice and Gods true Worship. Lastly,
whatsoever in Religion is Holy and Sublime, in Vertu
Amiable or Grave, whatsoever hath Passion or Admiration
in all the Changes of That which is call'd Fortune from
Without, or the Wily Suttleties and Refluxes of Mans
thoughts from Within ; all These things with a Solid and
Treatable Smoothness to Paint out and Describe. Teaching
over the whole Book of Sanctity and Vertu, through all the
instances of Example, with Such Delight to those, especially
of Soft and Delicious Temper, who will not so much as look
upon Truth her Self, unless they See her Elegantly Drest ;
that whereas the Paths of Honesty and Good Life appear*

now Rugged and Difficult, though they be Indeed Easy and
Pleasant, they would Then appear to all Men both Easy
and Pleasant, though they were Rugged and Difficult in-
deed. And what a Benefit this would be to our Youth and
Gentry, may be soon guest by what we know of the Corrup-
tion and Bane which they Suck in daily from the Writings
and Interludes of Libidinous and Ignorant Poetasters, who
having Scars ever heard of that which is the main Con-
sistence of a true Poem, the choys of such Persons as they
ought to introduce, and what is Moral and Decent to each
one, do for the most part Lap up Vitious Principles in Sweet
Pils to be Swallow'd down, and make the tast of vertuous
Documents Harsh and Sowr.

Another, a Shorter Account he gives of the Great
Business of Poetry in his Discourse *of Education* Written
Some Years Afterwards. He having directed What
were the Sciences which Youth should First Apply
themselves to, goes on Thus——*to which Poetry would*
be made Subsequent, or rather Precedent, as being Less
Suttle, and Fine, but more Simple, Sensuous, and Passion-
ate. I mean not here the Prosody of a Verse, which they
could not but have hit on before among the Rudiments of
Grammer; but that Sublime Art which in Aristotle's
Poetics, in Horace, *and the Italian Commentaries of*
Castelvetro, Tasso, Mazzoni, *and Others, teaches what*
the Laws are of a true Epic *Poem, what of a* Drammatic,
what of a Lyric, *what Decorum is, Which is the Grand*
Master-Piece to observe. This would make them Soon
Perceive what Despicable Creatures our Common Rimers,
and Play-Writers be, and show them What Religious,
what Glorious, and Magnificent Use might be made of
Poetry both in Divine and Human things.

Were I call'd upon to Define Poetry in General,

which *Milton* has not done in the Passages I have Cited, nor any where Else that I know of, I would do it by saying 'tis ORNAMENT. This Implies Fiction, for Dress, Lace, Gold, Jewels, &c. is not the Body. Poetry therefore is not Truth, but Somthing More Agreeable, at least than Meer Truth.

and its Business is, Consequently, to Awaken, to Please, to Allure; 'tis Address'd to the Imagination, to the Passions, and This Supposes Energy as well as Beauty.

Verse and Prose are Opposites, but Verse may be Destitute of Poetry, as Prose may be Poetick, by having all the Beauties of Poetry Except the Numbers. Verse, With, or Without Rime, is but One of the Advantages Poetry makes Use of, 'tis not Alone Worthy of That Name. 'tis Prosaick Verse.

Argument, History, even Oratory it Self is not Allow'd the Gaudiness and Splendour which Poetry demands; but should an Orator Deck Himself with the Utmost of These, without the Musick of *Numerous Verse* he would not be a Poet; for tho' Verse Alone is not Poetry, 'tis, strictly speaking, Essential to it.

as We are Most Easily Led, or Intic'd by Pleasure, Poetry has Proportionable Influence on the Mind, Whether to carry it to Good or Evil; Whether 'tis made Subservient to One, or the Other, 'tis no Less, or More Poetry Still. if you Ask What is the Most Excellent, the most Amiable Poetry, the Answer is Easy; 'tis That Whose Elevation of Language, Arrangement of Words, its Sentiments and Images are Directed, and made Subservient to, not Only the Delight, but the Improvement of Mankind. and This after All Terminates in Pleasure, as True Wisdom and

Goodness has the Greatest Tendency to our Happiness. in This Use of Poetry, and not its Power over Us, consists its Real, its most Important Dignity.

Poetry Pleases by a Peculiarity and Majesty of Stile and Language; its Numbers, its Rime (if us'd, and Skilfully) Pleases as Musick does, and as Painting, the Imagery of things, not only Real, but Fictitious: for Poetry is a Sort of New Creation, not only as it Produces to the Imagination What is Unknown to Nature, Such as Harpyes, Sphynxes, Gorgons, Hydraes, Centaurs, &c or a Sort of Men as *Shakespear's Caliban*, or the People of Romances, Men Better or Worse than ever were; but as it Raises and Embellishes (where 'tis possible) what is Seen in Nature, or Related in History, and by so doing shows Things Otherwise than they Really Are, or ever Were; and This not only agreeably Entertains the Mind, 'tis a Sort of New Acquisition; but it Helps Us oft-times to See Real Beauties, and which would Else have pass'd Unregarded, and perhaps makes us Fancy we See What in Truth we do not.

there is Another Pleasure in Poetry, Oftener Felt perhaps than plac'd to its Account; 'tis This. Much of Art is Essential to This kind of Writing, and to Observe the Address and Capacity of the Poet is vastly Pleasing. 'tis So for Example when we meet with a True Poetical Word, Phrase or Expression, an Apt Simile, a Beautiful Allusion, a Noble Sentiment, a Sublime Image, &c.

Besides the Pleasure we have in These Particulars, 'tis Some Addition to it when we Reflect, (as Self-Love will teach us) on our Own Ability to Discover, and lift up our Selves to the Perception of the Brilliant of these Beauties; and Thus, as it were, become Sharers in the

Honour of them.   There is yet a further Pleasure in
Thinking This is the Work of Our Friend, Our
Country-Man, at least of One of Our Species. 'tis true
This Kind of Pleasure is to be had from Prose, but not
the Degree.

Thought is the Life of the Mind, 'tis the *Intellectual
Being* (II. 147) and has the Universe, and Beyond what
is Real, even the Immense Regions of Fancy to range
and *Wander* in, and as it cannot be Limited by Time,
it Expatiates Eternity.   the Soul's Natural Vigour produces a Constant Succession of Ideas; but These are
Improveable by Art, by Frequent Reflection, Observation of what is offer'd to our Senses, or by Conversation;
Reading is Conversing only in Somwhat a Different
Manner from Discourse *Viva Voce*.   When we take a
Book in hand 'tis to Supply our Selves with Thoughts
which we could not Suggest from Within, or did not
Expect would Arise Spontaneously; We Read for
Amusement, Delight, Information, Instruction, Edifi-
cation, to Awaken or to put our Passions into a more
Vigorous Motion; in Short, to Rouze up the Intellec-
tual Fire which Then gives Us a Kindly Warmth, a
Wholesom Glow, a Lucid and Noble Flame;   or it
Pollutes the Mind with Black Exhalations, and Scorches,
or Torments Us.   Always the Mind is Fed, with its
Proper Nourishment, Ideas.   thus the Scripture, the
Best of Books, is said to be *Profitable for Doctrine, for
Reproof, for Correction, for Instruction in Righteousness.*
but None are Destitute of Some Juice, Somthing to
Feed the Mind; though Those where 'tis Richest and
in Greatest Abundance are to be Chosen.

'tis of no Small Consequence towards the Happiness
of Life to have a Lively, Inventive, a Great and Beautiful

Imagination, 'twill Always furnish Us with Delight, Fill up all the Chasms in Time, and Intervals of Business, and Sweeten even Those, which Most People seem to consider but as the Offals, if not the Incumbrance of Life; but the Happiest in This particular may be made Happier by Assistance from Abroad, by Conversation and Reading.

Paradise Lost is Such a Fountain in This Case as the Sun, VII. 364. Whence even These may in their *Golden Urns* draw Light. Here the *Morning Planet* may *Gild its Horns* ; Those too who are not So Expert at this Poetical Imagery may Richly *Augment their Small Peculiar* Here. All may Gather Somthing that will Adorn and Delight their Minds.

if Ever any Book was Truly Poetical, if Ever Any Abounded with Poetry, 'tis *Paradise Lost*. What an Expansion of Facts from a Small Seed of History! What Worlds are Invented, What Embellishments of Nature upon what our Senses Present Us with ? Divine things are More Nobly, more Divinely Represented to the Imagination than by Any Other Poem, a More Beautiful Idea is given of Nature than any Poet has Pretended to; Nature as just come out of the Hand of God, in its Virgin Loveliness, Glory, and Purity; and the Human Race is Shown, not as *Homer's*, More Gigantick, more Robust, more Valiant, but without Comparison more Truly Amiable, more So than by the Pictures and Statues of the Greatest Masters. and all These Sublime Ideas are Convey'd to Us in the most Effectual and Engaging Manner. the Mind of the Reader is Tempered, and Prepar'd, by Pleasure, 'tis Drawn, and Allured, 'tis Awaken'd and Invigorated to receive Such Impressions as the Poet intended to give it: it

Opens the Fountains of Knowledge, Piety and Virtue, and pours Along Full Streams of Peace, Comfort and Joy to Such as can Penetrate the true Sense of the Writer, and Obediently Listen to his Song.

in reading the *Iliad* or *Æneis* we Treasure up a Collection of Fine Imaginative Pictures as when we read *Paradise Lost;* Only that from Thence we have (to speak like a *Connoisseur*) More *Rafaelles, Correggios, Guidos,* &c.   *Milton's* Pictures are more Sublimely Great, Divine and Lovely than *Homer's,* or *Virgil's* or those of Any Other Poet, or of All the Poets, Ancient, or Modern.

to have the Mind Thus Stor'd, besides the Advantage of it intended by the Poet, is of no Small Importance to Us.   the Works of the Best Masters in Painting or Sculpture Deserve the Great Price they bear, upon Account of the Fine Ideas they give us whenever we please to have recourse to them, or as we happen to Remember them; a Well-Chosen Collection of Poetical Pictures, to Such as know How to Form them, Answers Much the same Purposes, but More may Possess Such, and at a Much Easier Price.

Paradise Lost not only Aims at a More Noble and More Extensive Moral, not only leads the Mind towards it by the Way of Pleasantness, All the Flowers in that Way are not only Fragrant, but Wholesom and Balsamick; All is Interesting, All not only Delight the Mind, but Contribute to make it Better,

"*What's* Hecuba *to Him, or He to* Hecuba ?

what does the War of *Troy,* or the Original of the *Roman* Name, say it was That of *Britain,* Concern You and Me ? the Original of Things, the First Happy, but

Precarious Condition of Mankind, his Deviation from Rectitude, his Lost State, his Restoration to the Favour of God by Repentance, and Imputed Righteousness; and That upon a Foundation which Cannot be Shaken. the Great Doctrines of the Christian Religion, Regeneration, Adoption and Glorification, Happiness Here, and For Ever; These Concern Us All Equally, and Equally with our First Parents, whose Story, and That of the Whole Church of God, this Poem sets before us; that is, These things are of the Utmost Importance, Such Importance as that what all the World calls Great are Comparatively Trifles, and Known to be So upon the least Serious Reflection. Without a Solid Establishment of Mind in These Sublime Truths, All Comprehended in a Just Idea of God, (So far as we are Enabled to Conceive of Him, and He has Sufficiently Reveal'd Himself to Us for That Purpose, More we Need not) whatever Happiness Any One may Seem to Enjoy, 'tis a Cheat, Precarious, and Will Fail, when the Mind is it Self, when Awaken'd by its Own Vigour, or by Some Adventitious Circumstance: Whereas Whoever Profits, as he May, by This Poem will, as *Adam* in the Garden, Enjoy the Pleasures of Sense to the Utmost, with Temperance, and Purity of Heart, the Truest and Fullest Enjoyment of them; and will Moreover perceive his Happiness is Establish'd upon a Better Foundation than That of his Own Impeccability, and Thus possess a Paradise Within Far more Happy than that of *Eden*.

O *Milton* thou hast employ'd all thy Vast Treasure of Wit, Learning, and Ability, all the Beauty, Energy, and Propriety of Words Our Language was Capable of, all the Sweetness and Harmony of Numbers thy

Musical and Judicious Ear furnish'd thee with, All the Fire and Beauty and Sublimity of Imagination Peculiar to thy Self, Added to what could be Supply'd by Those who have most Excell'd in That Angelical Faculty, in whatever Ages or Languages, All the Firmness, Force and Dignity of Mind thy Vertue and Piety Excited in thee, or Rewarded thee with; and together with All These a Genius Perfectly Poetical, if Ever Any Man's was, and That Regulated by a most Solid Judgment. All These thou hast Consecrated to Produce a Poem, more Instrumental than any Other Human Composition, to Calm and Purify the Mind, and through the Delightful Regions of Poetry, to Exalt and Fix it to the Mysteries, Sublimities and Practice of Religion; to a State of Tranquility and Happiness, the Utmost Mortality is Capable of.

NOTES

In the Notes the following abbreviations have been used :

Birch. An Account of the Life and Writings of Mr John Milton, prefixed to A Complete Collection of the Historical Political and Miscellaneous Works by Thomas Birch . . . 1753.

Newton. The Life of Milton, prefixed to *Paradise Lost*, The Seventh Edition . . . by Thomas Newton, D.D. 1770.

Todd. The Poetical Works of John Milton . . . with some account of the Life and Writings of Milton, by the Rev. H. J. Todd . . . 1826.

Masson. The Life of John Milton, narrated in connexion with the . . . History of His Time by David Masson, 1859-1880 : vol. i, second edition, 1881.

Trin. MS. Manuscript of Milton's Minor Poems, &c., in the Library of Trinity College, Cambridge.

Smart. The Sonnets of Milton, with Introduction & Notes by John S. Smart . . . 1921.

Paradise Lost, ed. H. Darbishire. The Manuscript of Milton's Paradise Lost, Book I, edited by Helen Darbishire, 1931.

Tercentenary. Milton Tercentenary. The Portraits, Prints and Writings of John Milton, exhibited at Christ's College, Cambridge 1908.

R.E.S. The Review of English Studies.

AUBREY

P. 1. Aubrey's minutes for the Life of Milton are in Part III of his Collections (with title-page inscribed thus : *Auctarium Vitarum à J. A. collectarum A° Dom.* 1681), Bodl. MS. Aubrey 8, folios now numbered 63 to 68, consisting of three sheets folded inside each other. The first sheet, which I call Sheet A, is the outside sheet, within which are folded two other sheets, Sheets B and C. Sheet A is of folio size, folded once, and is closely written over, so that all four sides are full, and the margins and interlinear spaces crowded with afterthoughts. Aubrey began to write on the first leaf, Af1, went on to Af2, then I think returned to Af1 verso, and finally filled up Af2 verso. On the four pages of this sheet he made his sketch for the whole life of Milton

down to his last illness and death, attempted an outline of his pedigree
and a list of his writings, and made notes from information given by
Christopher and Mrs Milton, amongst which appears a direction to
seek out Mr Edward Phillips.   He then took up another folio sheet of
different paper, Sheet B, slightly larger than Sheet A, folded once like
Sheet A.   Of this he only wrote on the two pages of the first leaf.   This
sheet is now folded within Sheet A, and was certainly used after he made
Edward Phillips's acquaintance, since it contains not only matter he
obtained directly from Phillips but also a list of Milton's writings and
a paragraph about his school teaching, both in the handwriting of
Edward Phillips himself.   Finally he used a half folio sheet, folded
across so that it forms a quarto-sized page.   This, Sheet C, is now
folded within Sheet B.   On this Mrs Milton has copied out the date
and hour of Milton's birth, and Aubrey has added some more information from Edward Phillips.   These three sheets folded within each
other have never before been printed in their right order.   As they are
bound up, A1 comes first, followed by B1, and then successively C1,
C2, B2, and finally A2, and they have hitherto been copied in that order,
whereas Aubrey used first the whole of Sheet A, then B, then C.

P. 1, l. 1.   *His mother was a Bradshaw*]   The crest on the left side
is Milton's (*cf.* note to l. 17 *infra*) : that on the right is the Bradshaws'.
His mother was Sarah Jeffrey : Aubrey puts . . . Jeffrey by mistake
as the grandmother in his family tree, *vide supra*, p. 8, and notes to
E. Phillips, p. 340 *infra*.

P. 1, l. 6.   *his Grandfather* . . .]   For the name of his grandfather
Aubrey must have applied to Christopher Milton, whose answer
" John, he believes," he records on the pedigree, Af2 verso.   His
name was in fact Richard, and he lived at one time at Stanton St. John,
as John Phillips says.   *vide supra*, p. 18.   The facts were established
by Mr Hyde Clarke from the books of the Scriveners Company, where
an entry describes John Milton, the poet's father, as " John Milton,
son of Richard Milton of Stanston (*sic*) Co. Oxon."   *vide Notes and
Queries*, vii. March 19, 1859.

P. 1, l. 7.   *Holton*]   This is written in to fill the gap which Aubrey
left for the name of Milton's family place.   He probably wrote it
first on Af2 verso (*q.v.*) in answer to the Quaere, *ubi vivit if not at
Shotover ?*

Wood prints Halton, and Malone in his transcript writes Halton,
which is the old name.   There is a brass in the South Transept of
Holton Church with the inscription :

> Hoc monumentum D. Johanni Brome de Halton
> in Comita : Oxon : . . . 1589.

P. 1, l. 17. *ye Spread Eagle*] *cf.* Wood's note, p. 35 *supra.* " The arms that Joh. Milton did use and seal his letters with were, Argent a spread eagle with two heads gules, legg'd & beak'd sable."

P. 2, l. 1. *He was borne . . .*] Aubrey learnt the missing facts by application to Mrs Milton. *vide infra,* note to p. 12, ll. 18-19.

P. 2, l. 5. *at fifteen . . .*] Milton was sixteen when he was admitted at Christ's College, on Feb. 12, 1624-5.

P. 2, l. 14. *ten yeares old, as by his picture . . .*] This portrait was one of those in the possession of Milton's widow when she died in 1727, (*vide infra,* note to p. 3, l. 10), and is mentioned in the inventory of her effects at Nantwich (*vide* Historic Society of Lancashire and Cheshire, vol. vii., article by J. F. Marsh). It is reputed to have been painted by Cornelius Jannsen, a painter of Flemish origin, working in London 1618-1643. Mr Charles Stanhope bought it from Mrs Milton's executors, and at his sale in 1760 it was bought by Mr Thomas Hollis. In 1761, a fire broke out at his lodgings in Bedford Street: " He walked out of the house taking in his hand the picture of the boy Milton." (*Memoir of Thomas Hollis, Esq.*) From him it passed to Mr Thomas Brand Hollis, then to Dr Disney, and Mr. Edward Disney. It was sold by Mr Disney to Mr J. Passmore Edwards who lent it to the Tercentenary Exhibition at Cambridge in 1908. Subsequently it was bought by Mr Pierpont Morgan, in whose library in New York it may now be seen. An inscription on the canvas reads: " Aetatis suae: 10. An. 1618. John Milton." *vide* Warton, Milton's *Poems,* 1785, p. 545; *On the engraved . . . Portraits of Milton.* by J. Fitchett Marsh, Historic Society of Lancashire and Cheshire, vol. xii.; and *Portraits, prints and writings of John Milton exhibited at Christ's College, Cambridge* 1908.

P. 2, *above* l. 16. *She went to her Mother at the K's Quarters*] Richard Powell left Forrest Hill for Oxford during the Royalist occupation. *vide* Todd, vol. i. p. 69. Extract from the First & Second Series of Royalists' Composition-Papers in his Majesty's Record Office:

" Richard Powell of Forrest hill deserted his dwellinge and went to Oxford, and lived there whiles it was a Garrison holden for the Kinge against the Parliamente, and was there at the tyme of the Surrender."

P. 2, l. 18. *Deborah was his Amanuensis . . .*] Aubrey is our sole authority for this.

P. 3, ll. 4, 5. *His widowe has his picture . . .*] This is the portrait known as the Onslow portrait. In 1721, Deborah Clarke, Milton's daughter, told George Vertue the engraver that her stepmother, living in Cheshire, had two portraits of Milton, one when he was a schoolboy (*vide* p. 2, *supra*), the other when he was above twenty. (B. M. Add. MS. 5016,* f. 71.) In 1731, this second portrait was in the possession of Mr Speaker Onslow and was engraved by Vertue. Onslow's friend, Lord Harcourt, greatly coveted the portrait, and Onslow had a copy made for him by Benjamin Van der Gucht. This copy has remained in the Harcourt family. On the back of the picture Van der Gucht has written the following inscription :

" This original picture of Milton I bought in the year 1729 or 30 and paid 20 guineas for it of Mr Cumberbatch, a gentleman of very good consideration in Chester, who was a relation and executor of the will of Milton's last wife who died a little before that time. He told me it hung up in her chamber till her death and she used to say that her husband gave it to her to show her what he was in his youth being drawn when he was about 21 years of age.   AR. ONSLOW.

" Mr Hawkins Brown (author of the poem De Animi Immortalitate) told me (8 Oct. 1753) that he knew this Mrs Milton, visited her often and well remembered this picture hanging in her chamber which she said was her husband.   A. O.

Compare this picture with that of Milton in his old age or in the print of it by White.

N.B. The above I transcribed from the writings I found on the back of the original picture of Milton belonging to Lord Onslow when I made this copy for the Earl of Harcourt in November 1792.

                                        BENJ. VAN DER GUCHT."

vide Tercentenary, p. 33.

P. 3, *above* l. 10. *Mris Eliz. Minshull* ...] Milton's third wife was daughter of Randle Minshull, yeoman farmer of Wistaston and Nantwich : she was born at Wistaston and baptized there December 30, 1638. Seven years after Milton's death, she returned to Nantwich, and died in 1727. *vide* papers by J. F. Marsh, Chetham Miscellanies, i., and Historic Society of Lancashire and Cheshire, vol. vii. p. 27.* For information about Milton's second and third wives *vide* Edward Phillips's Life, p. 77 *supra*.

P. 3, l. 16. *Dictionarie imperfect* ...] Aubrey's *Quaere* + means " make more inquiries." He adds some particulars on Sheet Af2. *vide* p. 4, *supra*, and Wood, p. 47, *supra*, with note, p. 339.

P. 4, *above* l. 15. *in the hands of Moyses Pitt*] Moses Pitt, a prosperous bookseller in St. Paul's Churchyard, printed Milton's Latin Letters of State in 1676. *vide* Masson, vi. 794-5.

P. 5, l. 10. *buried in St. Giles Cripplegate*] In a letter to Anthony à Wood, Jan, 12, 1675, Aubrey writes : Mr J. Milton is buryed at St Giles Criplegate, wch I will also see. Bodl. MS. Wood, f. 39.

P. 7, l. 11. *Mr Skinner*] Aubrey recognizes two Mr Skinners but does not get the Christian name of Daniel, the disciple.

The first is Cyriac Skinner, born 1627, to whom Milton addressed two famous sonnets. He was grandson of Sir Edward Coke, and friend of Andrew Marvell.

For the second Mr. Skinner, a much younger man, *vide infra*, note to p. 10, l. 1.

P. 7, ll. 12-17. *Jo: Dreyden . . . tagge his verses*] Dr Verrall considered this story " probably apochryphal," but an independent version appears in *The Monitor*, vol. i. No. 17, in 1713 :

" We shall here beg the Readers Pardon for mentioning a Passage told a Gentleman of our Society almost Forty years since by Mr Dryden, who went with Mr Waller in Company to make a Visit to Mr Milton and desire his Leave for putting his Paradise Lost into Rhime for the Stage. Well, Mr Dryden, says Milton, it seems you have a mind to Tagg my Points, and you have my Leave to Tagg 'em, but some of 'em are so Awkward and Old Fashion'd that I think you had as good leave 'em as you found 'em." *vide* R.E.S., vol. i. No. 1, p. 81.

cf. Richardson, p. 296, *supra*.

P. 8, *He had a middle wife*] Katherine Woodcock, described by E. Phillips as " daughter of Captain Woodcock of Hackney." *vide supra*, p. 77. He married her in 1656. For further particulars *vide* Smart, p. 122-3.

P. 10, l. 1. *Skinner, a merchant's sonne . . .*] This is the " Mr Skinner who was his disciple " mentioned by Aubrey on p. 7. He was the Daniel Skinner to whom Milton entrusted the MSS. of his *Letters of State* and *De Doctrina Christiana*. A large part of the copy of these MSS. in the Record Office is in Skinner's hand. He must have been the last of Milton's young literary friends. His age was probably little over twenty in the year of Milton's death. He has been identified as the eldest son of Daniel Skinner, Merchant of Mark Lane : he was elected major fellow of Trinity College, Cambridge, in 1679. An unsigned letter in the Collection of the Marquis of Bath at Longleat, giving information about Skinner's intention of printing Milton's MS. at Leyden concludes, " I am informed his father is in some office in the Custom House " (*Fourth Report of Historical MSS. Commission*, p. 231).

vide Papers relating to Milton in the State Paper Office, edited by W. D. Hamilton, Camden Society, 1859, and *Pepys & the Skinner Family*, R.E.S., No. 27, July 1931.

P. 10, l. 12. *Mr. Chapell . . .*] " William Chappell, afterwards Bishop of Ross in Ireland." *vide supra*, Wood, p. 36.

P. 10, l. 15. *Tovell*...] Nathaniel Tovey, Fellow of Christ's College, was Rector of Lutterworth, Leicestershire, from 1637, but was ejected about 1647, and died at Ayleston in 1658. *vide* Masson, i. 130.

P. 12, ll. 18, 19. *John Milton . . . morning*] This sentence is copied *verbatim litteratim* from the front page of Milton's Bible (now in the British Museum, Add. MS. 32310), in a hand which I believe I have identified as that of Elizabeth Milton, his widow. *cf*. her signature reproduced in *Chetham Miscellanies*, vol. i. In the inventory of her effects made at her death is " a large Bible " valued at 8s. Aubrey had made a note (*vide supra*, p. 11) : " Quaere Mr. Chr. Milton to see the date of his Bro. birth." It would appear that Christopher referred him to Mrs Milton, as possessor of the Bible, where the facts were recorded. If I am right about the third Mrs Milton's handwriting, the above is good evidence that the British Museum Bible, printed by Robert Barker, 1612 (the first quarto edition of the Authorized Version), was that copy belonging to Milton which came into the possession of his widow after his death. It was purchased by the British Museum on March 22, 1884, from Thomas Kerslake, a bookseller at Bristol. The entries made in Milton's hand on the blank page facing the beginning of *Genesis* are as follows :

" John Milton was born the 9th of December 1608 die Veneris half an howr after 6 in the morning.

Christofer Milton was born on Friday about a month before Christmas at 5 in the morning 1615.

Edward Phillips was 15 year old August 1645.

John Phillips is a year younger about Octob.

My daughter Anne was born July the 29th on the fast at eevning about half an houre after six 1646.

My daughter Mary was born on Wednesday Octob. 25th on the fast day in the morning about 6 a clock 1648.

My son John was born on Sunday March the 16th about half an hower past nine at night 1650."

Of the next entry Milton writes the first three words ; thereafter another hand writes at his dictation :

" My daughter Deborah was born the 2d of May being Sunday somwhat before 3 of the clock in the morning 1652.

my wife hir mother dyed about 3 days after. And my son about 6 weeks after his mother. 1652.

Katherin my daughter by Katherin my second wife, was borne yᵉ 19ᵗʰ of October, between 5 and 6 in yᵉ morning and dyed yᵉ 17th of march following, 6 weeks after hir mother, who dyed yᵉ 3rd of Feb. 1657."

Dr Birch saw another Milton Bible on January 6, 1750, the possession of Elizabeth Foster, daughter of Milton's daughter Deborah. This Bible originally belonged to Mary, Milton's first wife, and naturally descended to her children. " She showed me her Grandmother's Bible in *8vo* printed by Young in 1636, in a Blank Leafe upon which Milton had enter'd in his own Hand the Births of his Children, ... Anne . . ., Mary . . ., John . . ., Deborah . . ." B.M. Add. MS. 4244.

P. 13, l. 1. *Why do ye not . . . borne ?*] This is in Anthony à Wood's hand.

P. 13, l. 8. *His veine began at the Autumnall Æquinoctiall and ceased at the Vernall . . .*] *cf.* E. Phillips's corroborating, and Toland's conflicting, accounts, *supra*, p. 73 and p. 178. Mrs Milton said that "her husband used to compose his poetry chiefly in the winter" (*Newton*, p. lxxx.).

P. 13, l. 15. *In the 4th Booke . . . Tragoedie*] *cf.* E. Phillips's Life, *supra*, p. 72.

J. PHILLIPS

P. 17. This Life, which I ascribe to John Phillips (*vide* Introduction, *supra*, p. xvi *et seq.*), is here printed from Bodl. MS. Wood, D 4. After some hesitation I have adopted the more usual spelling *Phillips* for the name of both brothers. Aubrey and Edward Phillips write *Philips*, John signs himself *Phillips* at the end of his dedication to the *Satyr against Hypocrites*, *vide* facsimile, p. xviii, *supra*; Milton spells Phillips, *vide* note, *supra*, p. 336.

Malone meant to print this Life with Aubrey's notes for the Life of Milton. *vide* Bodl. MS. Eng. Misc. d. 26, where he writes :

" To be prefixed to the Anonymous Life of Milton : there is no date or author's name to this Life, which consists of only five leaves very fairly written ; but by a passage in it relative to passive obedience and non resistance, it appears to have been written in the year 1686 or 1687."

This Life, unsigned, has remained amongst Wood's papers in the Bodleian. For the character of the MS. and Wood's use of it, *vide* Introduction, *supra*, p. ix *et seq.*, p. xviii *et seq.*

P. 18, l. 9. *Stainton St. John*] There are still Miltons living in the neighbourhood. I notice the name of E. Milton in the Roll of Honour (for the War 1914-1918) hanging in the Church of Stanton St. John.

P. 19, l. 21. *the manners and Genius . . . no admiration.*] Edward Phillips also expresses contempt for the cringing French, *vide supra*, p. 69. *cf.* Milton's entry in his Commonplace Book (B.M. Add. MS. 36354), p. 180 :

" *Mores Gentium.*

A dangerous thing, and an ominous thing, to imitate with earnestnesse the fashions of neighbour nations : so the English ran madding after the French in Edward Confessor's time . . . god turn the omen from these days."

P. 30, l. 23. *Sr William Davenant when taken Prisoner . . .*]
Anthony à Wood writes in his life of D'Avenant :

" Having laid an ingenious design to carry a considerable number of
Artificers, chiefly Weavers, from France to Virginia . . . he did effect it so
far, that he and his company were ship'd in their way thither, and had got
on the main Ocean ; but being soon after seized on by certain Ships belonging to the Parliament of England, he was carried Prisoner, first to the
Isle of Wight an. 1650. and afterwards to the Tower of London, in order
to be tried for his life in the High Court of Justice, an. 1651, but upon the
mediation of Joh. Milton and others, especially two godly Aldermen of
York (to whom he had shewed great civility when they had been taken
prisoners in the North by some Forces under William Marquess of New-
castle) he was saved, and had liberty allow'd him as a prisoner at large."
(*Athenae Oxon.*, 1691, vol. ii. p. 293.)

Davenant wrote a letter from the Tower, October 9, 1652, thanking
Bulstrode Whitelock for his release : the letter only implies that he
had made a request to Whitelock for his liberty, and now that he was
free he thanked him " for the success of it " (*Whitelock's Memorials*,
1853, vol. iii. p. 462).

The service rendered to Davenant by Milton is supported by other
evidence, and two good witnesses suggest a reciprocal service.

vide Richardson, *supra*, p. 272, *et seq.*, and *cf.* old Jacob Tonson's
letter written 1732 :

" I was very intimately acquainted when young with one Mr. William
Davenant 2ᵈ Son to Sʳ William yᵉ Poet, this Gentleman was after of
Magdalen Hal in Oxford & published a Book printed there being a translation relating to old Authors in 8°. He was after unfortunately drownd
in france as he was Swimming. This Mr. Davenant told me that Mr.
Milton helped him in his study of yᵉ lattin & Greeke Authors, to whom
he used to goe in order to his Learning—That when his father was in the
tower he was very much assisted by Mr. Milton in his gaining his Liberty,
& if I am not very much mistaken he at the same time told me his father
in return upon yᵉ restoration was very helpfull to Milton, & Milton was
very acknowledging for it & uppon that score offered his willingness in
doing any thing that should be grateful to Sʳ William."

vide Paradise Lost. ed. Darbishire, p. xiv.

P. 32, l. 5. *ruddy complexion, light brown Hair . . .*] *cf.* the testimony of Deborah, quoted by George Vertue in a letter 1721 : " he
was of a fair complexion, a little red in the cheeks, and light brown
lank hair " (B.M. Add. MS. 5016*, f. 171).

P. 33, l. 11. *his Amanuensis*] Milton at one time hired a man to
read and write daily for him, *vide* Aubrey, p. 6, and J. Phillips, p. 33,
supra. But he also depended upon a highly select form of casual
labour, as John Phillips proceeds to tell : " the Youths that hee instructed servd him often as Amanuenses, & some elderly persons."

NOTES 339

We know that Edward and John Phillips both wrote for him; so did Daniel Skinner (*vide supra*, Note to Aubrey, p. 10) and most likely Thomas Elwood. *vide* Introduction, *supra*, pp. xvi. xix. xxvi.

WOOD

Wood's Life was first published in *Fasti Oxonienses*, 1691, pp. 880-884. *vide* Wood's annotated copy, Bodl. Wood, 431. a.

P. 35. Note] Milton's silver seal came into the possession of Mr James Payne on the death of Mr Foster, who had married Milton's granddaughter, Elizabeth Clarke. From Mr Payne it was bought by Thomas Hollis, who had it engraved. For a copy of the engraving *vide Memoirs of Thomas Hollis*, p. 533*. An impression of the seal is to be seen on the contract for the sale of the copyright of *Paradise Lost*, now in the British Museum, Add. MS. 18861.

P. 35, l. 3. *Incorporations* 1629.] Wood refers to his own paragraph under the year 1629:

" This year John French, M.A. and Fellow of *Merton* College was elected publick Scribe or Registrary of the University, who being a careless Man (tho a good Scholar) and more fit for another, than that, employment, hath omitted throughout all his time the Incorporations of the Canta-bridgeans . . ." (Wood, *Fasti Oxon.*, p. 865).

P. 47, ll. 19, 20. *Cyr. Skinner, living in Mark lane* . . .] Wood's mistake. It was Daniel Skinner who was the merchant's son of Mark Lane, and who received from Milton the MSS. of *De Doctrina Christiana* and the *Letters of State*. Aubrey distinguished the two Mr Skinners. *vide* notes, p. 335, *supra*.

P. 47, ll. 20-21. *Latin Thesaurus*] In his annotated copy of the *Fasti Oxonienses* (Bodl. Wood, 431. a.) Wood has pasted in a note on a slip of paper as follows:

" Jo. Milton. A Dictionary compleated and improved with great exactness from the several works of Stephens, Gouldman, Holyoke, Dr. Littleton, a manuscript of Mr. Joh. Milton &c for the use of Schooles— printed at Cambridge in qu. At the end of a sheet Almanack 1693."

The Dictionary appeared in Quarto, 1693, under the title " *Linguae Romanae Dictionarium Luculentum Novum. A New Dictionary in Five Alphabets* . . . the WHOLE Completed and Improved from the several Works of *Stephens, Cooper, Gouldman, Holyoke*, DR. LITTLETON, a Large Manuscript, in three Volumes, of Mr. *John Milton* &c."

The compilers state in the Preface to the Reader:

" We had by us, and made use of, a Manuscript Collection in three *Large Folio's* digested into an Alphabetical order, which the Learned Mr. *John*

Milton had made, out of *Tully, Livy, Caesar, Sallust, Quintus Curtius, Justin, Plautus, Terence, Lucretius, Virgil, Horace, Ovid, Manilius, Celsus, Columella, Varro, Cato, Palladius* ; in short out of all the best and purest *Roman* Authors."

cf. E. Phillips, *supra*, p. 72.

P. 47, l. 29. *Walter Raleigh* . . .] The reference is to Wood's *Life of Raleigh*, No. 458 in *Athenae Oxon.*, i., where in his list of Raleigh's writings appear :

" *The Prince, or Maxims of State. Lond.* 1642. . . . 'Tis the same with his *Aphorisms of State*, Lond. 1661. oct. published by John Milton.

The Cabinet-Council, containing the chief Arts of Empire and Mysteries of State. Lond. 1658. oct. This book was published by *John Milton* before-mentioned ; of whom you may see more in the *Fasti*, an. 1635." (*Ath. Oxon.*, i. 373.)

The *Cabinet-Council* was the only publication of Raleigh's works in which Milton had a hand. It appeared under the title *Aphorisms of State* in 1661, but is wrongly assumed by Wood to be the same book as " *The Prince or Maxims of State*."

E. PHILLIPS

P. 49. Edward Phillips was known by John Toland (*vide supra*, p. 178) to be the author of this Life, prefixed to the " *Letters of State*, written by Mr John Milton, . . . London, 1694." Birch saw a copy inscribed and acknowledged by Edward Phillips. *Birch*, Pref., p. 1. I have made here and there some slight alterations in punctuation and paragraphing in the interest of clearness.

P. 50, l. 28. *Born . . . in the year . . . 1606*] Phillips's mistake for 1608

P. 52, l. 2. *Sarah, of the . . . Castons*] Sarah Jeffrey. " There were Castons among her progenitors." Masson, i. 31.

P. 64, l. 19. *daughter to the . . . Lee*] James Ley, Earl of Marlborough. Captain John Hobson and his wife, Lady Margaret Ley, lived in Aldersgate Street and were near neighbours of Milton. Lady Margaret's family joined the Royalist cause, Captain Hobson the Parliamentarian. *vide* Smart, p. 62.

P. 66, l. 24. *one Blackborough* . . .] This relation seems to have been either Hester Jeffrey, who had married a Mr Blackborow, and who was a widow in 1657, or her son, Abraham Blackborow, who lived in London. Hester's brother, John Jeffrey, makes a bequest in his will, proved on September 21, 1657, to " cousins John and Christopher Milton." *vide Athenæum*, April 24, 1880. These Jeffreys were another branch of the same Essex family from which Sara Jeffrey, the mother of the poet, sprang. *vide* Masson, i. 33.

P. 72, l. 21. *Dictionary* . . .] *vide supra*, note to Wood, p. 47.

P. 73, l. 18. *Correction as to the Orthography and Pointing*] I trace Edward Phillips's hand in some of the corrections to the MS. of *Paradise Lost*. *vide Paradise Lost*, ed. H. Darbishire, Introduction.

P. 74, l. 15. *two Sonnets* . . .] The first was published in the *Poems*, 1673, the second first published by Phillips in this same volume, *vide supra*, p. 81.

P. 74, l. 31. *John Goodwin*] Milton was not in fact excepted along with John Goodwin. *cf.* Richardson, p. 271, *supra*.

P. 76, l. 7. *Earl of Anglesey* . . . *unlicens'd Papers of his History*] Published in 1681, under the title " Mr John Milton's Character of the Long Parliament and the Assembly of Divines." It was undoubtedly intended to be placed at the beginning of Book III of the History of Britain. There is a contemporary MS. of a portion of the digression in the library of Harvard University, headed : " To com in Lib. 3, page 110, after these words, ' from one misery to another.' "

Harvard MS. 14496, 34*.

This MS., written in a hand unknown to me, is certainly a copy of Milton's MS., reproducing his peculiar spellings, *e.g. thir, childern, enobl'd* altered from *enobled, Iland*. *vide Paradise Lost*, ed. H. Darbishire, p. 72.

P. 77, ll. 5, 6. *the Child* . . . *within a month after* . . .] The births and deaths of his son and his fourth daughter are recorded in his Family Bible now in the British Museum ; *vide supra*, p. 336, Note to Aubrey, p. 12.

P. 77, l. 26. *The Hebrew*] It is difficult to believe that the girls ever learnt to read Hebrew. Aubrey first wrote that Milton taught Deborah Latin and to read Greek and Hebrew to him, but he struck out *Hebrew* and wrote Q (=Quaere) above it. On a later page he writes that Deborah could read to him Latin, Italian, French and Greek,—with no mention of Hebrew. *vide* Aubrey, pp. 2, 3, 6, *supra*. Aubrey was scrupulous about matters of fact.

P. 79. At the end of this page the sentence follows : " Here is a Catalogue added of every Book of his that was ever publish'd ; which to my knowledge is full and compleat." On the succeeding four pages the four Sonnets are printed, and after them the Catalogue of works. This last I have omitted in the present edition.

P. 80. *Sonnets. To Oliver Cromwell, etc.*] These four Sonnets were here first published with many typographical errors, by Edward

Phillips.   Aubrey knew of those to Cromwell and Fairfax.   In a letter to Wood, endorsed by Wood " rec'd 25 May, 1684," he wrote :

Mr. J. Milton made two admirable Panegyricks (as to sublimitie of Witt) one on Ol: Cromwel, & the other on Th. Ld Fairfax, both wᶜʰ his nephew Mr. Philips hath ; but he hath hung back these 2 yeares, as to imparting copies to me for yᵉ Collect. of mine wth. you.   Wherefore I desire you in yʳ next, to intimate yr desire, of having these 2 copies of verses aforesaid. Were they made in the comendacion of yᵉ Devill, 'twere all one to me. 'tis the ὕψος yᵗ I looke after.   I have been told 'tis beyond Waller's or anything in that kind.   (Bodl. MS., Wood, F 39.)

The manuscript authority for the text of the Sonnets is as follows :

To Oliver Cromwell	Trin. MS. f. 47, in the hand of an amanuensis, numbered 16.
To my Lord Fairfax	Trin. MS. f. 47, written in Milton's own hand, numbered 15.
To Mr Cyriac Skinner.	Trin. MS. f. 49, in John Phillips's hand (*vide* Introduction, *supra*, p. xxvi), numbered 22.
To Sir Henry Vane.	Trin. MS. f. 48, in the hand of an amanuensis, numbered 17.

TOLAND

P. 83. *The Life of John Milton*, by John Toland, was first published as Preface to " *A Complete Collection of the Historical, Political, and Miscellaneous Works of John Milton, both English and Latin . . . To which is Prefix'd The Life of the Author, Containing, Besides the History of his Works, Several Extraordinary Characters of Men and Books, Sects, Parties and Opinions.   Amsterdam, Finish'd in the Year* MDCXCVIII." The book was, in fact, printed in London, anonymously, J. T.'s initials only appearing at the end of the Life.

P. 85, ll. 1-8. *I learnt some particulars . . . discover*] We have no clue to the identity of this Amanuensis (*cf.* note to J. Phillips, p. 33) ; the " daughter now dwelling in London " would be Deborah (*cf.* note to Richardson, p. 225) ; " his last wife," Elizabeth Minshull, was living at Nantwich (*cf.* note to Aubrey, p. 3) ; the nephew whose papers he perused must have been Edward Phillips, then, it seems, recently dead ; the other with whom he talked was John Phillips " the younger Nephew, now alive " (*vide supra*, Toland, p. 159).

P. 86, l. 5. *Christopher*] With Toland's unsympathetic account of Christopher Milton, *cf.* the kinder account by E. Phillips, p. 52, *supra*.

P. 96, l. 9. *two Greec Letters*] Two Greek letters of Diodati to Milton are in the British Museum (Add. MS. 5016, f. 64).

P. 134. *General Fairfax*] The Sonnets to Fairfax and Vane were first published by Edward Phillips. *vide supra*, E. Phillips, pp. 80-81 and note.

P. 165. *Cyriac Skinner*] The Sonnets to Cyriac Skinner and to Cromwell were first published by Edward Phillips. *vide supra* E. Phillips, pp. 80-81 and note.

P. 171, ll. 17-18. *This and another small Piece*] The two " pieces " appear in the Second Volume of "*A Complete Collection of the Historical, Political and Miscellaneous Works of John Milton*, 1698," to which Toland's Life is prefixed : they bear the titles, " *A Letter to a Friend, Concerning the Ruptures of the Commonwealth* " and " *The Present Means, and brief Delineation of a Free Commonwealth, Easy to be put in Practice, and without Delay. In a Letter to General Monk*." Under each title the words are added : " Publish'd from the Manuscript." The nephew from whom the worthy friend had them would be Edward Phillips ; *cf.* Aubrey, p. 4, *supra*.

P. 179, l. 18. *Homer ... without book*] Toland is our sole authority for this. Deborah Clarke said that Isaiah, Homer and Ovid's *Metamorphoses* were books which the daughters were often call'd upon to read to their father. She herself could repeat a considerable number of verses from both Homer and Ovid, *vide* Birch, Pref., p. 61.

P. 180, l. 10. *Ignorance or Malice of the Licenser*] Toland alone informs us of this obstructive behaviour of the Licenser, who must have been Thomas Tomkyns, Chaplain to the Archbishop. He duly signed the Imprimatur on the inside page of the covering sheet of the MS. *vide Paradise Lost*, ed. H. Darbishire.

P. 192, l. 25. *Cyriac Skinner*] *vide supra* note, p. 339, to Wood, p. 47, ll. 19-20.

RICHARDSON

P. 199. *Explanatory Notes ... by J. Richardsons, Father and Son*] Jonathan Richardson the elder (1665-1745), well known as a portrait-painter, and author of treatises on Painting, seems to have written the *Life of Milton*, but was assisted in the scholarly annotations to *Paradise Lost* by his son, Jonathan Richardson (1694-1771), in the manner he delightfully describes (*vide supra*, p. 312).

In printing Richardson's Life I have preserved the typographical peculiarities of the original. Richardson's ideas about the use of the capital letter for emphasis are set forth in his explanatory remarks about his notes on *Paradise Lost* :

" we have Offer'd a Specimen of *Emphasising*, which certainly would be of Great Use if Always done by Writers, the want of which, Especially at First Reading, Occasions Frequent Mistakes, and False Pronunciations, Somtimes so as to be Obscure, and Unintelligible ; and Somtimes Impressions are taken at First reading which are not Easily, if Ever Eradicated, though what the Writer was an Utter Stranger to. Somthing of This,

Marking where the Stress was, is done in Every thing that is Printed or
Written ; but not being Carefully observ'd Throughout 'tis of Little use,
the Reason of doing it at All is Good However for Constantly doing it ;
and indeed 'tis in a Manner as Necessary as Pointing, as 'tis done for the
Same Purpose, the Clearing and Establishing the Sense, and Immediately.
We have Us'd Great Letters, wherever any particular Weight is to be laid
on the Word ; and not Else, though at the beginning of a Paragraph in
Prose, or of a Line in Verse, where there is no Other Pretence for One than
Custom, and an Imagin'd Beauty in it ; for 'tis Imagination Only ; or if
it Really was Handsomer to the Eye ; or if So many Great Letters as We
put into the Page Look'd not So well as None at all, or very Few, as in the
Old Italian Books by *Giolito* or the *Giunti* and Some Others, is That Sufficient
to stand in Ballance with what is so much more Important ? "

P. 202, l. 7. *the Print Prefix'd*] This etching (see Frontispiece *supra*)
which appeared as the Frontispiece of his *Explanatory Notes and
Remarks on Milton's Paradise Lost*, was apparently made by Richardson
from a crayon drawing by Robert White from what is known as the
Bayfordbury portrait originally in the possession of Jacob Tonson ; *vide
Milton Tercentenary*, pp. 11-12. The painter of the Bayfordbury
portrait was probably Faithorne. According to Richardson (*vide supra*,
p. 229), this crayon drawing was the portrait which Deborah recognised
with such excitement : " 'Tis my Father ! 'Tis my Dear Father ! I see
him ! " De Quincey found in Richardson's etching a remarkably true
likeness of Wordsworth. *vide The Lake Poets : William Wordsworth*
in De Quincey's *Collected Writings*, vol. ii. ed. D. Masson.

P. 205, l. 7. *a Widow*] *cf. An Apology . . . Smectymnuus* : " I think
with them who both in prudence and elegance of spirit would choose
a virgin of mean fortunes honestly bred, before the wealthiest widow."

P. 205, l. 20. *. . . five Italian Sonnets . . . for the same Lady*]
There is no ground for the fancy that the Italian Sonnets were written
to Leonora, the famous Italian singer, to whom Milton addressed three
pieces of complimentary verse in Latin after hearing her sing in Rome.
Masson's conjecture that the Italian Sonnets were written in England
before the Italian journey is probably right. *cf.* Smart, p. 133 *et seq.*

P. 225, l. 31. *She that dy'd a few Years Since*] Deborah Clarke
who died in 1727. Addison visited her and gave her " a handsome
present of a purse of guineas," and Queen Caroline gave her fifty
pounds. *vide* Birch, Pref., pp. 76 and 77.

P. 227, l. 27. *about the year 50*] Milton's sight failed him in 1652.
He began to write, but another hand completed, the entry of Deborah's
birth, May 2, 1652, in the Family Bible, Brit. Mus. Add. MS. 32310.
Anne was born July 29, 1646, Mary October 25, 1648. *vide supra*,
p. 336, note to Aubrey, p. 12.

P. 238, ll. 1-2. *fragment . . . Printed . . . Anno 1681*] *vide* note to Edward Phillips, p. 76, l. 7, *supra*.

P. 240, l. 30. The note is as follows :

XII 583.   *add Love,*
        by Name to come call'd Charitie, the Soul
        of all the rest :

Charity from *Charitas* (Lat.) is Dearness. See IV. 756. Love to the Poor is shown by Alms, to All Men by putting the most Favourable Construction on their Words and Actions ; but Charity has a more Noble and Extensive Signification or it could not be said to be the *Soul* of all the Other Vertues, nor would St. *Paul* have Wrote to *Tim.* (1 *Ep.* i. 5) *Now the End of the Commandment is Charity out of a Pure Heart, and of a Good Conscience, and of Faith Unfeigned.* So 1 *Cor.* xiii. 13. *And now Abideth, Faith, Hope, Charity, these Three, but the Greatest of These is Charity.* That Here Intended then must be —— but let *Milton* Speak for Himself, He had done it Long before he Wrote This in his *Tetrachordon*, 'tis in *p.* 331. of his Prose Works.

" *Christ* having Cancell'd the Hand-Writing of Ordinances which was against us, *Coloss.* ii. 14, and interpreted the Fullfilling of All through Charity, hath in That respect set us Over Law, in the Free Custody of his Love, and left us Victorious under the Guidance of his Living Spirit, not under the Dead Letter ; to follow That which most Edifys, most Aids and furthers a Religious Life, makes us Holiest, and Likest to his Immortal Image, not that which makes Us most Conformable and Captive to Civil and Subordinate Precepts ; whereof the Strictest Observance may Oft-times prove the Destruction, not only of many Innocent Persons and Families, but of whole Nations. Although indeed no Ordinance, Humane, or from Heav'n can bind against the Good of Man, so that to Keep them Strictly against That End is all one with to Break them," he goes on, and Quotes *Cicero* in his Book of *Invention* saying, that *All Law we ought to refer to the Common Good, and Interpret by That, not by the Scrowle of Letters. No Man Observes Law for Law's Sake, but for the Good of them for Whom it was made.* whether *Milton's* Interpretation of the Word Charity is Right or No, 'tis His, and we Think Applicable to the Passage we are upon ; Further is not Our Concern, who are, not giving Our Own Meaning, but our Authors as far as we are Able ; at least St. *Paul* is Right, whom let Every one Interpret in the Sincerity of his Heart."

P. 268, l. 8. *Latin Thesaurus*] *vide* note to Wood, p. 47, *supra*.

P. 292, l. 12. *The Contract was in being a few Years since*] " This original contract with Samuel Simmons the printer," wrote Newton in 1749, " is . . . in the hands of Mr Tonson the bookseller, as is likewise the manuscript of the first book copied fair for the press." *The Life of Milton* prefixed to *Paradise Lost*, the Seventh Edition . . . by Thomas Newton, D.D. The contract is now in the British Museum, Add. MS. 18861.

P. 294, l. 2. *Notes by P. H.*] Patrick Hume.

P. 296, l. 9. *Sir W. L.*] Malone conjectures that this North-Country Gentleman was Sir Wilfred Lawson, of Isell, in Cumberland ; but dismisses the whole story in the following words : " Unless almost every species of incongruity and contradiction can authenticate a narrative, this anecdote must be rejected as wholly unworthy of credit." Malone's *Dryden*, i. pp. 114, 115.

P. 296, l. 14. *Tagg'd his Lines*] *cf.* Note to Aubrey, p. 7.

P. 303, l. 13. *Spelling and Pointing*] The MS. of *Paradise Lost*, Book I, which was used by the printer for setting up the text of the first edition, fully bears out Richardson's remarks about Milton's scrupulous care for spelling and punctuation. *vide Paradise Lost*, ed. H. Darbishire.

P. 304, ll. 3-4. *Their . . . Thir*] *vide* H. Darbishire, *op. cit.* p. 70, and note to p. 306, *infra*.

P. 304, l. 23. *the word Rhime*] Milton meant to spell Rime. *vide* H. Darbishire, *op. cit.* p. 52.

P. 305, l. 20. the Fault is in II 414] Ed. I. reads

Here he had need

All circumspection, and we now no less

In the *Errata* the correction is given : for *we* read *wee*.

P. 306, l. 2. *Six of the First Edition*] For a further investigation of the printers' corrections made in various sheets while the first edition was in the Press *cf. Monograph on the Original Publication of the Poem* by R. Herne Shepherd in the edition of *Paradise Lost*, with Text of 1667, published by Pickering in 1873.   I have myself noticed one uncorrected sheet bound up in a copy in the Bodleian, 4° H. 58, where *their* appears at Book V, 150 : the eight copies in the British Museum read correctly *thir*, as also every other copy I have seen. *vide Paradise Lost*, ed. H. Darbishire, p. 72.

P. 308, l. 16. *Pretence or Excuse to a New Editor*] Richardson's defence of Milton's text against the imputations of Bentley (*vide* his *Paradise Lost*, a New Edition, 1732) is fully justified.   Milton's copy of Book I, sent to the Printer, has been carefully corrected, not by one " ignorant and audacious acquaintance," called by Bentley " the Editor," but under Milton's supervision by at least five different hands, amongst which I recognise that of the scholarly Edward Phillips.   *vide Paradise Lost*, ed. H. Darbishire.

P. 313, l. 3. *the complicated Richardson*] The Jonathan Richardson, Father and Son, of the title-page.

INDEX

347